Circling the Canon

RECENCIES SERIES: RESEARCH AND RECOVERY IN TWENTIETH-CENTURY AMERICAN POETICS

MATTHEW HOFER, SERIES EDITOR

RECENCIES

This series stands at the intersection of critical investigation, historical documentation, and the preservation of cultural heritage. The series exists to illuminate the innovative poetics achievements of the recent past that remain relevant to the present. In addition to publishing monographs and edited volumes, it is also a venue for previously unpublished manuscripts, expanded reprints, and collections of major essays, letters, and interviews.

Also available in the Recencies Series:

For additional titles in the Recencies Series, please visit unmpress.com.

Circling the Canon

The Selected Book Reviews of Marjorie Perloff, 1969–1994

VOLUME 1

Marjorie Perloff   EDITED BY **David Jonathan Bayot**

University of New Mexico Press   —   Albuquerque

First paperback edition, 2021
Paperback ISBN: 978-0-8263-6275-9

Names: Perloff, Marjorie, author. | Bayot, David Jonathan, editor.
Title: Circling the canon, Volume I: the selected book reviews of Marjorie Perloff /
    Marjorie Perloff; edited by David Jonathan Bayot.
Description: Albuquerque: University of New Mexico Press, 2019. | Series: Recencies series:
    research and recovery in twentieth-century American poetics | Includes index. |
Identifiers: LCCN 2019012206 (print) | LCCN 2019018343 (e-book) | ISBN 9780826360519 (e-book) |
    ISBN 9780826360502 (printed case: alk. paper)
Subjects: LCSH: American poetry—20th century—History and criticism. | Poetry—Book reviews.
Classification: LCC PS325 (e-book) | LCC PS325. P377 2019 (print) | DDC 811/.509—dc23
LC record available at https://lccn.loc.gov/2019012206

Cover illustration courtesy of Steve Johnson on Unsplash
Designed by Felicia Cedillos
Composed in Minion 10.5/14.25

For Gerald Bruns
l'incomparable ami

Contents

Preface

> The place to which I really have to go is one that I must actually be at
> already. Anything that can be reached with a ladder does not interest me.
> —LUDWIG WITTGENSTEIN, *Culture and Value*

The impetus for this project was a lecture Marjorie Perloff gave on November 6, 2016, at The Arts House during the annual Singapore Writers Festival. The topic of the Round Table, which I was happy to attend as part of a large and enthusiastic audience, was "The Importance of the Book Review." In another sense, however, the book might have begun (at least as far as I can tell) on September 15, 2011, when Marjorie, with whom I had been corresponding about a Festschrift I was preparing in honor of my mentor (and Marjorie's doctoral student at the University of Maryland in the early 1970s), the Philippine critic Isagani R. Cruz, e-mailed me a copy of the keynote address she was to deliver at a festival organized by the Poetry Center in Wuhan, China, in honor of her eightieth birthday. Marjorie knew I was Chinese (although I was born in Manila and have always lived here) and thought I might be interested in her China talk.

The autobiographical essay in question was titled "Becoming a Critic." Here Marjorie observes that her "own development as a critic took a decisive turn in 1975 when [she] began to write [her] book on Frank O'Hara." She explains that "in the 1970s, the critical journals used to run omnibus reviews." In the course of my reading of Marjorie's autobiographical account so as to understand the trajectory of her "becoming a critic," I found myself going back time and again to an interesting and highly suggestive passage:

> If a journal asked you to do the annual poetry review, the editors would
> send you about 150 books and you could sort them out and decide which to
> include. In 1973, *Contemporary Literature* asked me to do the omnibus review.
> Among the hundreds of books arriving at my door . . . there was the Ron
> Padgett and David Shapiro *Anthology of New York Poets* (Random House,
> 1970), which included a sizable selection of O'Hara's poems. In the New York

art world, O'Hara . . . was something of a cult figure, but in the academy . . . no one had heard of him: we were busy dissecting Robert Lowell and Sylvia Plath . . . or, if we were more adventurous, Charles Olson. I found O'Hara's seemingly casual, graphic, and documentary "I do this I do that" poems a breath of fresh air . . . My omnibus review . . . centered on O'Hara. The next year, the MLA convention was in New York, and on the last day I found a free hour to visit the bookshop at the Museum of Modern Art in New York. Here I came across O'Hara's *Art Chronicles* [1975]—his reviews and articles about the Abstract Expressionists and related artists, produced while he was curator at MOMA. I asked Doris Grumbach, a writer-friend, who was then literary editor of *The New Republic*, if I might review the book. She said yes and the resulting review came to the attention of the art book publisher George Braziller and, next thing you know, I had a contract to write a book on O'Hara.

It is interesting to see how a (dis)interested review that centered on O'Hara's poems in a large anthology—poems that according to Marjorie are "seemingly casual, graphic, and documentary" and thus had provided her "a breath of fresh air"—sowed the seed of her interest in O'Hara that led further to another review (this one in *The New Republic*) on the poet's *Art Chronicles* in 1975 that was suggestively titled "They were There!" And from that review, a book was fortuitously born—one that opened for the critic (as well as for her readers for four decades) a brave new world of poetry or, more precisely, a different and differential way of knowing and engaging with "poetry" as, first of all, a practice in context, that is, a "language game." According to Marjorie "from then on, the avant-garde became my special interest."

Marjorie's readers would surely notice her own subsequent vigorous translation of her "special interest"—since the publication of *Frank O'Hara* (1977)—into a dozen more books. Written over a period of four decades, these books, though eclectic at first glance, do in reality cohere as a corpus of sustained critical inquiry into poetics. The Perloff corpus has no doubt played a role in the paradigm shift in poetry studies or, rather, poetic *practice* since the early 1980s, when Marjorie published *The Poetics of Indeterminacy: Rimbaud to Cage* in 1981. In 1990, in *Poetic License*, she referred to the earlier book as "an ongoing project . . . [toward] a revisionist history of twentieth-century poetics." In 2018, it's safe to say that no narrative-metanarrative of twentieth- and twenty-first century poetics—revisionist or otherwise—could disavow the constitutive force of Marjorie's scholarship in the figuration and reconfiguration of these narratives, no matter how controversial her specific readings might be for certain members of the poetry community as well as the academy.

A close reader of Marjorie's work can hardly fail to notice the importance she places on criticism as first of all a *practice* and a practice *within* a field. Like her maître à penser Ludwig Wittgenstein, Marjorie is persistently skeptical and resistant to generalization, metalanguage, and theory. For Marjorie, all these metadiscourses, no matter how useful they were at certain points in history, were "elucidatory" only *at certain historical contexts*, and should not be allowed to go on and become enshrined in scholarship as incontrovertible truths. In the scheme of Marjorie's poetics, these "truths" could be compared to ladders, as Wittgenstein would call them in the *Tractatus*, and thus, "when he has climbed out through them, on them, over them[,] . . . [h]e must so to speak throw away the ladder."

In Marjorie's view, these "ladders" tend to foster an uncritical disposition— one of complacency—among members of the poetic community who could be so taken by the prospect that theory, or the gesture of invoking it, is truth-building enough to warrant the critic's subscription to a (set of) notion(s) of poetry without having to "rock the boat" so to speak. The recourse to metalanguage certainly affords the poets-critics the convenience needed for them to peg and determine their poetic subjects in a certain way and according to foregone generalizations, overt or covert. But these easy recourses would, in the logic of Marjorie's poetics, only engender a weak set of poetic discourses that are devoid of firsthand knowledge of actual, current poetic practice—in both the textual and contextual sense.

It is in this context of understanding poetry and criticism (or poetry-criticism) that one begins to appreciate the significance of Marjorie's attention to the genre of the book review. Marjorie seems to be saying that this "timely" genre—the possibility of its datedness notwithstanding—is where a critic could make a critical difference on a discursive site where a differential disposition would certainly matter. Taking her cue from Wittgenstein, Marjorie would say as the philosopher does: that "the place to which I really have to go is one that I must actually be at already." And "anything that can be reached with a ladder does not interest me."

Where could that strategic place be other than where ideas ensuing from current book publications are forged and debated in a timely manner, and the canon formed and reformed in accordance with the exigencies of time—and not according to some dogmas from an alleged timeless zone? In both volumes of *Circling the Canon*, readers will witness Marjorie's polemical engagements with the poetry of card-carrying members of the poetic Tradition (e.g., Anthony Hecht and Robert Lowell), as well as those of the "other tradition" (e.g., David Antin and John Cage), and also those in between (e.g., Charles Olson and Adrienne Rich). And further, readers of these volumes will discover a treasure trove in Marjorie's witty and insightful polemics with literary theorists or antitheorists (both "metalinguists" as far as Marjorie is concerned), through the incarnations of, for instance, Harold Bloom, Helen Vendler, and Jonathan Culler.

As a matter of fact, Marjorie's acknowledgment of both the inevitability and the vulnerability of metalanguage is very much foregrounded in her choice of subjects for engagement. These are subjects other than poetry, yet they are inextricable from poetry as the latter's contexts—that is, as intertexts necessary in any responsible discourses on poetry, in the first place, as a "poetic artifice." After all, one must remember that for Marjorie, poetry—her prime object of concern—is a practice and will always be a practice in context(s). Thus, in these two volumes, readers will encounter Marjorie's reviews of works classified variously as anthology (e.g., in "Whose New American Poetry? Anthologizing in the Nineties"), biography (e.g., on David Moody's *Ezra Pound*), fiction (e.g., Joseph Roth's *The Hotel Years*), letters (e.g., on four volumes of letters by T. S. Eliot), translation (e.g., Richard Sieburth's translation of *Hymns and Fragments* by Friedrich Hölderlin), and visual arts (e.g., the concrete poetry of Augusto de Campos and Ian Hamilton Finlay).

––––––

Circling the Canon had yet another beginning. In 2012 when I took on the director's post of the De La Salle University Publishing House (Manila), I wrote to Marjorie to ask if it would be possible to work with her on a Marjorie Perloff reader. I tried to convince her that it's high time that we gather in one book a wide range of essays from all phases of her critical career—works published in her various books and representative of the main areas of her scholarship. She declared herself to be flattered by my suggestion, but also worried that her criticism was not important enough for such a volume. In the end, I suggested that we do something else: namely to put together a collection of her interviews, together with some personal essays. The result is *Poetics in a New Key*, published by DLSUPH in 2013 and the international edition released by the University of Chicago Press in 2015. Though the book turned out to be different from the project I had in mind initially, the outcome actually complements my earlier intention to present Marjorie's critical ideas and to do so via her key texts. It's heartening to read the words of Charles Bernstein about the book, "*Poetics in a New Key* is the perfect companion to Marjorie's many books, but, more than that, it is an ideal introduction to her thought." (It must be noted that this book opens with "Becoming a Critic: An Academic Memoir.")

In 2015, when I was made general editor of the *Critical Voices* series of Sussex Academic Press, I wanted to revive the reader project. And this time, I wanted to do a reader with a twist, so to speak. My intention was still pretty much the same: to introduce readers to the configurations of Marjorie's ideas by presenting her essays on key poets and thinkers, specifically those who have made defining marks in the development of her poetics over five decades. The twist lies in the fact that this new reader would consist entirely of essays that haven't been previously collected and included in any of Marjorie's books. Part of the plan was for us to include works that haven't been published earlier. Unfortunately, the plan didn't materialize due to complications of copyright issues. And in the end, Marjorie thought that it would be a good idea to come up with an unprecedented format for doing a book, namely, to publish and make her early essays accessible—without monetary demands on her readers— that is, on her own website. For this endeavor, Marjorie wanted us to focus on the uncollected essays and reviews she published during the predigital period from 1964 to 1994. The result is *Modernists, Avant-Gardists, Contemporaries: Essays of the First Three Decades, 1964–1994*, an online reader.

––––––––––

Circling the Canon is thus a book with many beginnings. The inception point, it seems, was a fascination I had with how much a book review—which is, after all, produced for a specific occasion at a specific moment—might reveal about a given critic's basic principles. And in helping Marjorie to assemble the pieces to be included in *Circling the Canon*, I have gained new respect for the book review as genre. Highly specific as these book reviews inevitably are, and more tentative in presentation than the chapters comprising Marjorie's scholarly books, they also have the advantage of casting a much wider net and encompassing a great variety of authors and topics. The book review allows Marjorie to comment on major writers from earlier periods outside her area of specialization—for example, Goethe and Heine—as well as to reassess problematic reputations like that of the poet Amy Clampitt. Again, reviews, being of the moment, can chart the process of critical change more fully than can a scholarly book, committed as it is to a particular argument.

I am happy to have been able to help Marjorie make what were difficult selections, given that the 64 reviews included here represent only about a quarter of her more than 250 published reviews. Recalling our fruitful years working together—a process that has taken many unexpected turns—I'm reminded of two sets of words by two of Marjorie's icons. The first is an observation made by Wittgenstein in *Philosophical Investigations*: "In the actual use of expressions we make detours, we go by sideroads. We see the straight highway before us, but of course we cannot use it, because it is permanently closed." And the second is by Gertrude Stein who said in "Composition as Explanation": "There was a groping for using everything and there was a groping for a continuous present and there was an inevitable beginning of beginning again and again and again."

And afterwards.

Now that is not all.

DAVID JONATHAN BAYOT

Manila, Philippines

February 2018

Acknowledgments

The idea for *Circling the Canon* came from Matthew Hofer at the University of New Mexico. Chatting one day with Matthew and my old friend Bob von Hallberg (Matt's mentor at the University of Chicago), Matt suggested that I might want to contribute a volume to his new series for the University of New Mexico Press to be called *Recencies: Research and Recovery in Twentieth-Century American Poetics*. Specifically, we talked of my book reviews, fugitive pieces that had been appearing in a great variety of journals for more than five decades. At around the same time, David Jonathan Bayot, the publisher of the De La Salle University Publishing House (DLSUPH) in the Philippines, who had approached me back in 2012 about reprinting my essays and reviews and had in the interim edited my interviews, first for DLSUPH in Manila and then for the University of Chicago Press (*Poetics in a New Key*, 2013), also expressed interest in the book reviews and offered to track them down, digitize the earlier ones, and help me to choose among them so as to assemble these two volumes. Throughout the process, David's intellect, judgment, and humor, not to mention the hard work of actual editing, has been indispensable, even as Matt Hofer's enthusiasm and confidence in me made the actual publication possible.

Al Filreis and Yunte Huang, my originally anonymous readers for the University of New Mexico Press, gave invaluable advice as to selection, organization, and revision. I also wish to acknowledge the help and confidence of my many editors over the years. Two, alas—Bill McPherson of the *Washington Post* and L. S. Dembo of *Contemporary Literature*—are no longer with us, but let me thank some of the others, beginning with Doris Grumbach (*New Republic*), Herbert Leibowitz (*Parnassus*), and Clayton Eshleman (*Sulfur*), and including Mary Jo Bang, Joshua Cohen, and Tim Donnelly (*Boston Review*), Calvin Bedient (*Lana Turner*), James Campbell (*Times Literary Supplement*), Jeffrey di Leo (*American Book Review*), Ben Mazer (*Battersea Review*), Michael Miller and Albert Mobilio (*Bookforum*), Claude Rawson (*Modern Language Review*), Michael Schmidt (*PN Review*), Philip Terzian (*Weekly Standard*), and Arthur Vogelsang (*American Poetry Review*).

At the University of New Mexico Press, Elise M. McHugh has been an exemplary editor, attending to all the details of production and planning with good humor and grace.

As always, my wonderful circle of friends, colleagues, and relatives, especially my daughters Nancy Perloff and Carey Perloff, have given me enormous support. But this may also be the place to thank a few of the great literary friends I have lost in recent years: David Antin, John Ashbery, Matei Calinescu, Michael Heim, Judd Hubert, Renée Hubert, and Herbert Lindenberger. The most important person on this list of the deceased is, of course, my late husband, Joseph K. Perloff (1924–2014). How sad that Joe cannot read this particular book as he had read all the others.

This book is dedicated to a fellow octogenarian, Gerald Bruns, whose work in critical theory and poetics has long been an inspiration to me and who, in the course of the last year or two, has read every one of these reviews and essays and offered incisive feedback. How blessed I am to have had the counsel of such a discerning friend and critic.

MARJORIE PERLOFF
Pacific Palisades, 2019

Circling the Canon

In November 2016, when I was a guest speaker at the Singapore Poetry Festival, I was asked to participate in a panel listed as "The Importance of the Book Review." I expected little of this session, given the relatively low status of book reviewing in the United States, where, especially in the case of poetry, reviews tend to be little more than expanded blurbs, written for the inner circle of fellow poets and prize committees. In Singapore, to my surprise, interest in book reviewing runs very high: many of the would-be reviewers I met at the session hold jobs in fields ranging from finance to tourism, but they are evidently anxious to learn the craft of reviewing so as to make a palpable difference in the reading choices of their fellow citizens.

I cautioned the audience that in the United States, many factors now play against the serious book review: the sheer volume of publications, the dissolution of shared values and recognized literary canon, the competition from the blogosphere, and the relatively low status of book reviewing in evaluating a candidate's dossier for a new academic position or for tenure. But in a young and proudly independent nation like Singapore, the audience was not to be deterred: evidently, its members are looking for the means to become certified judges—professional arbiters of their own literary scene. Listening to their lively discussion, I began to think that perhaps the book review is not such a dying species after all. Then, too, in the past few months, a single very favorable review in the *New York Review of Books*—Adam Kirsch's piece on my *Edge of Irony: Modernism in the Shadow of the Habsburg Empire* (2016)—evidently catapulted the book to a few weeks of best-seller status on Amazon.com. Even in the age of social media, it seems, reviews do make a difference.

At around the same time, Matthew Hofer, the editor of the new Recencies Series for the University of New Mexico Press, suggested that it would be valuable to publish a selection of the hundreds of book reviews—literary and academic—I have written over the five decades since I entered academe in 1965. Rereading these reviews, especially the predigitized ones, I was struck by the energy and vigor of the literary culture of the later twentieth century. It was a period, let's recall, when it was possible to obtain a university teaching position based on one's provocative and challenging reviews of such books as Paul de Man's *Blindness and Insight* or Jacques Derrida's *Of Grammatology*, especially if the review appeared in, say, *Critical Inquiry* or *Diacritics*. Similarly, a poet featured on the cover of *American Poetry Review*, interviewed for the *Paris Review*, or perhaps the subject of a *New Yorker* profile could count on reviews that would attract a sizable audience on the college campus circuit. In the United Kingdom, for that matter, where literary periodicals have always had a more stable and specific audience than in the United States, critics like Terry Eagleton and Frank Kermode were probably best known for their challenging reviews, later to be collected into volumes that were in turn reviewed by others.

The commissioned book review, at least in my own case, has not necessarily duplicated or even overlapped with the subjects of my essays and books. The authors most frequently discussed in the books—Gertrude Stein, Ludwig Wittgenstein, Marcel Duchamp, John Cage, Susan Howe, Charles Bernstein, Kenneth Goldsmith, and many Language and experimental poets—do not figure largely in reviews because the latter tend to deal with specific books assigned by specific journals. There are, of course, exceptions: Ezra Pound, Samuel Beckett, John Ashbery, and Frank O'Hara are crossover figures. In general, however, my book reviews can be said to provide both background and context for my own areas of special interest: in Cagean parlance, they thicken the plot.

Reviewing assignments, as I explained to the Singapore audience, can be fortuitous. The first review I ever wrote (1969) was of Anthony Hecht's volume of poems *The Hard Hours* (1967), billed by his publisher Atheneum as a "breakthrough" volume of verse. A friend had recommended me to a little Canadian magazine called *The Far Point*, now long defunct. As a recent PhD (with a thesis on W. B. Yeats's use of rhyme), I took the commission very seriously and read my way through as much of Hecht's poetry, past and present, as I could find, as well as commentary on Hecht by such of his fellow poet-critics as Richard Howard. I was trained to be what is now often dismissively called a "close reader"; more specifically, I accepted—and still do—the Modernist axiom that form and meaning are inextricable, which is to say that any visual, sound, or syntactic device also functions as a semantic one. Reading *The Hard Hours* from this perspective, I'm afraid I found Hecht's lyrics rather too mannerist for my taste, his ironies too reliant on what Wordsworth censured as "known habits of association."

In the same year, I wrote my first review of two scholarly books, this time for the journal *Contemporary Literature* (University of Wisconsin Press), which is still going strong. The books under consideration were Harold Bloom's *Yeats* and Allen Grossman's *Poetic Knowledge in the Early Yeats*, the latter evidently a revised dissertation. Not being an Ivy Leaguer (I did my graduate work at the Catholic University of America in Washington, DC, where my family was then based), I didn't have the temerity to be afraid of the great Harold and had no idea that Allen Grossman, of whom I had never heard, would soon count as a revered poet and mentor to the students in the Writing Seminars at Johns Hopkins. Both books dealt—though Bloom's much more broadly—with issues of Yeats's attraction to Theosophy and the Occult. Given my *literary* training and predisposition, I felt there should have been more attention paid to the fabric of the poetry itself: Bloom, moreover, was curiously dismissive of Yeats's later poetry, which I revered, favoring instead the early pre-Raphaelite poems like "Had I the heaven's embroidered cloths." In retrospect, I think I underrated the originality and strength of Bloom's strong reading of Yeats's late Romanticism. But I learned in the process how difficult it is to summarize another scholar's argument and to relate it to those of others—in this case, Grossman's. And in those days, decorum was very important: one tried to be judicious but polite and respectful. The ad hominem attacks one now comes across in the blogosphere simply didn't exist.

It was in the wake of publishing *The Poetic Art of Robert Lowell* in 1973 that I began to be invited to review new books of poetry as well as of biography and poetry criticism. Lowell was then in midcareer and there was much excitement about his work and that of his fellow "confessionals," from John Berryman and Randall Jarrell to Sylvia Plath and Anne Sexton. I was particularly interested in Plath, whose posthumously published *Ariel* (1966) spoke so strongly to my generation. "Viciousness in the kitchen! / The potatoes hiss": those opening lines of "Lesbos" daringly set themselves against the still genteel poetry to which we were then accustomed, and I took up the challenge of trying to understand Plath's curiously animistic poetry, its qualities often obscured by the romantic legend brought on by her untimely suicide at age thirty-one in studies like A. Alvarez's highly speculative *The Savage God*.

Then something surprising happened. It was the age of the omnibus poetry review and I was asked to write one for *Contemporary Literature*. I must have received more than a hundred books in the mail, many of them mere throwaways. But there were volumes that stood out: A. R. Ammons's *Briefings* and *Uplands*, John Berryman's *Love & Fame*, the *Collected Poems* of James Wright, and, best of all, a large volume with a red and white cover called *An Anthology of New York Poets*. Its editors were Ron Padgett and David Shapiro, themselves second-generation members of what came to be called the New York School. It was in this anthology that I first (and belatedly given that *Lunch Poems* had been published by City Lights in 1964) read the poems of Frank O'Hara as well as his "Personism: A Manifesto." I was instantly captivated by the colloquial immediacy and uncanny sense of *presence* in O'Hara's lyrics, and the anthology became the center of my review. I distinguished as well as I could between O'Hara and his many disciples included in the volume—for example, Allan Kaplan and Jim Brodey. It was one thing, I argued, to imitate Frank's *manner*, but in the hands of others, his "I do this, I do that" structures did not always transcend the trivial.

Oddly, however, I said nothing at all about John Ashbery, whose poetry was given even more space than O'Hara in the anthology. I cannot now recall why I did not yet recognize the greatness of Ashbery, whose books were soon to be so central to my own poetics: witness my 1977 review of the wonderful *Houseboat Days* for the *Washington Post*. Perhaps I found poems like "Leaving the Atocha Station" and "These Lacustrine Cities" too difficult, too surreal, to process. But in my omnibus review (1973), I did try to link O'Hara to Ammons—a conjunction rarely made that still seems right to me. Indeed, it was reviewing that gave me the chance to try to counter the usual dichotomies and standard associations. And I was soon working on a book on O'Hara, a poet who continues to be central to my own pantheon.

In the meantime, I found myself frequently reviewing for the *Washington Post*'s Sunday *Book World*, one of the free-standing newspaper book reviews that no longer exist. Through my Catholic University poet-friends Tim Dlugos and Terrence Winch (the former, sadly, an early victim of AIDS, the latter still going strong and producing witty short poems), I came to know the *Post*'s book editor, the late William McPherson, who won the Pulitzer Prize for Distinguished Criticism in 1977 and wrote what was to become a kind of cult novel, *Testing the Current* (1984). Bill gave me repeated assignments to review such then-prominent poets as James Wright and Richard Hugo, Thom Gunn and Mona Van Duyn.

Another great Washington venue of the period was *The New Republic*, in those years a central node for liberal political discussion, including book reviews. The literary editor Doris Grumbach, a passionate Leftist activist, had been a college professor, journalist, and novelist: in retirement (in 2018 she celebrated her 100th birthday), she was to write a series of interesting memoirs. Doris's own fiction was by no means experimental, but she was extremely open to new ideas, and was happy to have me review such then-considered oddball items as Frank O'Hara's impressionistic art criticism, collected under the title *Art Chronicles*, Ed Dorn's mock-epic *Slinger*, or David Antin's *Talking at the Boundaries*, not to mention William Chace's controversial study of the politics of Ezra Pound and T. S. Eliot or the new edition of Pound's *Gaudier-Brzeska*, that manifesto in the guise of an elegiac memoir of the sculptor Gaudier, "mort pour la patrie" in World War I at the age of twenty-three.

One of my *New Republic* reviews, not included in this collection, got me into serious trouble. In 1975, Robert Lowell published an embarrassing sonnet cycle called *The Dolphin* that dealt with his painful divorce from Elizabeth Hardwick and marriage to Caroline Blackwood in England. In these perhaps hyperconfessional lyrics, Lowell made extensive use of the actual correspondence between himself and Hardwick, much of it about their daughter Harriet, who, as presented in these (to me) maudlin poems, emerged as an irritatingly virtuous child, even as the portrait of Hardwick herself was curiously cloying. When I said as much in my review, Elizabeth Hardwick was incensed, and I received angry phone calls from someone who purported to be her cousin and from various editors. I protested that I was talking of the Lizzie and Harriet *in the poetry sequence*, not the *real* Elizabeth and her daughter Harriet, on whom I had never laid eyes, but the damage was done. I think Lowell himself forgave me—the one time I met him at a Library of Congress event he was very kind—but Hardwick, soon to be the *eminence grise* at the *New York Review of Books*, never did.

Serious reviewing is always risk-taking: one is sure to offend someone. In the 1970s, along with my more journalistic criticism, I was also writing regularly for the British *Modern Language Review* (*MLR*), its affiliate *The Yearbook of English Studies* (*YES*), and related scholarly journals in the United States. At *MLR*, then edited by the noted British scholar Claude Rawson, himself a fiercely brilliant and combative reviewer (whom I had come to know when he was a visiting professor at the University of Pennsylvania), the audience was almost wholly an academic one, but, in those years, engaged and exacting. My review of Donald Davie's little book on Ezra Pound for *MLR* provoked various scholars as well as Davie to respond, and a friendly if argumentative correspondence began that ended only when, in response to my *Frank O'Hara: Poet among Painters* (1977), Davie, to my dismay, voiced his strong disapproval of O'Hara's "queer" sensibility and subject matter. Davie's was, fortunately, a kind of last hurrah: by the early 1980s, the gay poetry scene had come into its own.

Reviewing scholarly books, at any rate, prompted a good deal of debate. A University of Connecticut professor named Charles Boer had written a book on Charles Olson's tempestuous late years, which I reviewed for the *Yearbook of English Studies*. This hagiographic memoir, written in the second person, repeatedly commended its subject for his rude and nasty behavior. It was full of commentary like "You greeted your first class [at the University of Connecticut] with a long blast of the foulest language you could muster," hoping to scare away the more timid students, especially the women. "This," Boer fondly recalls, "was a tactic you had used effectively at Buffalo." And Boer further commends Olson for bullying the patient who shared his semi-private hospital room, succeeding in getting the poor fellow patient transferred. This account gave me a chance to consider the larger relationship of ethics to aesthetics, calling into question Boer's unstated assumption that poets are not subject to the ethical norms that govern ordinary behavior.

Throughout the eighties and nineties, I continued on this dual track, moving between scholarly journals and more journalistic venues. I should note that in those days, the two were not that different, there being, on the one hand, less specialized jargon in scholarly reviews than there is today, and, on the other, a greater willingness of newspapers and little magazines to take on literary criticism. In the 1980s, for example, I had the good fortune to serve as a correspondent for the poet Clayton Eshleman's little magazine *Sulfur*. Eshleman was a superb editor: his was a journal focusing on the more experimental poetries of the Americas as well as Europe and he gave the journal's "correspondents" largely free reign. It was in *Sulfur* that I was able to write about Laurie Anderson's performance art or Kathleen Fraser's collaborations with Sam Francis; in *Sulfur* that I could dissect Jerome Rothenberg and Pierre Joris's excellent edition of the poetry of Kurt Schwitters; in *Sulfur* that Kenneth Goldsmith's collaborations with Joan La Barbara could be remarked upon. As a correspondent, moreover, I was given the leeway to take on the curious cult of Amy Clampitt, an obscure middle-aged woman, who began to publish poems only in her fifties and had been taken up by Helen Vendler and *New York Review of Books* critics. In *Sulfur*, I could argue my case against the pretensions of what I took to be Clampitt's mawkishly retro poetry. I also explored, in another *Sulfur* review of the period, the central assumptions governing Vendler's choices for *The Harvard Book of Contemporary American Poetry*—an anthology that omitted not only Ezra Pound but also the poets in the Pound tradition like Robert Creeley.

Throughout the eighties and nineties, I did much reviewing of poetry in translation. German is my native language; I am at home in French and know a little Italian, Russian, and Portuguese. I could therefore work with these languages although I make it a point never to review poetry in a language—say, Polish or Chinese—that I cannot as much as sound out. Given their reliance on meter and rhyme, the great German poets of the nineteenth century are notoriously difficult to translate, but I was happy to call attention to Hal Draper's ambitious Heine, Christopher Middleton's Goethe (both for *American Poetry Review*), and Richard Sieburth's Hölderlin for *Parnassus*. It was a pleasure to review Paul Auster's *Random House Book of Twentieth-Century* for *American Poetry Review*, Max Jacob's

The Dice Cup for *Sulfur*, and Donald Revell's rendition of Apollinaire's *Alcools* for the *Boston Review*. Jacques Donguy's French edition of Augusto de Campos's concrete poetry gave me access to the wordplay and punning of this great Brazilian poet who is one of my heroes: I reviewed Donguy's *Antologia despoesia* for *Western Humanities Review*. Again—and here I had to struggle but the effort was worthwhile given the strength of the poetry—I reviewed new translations of Vladimir Mayakovsky and Anna Akhmatova for various journals.

Poetry in translation (the subject of roughly a third of the reviews in both volumes) has given me the unique opportunity to write about major poets outside my own area of specialization: Goethe and Heine, Hölderlin, Rilke and Schwitters, Mallarmé and Césaire, Apollinaire and Max Jacob, Mayakovsky and Akhmatova. The challenge here is not only to get linguistic matters right but to encourage Anglophone readers to adjust their perspective. In these reviews, I am not participating in the current fashionable debate on translation theory or the politics of translation, my interests being largely practical: How can, say, Heine's ballad stanzas be made palatable to a contemporary audience and retain enough of their literal meanings? And I adhere to the old-fashioned view that there are more and less adequate translations, that the aim, at least for the translator of major poets, is to be faithful to the spirit of the original.

My most controversial reviews no doubt appeared in Herbert Leibowitz's *Parnassus: Poetry in Review. Parnassus*, which appears at irregular intervals, is one of the few journals that covers the gamut of contemporary poets, but its editorial aim is to match poets with reviewers who are not partisans of their work so that there will be real critique. William Logan is a *Parnassus* regular. Thus, the editor convinced me to take on two poets whose fame struck me as out of all proportion to their merit: Philip Larkin and Laura Riding. I had never reprinted my long review essay on Larkin (*Parnassus*, 1994), even though the essay—on Andrew Motion's biography as well as Larkin's *Collected Letters* along with the poems—won that year's Terrence du Près Prize for excellence in reviewing. I was afraid my friends and colleagues, many of them Larkin admirers, would find my piece too negative. The same reluctance to reprint held true for a second *Parnassus* piece—this one in 1998 on Laura Riding's poetry and her convoluted philosophical treatise *Rational Meaning*. Riding was something of a heroine for the experimental poets—for example, Charles Bernstein—of the 1990s; she was held to be a female (and Jewish) forerunner of Language poetry. Today, however, one hears much less about Riding, and because the review in question was excessively long and the Riding controversy has been largely eclipsed, I have not included this essay here. In the case of Larkin, however, I continue to try to understand what others see in him, for to read his poems and especially his letters in the second decade of the twenty-first century, is to be dismayed by the poet's openly racist slurs and his peevish misogyny. I felt then—and still do—that racism and sexism compromised a poetic vision that was, even aside from these issues, an oddly shrunken one.

Should one refrain from writing negative reviews? In recent years I have come to agree with Frank O'Hara that "it will go away without me," that, at a time where poetry gets so little attention, there is no point in writing a "bad" review. Still, when a particular poet is universally celebrated and has won countless awards, when, as is often the case, his or her reputation is inflated, it may be useful to step back and take another look. Larkin's poetry presents such a case as does that of the Lowell of *The Dolphin*.

Looking back over my reviews, I find that I have also been rather hard on anthologies, each one claiming to represent, in its own way, the "real thing." With the dominance of the digital over the print book, the anthology wars have cooled quite a bit: after all, instructors can now change assignments at will: they are no longer dependent on the structure or content of the class textbook. But in the eighties and nineties, it was quite different. My long review essay "Whose New American Poetry? Anthologizing in the Nineties," written for a Cornell University conference and published in *Diacritics* (1995), argues that, in a blind test, readers often couldn't tell the insiders from the outsiders—for example, Denise Levertov, very much a "new American poet" from A. R. Ammons, who was taken to belong to the Establishment canon. I have not until now reprinted this *Diacritics* essay because I knew I was stepping on too many toes. But now that the controversies in question have receded, it may be useful to reconsider the anthology wars of the period.

Since the turn of the century, my favorite reviewing venues have been two: *Bookforum*, where I was able to introduce what is primarily an art audience to the writings of Gregor von Rezzori, Joseph Roth, and Karl Kraus, and the *(London) Times Literary Supplement (TLS)*, which has, over the years, generously invited me to write on poetry, poets' biography, literary criticism, art, and, most recently, even film: specifically Ezra Edelman's astonishing film documentary *OJ: Made in America*, which won the 2017 Academy Award for Best Documentary. *TLS* editors tend to be exacting and demanding: if one goes over the word limit, every excessive word, awkward construction, or repetitive phrase is likely to be pruned. Indeed, even when word limit is observed, there is always plenty to excise and to rephrase more concisely and cogently. Reviewers are free to voice whatever view they hold, provided they make their case with sufficient detail and with accuracy. And it is an unwritten rule—no doubt dating back to the days when the *TLS* review was anonymous—that one doesn't review one's friends, or indeed one's mentors or students.

The question remains: why allot time to reviewing when one might be writing one's own books and articles? I have heard many friends and colleagues declare that they never write reviews; they want to be left alone to do their own work and not summarize the arguments or evaluate the literary oeuvre of others. Of course, the persons in question do "review" in that they write many fellowship recommendations, but these are usually anonymous and, by definition, positive. Fear of giving offense and a certain absence of curiosity are strong motives in avoiding the book review. But in declining to do so, writers and scholars are missing out on a unique opportunity, which is to move outside their particular discourse radius. I don't know enough about garden sculpture to write a book about Ian Hamilton Finlay's *Little Sparta*, but I believe I know enough about his writing practice to review a book about Finlay's concrete poetry or a compendium of his short stories. Again, I am not an art historian, but I can evaluate Mary Jacobus's treatment of Cy Twombly's literary references or Rosalind Kraus's reassessment of Picasso from a Frankfurt School perspective. I don't have the expertise to edit and annotate the letters of T. S. Eliot or of Samuel Beckett, but I can appreciate how much light the correspondence sheds on the primary work of these writers.

So much for the reviewing process. What, then, of the readership for a collection of reviews such as this one? What makes a newspaper or even a scholarly review more than one more bit of ephemera? Here history comes in. Reading these rather eclectic reviews—reviews long and short that touch on such varied bases as Lorine Niedecker's "Objectivist" poetry and the Nobel Prize–winner Elfriede Jelinek's "pornographic" fiction, William Gass's translations of Rilke and Donald Revell's of Apollinaire, the responses to Mina Loy's feminism versus that of Adrienne Rich—the reader may, I hope, gain perspective not just on my own views but on the evolution of our poetic culture from the late 1960s to the present. The complexities of literary history are endlessly puzzling. Who now reads Richard Hugo or Mona Van Duyn? Conversely, who today does not know the names Allen Ginsberg and John Ashbery? Who knew in 1984 that Paul Auster, first known as a translator of French poetry, would become a famous novelist? That the radical and difficult Tom Raworth (designated the "one" British poet referred to in the title of Jacques Roubaud's avant-garde French anthology of American poetry called *49 +1*) would come to have his *Collected Poems* published by the established Carcanet Press and reviewed (by myself among others) in the pages of the *TLS*? Then again, certain of my reviews, like those of Hugh Kenner's *A Homemade World* (*Washington Post*, 1975) and *A Sinking Island* (*Scripsi*, 1989), may remind contemporary readers how willing earlier critics were to go against the grain, to quarrel with received opinion.

A sequence of book reviews like the following can, or so at least I hope, provide us with an important chapter of literary history. Today, in the age of social media when everything happens so quickly, when reputations are made overnight only to be ignored by the next set of reviewers, it is easy to forget how continuously and inexorably canon reform operates. What has happened to the reputation of the counterculture poetic guru of the 1960s Charles Olson, and why? What were the cultural values that made Theodore Roethke (I recall directing at least three doctoral dissertations on his work) a model poet for the late 1960s and early 1970s and yet now all but forgotten? How is it that the *New York Review of Books* publishing house has come to revive the once taboo writings of Gregor von Rezzori?

Rereading the reviews collected in these pages, I take a certain satisfaction in having been largely on the right side of literary history. Some of my enthusiasms have turned out to be excessive; conversely, such poets as Larkin and Seamus Heaney continue to be very popular. But on the whole, I feel I have called the shots pretty accurately: Ed Dorn's *Slinger*, for example, which I first reviewed for the *New Republic* in 1975, is now being treated to an anniversary edition by Duke University Press. O'Hara is one of the most popular and admired poets in America, and the Concrete Poetry of the Noigandres group in Brazil has finally come into its own.

This is not to say that my own poetics—the concern, to put it succinctly for questions of language over questions of lyric, not to mention cultural and political issues—has escaped critique. Then again, the book review is by definition a site of controversy. Thus, I can only hope that my own "map of misreading" will stimulate a renewed debate about the writing of our recent past. Think how thoroughly the poetry world has changed between the publication of Anthony Hecht's *The Hard Hours* and the present! Or is it perhaps a case of plus ça change? In the words of Frank O'Hara's "Naphtha":

> I am ashamed of my century
> For being so entertaining
> but I have to smile

MARJORIE PERLOFF
Pacific Palisades, 2018

CHAPTER 1

The Hard Hours

To criticize a book of poems that has won such universal acclaim—not to mention the Pulitzer Prize—as Anthony Hecht's *The Hard Hours* may sound ungrateful or even perverse. Nevertheless, I propose to argue here that, despite his careful control of rhyme and stanza forms, his up-to-date idioms, and clever literary and mythological allusions, Hecht is not the major poet his admirers claim him to be.

Hecht's first volume, *A Summoning of Stones*, the greater part of which is reprinted in *The Hard Hours*, was published in 1954. Arthur Mizener remarked, after praising the elegance and charm of the collection, that Hecht's poems were perhaps "too charming," that he was "committed to the established style." This is a comment worth considering. What one misses in such poems as "La Condition Botanique," with its witty reflections on the difference between the human and the vegetable kingdoms, is an individual poetic voice.

The spirit that hovers over the whole collection is that of Wallace Stevens, the gaudy Stevens of the blank verse poems of *Harmonium*. Even the titles of the poems—"Discourse Concerning Temptation," "A Deep Breath at Dawn," "Alceste in the Wilderness"—might be Stevens titles. Sometimes Hecht intentionally writes a parody Stevens poem as in "Le Masseur de Ma Soeur," which is his amusing version of "Le Monocle de Mon Oncle." But all too often the poems are not quite parodies, not quite self-sustained lyrics—they are merely derivative. "As Plato Said," for example, consists in large part of lines and phrases from "Le Monocle": the passage beginning with the line, "The sheep come out of the hills, the sheep come down," is a case in point. One could, I suppose, argue that "As Plato Said" is also a parody of "Le Monocle"—its speaker opts for sex while Stevens's Uncle rejects it—but in this case the poem is no more than a coterie

Review of *The Hard Hours*, by Anthony Hecht. *The Far Point* 2 (Spring–Summer 1969): 45–51.

joke. If, on the other hand, Hecht is serious—and I think he is—what is one to make of the consistently Stevensian idiom?

I stress this point because I believe that *The Hard Hours* is again an example of the "established style," even though Ted Hughes claims on the dust jacket that Hecht has "shed every artifice" and now writes with "absolute raw simplicity and directness." The new collection merely exchanges one established convention for another. The poet's earlier aestheticism gives way to either of two modes: the confessional or autobiographical poem as invented by Robert Lowell and his followers, or the poem of religious meditation in the tradition of Eliot and the later Auden. Only rarely, as in "The Dover Bitch," does Hecht return to his earlier style.

The confessional poem is particularly hard to write; it requires a strong sense of place and of personal history as well as the ability to regard oneself with detachment, to make a drama out of one's own life. Lowell, the master of this mode, can make the most trivial incident from his past assume importance because he provides it with a rich context of history, geography, and family identity. The scene of a poem like "Terminal Days at Beverly Farms" is not just New England but a particular country house owned by his parents in the 1930s; the characters, Admiral and Mrs. Lowell, are two-dimensional figures whom the poet adores even as he castigates the "round boulder," which takes on symbolic connotations and is related to all the other images in the poem.

The creation of a specific locale, a context at once concrete and symbolic, is precisely what one misses in Hecht's new poems, although he obviously attaches importance to what Eliot called the objective correlative. In a recent essay for the *Hudson Review*, Hecht wrote that a lyric poem must "delight our faculties" by its "rendering of the substantive particularity of the diverse elements that compose our world." Not only must it render concrete particulars, it must also give us that "sense of their significant relationship to each other" that "Gerard Manley Hopkins calls 'inscape.'" Judged by his own high standard, Hecht's personal poems are less than successful.

In "A Letter," for example, the poet complains to his mistress of his frustrated love for her. They cannot be together because they know "Others are bound to us, the gentle and blameless"—for example, the poet's two sons. The lover's dilemma occurs in a vacuum: who is he and what kind of woman does he love? Who is responsible for the trying situation described by the speaker? It does not help much to know that he cannot forget his beloved because, in a phrase reminiscent of a dozen popular songs, "the crocus is up, and the lark, and the blundering / Blood knows what it knows." The only specific incident cited is the following:

You may remember that once you brought my boys
Two little woolly birds.
Yesterday the older one asked for you upon finding
Your thrush among his toys.
And the tides welled about me, and I could find no words

Here if anywhere in the poem, Hecht tries to objectify the speaker's anguish, but the image of the "little woolly birds" is merely embarrassing. The picture that comes in my mind is that of the tall gracious lady of minor Victorian fiction, hiding her tears as she hugs the dear children of the man she loves, and producing her thoughtful little present in the form of two birdies made of wool. The image is neither sharply articulated nor is it related to the images used to convey the urgency of the poet's longing: crocus, lark, sun, ocean, and blood.

The narrator of "A Letter" is full of self-pity. In the last stanza, he stoically declares that he will "continue as before / Doing some little good," but that he wants the lady to know "that all is not well / With a man dead set to ignore / The endless repetitions of his own murderous blood." These lines are annoyingly sentimental because the reader has not witnessed the speaker's struggle to forget his love. On the contrary, the poet seems to make every effort to indulge his daydream. Anyone who spins such fine phrases as "The sun plants one lithe foot / On that spill of mirrors," can hardly be very miserable.

In its failure to dramatize the poet's situation, "A Letter" is neither better nor worse than most of the confessional poems in the volume. "A Hill," for example, opens with the statement, "In Italy, where this sort of thing can occur, / I had a vision once," but the remainder of the poem fails to make clear why the animated street scene in sunny Florence should be the catalyst of the poet's somber and frightening vision of his own death. Landscape and emotion fail to cohere. Again, in "Behold the Lilies of the Field," the chain of events described in the opening verse paragraph is incommensurate with the speaker's overwrought emotional state. The scene is the analyst's office; the patient on the couch recalls a childhood incident in which his mother flattered a friend on the phone and then, having hung up, said to her children, "God what a bore she is!" This single bit of information is supposed to convince us, as it has convinced the speaker, that mother is a moral "whore" who has lost "all sense of honor." But the memory is so vague and trivial that it cannot carry the weight of the anxiety and guilt manifested by the patient in the bizarre dream that he now recalls for his analyst.

In "Adam," which furnishes the title of Hecht's volume, the speaker ponders the parallel between God's creation of Adam and his own paternity. Both he and God have created men, but his own creation is not an occasion for joy because his son, from whose mother the poet is evidently divorced, lives far away: "Where your men speak / A different mother tongue." Thus it is only the "empty air" that listens when the poet tells his son that "there will be / Many hard hours, / as an old poem says, / Hours of loneliness. / I cannot ease them for you; / They are our common lot." Such eminent critics as Daniel Hoffmann and Philip Booth have found these lines "moving" and "eloquent," but it is difficult for me to see anything beyond flat, expository statement in the stanza. As in the case of "A Letter," the speech is given an ill-defined context. One has no idea, for example, whether the father is a victim of circumstances or whether he is partially responsible for his isolation. If, moreover, "hard hours" are "our common lot," why bother to talk about it? And what does the fact that "an old poem says" that life is hard have to do with anything?

There is much irony in Hecht's confessional poems—in "The End of the Weekend," for example, the rapacious bat drops its prey on the roof at the very moment that the lustful couple beneath it is about to make love—but the irony is usually directed toward others, not against the poet himself. "The Vow" is a good example of this failure to secure proper distance. The poet's solemn speculation on the value of life is prompted by his wife's recent miscarriage. In the face of her acute depression, the poet wonders whether their union of "Jewish diligence and Irish jest" is perhaps "too bold a mixture to inform / A simple child." But because he is instinctively an affirmative person, he swears, in the concluding stanza, that a child will indeed bless their union. After all, he and his wife are still in love: "The flames are lit / That shall refine us."

This oath is, at best, inappropriate as are the earlier references to harps and tablets. The poet poses as dragon killer, rescuing damsels in distress from the fiery furnace, when in fact he is simply going to take his pleasure once again. The theme that one must bear one's suffering in the hope of a better future is out of proportion to the narrative itself, for a miscarriage is, after all, a rather common event. This is not to say that an excellent poem could not be written on the subject. Think, for example, what Sylvia Plath can do with a cut thumb or a broken leg. But "The Vow" is banal because it does not render the process of suffering itself. Hecht once again uses an experience to make his particular point.

The religious poems raise similar problems. The most ambitious poem in *The Hard Hours* is the ten-page "Rites and Ceremonies," a poem in four parts that Daniel Hoffmann has called a "riposte to Eliot's *Four Quartets.* There is no doubt that Hecht has the *Quartets* in mind. Like Eliot, he relates the natural to the supernatural, time to eternity, and man to God; like Eliot, he juxtaposes formal lyrics of great metrical variety with free verse paragraphs that exploit natural speech rhythms; he alternates realistic narrative and formal prayer. The language of "Rites" echoes not only the *Quartets* but also "The Waste Land" and "Ash Wednesday": it has a "Fire Sermon" like the former and liturgical references like the latter. The phraseology of "Ash Wednesday" runs through "Rites": "even among these Rocks" becomes "even among these snows," and the final prayer of "Rites" is an adaptation of Eliot's "Will the veiled sister pray" passage in part 5.

The voice of Hopkins is also heard in Hecht's poem. The opening prayer is an adaptation of the first stanza of "The Wreck of the Deutschland": witness such lines as "Furnisher, hinger of heaven, who bound / the lovely Pleaides . . . and caused to grow / veins, brains, bones in me, to breathe and sing / fashioned me air." Hecht evidently intends these echoes to be ironic; unlike the Christian God of Hopkins and of Eliot, his is secular and Jewish; He is the God "in whom we *doubt*." But, as in the case of the adaptations of Stevens found in *A Summoning of Stones*, it is hard to tell whether Hecht's attitude toward Eliot and Hopkins is serious or satirical. He makes no attempt to disprove or to reject their theology, but his own is clearly different. Why, then, is his poem so heavily dependent on theirs?

In part 1, "The Room," the poet visits Buchenwald twenty years after the war and wonders, in Job-like fashion, how a God who did not prevent the terrible sufferings of the Jews could be a just God. Part 2, "The Fire Sermon," presents an analogous situation in the Middle Ages: during a particularly bad plague year, two Jews are tried for poisoning the wells and are burned at the stake. Part 3, which begins with the matter-of-fact observation that "The contemplation of horror is not edifying," presents a third frightening scene: A Breughelesque pre-Lenten Carnival of Misrule in Renaissance Venice where once again the Jews are victimized. Finally, in "Words for the Day of Atonement," the poet tries to come to terms with the devil and suffering described in the previous sections. "Merely to have survived," he says, "is not an index of excellence." The wicked are still in power and the good still suffer. But, the poet now affirms, God, the Maker of all things, is still in His heaven in all His greatness and mercy. He will always help those Chosen People who have faith in Him; to them he shall "come down like rain upon mown grass."

"Rites and Ceremonies" has greater precision than Hecht's confessional poems, but like them it ultimately fails to cohere. The elaborate theological and philosophical correspondences that unify the disparate section of *Four Quartets* are not to be found in Hecht's poem. There is the terrible suffering of the Jews on the one hand. There is God on the other. But it is not made clear how the two can be related. What, for example, does the poet mean by the word "sin"? Are his own "sins" connected with the evil of Buchenwald? Hecht asserts that God is not dead, but he does not convincingly present a world that He inhabits. Like the speaker of Sylvia Plath's "Getting There," the poet declares in part 1 that "I am there. I am pushed through / With the others to the strange room," but the mood is not sustained. Literary and historical anecdotes are substituted for the experience itself; these anecdotes, moreover, do not enlarge the poem's range of meaning; they merely stress the obvious fact that there have always been evil and sadistic people in the world.

One is forced to conclude that Hecht is neither the confessional poet of our decade nor its religious bard. He is, I think, much more at home in the witty, aphoristic poems of the *Seven Deadly Sins* sequence. These short, impersonal lyrics with their sing-song Mother Goose rhythms and biting rhymes remind one of some of Pope's heroic couplets. Here, for example, is the frightening little poem "Lust," in which Christ's sacrifice is described in such ugly erotic terms that one wonders what mere human beings are like:

> The Phoenix knows no lust, and Christ, our mother,
> Suckles his children with his vintage blood.
> Not to be such a One is to be other.

The poet whom Hecht most resembles is not one of those who have so obviously influenced him—Eliot, Hopkins, Stevens, Lowell—but a poet of an earlier epoch, such as Edward Arlington Robinson. Like Robinson, Hecht lacks range and profundity, but both are masters of the low-key, minor irony. "Third Avenue in Sunlight" is nothing if not a latter-day "Miniver Cheevy," and "Rites and Ceremonies" is much closer to "The Man Against the Sky" than to "Ash Wednesday" or the *Four Quartets*. Like Robinson, Hecht is the product of a time of tension between dying and birth. He knows, but cannot always communicate, the aimless frustrations and longings of the modern urban agnostic.

CHAPTER 2

Yeats as Gnostic

I n 1964, Richard Ellmann remarked, "Yeats is in some present peril everywhere of being swallowed up by the great whale of literary history. . . . the search for his sources and analogues has become disproportioned, and . . . a tendency is growing to turn all that marvellously innovative poetry into a resumé of what other people have written. An inspired resumé, of course, but still a resumé."

Seven years later, these words seem peculiarly prophetic. Reading these two learned and closely argued studies of Yeats, one begins to have the uneasy feeling that the most "marvelously innovative" poet writing in English in the twentieth century is being slowly buried under the accumulating weight of his sources. For Allen Grossman, *The Wind among the Reeds* of 1899, a volume that "represents a poetic moment in which the determining conditions both of Yeats's later writing and of the Modern movement in poetry can be seen with singular clarity," is read as an "inspired resumé" of the European tradition of Wisdom. For Harold Bloom, Yeats's poetry, at its best, carries on the Great Tradition of Blake and Shelley, and, at its worst, is a confused, antihumanistic distortion of the true visionary Romantic mode. Both books rest on the unstated critical premise that the function of poetry is to convey both moral value and truth; both argue that Yeats was essentially a Gnostic. It is in their attitude toward Gnosticism that Grossman and Bloom part company. Where Grossman treats the term neutrally as the cornerstone of Yeats's system in the nineties and believes that Yeats outgrew his yearning for gnosis as he matured, Bloom, for whom "Gnosticism" seems to have the status of a dirty word, argues that Yeats became more and more absorbed in his search for a "dehumanizing divinity" and that his poetry suffered accordingly.

Grossman's thesis is that *The Wind among the Reeds* must be read, not as a

Review of *Yeats*, by Harold Bloom, and *Poetic Knowledge in the Early Yeats*, by Allen Grossman. *Contemporary Literature* 12 (Autumn 1971): 554–61.

collection of isolated lyrics but as a single "mythological poem" about the "search for poetic knowledge." The book's central myth is the contest of the "creative fire-self" or "figure at the center" with his father image, "the cherubic Warder of Eden, the cabalistic Jehovah," for possession of the White Woman who is both Beloved and Mother. The prize of this contest is poetic knowledge, but because Yeats gradually realized that consummation with the White Woman was equivalent to death, he renounced knowledge for living, eternity for identity, and emerged into the twentieth century as a Modern poet who could reevaluate his former structures from the new perspective of irony.

The latter part of Grossman's argument must be taken on faith because he never shows us what the "new Yeats" is like or why he, unlike so many other writers of the 1890s who were influenced by occult literature, "ceases to be a mystic and become an artist" after 1900. I am not convinced, in short, that *The Wind among the Reeds* is the watershed in Yeats's career that Grossman claims it to be. As an exposition of the volume's recurrent themes and symbols, however, the book is extremely interesting.

The first three chapters are the most important; Grossman groups the poems in the volume according to their date of composition and discerns that, whereas the first chronological group is characterized by eclecticism of style and derivative thematic motifs, the second section, which includes such poems as "Aedh Laments the Loss of Love," introduces the major icon of the book, the immortal White Woman of the pale trance and "hair tent," who is "the fallen aspect of Sophia as she can be found in the early history of Gnosticism." Grossman gives a fascinating account of the transmutations of this icon in occult literature and shows how the Sophia figure gradually merged in the poet's imagination with the image of Ireland herself, the Great Mother and Muse. In the same vein, he carefully traces the symbolic transformations of the wind and reed images. The reed bowed by the wind, for example, first signifies the poet's "self-image as the overthrown artist," an image derived from pre-Raphaelite painting, but after his contact with Hermetic writings, Yeats transformed "the symbol of the reed in water into the anima mundi itself, a gigantic mystical plant which is the source not only of poetry but of all life."

Less convincing are the later chapters, which deal with Yeats's early personae. Grossman himself admits that since Yeats generally assigned poetic speakers to particular poems only after their composition and publication, "it is difficult to determine the appropriateness in each case of the speaker to the poem." This admission undercuts such elaborate distinctions, based on alchemical texts, as those between Aedh, "the birth of the element, Fire of Fire," Hanrahan, "Air of Fire, the life of the element," and Robartes, "the Ideal, Water of Fire." In the poems cited, at least, such symbolism often seems extraneous.

This raises a more serious question about the whole study. To what extent does Grossman's source hunting illuminate the poems themselves? The little lyric "Breasal the Fisherman" (later called "The Fish"), for example, contains the metaphor, well known in folklore and fairy tale, of the poet as fisherman and his beloved as the slippery fish who eludes his net. The poem clearly refers to Yeats's frustrated longing for Maud Gonne, and its barely veiled reproach does not seem in any way obscure. But Grossman reads it in the light of Hermetic tradition: "The fish is the prima materia, the lapis philosophorum, the ultimate identity of the self, and Yeats is in search of it the more hopelessly because the moon, symbol of subjectivity, has set, and the creature of the moon is not to be found elsewhere." The whiteness of the woman is related to the "symbolic mercury" that dissolved and purified imperfect bodies, while the "silver cords" and "pale tide" refer to the "state of Luna," which is the alchemists' equivalent of "the Illuminative way." But by this time, we have lost sight of the poem itself, which is, after all, a fairly rudimentary version of what Bloom calls "the dramatic lyric of internalized quest." The overingeniousness of this and similar readings is matched by an opaque verbal style that frequently lapses into jargon. Thus, Grossman writes, "The notion of Art for Art's Sake proposes a self-referent system in which energy circulates endlessly without outlet"; he talks of the "estranging exigencies of idealization and concealment" or "the withering away of techniques of personal idealization." In such phrasing, the occult has become manner as well as matter.

Harold Bloom's Yeats is a much more ambitious, comprehensive, and original study than Grossman's; it has already been hailed as a classic by some reviewers, and it will surely be studied and hotly debated not only by Yeats scholars but by critics in general for years to come. Bloom's aim is admittedly polemic. He asserts on his first page that "Yeats, Hardy, and Wallace Stevens seem to me the poets writing in English in our century whose work most merits sustained comparison with the major poets of the nineteenth century," whereas "Eliot and Pound may prove to be the Cowley and Cleveland of this age." This sets the tone for Bloom's attack on the prevailing academic view of Yeats, the "false Romantic" aesthete of the 1890s who went to school to Donne and Ezra Pound, and, having purified his style and adopted modern colloquial idiom, became a great creator of symbolic systems, a prophetic poet who celebrates man's heroic drive to transcend the base and the commonplace.

Against this orthodoxy, Bloom argues that "Yeats's true context is the English Romantic tradition from Spenser through Pater and the Tragic Generation." Although many critics of the last decade—notably John Bayley, Frank Kermode, and Robert Langbaum—have explored Yeats's place in the Romantic tradition, Bloom's argument is much more sweeping. Romanticism is seen not as one of many influences on Yeats's poetry but as the only influence that matters. The word "influence" is defined as "a variety of melancholy or an anxiety-principle. It concerns the poet's sense of his precursors, and of his own achievement in relation to theirs. . . . In this revisionary sense, in which the poet creates his own precursors by necessarily misinterpreting them, poetic influence forms and malforms new poets." Yeats's poetry is viewed, in short, as "a series of swerves away from the precursors," in which the poet struggles to find his own aesthetic identity.

This is a refreshing view of poetic influence, because all too often scholars fail to consider the degree to which a given poet may misunderstand or transform his source. Grossman's reading of "Breasal the Fisherman" is a case in point. In any case, Bloom's discussion of Yeats's "swerves away from the precursors" in his first five chapters is fascinating, although I think that the influence of Wordsworth and Coleridge—and particularly of the greatest European Romantic, Goethe—is consistently underrated. Yeats's great autobiographical poems from "The Wild Swans at Coole" to "A Bronze Head" surely have more in common with Goethe's "Ilmenau" or with "Tintern Abbey" and "Frost at Midnight" than with the internalized quest romance of Shelley or with Blakean apocalypse. Perhaps for this very reason, Bloom generally plays down these poems and concentrates on the visionary lyrics written in the Blake-Shelley tradition.

Bloom gives a superb account of the Yeatsian versions of the Alastor quest romance in such early works as *The Isle of Statues* and *Oisin*. Although Shelleyan images and symbols continue to operate in the later poetry (the "alastor" or "avenging daimon," for example, stands behind the Yeatsian anti-self), Yeats, who "hungered for belief," became increasingly dissatisfied with a poet whom he correctly understood to be "the most heroic of agnostics." "He in effect blames Shelley for not being Yeats—for not seeking the support of a popular mythology, or of magic and occult tradition." Longing for an "antithetical poetic father to take Shelley's place," he turned to Blake, a poet with whom he could identify, ironically enough, only because he read him "with great inaccuracy and deliberately befuddled insight."

The chapter on Yeats's version of Blake is perhaps the best in the book. Here Bloom's profound knowledge of Blake and his careful discriminations leave us in little doubt that Yeats's misunderstanding of Blake was indeed radical. "Yeats's Blake becomes a Gnostic, with profound results for Yeats's own 'system' and poetry. Blake was vehemently set against all dualisms, Pauline or Cartesian . . . But Yeats . . . shared always the Gnostic sense of longing acutely for the soul's fortunate destiny after the body's death, a longing that is the negation of Blake's apocalyptic desires."

This argument, buttressed first by a careful reading of the Ellis-Yeats edition of Blake (1893) and later by a rigorous examination of the Gnostic distortions of Blake in *A Vision*, is wholly convincing, but difficulties arise when description gives way to evaluation. In Bloom's analyses of the poems and plays, Blake and Shelley, along with that major Modern poet of a "diminished but authentic Romanticism," Wallace Stevens (p. 215), are consistently used as moral norms against which Yeats's poetry is measured and found wanting. The underlying assumption, which is neither defended nor so much as discussed, is that the Modern poet should be a Romantic visionary who seeks "to make a more human man" (p. 471), that he must rigorously cast out all traces of sacramentalism and mysticism, so as to devote himself to the task of building Jerusalem here and now on his own soil. Because Yeats continued to hunger for spiritual knowledge and could not be satisfied with the idea that salvation is to be realized in historical process rather than after death, he is therefore judged to be inferior to his great Romantic predecessors and dismissed as a Jungian apostle of the irrational. The most revealing expression of Bloom's ethical bias is found in the following passage: "The most admirable restraint of imagination, in our time, is to be found in the writings of Freud, who does not quest after a cure that cannot be found. . . . he understood that poetry might be a discipline roughly parallel to psychoanalysis, one in which the poet and his reader, like the analyst and his patient, would find not cure but a balance of opposites, not ultimates beyond knowledge but self-knowledge, not a control over fate but self-control."

It is quite true, of course, that Yeats is not the poet of self-knowledge and self-control, but then why should he be? The moral presupposition behind this passage colors all of Bloom's readings and ultimately vitiates many of his conclusions: he is, in the end, no fairer to Yeats than the New Critics were to Shelley. Thus, the allegory of *Oisin* is preferred to the "mere complication" of "Among School Children" because the early poem has a "completeness of mythic structure," because, in other words, its convention is still that of Shelleyan quest romance. The poems of the middle period, on the other hand, are dismissed as inferior because they exhibit "insufficient self-dramatization," a charge that is particularly disconcerting, for how much "self-dramatization" is there in *Oisin*, "King Goll," or the *Rose* poems Bloom greatly admires? But the most irritating chapters are those that deal with Yeats's mature poetry. One must take some of Bloom's sweeping dismissals (e.g., of the Byzantium poems) with a grain of salt because he sometimes seems mainly anxious to *épater le professeur*. But in many cases his rejection is entirely serious and follows from his ethical premise. To take just one example, let us consider his treatment of "Leda and the Swan."

Bloom proposes to compare Yeats's treatment of "God as rapist" to Shelley's version of a similar theme in act 3 of *Prometheus Unbound*, where Jupiter learns to his dismay that he has not begotten a son upon his mortal victim, Thetis, after all, and that instead the fearful Demogorgon arises "to fill the vacuum of heaven." What Bloom particularly relishes is the Shelleyan irony that not only Thetis but even Jupiter turns out to have precious little knowledge or power, that Jupiter is, in fact, "a rather poor version of God." Shelley's theme is thus that "the human involuntarily thwarts God's design merely by being human," whereas Yeats unfortunately tries to convince us that the rape of Leda inaugurated a new historical cycle, a notion that Bloom, along with Yvor Winters, finds rather absurd: "I wish . . . that the Yeats sonnet had just a touch of the Shelleyan skepticism about divine power and knowledge." The revisions, moreover, are unfortunate because Yeats sacrifices "clarity and fullness for the sake of dramatic shock"; when, for example, the line, "Did nothing pass before her in the air?" becomes "So mastered by the brute blood of the air," the nature of Leda's vision becomes too obscure.

Here the limitations of Bloom's critical method become obvious. The poem is judged purely on ethical and philosophical grounds: philosophically, it evidently misses greatness because it does not question divine power; ethically, it is suspect because it does not teach us how to live. What Bloom ignores is that the revisions purposely move in the direction of suggestiveness, mystery, and ambiguity, for the poem, far from making statements about divinity, knowledge, and power, merely presents that cataclysmic moment when the two polar opposites—male and female, divine and human—come together, and suggests the enormous passions and pain such a union entails. Yeats's focus, as Richard Ellmann and Helen Vendler have shown, is not at all on Zeus but on Leda. What does it feel like, the poem asks, to be completely taken out of oneself, removed from all ordinary experience, and then to be dropped back to earth? It is a question Yeats did not pretend to answer definitely.

Despite these reservations, I find that when Bloom let his superb critical instinct get the better of his moral bias, his readings are usually excellent. No one, I think, has written as perceptively on *Four Plays for Dancers*, showing how Yeats, unlike Pound, assimilated Noh to the Romantic tradition. Again, no one writing prior to Bloom's book quite dared to say that, despite Eliot's unusually generous praise, *Purgatory* is a drama of "eugenic tendentiousness" that foolishly advocates violence, that Lear's "tragic joy" in "Lapis Lazuli" is asserted rather than shown, or that "Under Ben Bulben" is a snobbish piece of rhetoric written by an old man whose powers were obviously declining. Certainly, this book will make us all see Yeats with new eyes and rethink our own positions. How unfortunate, therefore, that Bloom, who abhors dualisms, falls into his own trap by making the question of Yeats's Gnosticism versus the desirable visionary humanism of Blake and Shelley such an either-or disposition.

CHAPTER 3

Extremist Poetry

Some Versions of the Sylvia Plath Myth

As the Sylvia Plath cult continues to grow, it becomes more and more diffi-cult to talk about her poetry as a verbal act. The cult prefers to see its high priestess as the *belle dame sans merci* of the early sixties, dangerous not only to her would-be lovers but to herself, a courageous free spirit who sacrificed her life for her art, a brave gambler who lost the gamble. Thus, it is now almost un-American—or un-British for that matter—to question the artistic merits of Sylvia Plath's posthumously published volumes of poetry, for anything Plath wrote is rapidly taking on the status of a sacred text.

On the surface, A. Alvarez's memoir of Sylvia Plath, which first appeared in *New American Review* 12 (1971) and is the opening chapter of *The Savage God*, would seem to dispel the more melodramatic versions of this myth. Con-vinced that Sylvia Plath did not really intend to die when she put her head inside her gas oven, Alvarez laments that out of her suicide "a whole myth has grown . . . a myth of the poet as a sacrificial victim, offering herself up for the sake of her art." Yet despite Alvarez's moving and understated account of Plath's last days in her pathetic little flat near Primrose Hill, his careful account of her brave efforts to appear "normal" and competent, and despite his protes-tations that what matters is Plath's poetry, not extra-literary gossip about her private life, I believe that Alvarez himself is finally guilty of championing the myth rather than the poetry. One begins to suspect, in fact, that Ted Hughes may have had at least some cause to be incensed about the publication of the Alvarez memoir.

Why do people commit suicide? Again and again in *The Savage God*, Alvarez modestly insists that he has no real answer to this question. The stated aim of his

Review of *The Savage God*, by A. Alvarez; and *Crossing the Water and Winter Trees*, by Sylvia Plath. *Journal of Modern Literature* 2 (November 1972): 581–88.

book is simply "to counterbalance two prejudices: the first is that high religious tone . . . which dismisses suicide in horror as being a moral crime or sickness beyond discussion. The second is the current scientific fashion which, in the very process of treating suicide as a topic for serious research, manages to deny it all serious meaning by reducing despair to the boniest statistics." And, having presented a variety of current theories on suicide as well as some fascinating case histories of suicidal artists, Alvarez concludes on the last page of his book that suicide cannot properly be explained, that it is simply "a terrible but utterly natural reaction to the strained, narrow, unnatural necessities we sometimes create for ourselves."

But one wonders if Alvarez is not protesting too much. Despite the sweet reasonableness of his middle chapters, which give a short, incisive account of changing attitudes to suicide from the Greeks to the present, followed by a very lucid critique of common fallacies about suicide (e.g., that suicide is promoted by bad weather, that it is a national habit, that it is more common among young people than old ones, that people commit suicide for unrequited love), Alvarez does have his own theory about the relationship of suicide to art in the twentieth century, and it is this theory, rather than the very interesting discussion of early Christian attitudes to suicide or of Freudian concepts of "primary aggression," that is the heart of *The Savage God*.

We might note, to begin with, that the conceptual and historical study of suicide found in Alvarez's middle chapters is framed by two personal memoirs: the first that of Sylvia Plath, the second, a rather puzzling and sometimes embarrassing account of Alvarez's own suicide attempt at Christmas 1960. "I wanted," writes Alvarez, "the book to start, as it ends, with a detailed case history so that whatever theories and abstractions follow can somehow be rooted in the human particular. No single theory will untangle an act as ambiguous and with such complex motives as suicide. The Prologue and Epilogue are there as reminders of how partial every explanation must always be."

But when one looks at the book as a whole, these personal chapters seem to have quite another function from the stated one. Both Plath and Alvarez are viewed as emblematic of the artist, of the special sensibility whose fate it is to wrestle with the knowledge of his or her own death. The difference between the two, Alvarez's account of his own suicide attempt implies, is one of degree: in his own makeup, the artistic sensibility was only one element, and therefore, when the youthful attempt failed, he was reborn a wiser, calmer, if a less exciting and creative human being, a man no longer expecting answers to ultimate questions—in short, an Odysseus or Aeneas who has gone down into the realm of the dead, returning to tell the rest of us what it feels like to kill oneself.

Like Melville's Ishmael, he has earned the right to say with Job, "And I only am escaped alone to tell thee."

The core of Alvarez's argument about the relationship of suicide to Modern art is an outgrowth of his earlier analysis of Extremist Art in *Under Pressure* (1965). It can be summarized briefly. In an age of world wars, extermination camps, atomic explosions, and genocide, an age of mass democracy, mass technology, and dehumanization, the artist has only two choices. He can practice "Totalitarian Art"—the art that "tackles the historical situation frontally, more or less brutally, in order to create a human perspective for a dehumanizing process." Beckett is Alvarez's prime example of Totalitarian Art: his characters "lead posthumous, immobile lives, stripped of all personal qualities, appetites, possessions, and hope." Only language remains, language ritualized and stylized to capture the full horror and grim humor of a Life-in-Death, a world that God has abandoned. Such "minimal art" in which the hero is "deindividualized" is one form of suicide; it abdicates all claims to a world of human choice, desire, or will.

The other alternative is what Alvarez calls Extremist Art. The Extremist Poet cannot believe in the existence of a world outside his own self; consequently, he presses deeper and deeper into his own subterranean world of psychic isolation, breakdown, and neurosis, confronting the confusions of his own inner life "along that friable edge that divides the tolerable from the intolerable." In facing the abyss in the depths of his soul, the Extremist Poet finally confronts his own absurd death. His double duty is thus "to forge a language which will somehow absolve or validate absurd death, and to accept the existential risks involved in doing so." Sylvia Plath, for example, seems to have decided "that for her poetry to be valid, it must tackle head-on nothing less serious than her own death, bringing to it a greater wealth of invention and sardonic energy than most poets manage in a lifetime of so-called affirmation." Her *actual* suicide, then, was simply "a risk she took in handling such volatile material," a "last desperate attempt to exorcise the death she had summed up in her poems."

Sylvia Plath, Alvarez suggests, is thus the archetypal Modern artist, the emblem of a century characterized by its "sudden, sharp rise in the casualty rate among the artists." As art turns further and further inward, it inevitably becomes more dangerous to its creator, for life, Alvarez repeatedly insists with a kind of Paterian or Wildean fervor, imitates art. "Before the twentieth century," he writes, "the gifted artists who killed themselves or were even seriously suicidal were rare exceptions. In the twentieth century the balance suddenly shifts: *the better the artist, the more vulnerable he seems to be*" (my italics).

This is the heart of the matter. Alvarez assembles an impressive list of artists to illustrate his thesis: Arshile Gorki, Jackson Pollock, Mark Rothko among the painters; among writers, Hart Crane, Randall Jarrell, Delmore Schwartz, Cesare Pavese, Vladimir Mayakovsky, Virginia Woolf, Ernest Hemingway, not to mention such psychological suicides as Dylan Thomas, who willfully drank himself to death, or Kafka, who "wanted to turn his premature natural death from tuberculosis into artistic suicide by having all his writing destroyed." It is perhaps also significant that John Berryman, whom Alvarez calls one of the leading Extremist Poets of our day, committed suicide shortly after the British publication of *The Savage God*, almost as if to confirm Alvarez's thesis.

Nevertheless, I find this thesis highly questionable. If one makes a list of major twentieth-century writers, a very different picture emerges. In France, after the tragic suicide of Nerval in 1855, and the self-proclaimed "litteraturicide" of the nineteen-year old Rimbaud in 1873, only the Dada poets seem to fit into Alvarez's scheme, and he himself insists that "Dada was knowingly a dead end; its aims were incompatible with art in essence." None of the following committed suicide: Proust, Gide, Mauriac, Valéry, Apollinaire, Claudel, Cocteau, Perse, Bonnefoy, Supervielle, Genet, Sartre, Camus—all major Modernists. Of German writers, the most notable suicide cases are Trakl and Toller; again, the major figures—Rilke, Brecht, Mann, Benn, Hesse, Musil, and I would add Kafka, even though he wanted his writing destroyed—did not take their own lives. Of English and American poets, we may set the suicides of Plath, Jarrell, Crane, and Thomas over against those who lived on: Yeats, Eliot, Pound, Stevens, Auden, Williams, Frost, Moore, Bishop, Roethke. Among the novelists, the suicides of Woolf and Hemingway can hardly be considered normative when one considers the nonsuicides of Joyce, Lawrence, Conrad, James, Forster, Ford, Faulkner, Bellow, Malamud, Mailer, or Murdoch. Can we agree that "the better the artist, the more vulnerable he seems to be"?

I am not saying that these writers were not, at some point in their lives, given to suicidal thoughts. But so were poets of earlier ages. Goethe, as Alvarez himself notes, tested his own attitude toward suicide by keeping a dagger at his bedside and trying, night after night, to send the sharp point an inch or two into his heart. When he realized that he simply *could not* perform the act, he threw the dagger away and decided to live. The important point here is that in Goethe's case, as in that of many poets, the will to live triumphed over the more morbid suicidal impulses. One might even argue, contrary to Alvarez's theory, that the artistic drive itself has kept many writers alive—if Yeats, for example, became, in the final decade of his life, the heroic "Wild Old Wicked Man," it was not, as Alvarez, implies, because he invented a pseudo-religion to allay his self-doubts, but because he knew that he was at the height of his poetic powers. Again, Proust became in his final years an ardent fighter against the death he had actually longed for two decades earlier when his mother died, because he simply had to finish his great novel. The best twentieth-century poets, perhaps, have been those who could transcend their own death wish, moving beyond death to a larger vision encompassing both life and death.

Alvarez is surely right in arguing that the contemporary poet is peculiarly committed to the truths of his inner life, to an art that is profoundly autobiographical. But his insistence that such an inward search necessarily places the artist on the narrow precipice between life and death strikes me as essentially a Romantic and specifically a fin-de-siècle myth, analogous, say, to the Werther myth that Alvarez treats quite objectively in his chapter "The Romantic Agony." Even Robert Lowell, Alvarez's Extremist Poet par excellence, has expressed some hesitation about the new myth of the artists' vulnerability. In his obituary essay on Berryman for *The New York Review*, Lowell writes, "I must say something of death and the *extremist* poets as we are named in often prefunerary tributes. Except for Weldon Kees and Sylvia Plath, they (i.e., Berryman, Jarrell, and Thomas) lived as long as Shakespeare, outlived Wyatt, Baudelaire, and Hopkins, and long outlived the forever romantics, those who really died young. John himself lived to the age of Beethoven." This is a very telling point. The ostensibly "sharp rise in the casualty rate among the artists," like the rise in divorce rate, may have something to do with the simple fact that we live so much longer today than did our ancestors.

I cannot, then, view Sylvia Plath's suicide as an attempt "to get herself out of a desperate corner which her own poetry had boxed her into." If we accept this explanation, what shall we make of the fact that, at the time of her first suicide attempt, Plath was writing rather careful and derivative poetry, in no way confronting her deepest self? Yet this first attempt was, Alvarez himself argues, much more carefully planned and likely to succeed than the final one. It seems more likely, then, that Plath committed suicide, not as a "last desperate attempt to exorcise the death she had summed up in her poems," but as an act of despair in the face of a renewed attack of mental illness. "How did I know," says the heroine of *The Bell Jar*, "that someday—at college, in Europe, somewhere, anywhere—the bell jar, with its stifling distortions, wouldn't descend again?" Evidently it did in February 1963. And the facts of Plath's life suggest that if this particular suicide attempt had failed, as it well might have since the au pair girl arrived just a few hours after the poet turned on the gas, there would have been another one some other time. The pattern was too well established to change.

All this is in the realm of speculation, but such speculation is naturally prompted by the elusiveness of Alvarez's central argument. We are on firmer ground, at any rate, when we talk about the poems themselves. But here we run into another problem, for unfortunately Ted Hughes' editions of Plath's previously uncollected poems—*Crossing the Water* and *Winter Trees*—serve her poetry at least as badly as Alvarez's memoir serves her biography. These two slim volumes of poems must surely be regarded as one of the scandals of recent publishing history.

The dust jacket of *Crossing the Water* announces, "The poems in this collection were written in the period between the publication of *The Colossus* (1960) and the posthumous book *Ariel* (published in England in 1965). As a group, they illuminate an extremely important period in Sylvia Plath's life; they also mark the point at which her work moved beyond great promise and competence and began to burn with genius." But a quick check through the biography compiled by Mary Kinzie, Daniel Lynn Conrad, and Suzanne D. Kurman for Charles Newman's symposium *The Art of Sylvia Plath* (Faber, 1970) makes clear that these are not, in fact, primarily "transitional poems" as they are subtitled. Of the thirty-eight poems in the volume, eleven were published before the end of 1960, and internal evidence suggests that an additional six were written in late 1959 or early 1960.[1] Almost half the poems in the volume, in other words, belong to the period of *The Colossus*. On the other hand, certain poems in *Crossing the Water* are contemporaneous with poems in *Ariel*. "In Plaster," for example, is the companion poem of "Tulips" (*Ariel*, p. 10); both were written in March 1961 when Sylvia Plath was in the hospital, recovering from an appendectomy.[2] To consider *Crossing the Water* a transitional volume is therefore puzzling to say the least. One wonders what Ted Hughes meant when he said in a BBC broadcast, reprinted in *Critical Quarterly* (Summer 1971), that "this work from the interim is fascinating and much of it beautiful in a rich and easy way that we find neither in *The Colossus* nor *Ariel*." Which *Colossus*, which *Ariel*? For the confusion is compounded by Hughes's prefatory note to *Winter Trees*: "The poems in this volume are all out of the batch from which *Ariel* poems were more or less arbitrarily chosen and they were all composed in the last nine months of Sylvia Plath's life." But, leaving aside the radio play "Three Women," of the eighteen poems in *Winter Trees*, three—"Lesbos," "The Swarm," and "Mary's Song"—had appeared in the US edition of *Ariel* (1966), although not in the 1965 British edition.

To make matters even worse, many Plath poems, published in periodicals in the early 1960s, are not included in either volume. Thus "Ouija" originally appeared in *Hudson Review* (Fall 1960) together with "Electra on Azalea Path"; the first is included in *Crossing the Water*, the second omitted. No explanations are given. Yet "Electra," an earlier variant of the famous "Daddy," seems at least as relevant to a study of Plath's interim work as does "Ouija." Again, all the poems published in the March 1962 issue of *Poetry*—"Widow," "Face Lift," "Heavy Women," and "Love Letter"—find their way into *Crossing*, with the exception of "Stars Over Dordogne." Why is this omitted? "Purdah," published

posthumously in *Poetry* in August 1963 appears in *Winter Trees*, but its companion poem "Eavesdropper" does not. And one of Plath's most interesting poems,
"The Jailor," published in *Encounter* in October 1963 is not reprinted in *Winter Trees*, although "Thalidomide" and "Childless Woman," printed in the same
issue, are.

Surely such careless posthumous publication of Plath's work is a disservice
both to the poet's memory and to her readers. The absurdity of making sweeping
conclusions on the basis of these badly edited volumes is illustrated by a comment of Lyman Andrews in the *London Sunday Times*, reprinted on the dust
jacket of *Crossing the Water*: "Assurance was sometimes lacking in her earlier
poems, and in the last poems at times there was a loss of control, while these
poems are an almost perfect marriage of strength and elegance." A remarkable
feat indeed, considering that half the poems in the volume were written at the
same time as half the poems in *The Colossus*!

My own view is that *Crossing the Water* does not generally rise above the
level of *The Colossus*. Despite such notable exceptions as "I Am Vertical" and
"Parliament Hill Fields," the poems in *Crossing* tend to be ingenious rather than
intensely moving. "Insomniac" is a good example. Ted Hughes calls this poem,
which won the Guinness Award at the 1961 Cheltenham Festival, "an egg from
The Colossus and *Ariel* is just cracking out of it." Superficially, "Insomniac" does
look ahead to the *Ariel* poems, in its concern for extreme psychic states, for the
sufferings of the individual who cannot adjust his mental landscape to that of
the outside world, here symbolized by the insomniac, for whom the slightest
sound or glimmer of light become threatening intrusions, forcing him further
and further into the dark chambers of his hyperactive mind.

Yet the poet herself seems to be standing *outside* the experience portrayed,
carefully commenting in the third person on the insomniac's anguish, rather
than exploring the movement of the mental process itself. In conceit after dazzling conceit, she defines his state of mind: the stars in the night sky are "much-
poked periods" in blueblack carbon paper, peepholes letting in the "bonewhite
light, like death." The insomniac's pillow takes on the irritating texture of desert
sand; his past haunts him like an "old, granular movie"; "Memories jostle each
other for face-room like obsolete film stars." Again, sleeping pills are seen figuratively as "Those sugarly planets whose influence won for him / A life baptized
in no-life for a while," but because the insomniac has built up an immunity to
them, they have become "worn-out and silly, like classical gods." And so on.

There seems to be nothing behind these clever analogies. The line "His forehead is bumpy as a sack of rocks," for example, recalls "le front plein déminences"
of Rimbaud's seven-year-old poets, but whereas Rimbaud, in the poem of that
title, establishes an elaborate thematic contrast between images of dryness and

rigidity on the one hand, and those of dampness, succulent grass, and fragrance on the other, thus defining the world to which the poet longs to escape, Plath's poem has no such central design. Pills alternately resemble communion tablets or classical gods; cats howl like "damaged instruments"; parental faces appear like flowers swaying on their stalks, but ultimately there is no reflexive relationship between these individual metaphors, and the poem, despite its complicated surface, does not really say much more than that insomnia is a highly unpleasant experience.

Very few of the poems in *Crossing the Water* have the oracular, transfiguring vision of Sylvia Plath's best poems—"Ariel," "Words," "Little Fugue," "Fever 103." Too often the poet seems concerned with the individual detail rather than the total construct: the sheep of "Wuthering Heights" are "All wig curls and yellow teeth / And hard, marbly baas"; the candles, dimly lighting the room where she is nursing her baby, are "the last romantics," "Upside-down hearts of light tipping wax fingers," and "Nun-souled" in that they "burn heavenward and never marry." But the poet does not identify with her images as she does in *Ariel*; she remains too detached, too knowing; she strains for effects that her materials won't yield.

Winter Trees raises slightly different problems. The fifteen "new" poems in the volume all stem from Sylvia Plath's "great period"—the last nine months of her life. On the whole, they could easily be included in an expanded edition of *Ariel*; they burn with the same central passion to destroy the old ego and create a new self, to undergo death and rebirth, to enter the lives of animals or plants, thus transcending one's humanity. In "Gigolo," for example, we are squarely in Plath's unique world of angst and animism:

> Pocket watch I tick well.
> The streets are lizardly crevices
> Sheer-sided, with wholes where to hide.
> It is best to meet in a cul-de-sac.

Nevertheless, the effect of reading these poems is oddly deflating. Sylvia Plath is, after all, a poet of narrow thematic range, and passages like the following, which immediately recall the *Ariel* poems, take on air of déjà vu:

> And my baby a nail
> Driven, driven in.
> He shrieks in his grease. ("Brasilia")

The womb
Rattles its pod, the moon
Discharges itself from the tree with nowhere to go. ("Childless Woman")

The sun blooms, it is a geranium. ("Mystic")

The blood that runs is a dark fruit. ("The Other")

Any reader can compile his own list of comparable passages, lines that often look like first drafts of the *Ariel* poems, and one begins to wonder whether Sylvia Plath is really the major writer Alvarez describes, or whether she is not perhaps an extraordinarily gifted minor poet, whose lyric intensity seemed more impressive when we encountered it in the slim and rigorously selected *Ariel* than when we view it in the new perspective afforded by the publication of her uncollected poems. That her influence on younger writers is currently a major one cannot be doubted. But we will have to wait for a *Collected Poems*, now projected by Faber & Faber for 1973 (and hopefully more carefully edited than *Crossing the Water* and *Winter Trees*!) before we can begin to determine the real place of Sylvia Plath in the history of modern poetry.

Notes

1.   The eleven poems published before the end of 1960 include the following: "Candles," "Black Rook in Rainy Weather," "Metaphors," "Maudlin," "Ouija," "Two Sisters of Persephone," "Who," "Dark House," "Maenad," "The Beast," "Witch Burning." Of these, the two earliest are "Two Sisters of Persephone," first published in the January 1957 issue of *Poetry*, and "Black Rook in Rainy Weather," originally published in *Granta* in May 1957. All the rest, except for "Candles," which appeared in *The Listener* on November 17, 1960, were first published in the British edition of *The Colossus* in the late fall of 1960. Five of these poems— "Who," "Dark House," "Maenad," "The Beast," and "Witch Burning"—were originally part of the seventy-poem sequence, *Poem for a Birthday*, written at Yadoo in late 1959. The remaining two poems in this sequence—"Flute Notes from a Reedy Point" and "The Stones"—were published as separate poems in the US edition of *The Colossus* (1962).

I believe that the following poems were written before 1960: "Private Ground," "Sleep in the Mojave Desert," "Two Campers in Cloud Country," "On Deck," "Crossing the Water," and "Finisterre." Most of these poems refer specifically to the camping trip across the United States and Canada that the Hugheses took in the summer of 1959. Since Plath's poems always stem from her immediate experience, it is highly unlikely that she would have used such settings as Rock Lake, Canada, or the Mojave Desert a year or two after the trip. After she returned to England in December 1959, she never came back to the United States.

2.   Ted Hughes calls "In Plaster," "the weaker twin" of "Tulips" and says that it was written "at the same time and in almost identical form." Charles Newman, ed., *The Art of Sylvia Plath: A Symposium* (Bloomington: Indiana University Press, 1971), 193.

CHAPTER 4

Poetry Chronicle, 1970–1971

> —Hello America let's tell the truth!
> *Robert Lowell is the least distinguished poet alive.*
> And that's just a sample
> Of what it's going to be like now that us poets are in charge
> Of poetry, at last.

These lines from Peter Schjeldahl's "To the National Arts Council" may not have any particular literary distinction, but I find them peculiarly prophetic of the new turn poetry is taking in the seventies. Reading the thirty-odd poets under review here, one is especially struck by the growing cult of Frank O'Hara, whose disciples, the former New York underground, once associated only with such coterie periodicals as *Mother*, *Locus Solus*, and *Angel Hair*, have begun to take over the literary scene. It is particularly ironic that, five years after his death, Frank O'Hara's *Collected Poems* should now have appeared in an expensive glossy edition, brought out not by his former publishers—Tibor de Nagy Gallery, Grove Press, or City Lights Books—but by the venerable Alfred A. Knopf, and that O'Hara's poetry, largely ignored by the Establishment during his lifetime, should win the National Book Award for 1971. Meanwhile his followers have gained steady ground. Thus, Random House has published Ron Padgett and David Shapiro's five-hundred-page *Anthology of New York Poets*, dedicated to O'Hara's memory, and a number of the younger poets included in this anthology—for example, Tom Clark, Lewis MacAdams Jr., and Clark Coolidge—have recently published first volumes with established presses.

For the New York poets, O'Hara is the Hero: he is invoked, eulogized, and openly imitated on page after page, and his untimely and bizarre death at the

Contemporary Literature 14, no.1 (Winter 1973): 97–131.

age of forty has prompted a flurry of O'Hara elegies, such as Allen Kaplan's "Thinking of Frank" and Lewis MacAdams' "Red River." And, although the twenty-seven poets (twenty-six men and one woman!) included in the Padgett and Shapiro anthology may protest against the "New York" label, they do, in fact, form a school in that they all cultivate improvisation, immediacy, documentary images that establish a precise context; racy, purposely outrageous diction, and a very loose free verse line.

Not surprisingly, then, a Robert Lowell, with his strong sense of poetic convention, historical tradition, and the niceties of prosody, is viewed by New York antipoet like Peter Schjeldahl as the Enemy. The autobiographical elegiac mode inaugurated by Lowell's *Life Studies* still has its adherents—witness the new books by James Scully, Barbara Harr, and Bill Tremblay, as well as Denise Levertov's *To Stay Alive* and John Berryman's *Love & Fame*—but the real action now seems to be elsewhere: either in the poems or manifestoes of the New York School, or in the work of what I should like to call the poets of the Rimbaud tradition—the oracular, visionary, intensely lyric mode of Galway Kinnell or of James Wright. I shall discuss the important new books of these and other Rimbaldian poets later on. For the moment, let us consider the achievement of O'Hara and his followers.

It is a paradox that at a time like ours, when every other would-be poet is greeted by some friendly reviewer as "dazzling," "vibrant," or "chillingly accurate," the real innovator like O'Hara should often be dismissed or ignored. Neither M. R. Rosenthal in *The New Poets* (1967) nor Monroe K. Spears in his *Dionysus and the City: Modernism in Twentieth-Century Poetry* (1970) so much as mentions O'Hara, an omission all the more remarkable when one notes that Spears devotes eight pages to James Dickey, Rosenthal nine to Anne Sexton and twenty-four to Allen Ginsberg. Raymond Roseliep, who did review O'Hara's *Lunch Poems* (1964) for the February 1966 issue of *Poetry*, complained that one could never tell when O'Hara was being serious, that many of the poems were "offensive," and that the whole book was characterized by a "wearisome cataloging of personalia."

Until very recently, then, O'Hara was regarded as something of an enfant terrible, a Pop Poet who claimed, in his "Personism: A Manifesto," that "I don't even like rhythm, assonance, all that stuff. You just go on your nerve." The *Collected Poems* belies this brash assertion at every turn. O'Hara was nothing if not learned. His command of language and verse forms, his knowledge of European literature rivaled not only Lowell's but Eliot's and Pound's; he could, when he wanted to, write fine sonnets, aubades, or eclogues. His aesthetic, for that matter, was no more revolutionary than Wordsworth's. "It may be," O'Hara wrote, "that poetry makes life's nebulous events tangible to me and restores their detail; or conversely, that poetry brings forth the intangible quality of incidents which are all too concrete and circumstantial." One thinks immediately of Coleridge's famous statement, in chapter 14 of the *Biographia*, that Wordsworth's aim in *Lyrical Ballads* was "to give the charm of novelty to things of every day . . . by awakening the mind's attention from the lethargy of custom, and directing it to the loveliness and the wonders of the world before us."

But although O'Hara's poetics is essentially romantic, he parts company with Wordsworth on one important point. For him, poetry, far from having its origin in emotion recollected in tranquility, is the expression of what is happening *now*. Unlike the confessional poets, who find the meaning of their present existence to be firmly grounded in the past, O'Hara seeks to remove what Coleridge called "the film of familiarity" by placing the poet's self squarely at the center of the poem, in the very process of discovering his world. Not analysis of emotion but its coming into being is what counts, and the reader's job is, accordingly, to participate in the poet's act of discovery. William Carlos Williams' "No ideas but in things," which is certainly a cornerstone of O'Hara's aesthetic, thus has as its unstated corollary something like "No things until the poet names them and makes them his own." Here, for example, is the opening of O'Hara's "A Step Away from Them":

> It's my lunch hour, so I go
> for a walk among the hum-colored
> cabs. First, down the sidewalk
> where laborers feed their dirty
> glistening torsos sandwiches
> and Coca-Cola, with yellow helmets
> on. They protect them from falling
> bricks, I guess. Then onto the
> avenue where skirts are flipping
> above heels and blow up over
> grates. The sun is hot, but the
> cabs stir up the air. I look
> at bargains in wristwatches. There
> are cats playing in sawdust

The structure of this poem may look random, the details—Coca-Cola signs, hours of the day, objects seen in store windows—are seemingly trivial, but in O'Hara's imaginative reconstruction of New York City, everything is there for a purpose. We might note, to begin with, that the speaker's thought processes constantly return to images of life, vitality, animation, motion. From the "hum-colored / cabs" to the skirts "flipping / above heels," everything is in motion. Even the sign above Times Square "blows smoke over my head, and higher / the waterfall pours lightly."

But what particularly delights the poet is the paradox of heat and motion: no matter how hot the New York Streets, their life force remains intact:

> A
> Negro stands in a doorway with a
> toothpick, languorously agitating.
> A blonde chorus girl clicks: he
> smiles and rubs his chin

At this point, "Everything suddenly honks," and the moment ("12:40 of / a Thursday") is endowed with radiance.

Just as "languorous agitation" gives way to "clicking," so the poet finds "great pleasure" in the conjunction of opposites of "Neon in daylight" or in the absurd tableau of the lady unseasonably wearing foxes, who "puts her poodle / in a cab." Such unexpected juxtapositions are pleasurable because they allow the poet, who remains essentially "A Step Away from Them," from the blondes, Puerto Ricans, and laborers on the Avenue, to create new patterns in space, new compositions of color, texture, and light.

But the vibrancy of the lunch hour would not seem special if the poet did not remember, near the end of the poem, those of his friends—Bunny, John Latouche, and Jackson Pollock—who can no longer experience it. The faint undertone of death, captured in the final image of the Manhattan Storage Warehouse, soon to be torn down, qualifies the poet's response and heightens his awareness of being alive. The poem has, in short, been moving all along to the central recognition of the affinity of life and death, to the perception that death is, as it was for Wallace Stevens, the mother of beauty. The poet's knowledge that he is mortal makes the final glass of papaya juice and the awareness that his "heart"—a book of Reverdy's poems—is in his pocket especially precious and poignant. Death, in short, is always in the background, but the trick is to keep oneself on top of it, to counter despair by participating as fully as possible in the stream of life.

Of course, "A Step Away from Them" would be spoiled if it included any statement as bald, abstract, and pretentious as the one I have just made, and indeed the only place in the poem where O'Hara is perhaps guilty of such a lapse is in the question, "But is the / earth as full as life was full of them?" a question that did not need to be asked because its answer was already implicit in the poem's network of images.

It is interesting to compare "A Step Away from Them" to Allen Kaplan's "Traffic":

> How pleasant to walk the streets.
> The warmth of a hand has been lingering on my side,
> while cars disappear and come, honking occasionally, as a thought
> going through my
> brain.
> How is it I do not love the girl who stayed with me
> and touched my side while she slept last night?
> Honk, honk! Another thought, Honk!
> . . . .
> See, two teen-agers walking wearing vinyl skirts, so short and yellow
> So like enthusiasm their hair falls abundantly. Look,
> their knees are naked savages
> I remember Michael, my friend, saying whatever brings you into
> the New
> is a positive good. Forward!

Here again are the honking cars, the sensuous images of attractive passersby, the casual references to friends, the poet's joie de vivre as he makes his way through the traffic. But Kaplan's poem does not, I think, manage to sustain our interest because its themes seem predetermined, and the poet is only going through the motions of coming to some sort of epiphany. When, for example, he says, "See, two teen-agers walking . . .," he is not really addressing anyone, and the image is awkwardly used as a stepping-stone for the poet's announcement of a change of heart:

> My spirit rises out of myself to be greeted in midair by loveliness
> of the girls.
> My love turns spiritual in midair!

This rather pat assertion is followed by a paean to life:

> How marvelous that short skirts bring youthful knees into our city.
> How marvelous is Michael's idea that shapes today for me.

O my own body, and Michael, all my friends,
the traffic where cars may gently bump like curious strangers
                        who are open-hearted,
and the thoroughfare of my head with its traffic passing,
        and the light of this hour
                    are OMNIPRESENCE

In the O'Hara passage, the syntax is purposely ambiguous. Does "with yellow helmets / on" refer to the laborers, the torsos, or the "sandwiches / and Coca-Cola"? Or again, although "They" has as its antecedent the noun "helmets," it confusingly seems to refer back to "sandwiches" as well, since "helmets" is embedded in a prepositional phrase. This running together and ambiguous positioning of phrases forces us out of our habitual responses and makes us see the objects in O'Hara's urban landscape as parts of a new world. O'Hara uses this device again and again:

                . . . I read
Van Vechten's SPIDER BOY then a short
story by Patsy Southgate and a poem
by myself it is cold and I shiver a little
in white shorts the day begun
so oddly not tired not nervous.

Here the phrases "by myself," "in white shorts," and "so oddly not tired not nervous" act as what we might call "floating modifiers," pointing both forward and backward. By contrast, Kaplan's syntax is perfectly straightforward, and the neat logic of his subject-verb-object units belies the supposed spontaneity of the speaker's thought processes. Kaplan is, for that matter, a fairly academic poet: in "Ars Poetica," we find the passage:

During my graduate studies in English literature,
I perspired
all over Despair
like a detective shadowing spirits like Dante up to
the only
hilltop of Affirming
located just above Resignation.
But, Leroi, you and I might call "Hey, why all this?"
because the pleasure

of poetry was actually born
one day
on your lawn
under the spray of your water sprinkler.

If poetry is, as Ezra Pound said, language charged with meaning, then this passage seems to be, despite its elaborate simile, its allusion to Dante, and its ostensible Personism in the address to Leroi, pure prose. The lineation, for example, is entirely arbitrary; the lines could be cut in other places without any particular gain or loss. But at least "Ars Poetica" is not as self-indulgent as the following poem by Ted Berrigan, found in the *Anthology of New York Poets*:

Personal Poem #7

for John Stanton

It is 7:53 Friday morning in the Universe
New York city to be somewhat exact
I'm in my room wife gone working Gallup
fucking in the room below
                    had 17 ½ miligrams desoxyn
last night 1 Miltown, read Paterson, parts
1 & 2, poems by Wallace Stevens & How Much Longer
Shall I Be Able to Inhabit the Divine Sepulcher
(John Ashbery). . . .
                    Had steak & eggs
with Dick while Sandy sweetly slept.

At 6:30 woke Sandy
fucked til 7 now she's late to work & I'm still
high. Guess I'll write to Bernie today
and Tom. And call Tony. And go out at 9 (with Dick)
to steal books to sell, so we can go
to see A NIGHT AT THE OPERA.

Here are all the O'Hara trappings: the precise time references, catalogs of books read, drugs taken, people seen and phoned, the slangy run-on sentences and broken phrases, the racy diction, and improvisatory manner. The difference is that in Berrigan's poem nothing adds up. From the coy proclamation that it is "7:53 Friday morning in the Universe" to the equally coy suggestion in the final line that it is OK to steal books so long as one uses the proceeds for such

worthwhile artistic pursuits as seeing the Marx Brothers, we are confronted by
a series of details that impress us with nothing so much as the poet's sense of
self-importance. One of O'Hara's most endearing traits is surely his humility, his
ability to say:

> and Joe has a cold and is not coming to Kenneth's
> although he is coming to lunch with Norman
> I suspect he is making a distinction
> well, who isn't

Berrigan, by contrast, seems to think it very important that he had "17 ½ mili-
grams desoxyn," read Williams and Ashbery like any young poet worth his salt,
and "fucked til 7" with Sandy. None of these details remove the "film of familiarity" from the trivia of everyday existence, and one can only be grateful that the
day has no more than twenty-four hours in which to make love, phone calls, or
steak and eggs.

I should like to digress for a moment to speak of the sophomoric attitude
toward women displayed in the work of the lesser New York poets. In their sexist
fantasies, the poet seems to be eternally in bed, waking up just long enough to
make love to his girl, who is consequently late for work like Berrigan's Sandy.
When he isn't having sex, he fondly watches his girl putter around the kitchen
or takes dope while she is out earning enough to support him. Consider the
following poem by Tom Clark:

> I'm still lying in bed
> when you came in
> to get dressed
>   but I wake up quickly
> when you slip
>   out of your nightie
> and I say come here
> . . . .
> and you bend over the bed
> and your tits wobble
> down like small melons
> . . . .
>   and when I bite them
> the nipples stand up
> and then you stand up

and put on your clothes
and go in the kitchen
and bake a chocolate cake
for Lewis' birthday tomorrow.

This looks almost like a parody of the macho poem: the prone male, the efficient, already up-and-dressed female, the male's invitation to bed as a brief interlude before the female hurries off to the kitchen to bake a chocolate cake, while the male poet uses the blessed aftermath of the little scuffle to luxuriate in bed composing his poem! And the "Lewis" of Clark's poem is probably Lewis MacAdams, who formerly coedited *Mother* magazine with Peter Schjeldahl, and whose *The Poetry Room* is full of references to girls who are cooking up fresh vegetables in the double boiler or painting walls, and who are only too happy to shed their tight red, paint-covered jeans when the poet, who has been watching all this homey activity, calls.

Such solemn and simple-minded fantasies of male domination are curiously prevalent in contemporary poetry. Gary Snyder, whose *Regarding Wave* is in many ways the West Coast-Zen counterpart of New York "naked poetry," puts it this way:

Motorcycle strums   the empty streets
Heading home at one a.m.
        ice slicks shine in the moon
                I weave a safe path through
Naked shivering light flows down
Fills the basin over Kyoto
and the plain
            a ghost glacier dream
. . . .
Tires crackle the mud-puddles
The northern hills gleam white
        I ought to stay outside   alone
                and watch the moon all night

The poet has his own world of serious male concerns that keep him out late, and even when he returns home, the ghostly beauty of the night world makes him long for solitary communion with the moonlit landscape. But then he remembers that his wife—no sensitive moon-watcher, she—is waiting for him in bed:

But the bed is full and spread and dark.
I hug you and sink in the warm
      my stomach against your big belly

     feels our baby turn.

For Snyder, as for many of the New York poets, women are especially desirable
when pregnant or shortly after giving birth. In "Not Leaving the House," the poet's
sexist fantasy turns into a Rousseauistic dream of an erotic-ecological paradise:

When Kai is born
I quit going out

Hang around the kitchen—make cornbread
Let nobody in.
. . . .
We sit and watch
       Masa nurse, and drink green tea.

Navajo turquoise beads over the bed
A peacock tail feather at the head
A badger pelt from Nagano-ken
For a mattress; under the sheet;
A pot of yogurt setting
Under the blankets, at his feet.

This is very idyllic, very pretty, but one wonders what will become of the poet's
equanimity when Kai first tosses those blankets aside and stands up.

    O'Hara, fortunately for us if not for him, was no such innocent. If his love
poems avoid the sentimentality of Clark's and Snyder's, it is not because O'Hara,
as a gay man, had no use for the big bellies of luscious women, but because he
recognized that the "I" is just as vulnerable and foolish as anyone else, that there
are no happy endings replete with Navajo beads and yogurt pots. "When the
tears of a whole generation are assembled," he says in "St. Paul and All That,"
"they will only fill a coffee cup / just because they evaporate / doesn't mean
life has heat." Even when O'Hara's love poems are willfully outrageous in their
scatological fantasies, they are usually redeemed by the poet's sense of humor, a
sense of the absurd largely absent in the pornographic poems of John Giorno,
or of Ed Sanders, whose imagination, judging from his "Soft Man 1" or "Elm

Fuck Poem" (*NYP*, 374, 371), does not transcend *Playboy* bawdy. O'Hara has the ability to take any cliché, accepted Great Idea, or Universal Sentiment and turn it inside out. Here, for example, is what he does with two favorite middle-class clichés heard around New York: (1) New York is a *dirty* city, and (2) watch out for all those New Yorkers with their dirty minds!:

> Is it dirty
> does it look dirty
> that's what you think of in the city
>
> does it just seem dirty
> that's what you think of in the city
> you don't refuse to breathe do you
>
> someone comes along with a very bad character
> he seems attractive. is he really. yes. very
> he's attractive as his character is bad. is it. yes
>
> that's what you think of in the city
> . . . .
>
> and you take a lot of dirt off someone
> is the character less bad. no. it improves constantly
> you don't refuse to breathe do you

Here the nursery rhyme repetitions, the tone of wide-eyed innocence, and the silly refrain slyly work the reader around to the realization that *dirt* is what he has really been longing for all along, that it is the very breath of life. The comic logic of the poem is implacable.

Equally as funny as Frank O'Hara and often just as inventive and imaginative is Kenward Elmslie, a poet represented in *New York Poets* who has not yet found the audience he deserves. "Shirley Temple Surrounded by Lions," for example, is a delicious parody of the "kissy" child films of the thirties, replete with "kapok on a sidewalk," cookie forests full of "yowly" hounds, freckles that enlarge into "brown kingdoms," and an "albino industrialiste" pursued by a lifeguard while the gardenias and mimosas get "anti-droopage stuffing." An Elmslie poem usually begins with a perfectly ordinary situation and then rapidly turns the poet's reverie inside an airport lunchroom, where he watches the "travelling nuns" weaving "sleeping babies on doilies of lace," and rapidly gives way to a megalomaniac dream of

Whitmanesque travels, culminating in a new vision of Creation, in which "The whip cracks" and "Albatrosses settle on swaying weeds." Again, in Duo-tang," Elmslie uses an *abcdef* rhyme scheme, repeated four times (note such rhymes as "Frank" / "blank" / "sank" or "emotional stance" / "Grant's" / "took off his pants") to heighten the comedy of his malicious portrait of a fretful Prufrock, masturbating on the beach.

A similar inventiveness and wit characterize Michael Benedikt's second book, *Sky*. Like O'Hara, Benedikt, an editor of *Art News*, incorporates his experience of the visual arts into his poetry. In the opening poem, "Water," for example, the poet, rapidly shifting his perspective somewhat in the manner of a cubist painter, presents a dazzling montage of images, each one comically suggesting what it feels like to hear, touch, and see water—whether from the bottom of a boat, the inside of a teacup, or

> here in the bathtub
> I can hear the swishing of two feet that float
> The lifting of little hairs from the ankle, and also the big hairs.

Again, in "Clement Attlee," Benedikt resolves the portrait of the first postwar English Laborite and somewhat socialist prime minister into a series of metonymic images—a pair of earmuffs, a bear, a boot, "a shiny bald head," "a bristly walrus moustache," "checquered knickers," "a walking stick," and "a frayed black monocle"—thus nicely setting up Attlee's endearing obsolescence as a norm against which to measure the more bizarre manifestations ("twelve students from nursery school . . . discussing the New Order") of our own time.

The danger of this sort of poetry is that it all too easily lapses into the merely cute. Benedikt's syntax is much less dense and economical than O'Hara's, and his long loose free verse lines sometimes go slack, as in "Passing Through Troy," whose opening line, "Get the children of America out of Troy, New York!" recalls O'Hara's "Mothers of America / let your kids go to the movies!" The trick in writing such an exclamatory catalog poem, which wittily debunks the myth of Smalltown, USA, is to vary tone and rhythm sufficiently so as to avoid belaboring the obvious. Benedikt does not always accomplish this:

> O children of the universe (who live in Troy, New York)
> The mind moves on
> We have just scratched the surface of the problem
> And soon I will be out of the suburbs, even, of Troy, New York
> But the children of the universe (and of Troy, New York)

> I make this suggestion: that the ugliness of Troy, New York,
>   may be transcended. . . .

But by this time we are too tired of Troy, New York to care. Benedikt has such resourcefulness and charm that one hopes he can devise a more flexible prosody and syntax to embody his comic vision.

Peter Klappert, the 1970 winner of the Yale Younger Poets Competition, has an imagination not unlike Benedikt's. *Lugging Vegetables to Nantucket* is, as Stanley Kunitz says in the foreword, "recklessly clever." The volume's central poem, "The Babysitters," is a carefully wrought study of the pretensions and snobbery of the literary set; the babysitters of the title are the poet's friends who have seen him through difficult times, but from whom he now wishes to break loose. The setting is an alcoholically bitchy evening party; the narrative is divided into seven sections, based, according to the poet (p. xii), on the Lasswell Formula, by which any communication is divided into seven elements: (1) who, (2) says what, (3) to whom, (4) under what circumstances, (5) by what means, (6) with what purpose, and (7) with what effect. The voice shifts as the poet alternately talks to himself, to his "babysitters," and to his sweetheart Elsie, who, as he realizes at the end of the poem, no longer loves him. Sometimes "The Babysitters" does not rise above sophomoric parody of Eliot ("Cigarette smoke eddied in the patterns / Lanterned by the fire on the walls" [p. 13]) or of Baudelaire ("You! Malignant Lepidopterist!"). But Klappert can be genuinely funny as in this portrait of the literary clique's guru:

> And our condescending confucian
> focuses into a yawn: a rebirth is reborn.
> (who had his ears in the clouds and failed to sleep.
> . . . .
> who carefully had not neglected to breathe
> who made up schedules of himself, who made up timetables,
>   who stood in the rain and missed every bus
> who touched on the subject touching the subject.

Here and in the "Pieces of the One and a Half Legged Man," Klappert fuses the conversational, improvisatory Personism of O'Hara with the more studied elegance of James Merrill. In its use of puns, wordplays, allusions, onomatopoeia, sound repetition, and parody rhythms, "The Babysitter" recalls both Merrill's "The Summer People" and his "The Thousand and Second Night." Like Merrill, Klappert combines a slightly mannered verse with a flexible prose; like

Merrill, he uses the device of crossing out words and lines so as to suggest spontaneity. *Lugging Vegetables to Nantucket* has enormous virtuosity and intelligence; now Klappert must go beyond these qualities to create his own world.

A poet's wit is difficult to imitate; his verbal mannerisms or visual devices
can be copied much more readily. Among the thousands of minor poems that
O'Hara tossed off for friends in the way that most of us make phone calls, one
finds word games such as the following:

Yet   while   eat   possible   exact   slap
   Wilt   acceptable   moan   adverse   creep
cannever   wait   whereof   revolt   struck

No doubt, O'Hara, who was never pompous about his work, regarded such
exercises as mere verbal play. A number of the New York poets, however, partly
influenced by O'Hara's experiments and partly by those of the Black Mountain
poets, have recently practiced a form of minimal poetry perhaps influenced by the
painting of Sol LeWitt and Donald Judd. Here are two poems by Aram Saroyan:

'
aren't

ly   ly
ly   ly

The Anthology of New York Poets also includes his poem "crickets"—a vertical
column, single-spaced, of the word "crickets" all the way down the page. But
Clark Coolidge almost outdoes (or, should I say, underdoes) Saroyan. The dust
jacket of his new book *SPACE* announces:

At first glance, Clark Coolidge's poems appear to be completely impenetrable parades of apparently unrelated words arranged in meaningless
patterns across the page. If you keep reading, though, the poems begin
to have a strange effectiveness, and eventually you begin to see the words
themselves in an entirely new and exhilarating way. Coolidge's structures are reductive. Syntax—the systematic connection between words
which gives linear discourse its character of extended meaning—is simply
removed. This leaves our attention open to the ways in which words can
become instruments of a visual order and of an order of sound that is
abstract but not meaningless.

But when Coolidge writes:

> mount
> cull band loom bound
> arkansas

I wonder if the "strange effectiveness" is not in the mind of the beholder. If we rewrite the poem as follows:

> fount
> bull sand bloom wound
> indiana

or with any other comparable arrangement of nouns and verbs, we can claim, just as plausibly, that the result is "abstract but not meaningless" or that words are "organisms with patterns of existing which are specific to themselves, inexplicable and marvelous" (see dust jacket of *SPACE*). Coolidge's experiments recall e. e. cummings, as such titles as "Nothing at Newbegins" indicate. Kenneth Patchen, for that matter, was playing with similar reductive syntactic structures and abstract typographical positioning as long ago as 1946, as the recent reissue of his *Panels for the Walls of Heaven* in New Directions' *In Quest of Candlelighters* reminds us. Coolidge and Saroyan's experiments here can be traced back to Patchen, cummings, Williams—and ultimately to Ezra Pound—but in highly attenuated form.

II

So much for New York poetry and related experiments in open form. Side by side with the experimental verse of the O'Hara school, one continues to find a sizeable body of confessional poetry, more or less modeled on Lowell's *Life Studies*. But whereas Lowell understood that autobiography is always a judgment of the present on the past, that the autobiographical poet must select key incidents of his past life and arrange them in coherent and meaningful patterns, most of the recent confessional poets make the unfortunate assumption that anything is interesting and important so long as it really happened to them. Thus, in *The Mortgaged Wife*, Barbara Harr indulges in a series of painful reminiscences about her childhood in Kansas City, her religious uncertainties, her unfortunate marriage, divorce, and so on. Harr has a strong urge to relive her past and to engage in self-analysis, but the incidents and images she so solemnly details have a kind of ladies' magazine redundancy, and her language is almost flatly denotational:

> Sandra, lady, mother, wife of sorrows,
> I remember your green jumper
> the first day of school.
> You made a mess of the finger paints.
> I didn't tell. We were friends.
>
> . . . .
>
> At eight or nine years old, Sandy,
> we dug in my daddy's garden.
>
> . . . .
>
> We tried my mother's recipe
> for crumb cake with sweet topping,
> but used, in error, the rancid lard
> and could not eat our cake.

All very sweet, but it does not distinguish the poet and her friend Sandy from all the other little girls of America, or make clear why both have become bitter, frustrated, and alcoholic. The obvious implication—that sensitive American girls growing up in the fifties could have no other fate—is not exactly compelling.

Similarly, in his second book, *Avenue of the Americas*, James Scully gives us vignettes of his boyhood at a strict Catholic school—his friendships, love affairs, and early intellectual interests. Scully's aim is, in his own words, "Not to explain, explanations violate reality, but to burn off the mist that obscures it" (see dust jacket). But unfortunately, Scully is explaining all the time. In one of his most ambitious poems, "Letter to Grandin," the disillusioned poet, writing to the closest friend of his youth, reminisces about the days before "the old crowd broke up / like aborigines," the days of "hope and dream, openhearted bull session / beer and cheap wine. . . . Cigarette butts heaped in ashtrays / like broken crutches at Lourdes." Everyone, of course, remembers such things, and some of us might even agree with Scully that "I don't think I've ever been happier," but the typicality of this feeling does not make "Letter to Grandin" any less sentimental or tedious. Growing up is painful: the poet has now "stumbled into a family"; he has two small children who sometimes wake up in the middle of the night, "howling with the nightmare," and he feels that he and his wife Arlene are "useless parents." This malaise evidently in the nature of things: "*The Dreadful has already occurred /* that's what Heidegger learned." But the poet finally consoles himself with the thought that his wife Arlene "grows lovelier than ever," that he loves her ("except when my heart is ill, unbelievably ill"), that John and Deirdre are, after all, "our son" and "our daughter," and that, "after all these years," he can finally talk frankly and freely to Grandin.

Scully is nothing if not sincere, but the main impression produced by *Avenue of the Americas* is that it takes more than an amalgam of childhood reminiscences, memories of mental hospitals, and expressions of *Angst* to produce a "Waking in the Blue" or a "Skunk Hour." Bill Tremblay's first volume, *Crying in the Cheap Seats*, raises similar problems. The publishers tell us that Tremblay's "searching narration should speak particularly to and for the generation that came to awareness in the late fifties and early sixties by means of a poetry that lives through urban immensities, senseless riots, cruel assassinations, insane war, and comes to itself with no answer but an endless quest." But the longest poem in Tremblay's book, "A Time for Breaking," again gives evidence of an inability to transfigure the particulars of one man's life. The speaker is a college instructor who finds his world falling apart as a result of Nixon's invasion of Cambodia:

> even the wind protests more loudly
> we walk alone clutching our guts
> crying what can I do?
> nothing

"We make out of the quarrel with others, rhetoric, but of the quarrel with ourselves, poetry," said Yeats. In "A Time for Breaking," Tremblay consistently quarrels with others. He is indignant about all the right things—Cambodia, Kent State, the military-industrial complex, the police, the silent majority— and posits, predictably enough, that in these troubled times, marriages dissolve ("Cynthia calls in mid-week / crying Phil and Dee Dee have broken up"), people attend group therapy sessions, join communes, quit their jobs, and often lose their minds. To top it off, right after the Cambodia crisis, the poet's father dies, and, having flown West to attend the funeral, he feels that "some part of me is dead." But in the end, he does come back to his wife Cynthia as well as to his love for literature, and the poem concludes with an account of a "guitar and banjo pickin' sing and beer blast" that raises the speaker's spirits:

> and I'm getting to the point where I don't
>   give a shit anymore
> about losing my job or being a black sheep

I'm going to write about the spirit I know is
  there in man
and find a way to be happy and loving
and let the old crap of the past go at last
and live free

"A Time for Breaking" is, unfortunately, a very representative poem of our time. Written in a slack free verse that is in fact indistinguishable from ordinary prose, the poem is no more than a series of journalistic platitudes, loosely strung together. If this is poetry, so is anything else anyone cares to write.

It is distressing to report that even Denise Levertov's new book, *To Stay Alive*, contains a quantity of bad confessional verse. Her anti-Vietnam War poems, written in casual diary form, sound rather like a versified newspaper editorial— the same righteous indignation, the same uncompromising moral zeal and self-important tone. It is difficult to believe that the poet who, as one of the most promising heirs of William Carlos Williams, wrote, "The world is / not with us enough / O taste and see," should now resort to the flat abstractions, the facile polemics, and the careless rhythms of *To Stay Alive*. Here is a sample of the book's verse:

Revolution or death. Revolution or death.
Wheels would sing it
    but railroads are obsolete,
we are among the clouds, gliding, the roar
a toneless constant.
     Which side are you on?
Revolution, of course. Death is Mayor Daley.

Juxtaposed with such passages are snatches of actual letters to friends concerning the pending indictment of the poet's husband, Mitchell Goodman: "I understand that Mitch may have to go to jail and that it will be a hard time for him and for me, yet, because it's for doing what we know we must do, that hardship is imaginable, encompassable, and a small thing in the face of the slaughter in Vietnam and the other slaughter that will come. And there is no certainty he will go to jail."

This may well be moving, but its place in a poem seems questionable. But, poetry aside, *To Stay Alive* is not even particularly good rhetoric: the speaker herself seems too implausibly innocent of the crimes that "fevered Amerika" is committing. One would think that never before in history had any country waged an unjust war, that all Vietnamese are saints, all American politicians villains. It is revealing that in "Looking for the Devil Poems," which describe the poet's brief respite from political turmoil during a summer vacation in Europe, she expresses feelings of guilt because she is having a happy time in sunny Italy:

> Cop-out, am I,
> or merely,
>   as the day fades
>
>   (and Amerika
>   far away
>   tosses in fever)
> on holiday?

Subconsciously, perhaps, Denise Levertov feels that writing poetry at a time of "revolution or death" is itself a cop-out, that the good man (quite literally, her husband Mitchell Goodman) must dedicate his life to the struggle. This may explain why Levertov's new poems are so casually—and it seems hastily—assembled, but one can only hope for a change, if not a heart, then at least of purpose.

The mode of John Berryman's *Love & Fame* resembles that of *To Stay Alive*, but Berryman's speaker is the antithesis of Levertov's solemn "I." The voice of *Love & Fame* engages in no polemics, takes little interest in major political events, and has astonishingly few principles. Instead, he reminisces, in poem after poem, about his childhood days at PS 69 in Jackson Heights, his ups and downs at Columbia, his sexual adventures, his fellowship at Cambridge, his "arrival" as a poet, and his later bleaker days, especially those spent in a mental hospital in the Midwest. Much of the book is local gossip in the purest sense of the word. If one is interested in Berryman, then reading these poems, so revelatory of his basic attitudes and concerns, is certainly mandatory. If, on the other hand, these poems are read as poems, they must disappoint those readers who admired the *Dream Songs* for their wit, their range of mood, the originality of their syntactic dislocations, their wry dialogues between Henry and Mr. Bones.

Love & Fame is, I believe, a poetic dead end, a touching counterpart in verse of Berryman's actual suicide a year after the book's publication. The aesthetic principle behind these poems seems to be that anything can be included if Berryman feels like it, that the poem can start or stop anywhere, that anything is interesting if it happened to him. "Down & Back" is typical. It begins with fond reminiscences about the poet's sexual attraction to a "nice" girl named Atherton, who toyed with him but refused to go to bed with him:

night on night till 4 till 5 a. m.
intertangled breathless, sweating, on a verge
six or seven nerve-destroying hours.

At the end of vacation, she goes back to Smith, leaving the poet "sore & cha-
grined / with a hanging head & no interest / in anything." As a result, he flunks
his eighteenth-century literature exam for Mark Van Doren's course. Since Mark
is a special friend, the poet bravely admits to him that "of the 42 books in the
bloody course / I'd only read 17":

> He liked my candour
> (he wrote) & had enjoyed the exam
> but had no option except to give me F in the course—
>
> costing my scholarship.

In the remainder of the poem, Berryman recalls how he got back into Mark's
good graces by cramming all summer, even writing "an abridgment of Locke's
Essay" that Van Doren wanted to have published "but we found out there was
one in print already." The happy ending follows:

> Anyway he changed my grade retroactively & talked to the Dean.
> My scholarship was restored, the Prodigal Son
> welcomed with crimson joy.

The end. This poem, like its neighboring ones, has no unifying pattern, no
larger meaning that transcends the partly dreary, partly amusing particulars
recounted, no special mood beyond the jocular-sophomoric. The poem's division into four-line stanzas with occasional approximate rhyme or consonance
seems arbitrary; a series of prose paragraphs would do just as well. It is never
clear why Berryman assumes that others will be interested in the exams he
flunked, the girls he either did or did not sleep with, and so on. The supposition
is simply that these things matter because they happened to someone whom we
now recognize as a *Poet*. "Look at me," the speaker implies, "I'm human too! I
flunked eighteenth-century lit."

But despite such attempts to be endearing, the voice that runs through the
rather stale reminiscences of *Love & Fame* is generally unsympathetic. As in the
poems of Berrigan and Clark, Berryman's women are seen as so many bodies
to knock up, and he annoyingly gloats over his supposed sex appeal (see, e.g.,

"Thank You, Christine"). Friends and fellow poets are mere sounding boards for his brilliance; he is always reminding the reader that he is famous, that everyone recognizes him, that despite his many vices, even "the most passionate & versatile actress in Cambridge" succumbs to his physical charms. Underneath the bravado that runs through *Love & Fame*, one senses a desperate urge for recognition, for acceptance from a poet who cannot really accept himself. Ultimately, then, the interest of *Love & Fame* is largely extra-literary; the book is a gold mine for Berryman's future biographers.

III

Classical rhetoricians distinguished between three styles: the *low* or plain-colloquial, the *middle* or observational-meditative, the *high* or ceremonial-grand. According to these categories, O'Hara and the New York poets generally favor the low style; the confessional poets, the mixed or middle. I turn now to the new poetry written in the high style, concluding with that of A. R. Ammons, although Ammons, who shifts easily from sublime exclamation to casual slang, is actually sui generis, a poet too extraordinary to be pigeonholed.

Unlike the New York poets who cultivate spontaneity, colloquial idiom, the improvisatory gesture, the celebration of the mundane, the poets of the high style are concerned with the articulation of a vision that demands a heightened speech. Thus, although they resemble both the New York group and the confessional poets in their exploitation of the first-person singular, their "I" is less Wordsworthian than Rimbaldian, an exclamatory, hallucinatory, oracular "I" whose function is to utter rather than to address. Rimbaud's famous "Je est un autre" (I am somebody else), his "C'est faux de dire: Je pense. On devrait dire: On me pense" (It is wrong to say: I think. One should say, "I am being thought) could act as epigraph to the poetry of, say Kinnell or Wright. In lyric poetry of this sort, language must be extraordinary, and sound must be fully orchestrated so as to convey the poet's all but inexpressible and momentous experience of otherness.

The Modern oracular movement is peculiarly international. Pablo Neruda and César Vallejo are both Rimbaldian poets, as is the Hungarian Ferenc Juhász, a generous selection of whose poetry, written between 1949 and 1967, has recently appeared in English translation. Strictly speaking, poetry in other languages falls outside the scope of this review-essay, and I am furthermore reluctant to talk about poetry I cannot read in the original language. But Kenneth McRobbie and Ilona Duczynska have done such an admirable job in editing and translating Juhász's poems that I will venture a few comments on this exciting book.

The first thing that strikes the Anglo-American reader of Juhász's poetry is its sheer intensity of feeling. When one compares *The Boy Changed into a Stag* to, say, Jon Silkin's *Amana Grass* or Sandra McPherson's *Elegies for the Hot Season*—both very accomplished collections of visionary lyrics—one notes that British and American poets, even when they want to convey ecstasy, as McPherson does in "The Wedding," or violence and cruelty, as Silkin does in "Amana Grass," never quite express the naked and almost unbearable passion found in Juhász's work. *The Boy Changed into a Stag* has none of the self-consciousness characteristic of much of our visionary poetry; it has a strange sense of inevitability, as if its maker were not so much writing a poem as uttering a cry from the heart.

Juhász's chief technical devices are two: repetition, whether of word, phrase, or line, and the catalog. He piles up strings of nouns, verbs, or adjectives in long paratactic units. Here is an example from the prose poem "At Childhood's Table":

> I shall go out to the silent field of rotting wreaths, torn white crepe-paper-bandaged wreath-wires, frozen petalled flowers, bones lying in cancered mud, bare, wind-whistling poplars, acacias, sumachs, elder bushes, lilacs, crudely carved Jesuses not yet freshly white-washed, sorrowful faces of the Virgin green-spotted with death, marble crowns of thorns, rusty tin candle-holders, wet candle-stumps, to the graveyard at home, and I shall thump on my father's grave.

In the following passage from a later poem, "Power of the Flowers," Juhász uses anaphora, internal repetition, and strings of appositive phrases:

> flowers, you who have lived through the past, what know you of me,
> what do you know of my heart, why it lives so avidly,
> why proud faith is beautiful, why I find pain in the rain showers,
> why my consciousness puts forth heavy-scented, undyingly fair
>   flowers?
> Flowers, timeless ones, yet easily broken as I have seen,
> with narrowing leaves for shoulders, hips of gelatine,
> gland-browed, lips growing from larynx, and tenderness in your
>   thorns,
> my flowers, fragile dreams, pliant-ribbed, spear leafed ones,
> my flowers, black tongued, cold collared, milk within you for
>   blood circulating.

An American reader may find this rather baroque, but Juhász generally brings it off because his incantatory, exclamatory repetitions do have a sense of direction. In the prose poem "Crown of Hatred and Love," for example, the first section, written in prose, is based on the repeated refrain, "Oh how I hated that village":

> Oh how I hated that village, crown of thorns around my timid child's heart, at whose whimpering response to some pulsation, some birdcall from the constellations, it would bite with round tangled mouth, cruel teeth-circle, so that my larva-soft flesh bled from within towards the surface, towards the stars. . . .
>
> Oh how I hated that village, closing around me like a spined mollusc, each thorn's tip a tenacious leech's mouth, a belly beneath the hard grey shield.

In the course of the poem, the obsessive nature imagery—insects, animal teeth, tendrils—defines the poet's sense of constriction, of imprisonment. But gradually another note appears in the poet's impassioned utterance: "O my village, you flower-fragrant calf's moist cherry-muzzle thirsting for the udders of the world-mists netted with rubies, why did I hate you? My morning's gold-fenced flower garden, why did I dread you?" And in the second (or verse) half of the poem, the "brown towers of burrs from hawthorn and thistle" become "tatters of mourning in a burned-out chapel," as the poet comes to the anguished realization that the village he hates and the father he has feared and avoided are the very fountainhead of his being.

A similarly passionate dialectic of hatred and love is found in the brilliant title poem, which W. H. Auden has called, rightly, I think, "One of the greatest poems written in my time." It begins once again with a refrain: "Her own son the mother called / from afar crying . . ." and presents, in mythic terms, the terrible tension between an old peasant mother and the alienated son who can escape her magnetic pull only by turning himself into a stag. The passage in which the process of metamorphosis itself is described is especially fine:

> In the far forest the lad heard,
> at once he jerked up his head,
> with his wide nostrils testing
> the air, soft dewlaps pulsing
> with veined ears pricked, harkening
> alertly to those tones sobbing.

As a stag, the poet cannot return home: "my horns would fell you, / I'd toss your body, / if I should come home / down i would roll you, / tread your loose vein / breasts mangled by hooves." The imagery continues in this cruel vein, and all the mother's reminders that "you loved Irene B., your friends were V. J. and H. S. the wild orchid-bearded painter," make no difference. Only when she suddenly mentions his dead father does the spell break. For the poet's father is clearly the dominant presence in his life, a figure analogous to Roethke's "Papa," but even more amazing and frightening:

> I saw the bristles sprout from your chin
> blackened by morning.
> . . . .
> Oh, and I thought your hair, your beard, would overgrow
> the whole room.

But Juhász is no sentimentalist; his father is dead and so he cannot and does not want to go home again, despite his mother's anguished pleas. Cruelly, he tells her:

> mother, my mother I cannot go back
> pure gold seethes in my hundred wounds,
> . . . .
> each branch of my antlers is a dual-based pylon,
> each prong of my antlers a high-tension wire.
> . . . .
> teeth are iron bridges, and in my heart surge the
> monster-infested seas.

In Juhász's powerful myth, the Mother, an abstract, generic female figure like those of Lorca, finally loses the Prodigal Son, whose future depends on his ability to cut the knot. To be human, the poet implies, is to suffer, and accordingly, the greatest virtue one can exercise is energy—the power to survive in the marvelous but terrible world of nature.

In its stress on primal energy, on the will to survive, *The Boy Changed into a Stag* has affinities with Ted Hughes's *Crow*. For the tough little black bird of Hughes's title is emblematic of the last survivor, the force remaining in the universe once it has been destroyed by atomic quality is, both literally and figuratively, a black humor that enables him to outlast man and outsmart God, a God who is, at best, a rather confused and inept personage. In "A Childish Prank," for example, God is wondering how to endow the bodies of man and woman with a soul, but "The problem was so great, it dragged him asleep." Now Crow steps in, laughing:

> He bit the Worm, God's only son,
> Into two writhing halves.
>
> He stuffed into man the tail half
> With the wounded end hanging out.
>
> He stuffed the head half headfirst into woman
> And it crept in deeper and up
> To peer out through her eyes
> Calling its tail-half to join up quickly, quickly
> Because O it was painful.
>
> Man awoke being dragged across the grass.
> Woman awoke to see him coming.
> Neither knew what had happened.

So Crow maliciously twists God's well-meaning but blunted purpose by making human love no more than joint sexual participation in evil (the Worm). And of course, the Worm is "God's only son."

"A Childish Prank" is, like many of the *Crow* poems, dramatic and economical; it drives on with relentless wit to its climax, using no waste motion, no excess verbiage. Hughes's flat statements, his abrupt rhythms, his effective repetitions make this a lyric of great virtuosity.

But a little of *Crow* goes a long way. The same ironies are stressed again and again, and the poet's sarcasm becomes increasingly heavy handed. "Crow's First Lesson" is that in our posthuman world, love is a meaningless concept: when God tries to teach Crow to articulate the word "love," Crow can only retch, and "Man's bodiless prodigious head / Bulbed out onto the earth, with swivelling eyes." At the second retching, "woman's vulva dropped over man's neck and tightened. / The two struggled together on the grass. / God struggled to part them, cursed, wept—"

These lines have been called Blakean, but whereas Blake knew very well that man himself was ultimately responsible for the perversions of love, freedom, and generosity he depicted, Hughes implies, here and throughout *Crow*, that the responsibility is that of some implacable fate, cruelly sporting with a helpless mankind. This emphasis on fate—reminiscent not at all of Blake, or, for that matter, of a poet like Juhász, but rather of such poets as Hardy and Housman—is especially apparent in "Crow's Theology," an ironic treatment of the Argument From Design, in which Crow begins by positing that surely God must love him, but then he begins to wonder, "what / Loved the stones and spoke stone? . . . And what loved the shot-pellets . . .?" Finally, he is forced to conclude that

> there were two Gods—

> One of them much bigger than the other
> Loving his enemies
> And having all the weapons.

The only design, in short, is one of cruelty and violence. Similarly, in "The Apple Tragedy," God arranges man's Fall as a sort of amusing game. He spurs on the innocent serpent, who only wants to be left alone, to seduce Eve, with the result that

> Now whenever the snake appears she screeches
> "Here it comes again! Help! O Help!"
> Then Adam smashes a chair on its head
> And God says: "I am well pleased"

> And everything goes to hell.

Man is the toy of the Gods who have destroyed his true world, replacing it with a terrible new one, unfit for human habitation, a world fit only for the tough, strong, fearless, and mindless energy of Crow.

Hughes's treatment of biblical themes suggests that he is essentially an out-raged Christian-turned-inside-out. He wants the Fall to have meaning and love to exist; he wants to believe that God made man in His image, but because cities are turning to rubble and "excreta poisoning seas" ("A Disaster"), he feels that one can only cope with life by adopting the ironic detachment and indifference of the subhuman Crow. Yet ultimately the poet's pervasive image of horror is too one-dimensional to have much impact. "The danger of poetry written in a monochromatic black," said Stephen Spender in *The New York Review of Books* (July 22, 1971), "is that it simply confronts us with the fundamental truisms such as 'Life is death' or 'Life is hell.'" Precisely. What sense of the poet's commitment. Where does he fit into the scarred, post-atomic landscape? How is he to blame for what has happened to love, friendship, kindness? The beast fables of *Crow*, it seems to me, are, despite all their sophistication, economy, and fine control of sound and rhythm, an easy way out. By adopting the Crow persona, the poet can be devastating and prophetic without working out the implications of the situations he dramatizes. *Crow* is, in short, devoid of tension, of the recognition of alternatives. Its ironies are those of the surface: one can comfortably read *Crow*, chuckling at the trick endings, as when Crow is asked, "But who is stronger than death?" and replies, "*Me, evidently*," without being particularly troubled or moved. The holocaust seems all in a day's work.

Galway Kinnell's *Body Rags* (1968) was a major poetic event. "The Bear" and "The Porcupine," which have already become anthology pieces, seem to me to have a peculiar excellence that goes beyond anything in *Crow*, for unlike Hughes's witty but essentially one-dimensional moral allegories, Kinnell's animal poems are explorations of the poet's deepest self, a self he can only discover by identifying imaginatively with the sufferings of wild, alien creatures. Both poets are haunted by violence, but whereas Hughes views violence as an abstract concept, generic to the contemporary human situation, Kinnell sees it always in terms of himself.

Kinnell's new book, *The Book of Nightmares*, is somewhat uneven. It consists of ten long meditative poems, in form like irregular odes, each made up of seven sections of varying length. In each case, the poet begins with an actual situation—trying on old shoes in the Salvation Army Store (3), trying to fall asleep in flophouse (5)—and then begins to meditate, moving backward and forward in time, as he tries to come to terms with the nightmares that confront the living. As in his earlier poems, Kinnell uses images of nature in its most elemental forms—bloody hen feathers, spiders, bare black rocks, skulls, the corpses of animals—to discover the deepest instincts of the submerged self.

"The Call Across the Valley of Not-Knowing" (8), for example, is a fevered meditation on loneliness and frustration in love. Wide awake as he lies beside his peacefully sleeping, enormously pregnant wife, the poet feels wholly isolated, viewing himself and his wife as "two mismatched halfnesses lying side by side in the darkness." The very house seems to be "sinking down / into ground rot," and the invisible fetus becomes a threatening little monster, about to "rouse himself / with a huge, fishy thrash, and re-settle in his darkness."

In part 2, the thought that all men and women are torn halves, searching for each other, takes the poet back to Plato's *Symposium* and to the memory of a chance encounter with another woman whom he might have loved if circumstances had permitted. The very memory of that wound, a wound caused by the inexplicable feeling of a single moment, is still dear to him. Yet in part 4, the poet's thoughts return to his wife, as he remembers a happier time of love-making, a time now romantically viewed in terms of blossoming. If their former relationship was blessed, so was his momentary contact with the sheriff of a little Southern jail, who took his fingerprints: "the animal gentleness of his hand on my hand" was a sign, a gift. And again (part 6) he wonders what would have happened if he had "stayed with that woman of Waterloo," the other woman; he wonders what happens if, by some miracle, our deepest desires were to be fulfilled. In the end, he concludes that "We who live out our plain lives" are cursed by the knowledge that, sooner or later, "the bear call," the call of the unknown, of the love we did not dare demand, of the irrational, will return to haunt us. And isn't it possible that next time we might say, "yes . . . yes . . .?"

"The Call Across the Valley of Not-Knowing" is a very brave poem, for the "I" admits that he has no core, no consistent identity he can count on. At any moment, he might betray his wife as well as himself, giving in to his desire for something other. Thematically, it is a much more rewarding poem than, say, the sexist reveries of Berrigan or Clark discussed earlier in this essay. The main fault of this and the other long lyrics in *The Book of Nightmares* is a propensity to depend rather heavily on cumbersome coinages like "halfnesses," "nightmared," or "biopsied," and to lapse into vague abstraction. In sections 3 and 4 of "The Call Across the Valley," we find too many passages like the following:

> And yet I think
> it must be the wound, the wound itself,
> which lets us know and love. . . .

>   . . . she and I once
> watched the bees, dreamers not yet
> dipped into the acids
> of the craving for anything. . . .

Here Kinnell dissipates the force of the dreamlike vividness of his best passages: the emotion is recounted as if from a distance rather than presented dramatically. The poet's voice loses its ecstatic urgency and becomes a shade of precious. Nevertheless, Kinnell is one of the best poets writing today; because his risks are so great, his very lapses seem preferable to the limited successes of many other poets.

Like Kinnell, James Wright is one of our finest visionary poets, and his *Collected Poems* must be counted as one of the major literary events of the past few years. Nevertheless, I find the thirty-three new poems at the back of the

Collected Poems something of a letdown. The real watershed in Wright's work was *The Branch Will Not Break* of 1963. In his first two volumes—*The Green Wall* (1955) and *Saint Judas* (1959)—Wright was a self-declared disciple of Robinson and Frost; he wrote regional poems characterized by their gentle irony, their ordinary people in ordinary places. His language is purposely flat, his rhyming stanzas modest and clean-cut. In the poems of the 1950s, we find vignettes of eccentric Ohio townspeople like the homosexual "Sappho," a group of fairly bloodless love poems like "A Girl Walking into a Shadow," and elegiac lyrics about Wright's parents. There is much graveyard and nature imagery and a good deal of quiet moralizing somewhat in the vein of Robinson's "Eros Turannos."

Between 1959 and the publication of *The Branch Will Not Break*, Wright did a number of fine translations, especially of the German poet Georg Trakl, whose poems he called "Attempts to enter and to recognize one's very self." Trakl's finest poems, written between 1912 and 1914, and heavily influenced by Hölderlin and Rimbaud, mark a fascinating departure from the then prevailing Symbolist aesthetic. They present highly subjective, hallucinatory, sharply etched images in short undeveloped scenes, apparently having no relation to one another. Their tone is exclamatory, their mode elliptical; they dramatize intense personal suffering. Here, for example, is part of Wright's translation of Trakl's "De Profundis":

> It is a stubble field, where a black rain is falling.
> It is a brown tree, that stands alone.
> It is a hissing wind, that encircles empty houses.
> How melancholy the evening is.
>
> . . . .
> Cold metal walks on my forehead
> Spiders search for my heart.
> It is a light that goes out in my mouth.

The deceptive parallelism, the pseudo-reference of "It is," the concrete visual imagery used to objectify the poet's nameless fear—all these are qualities that Wright took over in his own poetry. The predictable ironies and moralizing of the earlier poetry disappear, and in such marvelous short poems as "In Fear of Harvests," the poet dwells on the sheer force of the phenomenal world as it reflects his unmotivated anxiety:

> It has happened
> Before: nearby,

The nostrils of slow horses
Breathe evenly,
And the brown bees drag their high garlands,
Heavily,
Toward hives of snow.

In "Stages of a Journey Westward," Wright begins, as he did in earlier poems, with a reference to his native Ohio, but here the settings are dream images rather than actual places. The journey from Ohio westward to the Pacific and Alaska becomes symbolic of the self's journey from a childhood sense of border and a belief in rational control to a recognition that the soul's secret springs are those of violence and cruelty:

Defeated for re-election
The half-educated sheriff of Mukilteo, Washington,
Has been drinking again.
He leads me up the cliff, tottering.
Both drunk, we stand among the graves.
Miners paused here on the way up to Alaska.
Angry, they spaded their broken women's bodies
Into ditches of crab grass.

These poems of sharp, terrifying, and unrelenting vision gave Wright a central place in contemporary poetry. In his recent work, however, Wright returns to his earlier moralizing bent; he cannot resist the temptation to impose a *profound meaning* on incidents that cannot quite bear such weight. The longest and most ambitious of the new poems is undoubtedly "Many of Our Waters: Variations on a Poem by a Black Child," which was the 1969 Phi Beta Kappa Poem. In its seven free verse sections of irregular length, Wright wishes to explore, once again, the theme of the poet's isolation and the relation of life to death. But the introduction of the little black boy Garnie, who appears in a number of the "New Poems," is alien to Wright's highly personal vision: the documentary treatment of social phenomena is not his forte.

In the first section, Wright begins with a prose journal entry, which explains that Garnie's poem, the starting point of his own lyrical meditation, was spoken when the little boy looked down on a construction site in midtown Manhattan. After this fairly labored buildup, one expects to hear the gnomic utterance of a Rousseauistic Wise Child, but Garnie's words, evidently meant to convey the terror of death, are not sufficiently pointed:

You know
if a blind boy
ride his bicycle
down there
he might fall into that water
. . . .
they call it acid
and if that poor boy
drive his poor blind bicycle
into that acid
he drown
he die
and then
they bury him
up

This is less shocking than sentimental, as is part 2, "to the Ohio," a lyrical invocation to the "rotted but beautiful" river of the poet's boyhood. In lines that are alternately sublime and coy, the poem tries to recapture the innocence of childhood, culminating in the rather embarrassing lines:

This morning, I feel like that old child
You gathered so often
Into your rinsing arms,
And bathed, and healed.
I feel lonesome.
And sick at heart,
Frightened
And i don't know
Why.

help.

In parts 3 and 4, the poet vacillates between two concepts of poetry: that it is a constant struggle ("He gets up in the morning and curses himself / into black silence"), or that it is a wise passiveness, a sheer openness ("Work be damned, the kind / Of poetry I want / Is to lie down with my love"). The fifth part, with its realistic altercation, on the corner of 84th Street and Amsterdam Avenue, between the poet, planning an outing to the planetarium, his wife, annoyed by the delay caused by Garnie's wish to bring his brother along, and Garnie himself is, I think, the weakest in the poem. The speaker is evidently torn between two loyalties: that to Garnie and that to his wife and baby Gemela, but the motivations remain unclear. When, in part 6, Wright describes Gemela, asleep in their city apartment, as "face down the Hudson River / where the rats drift," one has the feeling that Wright needed another water image to sustain his central metaphor, but that in fact, the Hudson plays no real role here. The brief seventh section is meant to reinforce the theme, introduced in part 4, that there is more enterprise in walking naked: the poet remembers an idyllic nude swim in a mountain pool with his wife, when some deer, usually frightened of them, came very close because "It never occurred to them / what we might be." From here, Wright modulates into the conclusion that "I want to live my life, / And how can I live my life / Unless you live yours?"

This conclusion seems grafted on to the rest of the poem. Wright is straining to tell us that death shall have no dominion, that he opts for life, the life Garnie sees threatened by building excavators, but that persists in the timeless waters of the Ohio, in the image of the "small fawn, Gemela," asleep "face down on the Hudson," and in the memory of swimming with his love in the mountain pool. But the poem suffers from a certain blandness. Unlike O'Hara, who would have transformed that building excavation near Radio City into a new radiant configuration, Wright is ill at ease when trying to convey the mood and tempo of New York. His Upper West Side blacks are merely cardboard figures.

Wright is at his best when he writes what we might call the "epiphany poem"—a brief lyric in which contemplation of the external landscape suddenly gives way to insight into the world beyond. This kind of lyric—and the recent "To the August Fallen," a meditation on death, is a good example—links Wright to A. R. Ammons, whose *Uplands* and *Briefings* are probably the most significant of the new volumes under review here.

Relatively unknown until recent years although he published his first volume *Ommateum* in 1955, Ammons is now getting the attention he deserves. "Of the poets in my own generation," writes Harold Bloom in the Winter 1972 issue of the *Southern Review*, "Ammons seems to me the likeliest to attain a central position in our imaginative history." For Bloom, Ammons is "the most Emersonian poet we have had since Whitman's petering out after 1860," a Transcendentalist who has learned that intimations of immortality come only fleetingly, and that, accordingly, the most important virtue the poet can cultivate is that of patience.

"Seeking the Other in the Emersonian Not-Me of nature, the seer has learned indirection and finally resignation."

In his bemused and resigned attitude toward his search for transcendence, Ammons is, as Bloom notes, very much like Wallace Stevens. But his aesthetic, as presented in the poem "Poetics," is not quite like that of Stevens either. There is a special rationale behind Ammons' wholly unusual diction, punctuation, and syntax:

> I look for the way
> things will turn
> out spiralling from a center
> the shape
> things will take to come forth in
>
> so that the birch tree white
> touched black at branches
> will stand out
> wind-glittering
> totally its apparent self:
>
> I look for the forms
> things want to come as
>
> from what black wells of possibility. (*Briefings*)

In its emphasis on the process rather than product, on the act rather than its consequence, this poem recalls Williams' "Young Sycamore." Ammons believes that objects only "selve" themselves when they are allowed the freedom of unobstructed motion. It is the poet's duty to capture the "shape that may be / Summoning itself / through me / from the self not mine but ours." The result is what we might call "action poetry." The poem "Admission" is typical of Ammons' later work:

> The wind high along the headland,
> mosquitoes keep low: it's
> good to be out:
> schools of occurring whitecaps
> . . . .

leap and dive:
gulls stroll
long strides down the shore wind:
every tree shudders utterance:
motions—sun, water, wind, light—
intersect, merge: here possibly
from the crest of the right moment
one might break away from the final room. (*Briefings*)

The colon, used six times within the poem's thirteen lines, is Ammons' favor-ite form of punctuation. It is his way of insisting that meaning is always thrown forward, that only by pressing ahead, by allowing one idea or image to gen-erate another, can insight finally come. Ammons' free verse is extraordinarily fluid because his line lengths and syntax are always defying one's expectations. Thus, we have the surprising break between "it's" and "good" on the one hand, and, on the other, the unexpected joining together of "intersect, merge" with the new phrase "here possibly," which would logically belong in a new line. Again, our demand for syntactic parallelism is defeated by the first two lines, in which the noun phrase, "The wind high along the headland," is followed by the sub-ject-verb unit, "mosquitoes keep low." At the same time, Ammons forces the reader to be unusually attentive by using words in new contexts or giving them new meaning, as in "*occurring* whitecaps," "*shudders* utterance," "gulls *stroll* long strides down the *shore* wind," or "the *crest* of the right moment." As a result, the reader is wholly drawn into the experience of the poem. Adopting the poem's angle of vision, one finds it only natural that the buoyancy produced by the high wind "along the headland," the "occurring whitecaps," and the trees' mysterious "utterance" should induce the feeling that "one might break away from the final room." Everything in the poem moves, turns, revolves, intersects, and merges so that, finally, "Admission" to Otherness seems wholly within the realm of possi-bility.

Ammons can, of course, be accused of a certain monotony. One can argue that his poems are all of a piece, that all are delicate insights based on the con-templation of blades of grass, insects, laser beams, and so on. It is true that Ammons' poems rarely deal with persons and places with historical and social realities, that they have none of the burning passion of a Ferenc Juhász or the jaunty immediacy of the New York poets. But within his given limits, Ammons is a worthy heir to Wallace Stevens, as these lines from "Cut the Grass," reminis-cent of Stevens' "The Sense of the Sleight-of-Hand Man," suggest:

The wonderful workings of the world: wonderful,
wonderful: I'm surprised half the time:
ground up fine, I puff if a pebble stirs.
. . . .
when grassblades flop to the little red-ant
queens burring around trying to get aloft, I blame
my not keeping the grass short, stubble

firm: well, I learn a lot of useful stuff, meant
to be ignored: like when the sun sinking in the
west glares a plane invisible, I think how much

revelation concealment necessitates: and then I
think of the ocean, multiple to a blinding
oneness and realize that only total expression

expresses hiding. (*Briefings*)

Superficially, this meditation on the relation of sameness to difference, macrocosm to microcosm, would seem to be the antithesis of the Frank O'Hara poems with which this survey began, but as Ammons so nicely puts it, "the pleasure of / circles [is] driven into the next / moment." Although Ammons is our Emersonian Nature Poet, O'Hara our City Poet par excellence, although the latter is as devoted to pavement and the phonograph as the former to bird song and rock ledge, the two poets, interestingly enough, have a similar aesthetic. Ammons does not, of course, subscribe to O'Hara's Personism, but, like O'Hara, he conceives of poetry not as product but as process—as action, as a mode of continuous discovery, a bursting into being that is always taking place. Both think in terms of film or painting rather than of purely verbal art. The desire of both poets to avoid finish, to keep the poem as open-ended as possible, may usher in a bevy of trivial "I do this, I do that" poems, but a year that has witnessed the publication of *Briefings* as well as of O'Hara's *Collected Poems* is surely one in which poetry is alive and well.

CHAPTER 5

Roots and Blossoms

Theodore Roethke has been dead for ten years now, but although contemporary critics often dismiss his poetry as excessively narrow, both in scope and in style, among poets, judging from these three books, his influence continues to loom large. In the typical Roethke poem, the "I," presented as an archetypal seer figure and distanced from the "real" Ted Roethke, undergoes a hallucinatory, momentous experience of otherness. Merging his deepest self with what he called the "lovely diminutives" of nature—ferns, tendrils, bits of moss, cyclamen tips, weeds, minnows, lizards, meadow mice—the poet is reborn:

> I can hear, underground that sucking and sobbing,
> In my veins, in my bones, I feel it,—
> The small waters seeping upward,
> The tight grains parting at last.
> When sprouts break out,
> Slippery as fish,
> I quail, lean to beginnings, sheath-wet
> (from "Cuttings")

In *The Branch Will Not Break* (1963), to my mind his best book, James Wright beautifully adapted this visionary mode to his own purposes. His poems are shorter, quieter, gentler than Roethke's; they usually present the poet in a specific midwestern locale, contemplating a landscape that seems wholly alien until a sudden gesture or change in perspective momentarily unites poet and nature,

Review of *Two Citizens*, by James Wright; *The Lady from Kicking Horse Reservoir*, by Richard Hugo; and *Moly* and *My Sad Captains*, by Thom Gunn. *Washington Post: Book World* 6, September 1973, 6–7.

self and other, in a muted epiphany. Wright's well-known "Lying in a Hammock at William Duffy's Farm in Pine Island, Minnesota" is a good example; "In Fear of Harvests" is another:

> It has happened
> Before: nearby,
> The nostrils of slow horses
> Breathe evenly,
> And the brown bees drag their high garlands,
> Heavily,
> Toward hives of snow.

Two Citizens contain a few such "epiphany poems," particularly "You and I Saw Hawks Exchanging the Prey," in which the contending hawks are gradually and subtly associated in the poet's mind with his turbulent love for his wife. But in most of Wright's new poems, transfiguration gives way to protestation: the poet seems to be straining to assert his sense of place, his myth of the small-town Ohio of his youth. "The Young Good Man," for example, recalls a summer when all the poet's friends and relatives warned him not to eat the bitter crab apples growing in his backyard. But "One evening in August something illuminated my body," and the boy "found . . . A wild crab apple":

> I licked it all over.
> You are going to believe this.
> It tasted sweet.
>
> I know what would have happened to my tongue
> If I had bitten. The people who love me
> Are sure as hell no fools.

This rather simplistic account of instinct proving wiser than reason—but not too wise—remains inert because the remembered incident lacks all context; it is so obviously recalled because the poet needs an illustrative example. Similarly, in "Prayer to the Good Poet," in which Wright tries to relate his spiritual father, Horace, to his real one, "a good man in Ohio," who used to work in a factory and now "Lies alone in pain," the analogies seem strained and coy, as when the speaker tells Horace:

I worked once in the factory that he worked in.
Now I work in the factory that you live in.
Some people think poetry is easy,
But you two didn't.

In the long opening room, "Ars Poetica: Some Recent Criticism," the poet recalls how his childhood trust in America was destroyed by his initiation into pain and evil. His prime example is the deterioration of his pitiful, ugly, badly treated, ultimately mad Aunt Agnes, the family outcast, whose only meaningful act occurred on a day when the local boys tried to stone a poor goat to death, and she

Threw stones back at the boys
And gathered the goat,
Nuts as she was,
Into her sloppy arms.

In the final section of this poem, Wright insists that he doesn't want to sentimentalize this incident: "I don't believe my Aunt Agnes is a saint," and "I don't believe in the goat either," but in that case his conclusion "Hell, I ain't got nothing. / Ah, you bastards, / How I hate you," seems histrionic. On the book blurb, Wright states that he discovered America in "the shape of a beautiful woman who loved me and who led me through France and Italy." But one wonders if Fiesole or the village of Ohrid in Yugoslavia would seem so enticing to the poet if he spoke the language, for, as he says in one poem, "the language is only to me / The music of mountain people." Here to the detriment of the poetry, ignorance is bliss: anyone who has read, say, Verga's Sicilian stories knows that there is nothing inherently American in the ostracizing of ugly old eccentrics or in the stoning of runaway goats. *Two Citizens*, in short, tries to moralize its contrasting landscapes without fully establishing their distinguishing features.

One cannot level such an accusation at Richard Hugo's *The Lady in Kicking Horse Reservoir*. Like Wright, Hugo is, loosely speaking, a regional poet. Like the later Roethke, the region he celebrates is the Pacific Northwest, specifically his home state, Montana. If his new book is not a notable departure from his three earlier ones, this is perhaps all to the good, for although Hugo's limits are narrow, within those limits he is superb. The poems in this new volume could have as their epigraph Robert Frost's phrase "what to make of a diminished thing." Hugo's landscapes are like so many backdrops for James Dean's *East of Eden*;

they are uniformly bleak, alien, dehumanized, yet Hugo knows how to make these uninhabited wastes memorable, even desirable. Take the opening of "A Map of Montana in Italy":

> On this map white. A state thick as a fist
> or blunt instrument. Long roads weave and cross
> red veins full of rage. Big Canada, map maker's
> pink, squats on our backs, planning bad winters
> for years, and Glacier Park's green with my envy
> of grizzly bears.

Montana is seen here as a place unique in having absolutely nothing to offer. Overshadowed by Big Canada to the north and yet sharing its miserable winters, unable to boast even the Grizzly Bears of the great National Parks, this country merely is.

> With so few Negroes and Jews we've been reduced
> to hating each other, dumping our crud
> in our rivers, mistreating the Indians.
> Each year, 4000 move, most to the west
> where ocean currents keep winter in check.

In Hugo's imagination, this land becomes the paradigm for the starkest, barest, existential reality, and contemplating it from the distance of Italy, he understands perhaps for the first time, why our westerns have such universal appeal.

Hugo's Montana poems are never merely descriptive. As self and landscape meet, ironic changes occur. In "2433 Agnes, First Home, Last House in Missoula," the poet records his response to acquiring his first home, a house situated on the very edge of town, where civilization and wilderness meet. He begins smugly, "It promises quiet here," but as in Coleridge's "Frost at Midnight," the silence is so extreme that it becomes oppressive, and the new homeowner rapidly looks around for signs of life: "A green Plymouth . . . sitting across the street," "the lady in 2428" who "limps with a cane," the "chicken coop / in disrepair" further down the block. The slightest changes, whether visual or auditory, begin to preoccupy him: "in 2430 / a woman is moving, muted to ghost behind / dotted swiss curtains." By the end of the poem, he is guarding his privacy so jealously (although no one has so much as spoken to him!) that he resents the trespassing of "fifty buntings . . . nervously pecking my lawn." The poem is a delicately ironic version of the Romantic theme that the outer landscape is merely a reflection of the mental one, that nature is transformed in our image.

Like *Two Citizens* Hugo's book contains a selection of poems about touring Europe. Comparing the two, one concludes that coming to terms with one's own landscape paradoxically makes it much easier to travel abroad. I find Hugo's sharply etched, low-key images of Praed Street, London, or the Roman ruins at Chysauster more convincing than Wright's travel poems, which often sound like self-conscious versions of Lawrence's *Look! We Have Come Through!*

Thom Gunn's *Moly*, originally published in Britain in 1971, has now been brought out in this country together with an earlier collection, *My Sad Captains* (1961). It is not clear to me why this new edition of Gunn's work bypasses his 1967 book *Touch*, which contained what many critics felt to be his major achievement, "Misanthropos." *Moly*, in any case, is only a qualified success. Too often, in these new experiments with the Roethkean mode, Gunn's form seems to be at odds with his theme. Moly, the flower Hermes gave Odysseus to avoid the temptations of Circe (and which Joyce marvelously transformed in Bloom's little trouser button that pops to the tune of "Bip!" at the moment of crisis in Nighttown) must be taken as an ironic image in Gunn's book, for his poems concern, not the means of avoiding temptation but, on the contrary, the desire to be tempted, to be turned into Circe's swine. Moving away from his earlier Audenesque, third-person, impersonal, ironic manner, Gunn is now writing visionary lyrics. The opening poem, "Rites of Passage," describes the metamorphosis of a man into a stag, ready to battle his father:

> Something is taking place.
> Horns bud bright in my hair.
> My feet are turning hoof.
> And Father, see my face
> —Skin that was damp and fair
> Is barklike and, feel, rough.

One cannot help comparing this poem to Ferenc Juhász's famous "The Boy Changed into a Stag" but Gunn's lyric has none of the Hungarian poet's passionate intensity. For one thing, the six-line trimeter stanza rhyming *abcabc* is an oddly inappropriate vehicle for the experience of metamorphosis, and the mystery of the vent seems to be asserted rather than felt.

At least two poems in *Moly*—"At the Center" and "The Fair in the Woods"— deal with LSD visions. Again, these poems are so controlled, so carefully organized and sequentially structured that the very opposite of drug-induced hallucination seems to take place. Certain nature poems like "Flooded Mead-ows" and "Sunlight" are more successful, but even here one feels that Gunn is writing against the grain. "Sunlight" ends with the prayer:

> Great seedbed, yellow center of the flower,
> Flower on its own, without a root or stem,
> Giving all color and all shape their power,
> Still re-creating in defining them,
>
> Enable us, altering like you, to enter
> Your passionless love, impartial but intense,
> And kindle in acceptance round your center,
> Petals of light lost in your innocence.

This is very accomplished verse, written by a poet who has obviously mas-tered the variations of which iambic pentameter is capable, and whose meta-phors (e.g., sun=seedbed) are carefully worked out. Yet there seems to be noth-ing behind the elegant verbal structure of "Sunlight." One is not convinced that Gunn believes in the sun's power to change us, whether for better or worse. The ecstatic Lawrencian sun worship, the Roethkean ability to enter the life of the other, are absent.

CHAPTER 6

Mona Van Duyn's Disguises

Mona Van Duyn has won so many fellowships, honors, and prizes—including the coveted Bollingen Prize and a National Book Award—that one naturally comes to *Merciful Disguises*, which is in effect Van Duyn's *Collected Poems 1959–73*, although she modestly refuses to call it that, with great expectations. Yet seen in its totality, Van Duyn's work seems somehow slighter, less important than it appeared to be when her two best volumes, *A Time of Bees* (1964) and *To See, To Take* (1970), first appeared. There are many poems in *Merciful Disguises* that are charming, delightfully witty, and subtle; the poet's voice, moreover, is entirely her own: bemused, discriminating, detached, yet full of concern for those she loves. Going through the poems in sequence, however, I have the oddest sense that I am always reading the same poem. For one thing, there is astonishingly little development in verse technique. Here are two lines from the book's opening poem, "Three Valentines to the Wide World":

> I have never enjoyed these roadside overlooks from which
> you can see the mountain of two states.

And here is the very last, "Walking the Dog: A Diatribe":

> I have never seen a cicada, but
> nothing so pollutes
> the night with noise as those
> self-absorbed, ear-baiting singers.

It is hard to believe that fifteen years have intervened between the two.

Review of *Merciful Disguises*, by Mona Van Duyn. *Washington Post: Book World*, January 6, 1974, 3.

But it is not just a matter of verse form. Thematically, Van Duyn's range is fairly narrow: she generally begins with a specific observation, situation, or object, and then deduces delicate little insights from what she has just seen or thought about. But the gain in understanding, the looked-for epiphany is often so minor that one wonders whether it was worth the poet's trouble to bring her reader around to her position. Here, for example, is the opening of "A Spell of Conjunctivitis":

> The act of seeing a tree is the act of pressing
> an etched eyeball against the damp paper sky,
> carefully, carefully, and there it hangs, a fresh print.
> An elegant frme of fur defines the start as mid-trunk
> and the highest achievement as a slight tapering.
> But how insistently it gathers itself together,
> forcing the multitudinous scratchings out of which it is composed
> into a perpendicular, a tree, recognizably sycamore.

This careful account of what it feels like to see the world through eyes that are painfully smarting is both witty and original; we follow the poet's perspective as the "elegant frame of fur" gradually becomes something perpendicular and finally reveals itself to be a sycamore tree. In subsequent stanzas, the poem explores similar distortion of vision: the poet's dog "leaps through hoops of fur" and then "reappears . . . with several legs that require an instant to rejoin the body." The faces of her friends "are on balloons that drift and rise"; one resembles "a pirate with a gray patch on his eye," while others have "missing mouths." How precariously, the poet concludes, "They are delivered to my senses, and with what loss of self-containment!" Sight, in other words, is a precious gift, appreciated only when we momentarily lose it.

No one would want to quarrel with this observation, but it hardly seems to merit the complicated elaborations that bring us to it. For unlike Williams, whose "Young Sycamore" is a wholly new creation, an object in space seen as if for the first time as it "rises / bodily / into the air with / one undulant thrust," Van Duyn does not endow her sycamore with a sense of felt presence. Nor, on the other hand, does she use the diseased eye as a symbol of diseased moral and psychological vision as does Lowell in his marvelous "Eye and Tooth":

> My whole eye was sunset red
> the old cut cornea throbbed,
> I saw things darkly,
> as through an unwashed goldfish globe.

Here there are resonances quite beyond Van Duyn's range; her poem simply records the way any nice, sensitive person might respond to "A Spell of Conjunctivitis."

What Mona Van Duyn's poetry lacks, in short, is the quality the Russian Formalists called *factura* or density. If poetry is, as Pound put it, "language charged with meaning to the utmost possible degree," hers has a fairly low voltage. Too often, poems that begin with dazzling metaphors peter out because they go on for too long.

Van Duyn's tendency to overelaborate a fairly simple theme is reflected even in her verse line, which is almost always peculiarly long (ten to fifteen syllables), run on, and characterized by an unusually large amount of function words, conjunctions, and pronouns. There is little phrasal or clausal repetition, sound patterning, or ellipsis, and the long, rambling lines are so lightly stressed that the net effect is that of ordinary prose, as in this passage from "A Time of Bees":

> I tell you I swept up bodies every day on the porch.
> Then they'd stop, the problem was solved; they were there again,
> as the feelings make themselves known again, as they beseech
> sleepers who live innocently in will and mind.

It is one thing to strive for the effect of normal, colloquial speech but another to simply write the way one talks, as Van Duyn does here.

My favorite poems in *Merciful Disguises* are those that are forced by certain thematic necessity to have a more formal structure, to stick, as it were, to the rules. "Elementary Attitudes," for example, is a carefully structured four-part meditation on the four elements. Van Duyn's strategy is to take each element and think of all the things, people, objects, attitudes, or situations that the element connotes. The result is at once a literalizing of the element—no fires of purgation or lust here—and a wholly original treatment of it. The most delightful of the four sections is "Air," a witty diatribe against being "up in the air," both literally and figuratively. "I'll never climb Eiffels, / see Noh plays, big game, leprous beggars," says the poet somewhat ruefully. Hers is a world of "prunes / in the pot roast, kidneys in the wine and the restrained misery / of a hamburger-loving husband." Even in her backyard, there are only "prone / plants from far places that never adjusted to Missouri." Flying high is no pleasure for this poet who finds even breathing a nuisance and concludes, "I tend toward asthma and bronchitis."

All four parts of "Elementary Attitudes" display Van Duyn's very real strengths: the ability to turn a commonplace inside-out, the willingness to laugh at oneself. The later love poems are particularly successful in this regard. In "The Fear of Flying," the poet knows she is no starry-eyed ingenue. Yet even though she can see through her husband's poses with a merciless vision, she depends upon his pretenses more than on the "truth" of her situation, and so getting on a plane without him is painful.

> my world, my senses' home, familiar monster,
> it would seem that I still love you,
> and, like a schoolgirl deep in her first despair,
> I hate to go above you.

Poems like "Elementary Attitudes" and "The Fear of Flying" deserve to become well-known anthology pieces; I would add "A Day in Late October," which is to my mind the best of the many elegies on Randall Jarrell composed by his illustrious contemporaries, as well as the two witty feminist responses to Yeats's "Leda and the Swan," especially the first, in which Leda, far from putting on the god's "knowledge with his power," lives fairly happily ever after, married to "a smaller man with a beaky nose." But a little Mona Van Duyn goes a long way, and this 245-page collection of her poems, similar as they tend to be in mood, theme, and form, may well be more than all but her most devoted readers bargained for.

CHAPTER 7

The Poet and His Politics

To speak dispassionately about so delicate a subject as the "political identities" of Pound and Eliot is, even thirty years after World War II, almost impossible. In 1972 Pound was denied the Emerson-Thoreau Medal of the American Academy of Arts and Letters on the grounds that, despite the genius of his poetry, his political and social views made it impossible to honor him with a humanistic award. Such a judgment may strike us as unnecessarily harsh, perhaps even quaintly absurd. But then we remember that on the other side of the fence we have voices like Sister Bernetta Quinn's, an established Pound scholar who declared in her recent book, with reference to the poet's notorious Rome broadcasts of 1941–1943, "Pound attacked the Roosevelt administration, somewhat in the manner that more recent critics have assailed the policies of Johnson and Nixon"—an extraordinary statement that must send shivers down the spine of those of us who are alive today because Roosevelt fortunately did not listen to the likes of Ezra Pound.

Eliot's political pronouncements have given rise to similar—if less violent—controversy. In an especially interesting chapter of *The Real Foundations: Literature and Social Change*, David Craig argues that the so-called trenchant satire of *The Waste Land* is frequently no more than nasty sarcasm, directed against lower-class persons who happen to need false teeth, eat food from tin cans, or, like "the young man carbuncular" who is only "A small house agent's clerk," suffer from acne. Far from being the "centrally wise diagnosis of 'mass civilization' and its ills" it is generally claimed to be, *The Waste Land*, Craig suggests, is "primitivist" in its rejection of modern industrial society, a "defeatist"

Review of *The Political Identities of Ezra Pound and T. S. Eliot*, by William M. Chace; and *The Real Foundations: Literature and Social Change*, by David Craig. *The New Republic* March 16, 1974, 2–23.

poem that "projects an almost despairing personal depression in the guise of an impersonal picture society." Yet others—notably Russell Kirk and the makers of a recent BBC television special on Eliot, continue to view the poet as a gentle, kind, humane Christian, just short of being a saint, a voice in the wilderness preaching to the Philistines.

In such an emotionally charged atmosphere, the temptation is to do what the Bollingen Prize Committee did when it made its now notorious award to Pound for the *Pisan Cantos* in 1949—namely to insist that a man's poetry is not to be judged by his politics. Thus, in his well-known study of the *Cantos*, Clark Emery says, "Seen in their proper perspective in strict terms of literary criticism [Pound's Fascist sympathies] are of minor importance. The critical evaluation of *The Faerie Queene* or of *Paradise Lost* does not hinge upon the anti-Catholicism or anti-monarchism of their authors."

It is the great merit of William M. Chace's book that he refuses to take this way out. Convinced that whatever one's own political persuasions, one cannot understand the poetry of Pound and Eliot—both intensely political writers—without coming to terms with their political ideas, Chace proceeds to give us the most balanced, fair-minded, lucid exposition we have to date of these ideas, neatly avoiding the Scylla of polemic attack and the Charybdis of partisan whitewash. *Political Identities* is, moreover, a model of conciseness: each poet gets roughly one hundred pages, and within that short span Chace shows clearly what forces attracted both poets toward varieties of fascism, and what inconsistencies and sometimes sheer ignorance of fact colored their political thinking.

Thus Chace places the whole matter in a new perspective. His central argument is that Pound and Eliot were neither "uniquely political" nor "uniquely unwise in their views," which were simply an extreme version of the views held by a large number of their contemporaries. Their rejection of democracy begins in their family situation, which Chace defines, especially in Pound's case, as "nouveau-poor: refined, with pretensions of gentility, with a memory of rather better times, with little room for social mobility" and a consequent distrust of the "strangers"—particularly the Jews—who were displacing people like themselves "who could trace their American lineage back to the early years of the Republic."

If family background is one major factor, a second is the literary milieu of high decadence into which Pound and Eliot were born. Their partisan activities, Chace argues, must be viewed "as an awkward emergence from the Symbolist quarantine," the esthetic movement's dictum that "the poet must shut his door to the world of streets and speeches." Both Pound and Eliot began by insisting on the autonomy of poetry only to discover that the price the artist paid for divorcing his poetics from ethics was a painful isolation from his society. Both accordingly soon modified the purist stance of their celebrated early criticism and moved toward the position that poets should be the "unacknowledged legislators of the world."

In Pound's case the political doctrine was formulated as early as *Patria Mia* (1912), whose basic assumptions are two: (1) art is the best index of a nation's strength, and (2) although nature is bountiful, modern industrial democracy weakens that synthesis of human resources in which alone art can flourish. At age twenty-seven, then, Pound already regarded the financial inequity that is inherent in capitalist democracy as the cancer in the body of modern civilization and the root of human decay.

For a time, indeed, he flirted with Marxism, but, as Chace makes clear, Pound could never stomach an ideology that glorified the worker and advocated the overthrow of the class system, for by instinct he despised the masses and wanted to be a free individual with entrepreneurial literary energies that would transform the consciousness of the nation. If capitalism per se could not, then, be considered the Enemy, the answer was to put the blame on individual capitalists: the usurious Jewish financiers who had destroyed the very fabric of Jeffersonian democracy. From this initial deep-seated prejudice against the Rothschilds, the "Jewspapers" and the New Deal of "Franklin Finklestein Roosevelt," it was only a logical step to the hero-worship of Mussolini, that charismatic leader who would ostensibly provide the order and stability within which the artist could flourish. And soon Pound was declaring that history had been "keenly analyzed" in *Mein Kampf.*

The evolution of Eliot's political thought is similar. Like Pound's, Eliot's politics is rooted in his own personal situation, his sense of alienation at postwar chaos and the seeming collapse of Western civilization. His notorious declaration of 1928 that his position was "classicist in literature, royalist in politics, and Anglo-Catholic in religion" is seen by Chace, quite rightly I think, as a wholly negative statement: Eliot's "classicism" was in fact a thinly disguised urge to withdraw from a distasteful democracy into a private universe of his own making, and his Anglo-Catholicism is best understood as a means of separating oneself from the masses. "The Church," in Chace's words, "signified not union, but separation," and "Between the isolated Church . . . and the pagan world without, no contact exists or should exist." Accordingly—and here Eliot parts company with Pound—no secular ideology could ever be acceptable. Eliot's aim was not to solve social problems but to show "how men failed to achieve a society in which certain religious values could be appreciated."

The result of such a stance was *After Strange Gods* (1933), that embarrassing book Eliot chose not to reprint, in which he argued that in a proper society, "The population should be homogeneous . . . reasons of race and religion combine to make any large number of free-thinking Jews undesirable." Criticism, then, became more and more the search for heretics, such as that "parvenu scientist" Freud or Karl Marx, the "Jewish economist" who had "inverted Hegel." Ultimately Eliot could only retreat into his imaginary Christian society, a Utopia in which somehow the common people would let themselves be guided by the "Clerisy" of moral and ethical leaders as well as by the newly revived strong monastic orders.

What lesson can we draw from all this? David Craig would reply that it is only writers on the Left like Brecht and Sartre who have given us a convincing and realistic picture of modern industrial society. "The great novelist may not be interested in the social urgings behind 'equality' and the planning that it entails, but that doesn't free him from the duty to present fairly—which in terms of his particular art means a *fully dramatic* treatment—the sorts of situation in which the ideas he is canvassing . . . actually arose."

Craig's attack on *The Waste Land* is impressive, but if Chace's book teaches us anything it is that "the step from being authorities in poetry and criticism to thinking well of authoritarianism is the most important step Pound and Eliot took." It is almost hopelessly difficult for the poetic imagination to engage the intellectual complexity and deep contradictions of our political world. "Entry into the world of profound political consequence," he concludes, "is as difficult for today's liberal as it was for Pound and Eliot," and indeed, "it is foolish to look to most of the writers of our time for political wisdom."

But Chace's argument that the political vision of both poets everywhere informs their poetic vision is less convincing. For if this political vision is misguided, inhumane, confused, and sometimes downright evil, how can the poetry that it informs be, as Chace all along assumes it is, poetry of the first order?

Eliot's poetry, in this respect, presents fewer problems than does Pound's. Yeats's shrewd observation that as "a New England Protestant by descent, there is little self-surrender in his [Eliot's] personal relation to God and the soul," is not cited by Chace but it could serve as an epigraph to his critique of Eliot's later poetry. He considers 1930 a kind of turning point, arguing that in "Ash Wednesday," the struggle toward the spiritual life is ultimately subordinated to a tired Olympian disdain for "those who walk among noise and deny the voice." Moreover, Chace questions Eliot's declared intent of turning the theater into a communal enterprise: "His plays, the superficial appearance of *Murder in the Cathedral* notwithstanding, do not revive the spirit and the appeal of an *Everyman*. Still less do they cultivate, in the manner of a Shakespeare or even a Yeats, the latent aspirations, nationalistic or otherwise, of the people who might be watching them. They are a severely restricted drama."

Here Chace puts his finger on precisely what is wrong with what is to my mind one of the most overrated plays of the century, *Murder in the Cathedral*. He argues convincingly that the women of Canterbury who acts as chorus are presented as a lower order of being, capable of faith but not true perception: "For us, the poor there is no action, / But only to wait and to witness." The capacity for religious understanding and salvation is, in other words, "subtly linked with social standing." By the time of *Four Quartets* (1941), Eliot had swept away all ideology and politics from serious discussion. The world is pure folly devoid of sense. Depending on one's point of view, *Four Quartets* is therefore the most Christian and perfect of Modern poems, or an inert, static poem of withdrawal. Chace writes, "The cruel paradox of *Four Quartets* stems from the poet's stubborn reliance upon words as the single instrument for evoking and substantiating faith, coupled with an equally strong conviction on his part that in this world, an un-Christian world doomed to internal decay, no labor and no zeal can matter very much."

If one excepts the later pseudo-comedies, which do little to redeem the poet's early reputation, the rest, in Eliot's case, is silence. Political withdrawal and poetic isolation do go hand in hand. Pound's poetry is, however, quite another matter, and here I think Chace's case is weaker. He argues that the *Cantos* are problematic because "Pound's matter is often ill-served by his form." Pound yearns for an all-encompassing ordering principle, yet his poetics demands a "phalanx of particulars," discrete images and ideograms paratactically related and hence defying the very order the poet defines so eloquently in, say, Canto XIII: "If a man have not order within him / He can not spread order about him." This is a very good point and Chace also makes clear that although Pound is always yearning for order, his politics, like his poetry, is built upon the isolation of particulars— individual scapegoats such as Metevsky or heroes such as Martin Van Buren. But then Chace goes on to suggest that the most successful cantos are those like XXXIII, in which a series of instructional examples from history neatly illustrate the central theme: that money is misused by bankers and monopolists. True, here "aesthetic form and didactic intent are united," but I am not at all sure that this is a good thing. On the contrary I would argue that the best cantos are not those that provide clear-cut illustrations of Pound's political ideas, but precisely the more disorderly ones like the first Pisan Canto (LXXIV). For Pound, unlike Eliot, is not a consistent poet. As early as "Hugh Selwyn Mauberley" (1920), we find the most banal diatribes against war ("There died a myriad / And of the best . . . for an old bitch gone in the teeth, / For a botched civilization") side by side with the charming, witty satire of "Yeux Glauques" and of that epitome of the "pickled foetuses" of the 1990s, Monsieur Verog.

The truth is that Pound never did escape from the decadent quarantine that Chace speaks of. His work is the living embodiment of dissociation of sensibility. For there are only two things that Pound really knew about: the world of art and the world of his own life. When he writes of Uncle William (Yeats) "dawdling around Notre Dame" or of Wyndham Lewis "out in the privvy" he is incomparable. When, on the other hand, he expounds on the noble currency reforms made by the Bürgomeister of Wörgl in the Tyrol he is, quite aside from being morally offensive, just plain silly.

Silliest of all, to my mind, are the great set pieces like "Pull down thy vanity" (LXXXI), "Compleint, compleynt" (XXX), and especially the famous Usura Canto (XLV). At the risk of offending all Pound devotees, I suggest that Canto XLV, that well-worn anthology piece, is not a good poem. Critics have raved about its metrical brilliance and the power of its lyrical condemnation of *Usura*, and even Chace concedes that the canto's "undeniable effectiveness" is "to be explained by the astonishingly forceful way in which the poem simplifies a problem as complicated as the relationship of art, life, and society." But how much simplification is tolerable? When Pound writes, "Duccio came not by usura / nor Pier della Francesca; Zuan Bellin' not by usura," I want to close the book, not because these notions offend me, but because they are so foolish. Piero and Bellini may not have "come by" Usura—they only "came by" treachery, fraud, murder, rape, poisonings, and all those other crimes committed by their great Renaissance patrons. And what about those great artists who did "come by" Usura? In *How to Read* Pound declares, "No man can write really good verse unless he knows Stendhal and Flaubert." Yet surely no age was more aggressively usurious than that of the July Monarchy and the Second Empire.

In short, however convincingly one may theorize about the dependence of a poet's aesthetics on his politics, Pound happens to be sui generis. In reading the *Cantos*, one simply must separate the embarrassingly banal or prejudiced political passages from the great autobiographical and literary ones. Future selections from the *Cantos* will, I believe, omit large chunks of the Van Buren, Adams, and *Monte de Paschi* Cantos, not because these will offend readers but because they will bore them. The great autobiographical passages, on the other hand—for example, most of the Pisan sequence—will be seen for what they are: a poetic triumph, the formal breakthrough that paved way for the conjunction of poetry and prose, of high and low styles, of documentary realism juxtaposed with myth, that look ahead to Williams's *Paterson*, Lowell's *Life Studies*, Berryman's *Dream Songs*, or O'Hara's "To the Film Industry in Crisis." As the poet who invented the free verse line at its most "poetic," who taught poets how to juxtapose the most disparate images, to charge proper names with amazing weight and density, to endow army slang, foreign accents and quirky dialects with poetic resonance, Pound is our contemporary in the best sense of the word: contemporary poetry simply could not exist without his model.

Thus, although Chace's argument about the interrelationship of politics and poetry is entirely valid in the case of most poets, including Eliot, try as he may he cannot quite fit Pound into his scheme. For as Williams, Pound's lifetime friend, put it, "I could never take [Pound] as a steady diet. Never. He was often brilliant but an ass."

CHAPTER 8

Pound's Vorticist Textbook

Henri Gaudier-Brzeska, the French sculptor tragically killed in action on the Western Front when he was only twenty-three, was perhaps the most promising sculptor of his generation. Yet the only available edition of his sculpture and drawings, that of Mervyn Levy (October House, 1965), is hardly adequate: it omits some of Gaudier's most important sculptures, provides indifferent reproductions of the others, and Levy's brief introduction is, at best, sketchy. Reviewing the book for *Apollo*, John Parry asks: "Why doesn't some enterprising publisher reprint Pound's monograph?"

The enterprising publisher who did just that was James Laughlin of New Directions. In 1970 he brought out an enlarged edition of Pound's 1916 memoir, including thirty pages of illustrations as well as Pound's later notes on Gaudier. Now this edition has been reissued in paperback, and although the reproductions are disappointingly small and grainy, one must be grateful to New Directions for making readily available at low cost one of the central documents of our century on avant-garde art.

Pound's "Memoir" tells us little about Gaudier's personal life. The sculptor's bizarre semi-Platonic love affair with Sophie Brzeska, the Polish writer twenty years his senior whose name he adopted, and with whom he lived on and off during the last five years of his short life, is barely mentioned: Pound discreetly refers to Sophie as Gaudier's "sister," and those who want to know more about the romance must turn to H. S. Ede's rather histrionic *The Savage Messiah* (1931).

Nor can *Gaudier-Brzeska* be called, in any usual sense of the word, "art criticism." It is a seemingly random, repetitious, disorganized, and eccentric book, a miscellany of personal vignettes, tributes by fellow artists, a selection of

Review of *Gaudier-Brzeska: A Memoir*, by Ezra Pound. *The New Republic*, December 28, 1974, 21–22.

Gaudier's letters from the Front, reprints of his critical prose (part of the "Vortex" essay for *Blast* [1914], appears twice!), Pound's own "Vorticist" essays of 1914–1915, a "Partial Catalogue" of Gaudier's work, and Pound's preface to the Memorial Exhibition of 1918.

Yet today, more than half a century after it was written, we can begin to understand *Gaudier-Brzeska* as the formal equivalent of Gaudier's credo that "sculptural energy is the mountain," or of Pound's insistence that "the image is not an idea. It is a radiant node or cluster . . . a VORTEX, from which, and through which, and into which, ideas are constantly rushing." For all its seeming chaos, *Gaudier-Brzeska* does have a plan. Pound begins with the plain facts: the news of Gaudier's death as "part of the war waste," and reprints a moving obituary by Ford Madox Ford. He then moves rapidly from the "Vortex" essay and Gaudier's other manifestos back in time to his first meeting with the sculptor that took place in 1913 at an Albert Hall exhibition, when Pound, admiring a particular green clay statue, and making of its sculptor's unpronounceable name ("Brzkjk . . . Burrzisskzk"), was suddenly approached by a young, wolflike, bright-eyed "Greek god," who said gently: "Cela s'appele tout simplement Jaershka. C'est moi qui les ai sculptés." So began the great friendship that quickly led to Pound's posing for Gaudier. "Some of my best days," Pound recalls, "the happiest and most interesting, were spent in his uncomfortable mud-floored studio when he was doing my bust." Only after this account and the series of Gaudier letters does Pound suspend the narrative and pause to define vorticism in poetry as it relates to Gaudier's "vorticist" sculptures.

On closer inspection, the book may be seen to embody the aesthetic of *process* that is, in fact, its subject matter. We come to understand Gaudier's art only gradually, just as Pound himself did. The first time one reads the "Vortex" essay, phrases like "the PALEOLITHIC VORTEX . . . Early stone-age man disputed the earth with animals" sounds merely pretentious. But when they reappear one hundred pages later, after Pound has inspected them from all sides and puzzled out their implications, these odd elliptical statements begin to make sense. *Gaudier-Brzeska* is, then, as Pound says of Gaudier's "Vortex" essay, "a remarkable arrangement of thought"; it presents ideas in action, capturing fragments of Pound's aesthetic at the very moment of their formulation.

What is that aesthetic? *Vorticism* is, as most critics have noted, a slippery term, meaningless if we take it too literally as referring to an art based on the vortex or whirlpool—"a rapid movement of particles of matter round an axis" (NED). The "vorticist" art of Gaudier and Pound tended to ignore the "central axis" itself in favor of rapid movement, a movement "caught" and given form. Art historians generally agree that Gaudier's greatest innovation was his presentation of movement that is potential rather than actual as in *The Dancer* or *Boy with a Coney*. It is this energy that immediately attracted Pound to Gaudier's sculpture. It is interesting that he preferred the portrait bust of himself "two weeks before it was finished" because at that point "it was a *kinesis*, whereas it is now a *stasis*, but before the back was cut out, and before the middle lock was cut down, there was in the marble a titanic energy, it was like a great stubby catapult, the two masses bent for a blow."

The demand for energy was only a part of Pound's "New Aesthetic." The real thrust of *Gaudier-Brzeska* lies, I think, in its rejection of (1) Mimesis and (2) Symbolism in art. In the 1934 postscript Pound says, "The key word of vorticist art was Objectivity in the sense that we insisted that the value of a piece of sculpture was dependent on its shape." This belief in the irrelevancy of subject matter was one of Gaudier's central tenets. "We have arrived at an age," he says, "when men can consider a statue a statue. The hard stone is not the live coney. Its beauty cannot be the same beauty." Such statements struck a responsive chord in Pound: "the 'new form,'" he agreed, " . . . is not a mimicry of external life." For "the organization of forms is a much more energetic and creative action than the copying or imitating of light on a haystack."

The representation of external reality is not, then, the artist's business. The French Symbolists had, of course, already allowed this precept, positing that the poet creates his own imaginative world, a construct of internalized meanings and self-contained symbols. But both Gaudier and Pound equate Mimesis and Symbolism and reject both. "I shall arrive at my emotions," Gaudier declares, "solely from the arrangement of surfaces . . . the planes and lines by which they are defined." Pound applies the same principles to poetry: "Imagism is not Symbolism . . . to use a symbol *with an ascribed or intended meaning* is, usually, to produce very bad art." The image does not, then, stand for something else; it is the "poet's pigment"; it is "itself the speech." The essence of poetry is "precision . . . a refusal to define things in terms of something else." "If I were a painter," Pound posits, "I might found a new school . . . of non-representative painting . . . that would speak only by arrangements in colour." Thus, Pound was especially drawn to Gaudier's late sculptures, which, unlike his famous *Dancer*, a semirealistic nude, were abstractions from animal life. Of *Birds Erect* Pound says: "This is one of the most important pieces. The representative element is very slight . . . as a composition of masses, I do not think I have seen any modern sculpture to match it." And indeed, *Birds Erect* prefigures the abstract bird sculptures of Moore, Brancusi, and Lipschitz.

Whether poetry can ever become purely "nonrepresentative" is, of course, doubtful, for words inevitably have meanings, and it is here that the analogies between language and stone, poetry and sculpture break down. Yet the "presentational" mode advocated by Pound in *Gaudier-Brzeska*—the doctrine that good poetry depends upon the proper arrangement of surfaces, the "positioning" of stark literal images and word groups so as to "Make It New"—looks ahead to Pound's own *Cantos* and Williams's *Spring and All*, to the poetry of Black Mountain, the Objectivists, and the New York poets, and it culminates, logically enough, in the concrete poetry of our own day. A recent manifesto of concretism asserts: "We are here to proclaim the word in space. . . . We proclaim the word as well as proclaiming the emptiness around it. When we say 'line of poetry,' we mean line as line and not as length of sound. And to 'color a thought' is no longer a metaphor but real live color. If our words do not touch you, then you should touch them, feel them, even play with them." Here, conceivably, is a rationale for the fusion of poetry and sculpture.

Pound was convinced that the Gaudier Vortex of 1914 would become "the first textbook of sculpture in many academies before our generation has passed from the earth." No doubt this claim was extravagant, at least so far as the training of contemporary sculptors is concerned, but in an odd way Pound turned out to be right. For if Gaudier's aphoristic Vortex has not become "the first textbook of sculpture" in our academies, Pound's own essay-memoir on Gaudier is well on its way to becoming a "first textbook" for anyone interested in contemporary poetry and poetics. It is a commonplace book that takes nothing for granted, an *Ars Poetica* for an age that increasingly doubts that *art* is amenable to definition.

CHAPTER 9

Art Chronicles

> Why is it all right to be influenced by a
> dead artist and a scandal if you're
> influenced by a live one?
>
> —FRANK O'HARA, "Five Participants in a Hearsay Panel"

*A*rt Chronicles 1954–1966 contains only a selection of Frank O'Hara's extensive art criticism, but it is a beautiful book, with excellent reproductions as well as delightful photographs of O'Hara on street corners or at black-tie openings or making his way through the revolving doors of the Museum of Modern Art, where he worked from 1952 until his untimely death at forty in 1966. Read in conjunction with the *Collected Poems* (1971), this set of essays suggests to me that O'Hara will eventually emerge as the Ezra Pound of the postwar period. His poetry—brilliant, droll, exciting, iconoclastic—may not measure up to the *Cantos*, but like Pound, O'Hara helped to bring about a revolution in artistic sensibility.

He counted among his friends an astonishing number of the leading poets, painters, composers, and dancers of the 1950s and 1960s (e.g., John Cage, Merce Cunningham, LeRoi Jones [Amiri Baraka], Kenneth Koch, John Ashbery, Allen Ginsberg, John Wieners, Gregory Corso, Franz Kline, Robert Motherwell, Willem and Elaine de Kooning, Helen Frankenthaler, Larry Rivers). He collaborated with Jasper Johns on "poems/lithographs," with Al Leslie on films, with John Ashbery on plays, with Arnold Weinstein on musicals. He contributed poems to exhibition catalogs and literary criticism to little magazines. As curator of the Museum of Modern Art, he was responsible for major exhibitions of

Review of *Art Chronicles*, by Frank O'Hara. *The New Republic*, March 1, 1975, 23–24.

Pollock, Kline, Smith, Motherwell, and Nakian. At the time of his death he had at last secured de Kooning's agreement to organize a large retrospective of his paintings. Finally, as art editor and critic, first for *Art News* and later for *Kulchur*, he was for more than a decade one of the leading champions of abstract expressionism and its offshoots.

Despite—or perhaps because of—this great range of interests, the academic establishment, ready to enshrine an Adrienne Rich in a Norton Critical Edition, still refuses to take O'Hara seriously. His poems, written at odd moments of the day or night, are accused of frivolity, formlessness, and excessive in-jokes. No doubt, his art criticism will be similarly dismissed by certain academics as being too impressionistic. True, O'Hara is likely to refer to paintings as "tragic," "demonic," "sullen," "somber," "tender," "luminous," or "joyful," without backing up these adjectives with any overt theory of art. Yet his impressionistic criticism takes on a different cast when one notes that, like Pound, he had an unerring eye for genius, an amazing sense of the difference between the first-rate and the second-best.

It is too bad that of the fourteen pieces in this collection, four ("Franz Kline," "David Smith," "Robert Motherwell," and "Reuben Nakian") are introductions to catalogs, because the set piece is not O'Hara's forte. Its form is too confining: something must be said of the artist's life and background, the work must be treated chronologically, and generalization is the order of the day. But in his omnibus reviews, especially the Art Chronicles for *Kulchur*, of which only one (Summer 1962) is, regrettably, reprinted here, O'Hara's critical genius is unmistakable. In 1963, for example, O'Hara said of Mark Tobey: "[He] has done fine things in his own way . . . but they will never be major any more than Redon will ever challenge Renoir. . . . Not while Willem de Kooning and Barnett Newman are about." This is a judgment that time has certainly borne out. In the same review he distinguishes perceptively between the witty "found art" of Claes Oldenburg and the banal "constructed commonplace" spray-gun paintings of Niki de St. Phalle. "What hath Pollock wrought?" O'Hara asks in mock indignation. "You don't even have to put the thing on the floor any more and you can get someone else to finish it, as a boyfriend helps his girlfriend win a panda at Palisades Park."

This may be treating "art" with insufficient respect, but although O'Hara loves to ham it up, he is never merely modish. Today Oldenburg is recognized as a major artist, and who has heard of Niki de St. Phalle? Similarly searching is O'Hara's account of the opening of the Guggenheim in 1962. After praising the wonders of the building—daytime elevators that actually take you somewhere for pleasure rather than business, the ramp that "almost completely eliminates the famous gallery-going fatigue," and the dome that resembles "the home of an urbane and mildly eccentric person," O'Hara comments, very sensibly, on the uneven quality of the show itself. He admits that "Abstract Expressionists and Imagists" is a mixed bag but wonders what the public expected:

> What the title implies is a summary of achievement, but what you get is recent works by most of the important members of the movement. This is very interesting, if you want to look at paintings. Unfortunately many people wanted to see a justification, packaged in a new Sherry's container, with a card saying, "Because of this show you are entitled to keep on admiring Abstract Expressionism." Hence the criticism the Guggenheim has gotten about the quality of the show, some of it near hysteria: "A WEAK HOFF-MANN! HOW COULD THEY!" None of the reviewers seems to have thought, "How could he!"

Such good-humored—but ultimately quite serious—irreverence is typical of O'Hara. His point is that "the show reflects the living situation" and hence "keeps you fresh for looking. . . . A lot of people," he concludes, "would like to see art dead and sure, but you don't see them up at The Cloisters reading Latin." O'Hara wants us to look for ourselves; the "masterpieces" need not be prepackaged and labeled. But this is not to say that anything goes. In the same review, O'Hara insists that de Kooning is "the greatest painter after Picasso and Miro," and singles out from the welter of new shows in town those of Oldenburg and Jasper Johns. The latter's "meticulously and sensually painted rituals of imagery express a profound boredom, in the Baudelairian sense, with the symbols of our over-symbolic society."

This distrust of Symbolism lies behind O'Hara's passionate advocacy of the abstract expressionists, especially his groundbreaking essay on Jackson Pollock, written in 1959 when action painting was still an object of ridicule. Here is the poet's comment on Number 29 (1950): "A painting-collage of oil, wire-mesh, pebbles and shells composed on glass, it is . . . unique in that it is a masterpiece from opposite sites of viewing." He marvels at the painting's "reversible textures . . . the tragedy of a linear violence which, in recognizing itself in its own mirror-self, sees elegance." And this brings O'Hara to a discussion of *scale* in Pollock's abstractions: "The scale of the painting became that of the painter's body, not the image of a body, and the setting for the scale, which would include all referents, would be the canvas surface itself. Upon this field the physical energies of the artist operate in actual detail . . . with no reference to exterior image or environment . . . no need for the mediation of metaphor or symbol. It is Action Painting."

Not all the interviews and essays included in this book are as interesting as the monograph on Pollock. O'Hara can be annoyingly flip as in his reference to Nakian's background as "Armenian-familial and Brave-New-World-Dos Passos-USA social." But beneath the archness, O'Hara repeatedly demonstrates his profound understanding for nonfigurative art. In contrasting the black-and-white paintings of Pollock and Kline, O'Hara notes that whereas Pollock has "black paint seeping into unsized canvas, at once sensitive in surface and frequently grotesque in form," Kline's "forms are stark and simple, the gesture abrupt, rough, passionately unconcerned with finish." Against the accepted view that Kline was strongly influenced by Japanese calligraphy, O'Hara argues: "The whites and blacks are strokes and masses of entirely relevant intensity to the painting as a whole and to each other. . . . [They] are aimed at an ultimate structure of feeling rather than at ideograph or writing." If anything, Kline has influenced Japanese painters rather than vice-versa.

O'Hara was, then, always testing critical commonplaces; like Pound's, his approach to art was insistently individual, independent. By the mid-1960s, when the human figure began to reassert itself, O'Hara was one of the first to discern its new potential. One of the best essays reprinted in *Art Chronicles*, written shortly before the poet's death, deals with the "figurative" painting of Alex Katz, whose pictorial world is described as "a 'void' of smoothly painted color . . . where the fairly realistic figure existed (but did not rest) in a space which had no floor, no walls, no source of light, no viewpoint. . . . Katz's people simply existed, somewhere. They stayed in the picture as solutions of a formal problem, neither existential nor lost. . . . They were completely mysterious pictorially, because there seemed to be no apparent intent of effect. They knew they were there."

Here O'Hara reveals his profound understanding of the new aesthetic, whether in painting or poetry. In his own poems there are hundreds of figures, but they too seem to exist in a space with no viewpoint, functioning "as solutions of a formal problem." They manifest what O'Hara calls (with reference to Katz's portraits of his wife Ada) "presence." "They knew they were there." Today, almost a decade after the poet's death, we should know it too.

CHAPTER 10

Battle of the Books

"A poem," said William Carlos Williams in 1943, "is a small (or large) machine made out of words. . . . It isn't what [the poet] *says* that counts as a work of art, it's what he makes, with such intensity of perception that it lives with an intrinsic movement of its own to verify its authenticity."

Wallace Stevens had a very different conception of poetry. In 1946, when asked if he had read Williams's new long poem, he said: "I have not read *Paterson*. I have the greatest respect for [Williams], although there is the constant difficulty that he is more interested in the way of saying things than in what he has to say. The fact remains that we are always fundamentally interested in what a writer has to say. When we are sure of that, we pay attention to the way in which he says it, not often before."

"This," Hugh Kenner comments dryly, "is one of the most extraordinary misunderstandings in literary history." If Kenner is right, then Harold Bloom's *A Map of Misreading* is just such an "extraordinary misunderstanding." For Bloom follows Emerson in holding that "it is not meters, but a meter-making argument that makes a poem . . . In the order of genesis, the thought is prior to the form." Given this premise, Bloom naturally assumes that "Poetic influence . . . has almost nothing to do with the verbal resemblance between one poet and another." To which Kenner would no doubt respond, "What other significant resemblances between poetic texts are there?" For in Kenner's view, the function of words is not "to say things, just as a hole is to dig." Art is, on the contrary, that which "lifts the saying out of the zone of things said." Above all else, "a poet needs a passionate interest in the language, in the words people use, and the words they might use but do not."

Review of *A Map of Misreading*, by Harold Bloom; and *A Homemade World*, by Hugh Kenner. *Washington Post Book World*, June 22, 1975, 3–4.

And so, amazingly enough, here in 1975 the old dichotomy of content versus form—a dichotomy the New Criticism had supposedly put to rest once and for all—raises its ugly head once more. Given their antithetical definitions of poetry, Bloom and Kenner clearly have opposite notions of what constitutes the "Modern tradition." Kenner's basic premise is that "writers invent the criteria by which we must understand them." Accordingly, his aesthetic is derived from those who have consciously tried to invent a new American idiom, to "Make It New"—especially Pound, Williams, Marianne Moore, the Objectivists. But, according to Bloom, no poet can make anything new. He can only misread the poems of his predecessors "so as to clear imaginative space" for himself. Strong poets, Bloom argued in *The Anxiety of Influence* (1973), "wrestle with their strong precursors . . . Weaker talents idealize." And since Romanticism "is of course *the* tradition of the last two centuries," the best Modern poem is one that has wrestled most imaginatively with its Romantic predecessor.

The great poets of the twentieth century thus turn out to be Hardy, whose poetic father is Shelley; Yeats, especially when he actively engages his precursors, Shelley and Blake; Stevens, whose poetry is a "transumption" of the great Romantic quest lyric; and finally, John Ashbery and A. R. Ammons, two "spent seers" of our own day. But since no movement can make significant advances beyond Romanticism, the role of the contemporary poet is at best equivocal, and Bloom admits that even the poets he most admires, Ashbery and Ammons, "are rendered somewhat problematic by a cultural situation of such belatedness that literary survival itself seems fairly questionable." This is tantamount to saying that poetry is now dead. And it follows that a champion of the avant-garde like Hugh Kenner becomes the Enemy: "Modernism in literature," says Bloom scathingly, "has not passed; rather, it has been exposed as never having been there. Gossip grows old and becomes myth; myth grows older and becomes dogma. Wyndham Lewis, Eliot and Pound gossiped with one another; the New Criticism aged them into a myth of Modernism; now the antiquarian Hugh Kenner has dogmatized this myth into the Pound Era."

Kenner, who rarely concerns himself with what other critics have said, does not so much as mention Bloom. But reading these two books in conjunction is to be made aware of the real Battle of the Books currently being fought in our academies (Yale and Hopkins), which count Bloom and Kenner among their most celebrated members. It is perhaps not a fair contest, for *A Homemade World* presents Kenner at his most genial and confident, whereas *A Map of Misreading* is Harold Bloom at his weakest. It is a tired, crotchety, disillusioned book, full of contempt for contemporary poets and dislike for rival critics. Even Bloom's most faithful disciples may wonder whether his new applications are valid.

According to the blurb, *A Map of Misreading* "presents the first formal advance in the techniques of closely reading poetry since the early days of the New Criticism." It must be said right away that the book does no such thing. Bloom engages in precious little "close reading"; rather, he amplifies the theory, adumbrated in *The Anxiety of Influence*, that poems are neither about "subjects" nor about "themselves." "They are necessarily about *other poems*." A poet cannot choose his precursor any more than a man can choose his father; his fate is to struggle with all his might against his precursor and yet to recognize his imprint. The analogy is Oedipal: "Reject your parents vehemently enough, and you will become a belated version of them, but compound with their reality, and you may partly free yourself."

This theory is neither as outrageous nor as new as Bloom seems to think: Andre Malraux argued long ago that art is born of art, not of nature—a thesis E. H. Gombrich developed in his seminal *Art and Illusion* (1960), which demonstrates that all art is a struggle between personal style and existing convention, that no painter ever paints "what he sees," for "what he sees" is largely determined by what his predecessors have painted.

Bloom's originality—and I would say his real weakness as well—is thus less in the realm of theory than in his New Critical vocabulary, an amalgam of Freudian, Neoplatonic, and Kabbalistic terms. In *The Anxiety of Influence*, Bloom defined six phases of "poetic misreading" from *clinamen*, "which is poetic misreading or misprision proper . . . a 'swerve' of the atoms so as to make change possible" to *apophrades*, "the return of the dead," the condition in which the poem is "*held* open to the precursor" so that it seems as a though "the later poet himself had written the precursor's characteristic work."

These terms were confusing enough, but now, in his new book, Bloom complicates things further by bringing in the system of one Isaac Luria, "a sixteenth-century master of theosophical speculation":

> The Lurianic story of creation now seems to me the best paradigm available for a study of the way poets war against one another in the strife of Eternity that is poetic influence. Luria's story . . . has three main stages: *Zimzum, Shevirath hakkelim, Tikkun. Zimzum* is the Creator's withdrawal or contraction so as to make possible a creation that is not himself. *Shevirath hakelim* is the breaking-apart-of-the-vessels, a vision of creation-as-catastrophe. *Tikkun* is restitution and restoration, man's contribution to God's work.

Zimzum, Bloom explains, is the same thing as limitation; *Shevirath hakelim* is substitution; and *Tikkun* is a synonym for representation itself.

If we now look at the map on page 84, which is meant to serve as our guide to practical criticism, we find a set of amazing mathematical relationships between the six phases of the "Revisionary Ratio" (clinamen, etc.); the Lurianic terms (the "Dialectic of Revisionism"), and a six-term series of "rhetorical tropes" and "psychic defenses." Northrop Frye's cosmological charts are child's play by comparison. One has to go to the Lagado Academy of Projectors in *Gulliver's Travels* to find anything like it. But then Swift is a writer who plays no role in Bloom's Miltonic-Romantic canon even though he was obviously one of Yeats's central precursors.

Ironically, when Bloom does get around to reading poems, he really doesn't need his own terminology. His interpretation of Wordsworth's "Intimations" ode as a creative misreading of *Lycidas*, Shelley's "Ode to the West Wind" as a similar "misprision" of Wordsworth's "Intimations" ode, and of Tennyson's "Ulysses" as a belated version, via the Romantics, of Milton's Satan is both convincing and illuminating. Certainly, these poems are members of the same family. When he turns to the Moderns, however, Bloom misreads his own map. His own consciousness is so steeped in the poetry of Milton and the Romantics that it never seems to occur to him that twentieth-century poets do have other precursors available, that Stevens, for example is "misreading" Mallarmé and Valéry at least as much as he is "misreading" Shelley. Again, Bloom does not know what to make of Pound because he doesn't recognize this poet's particular precursors, ranging from the Provençal troubadours and Dante to Li Po and Confucius. His insistence that every Modern poem must be a belated version of a Romantic or Transcendentalist one, leads him to the amazing misjudgment that Robert Pen Warren "has become the major contemporary revisionist of the native strain in American poetry." Bloom's enthusiasm is prompted by Warren's recent "Sunset Walk in Thaw-Time in Vermont," a poem in which the sudden disappearance of a partridge-cock into the sunset prompts a shock of recognition in which the poet senses his mortality. The poem ends with a prayer that the poet's son will bless him, "For what blessing may a man hope for but / An immortality in / The loving vigilance of death?"

In judging such passages to be "powerful" and "moving," Bloom is committing his own ultimate apophrades. He longs so desperately to find "Tintern Abbey" in our time that he fails to discriminate between the Real Thing and the synthetic academic product. Kenner could no doubt show us that Warren may be *saying* something Wordsworthian or Emersonian here, but that his *making* is largely derivative.

To turn from *A Map of Misreading* to *A Homemade World* is, then, an enormous relief. Kenner has his faults too: if Bloom is often murkily obscure, Kenner can sometimes be unnecessarily flip, as when he writes, "And Bohemian doings were afoot in Manhattan, where an alert-faced young woman named Marianne Moore with her hair done up tight in a basketry of braids did not allow her proprieties to be breached at Village parties." The reference to Miss Moore's hairdo, alluding to Pound's "basketwork of braids" in "Hugh Selwyn Mauberly," is rather too cute a way of relating Moore to the Pound tradition.

But never mind. *A Homemade World* is both brilliant and fun to read—a rare combination. I am not sure the book has a unifying theme; the ostensible thesis that Stevens, Williams, Moore, Faulkner, Hemingway, and Fitzgerald "inhabited and created a common world—a homemade world scarcely at all indebted to European . . . models—and that they shared a common source of craftsmanship: a distinct doctrine of perception and language whose force and influence endure," is somewhat dubious because, as Kenner himself admits, the novelists were after one thing, the poets quite another. Kenner has very interesting things to say about the role of Nick as narrator in *Gatsby*, about Hemingway's commitment to Pater's doctrine of sensations, and Faulkner's technique of expansiveness, but the real center of *A Homemade World* is the discussion of Williams's invention (with Moore as precursor) of a wholly new kind of poem, an invention as indisputably American as the Wright Brothers' airplane or the Ford car.

Kenner's third chapter, "Something to Say," should be assigned reading for all graduate students in English. The title has a nice irony of its own. Kenner is, of course, arguing that the function of a poem is not to *say* but to *make*, yet the astonishing thing is that the chapter really does have "Something to Say"— something entirely new—about the too-much-discussed relationship of Stevens and Williams: The usual view is that these two poets belong to the Whitman tradition. As Adamic poets, both rejected the mythic mode of Eliot and Pound and forged a kind of antipoetic, a poetry of dissonance, decreation, and "things as they are." But for Kenner, Stevens and Williams are antithetical poets. Stevens's is a poetry of ideas; "the poetry . . . holds them, efficiently suspended, for discussion." His world is "empty of people" and contains no "human actions with agents good and bad. There is a great deal of language in these poems, with no one speaking it except the grave impersonal voice of poetry, and there is little variety of feeling." Indeed, the poetry often resorts to tricks of noble imagery," evasions, an elevated, artificial manner, all of which act to keep the real world at bay. Stevens is above all a painterly poet, the woman of "Sunday Morning" is a Matisse Odalisque, beautiful but static. Williams, by contrast, takes real words people use and real actions and events, and then positions those words so carefully that he creates a kind of "suspension system," an "audio-visual counterpoint." It would see, on the face of it, impossible to say anything new about "The

Red Wheelbarrow," Williams's famous little exhibition piece, but Kenner manages to say much that is new about it. He shows, for example, that everything in the poem "depends upon" its typography, that written out as a prose sentence, Williams's words become meaningless and absurd.

Kenner purposely overstates his case against Stevens in order to make his point, which is that, great poet though he is, Stevens looks back to the Romantics whereas Williams looks ahead to our world. Stevens's rhetoric, according to Kenner, is essentially conservative and so, despite its beauty and power, it could not have a major influence on poets of subsequent generations. Which is precisely why Bloom thinks Stevens is the greatest twentieth-century poet and dislikes Williams. It all depends on whether you are looking for the mode of the nineteenth century or that of the twentieth.

Obviously, Kenner, far from claiming objectivity or neutrality, wants to promote a particular school of poets. I personally think he overrates Moore and the Objectivists and underrates Stevens's late poetry with its bleak and bare trees, a poetry of brilliant syntactic positioning that has put the bombastic rhetoric of Crispin far behind it. But Kenner is quite right to insist that the Williams mode has, in fact, triumphed in our day, that the more recent typographical experiments of Creeley and Zukofsky are, like it or not, where poetry is going. This is not to say that Kenner likes experimentation for its own sake. He acutely dismisses e. e. cummings, still a favorite among young students, as "the supremely experimental, trifler with the sacred upper-case font," a poet who "finally altered no verbal environment except his own."

A good critic always sends us back to the text. This is what Kenner does so admirably in *A Homemade World*. He is willing to take contemporary poetry on its own terms, understanding that, despite the role convention plays, the poet does and must have some freedom of choice: "Styles are *elected*. . . . They need not be historical." Bloom would counter that styles can never be elected, that the poet engages in an endless struggle with a poetic father he could not and did not choose. This seems to me an overly deterministic view of literary history, forcing us to search in every new poem for echoes of the Primal Scene. I would prefer to replace the "Anxiety of Influence" with Kenner's more positive notion that "a language may be less a heritage than a code, and a code moreover that we are free to change."

CHAPTER 11

The Poet as Critic

One of the anomalies of Frank O'Hara's literary career is that he wrote so much but made so little effort to publish his work. Some of his best poems survive only because O'Hara enclosed them in letters to friends or because an enterprising editor like *Floating Bear*'s Diana di Prima would fish them out of his bureau drawers. Accordingly, when the *Collected Poems*, meticulously edited by Donald Allen for Alfred A. Knopf, appeared in 1971, even the poet's best friends were astonished by the volume's tremendous size: some 500 pages of closely packed print. Since then, many more poems, especially from O'Hara's early years, have come to light and will soon be published by Donald Allen under the title *Poems Retrieved*, a collection that runs to roughly 250 pages in typescript. Even if O'Hara himself might not have wanted to preserve all these poems—some are in-jokes, some casual addresses to friends meant as throwaways—his oeuvre is now beginning to be seen for what it really is: one of the central poetic achievements of our time.

O'Hara's critical prose, almost unknown outside New York art circles until quite recently, is an important adjunct to the poetry. Last year, George Braziller published a beautifully illustrated edition of O'Hara's selected art criticism called *Art Chronicles*. Now, in *Standing Still and Walking in New York*, Donald Allen gives us further essays on painting not included in *Art Chronicles*, as well as previously uncollected—and often unpublished—reviews, prefaces, autobiographical fragments, essays on poetry, music, and film comedy, and a long interview with Edward Lucie-Smith, conducted in 1965, a year before the

Review of *Standing Still and Walking in New York*, by Frank O'Hara, ed. Donald Allen. *Washington Post Book World*, January 25, 1976, 615.

poet's death. *Standing Still* by no means "completes the job . . . of rendering all of O'Hara's writing back into print" as Aram Saroyan has claimed. There is much still to come: aside from O'Hara's enormous correspondence, currently being edited by Donald Allen, the poet's still uncollected writings include a half-dozen plays, soon to be published by Full Court Press, his Harvard papers (journals, essays, a Commonplace Book, and many more poems), translations, short reviews for *Art News* and other periodicals, the interviews with David Smith and Barnett Newman, and the collaborations with painters like Larry Rivers and Norman Bluhm. Like *Art Chronicles*, *Standing Still* is, and was meant to be, a provisional volume; as such, it is both a valuable addition to the O'Hara canon and an important guidebook to postwar aesthetic.

The essays on art collected in *Standing Still* confirm one's sense that O'Hara was less a formal, systematic critic than a brilliantly intuitive judge of specific works by specific artists. When he tries to make theoretical generalizations, the results are not always happy. The 1954 essay "Nature and the New Painting," for example, begins with rather lame statements like "From the impressionists through the cubists to the present, art has always been involved with nature." Yet the same essay goes on to make precisely the right distinctions between "pure" abstraction and the mode of Grace Hartigan and Larry Rivers, both of whom found Abstract Expressionism ultimately too confining and invented ways of bringing the figurative element—stylized and fantastic shapes—back into painting. Indeed, O'Hara was one of the first critics to understand what Rivers was trying to do in his historical paintings. In his notes on *The Next to Last Confederate Soldier*, O'Hara remarks that the soldier "is not the subject of this painting, but the occasion of its appearance"; what seem to be "corny" and banal images of heroism are introduced only to be "lost in the linear acuity and tenderness and the cool, powerful masses of oncoming silence," creating the ironic distancing that makes Rivers's work so startlingly original.

The three *Art Chronicles*, written for *Kulchur* in 1962–1963 (only the first is included in the Braziller volume), testify to O'Hara's uncanny ability to discriminate between the first-rate and the second best, between de Kooning and Mark Tobey, between the run of Pop artists like Robert Indiana, and such great painters as Claes Oldenburg and Jasper Johns. Reviewing Oldenburg's 1963 show at the Green Gallery, O'Hara writes:

Where most of the other artists grouped by opinion into the "new realist" or "pop art" movement lend to make their art *out of* vulgar (in the sense of everyday) objects, images, and emblems, Oldenburg makes the very objects and symbols themselves, with the help of papier-mache, cloth, wood, glue, paint and whatever other mysterious materials are inside and on them, *into* art.

The same discrimination characterizes "David Smith: The Color of Steel," written for *Art News* in 1961. Unlike most abstract sculptures, O'Hara notes, Smith's figures have a peculiar sense of *presence*; placed on the lawn in front of the sculptor's house at Bolton's Landing, they resemble "people who are awaiting admittance to a formal reception"; they make us want, not "to *have* one," but "to *be* one." The viewer cannot, in short, be detached, for Smith's strategy is to invite "the eye to travel over the complicated surface exhaustively, rather than inviting it to settle on the whole first and then explore details." It is, in a fine distinction, "the esthetic of culmination rather than examination."

O'Hara's pieces on literature, dance, music, and film are much more casual, and often much slighter than his art criticism, which was, after all, a professional activity. (At the time of his death in 1966, he was a curator at the Museum of Modern Art.) The prefaces to books by Erje Ayden, A. B. Spellman, and Edwin Denby, for example, are gestures of friendship rather than serious critical assessments. Except for "Design Etc.," a lecture given at the Arts Club in 1952, with its surprisingly traditional distinctions between *design*, the "exterior aspect of art" (say, the diamond shape of a Herbert devotional poem), and *form*, "the poem's interior structure" (e.g., the Herbert poem as "traditional . . . metaphysical meditation"), O'Hara's literary criticism was almost occasional, prompted by attacks on poets he admired (as in the case of the Kenneth Koch pieces), or by his desire to spread the fame of unknown writers, as in his fine review of Ashbery's *Some Trees*, which O'Hara calls prophetically "the most beautiful first book to appear in America since *Harmonium*," and in his witty, learned review of John Rechy's *City of Night*.

The interview with Lucie-Smith not only contains much useful information about O'Hara's career at the Museum of Modern Art and his favorite poets (Pound, Williams, Auden); it also displays two of the qualities that distinguish O'Hara from many of his contemporaries: a wonderful sense of humor and a stubborn, even hard, common sense. When Lucie-Smith asks the poet about the "embattled vanguard" of the Andy Warhol underground, O'Hara replies characteristically:

Embattled? That's interesting. There is no underground and there is certainly no embattlement. Andy Warhol gets more publicity than any other single living American artist right this minute. . . . You cannot even open a fashion section of the *Herald Tribune* without seeing his name at least once a week. . . . And there's a whole Cinematheque on LaFayette Street to show those movies. . . . I don't mean . . . that it isn't a good thing; I think it's terrific. But it's not being underground; that's a lot of romantic nonsense.

Again, when Lucie-Smith talks rather solemnly of *happenings* as esoteric artworks, O'Hara notes drily that a happening is neither more or less than an improvised play, a genre we all know from our early childhood. As for the avant-garde, O'Hara refuses to theorize about its origins or its ontology, declaring that it is simply a reaction to boredom with other people's ideas: "If de Kooning says . . . what he is really interested in is Poussin, that's his way of not being bored with Kandinsky. . . . Now it may only work for two years, but that doesn't matter in the life of the artist as long as it energizes him to produce more works—that are beautiful."

O'Hara himself avoids boredom by being as attentive as possible to neglected art forms. One of the funniest essays in *Standing Still* is the previously unpublished "Apollinaire's Pornographic Novels." Many learned treatises have been written on pornography; O'Hara accordingly takes a matter-of-fact view:

Let's assume that pornography is . . . a work which is created solely to arouse the sexual passions. . . . It cannot have a serious literary intention. It must always be written for a small sum of desperately needed money. It must be indefensible to the postal authorities, even if it's a literary phenomenon (like *Fanny Hill*). It only rarely might be appealed to under the category of delight (as the Apollinaire novels could . . .), but delight is hardly a serious postal category. Far from being an element of literature where the writer finds himself intimately engaged with his primal forces, pornography is the most difficult, limited, boring, and laborious *genre* a writer could take on. And therefore it's an extremely interesting one. Personally, I wish the postal authorities would ban the detective novel, the autobiographical novel and the *roman à clef*, which, like the sonnet, are simple forms requiring only application, and let pornography run rampant.

The notion of banning the autobiographical novel (not to mention the roman à clef) is so wonderfully absurd that it forces us to reconsider our stereotypes of pornography. O'Hara now goes on to explain how Apollinaire makes use of literary convention:

The human body having only a certain fixed number of organs and orifices, this [writing pornography that isn't dull] is no small problem. . . .

Apollinaire nonchalantly commences each novel with a literary satire as the framework. *Memoirs of a Young Rakehell* starts as a spoof of the traditional French novel about "what happens to a boy who's just reached puberty during a summer in the family's countryplace" (and never has a boy had such a satisfactory summer, Colette or no Colette), and *The Debauched Hospodar* is a demented view of the Marquis de Sade's world told in the style of Jules Verne's *Michael Strogoff*. The one is an idyllic pastoral, the other a straightforward adventure story.

After this tantalizing preview, who could not want to read these novels? O'Hara wears his learning very lightly, but here and throughout the collection, one is impressed by the range of his reading, the justness of his comparisons, and the wit and discernment with which he approaches a work of art. *Standing Still* is not the sort of book one reads through once; it must be reread, dipped into, digested. One hates to call this modestly priced paperback a coffee-table book, because of the derogatory implications of that term, but *Standing Still*, with its delightful cover photograph of O'Hara and Rivers in the New York streets, is the kind of book one does want on one's coffee table, kitchen table—or any place where one can pick it up quickly and cite it to one's friends.

CHAPTER 12

The Poetry of Edward Dorn

—he will unroll the map of locations

Like his shape-shifting protagonist Gunslinger, that archetypal hero of the Wild West who also happens to be a Greek Sun God and a sophisticated New Philosopher expounding on Heidegger ("Hi! Digger"), the "pre-emption of the ultra-specific," and "Holy xit," Edward Dorn has been unrolling the map of locations for some twenty years now, and the publication of these two books, the first his collected lyric poetry, the second his extraordinary narrative poem *Slinger*, should finally earn Dorn the reputation he deserves as one of a handful of important poets writing in America today.

If Dorn has never been widely known (Richard Howard, for example, does not include him among the "41 leading contemporary poets" discussed in *Alone in America*), the reasons are not hard to find. Dorn began his career at Black Mountain College in the shadow of Charles Olson, his acknowledged master. Both poets were deeply influenced by the geographer Carl Sauer's essay, "The Morphology of Landscape" (1925), deriving from Sauer the conviction that "The thing to be known is the natural landscape. It becomes known through the totality of its forms"—a statement that Dorn uses as the epigraph for his long poem "Idaho Out." In an essay called "What I see in *The Maximum Poems*" (1960), Dorn praises Olson's attempt to give in language a *map* of one place (in this case, Gloucester, Massachusetts), and Dorn's fourth book (1965) is appropriately called *Geography*, a word he defined in a recent interview for *Contemporary Literature* as "the writing of earth, earth writing."

Yet despite such thematic links, Dorn is really quite unlike Olson; he is, for that matter, quite unlike any poet writing today. To call him a "regional poet" (he refers to himself as "a poet of the West"—not by nativity but by orientation),

Review of *Collected Poems* and *Slinger*, by Edward Dorn. *The New Republic*, April 24, 1976, 22–26.

misses the mark, for his central concerns are metaphysical and have, finally, nothing to do with his chosen region, the American West. Indeed, some of his best poems, written while he was teaching at the University of Essex, are "about" the topography of Oxford and the Cotswolds. Again, it is not with the San Francisco school or the Beats; unlike Gary Snyder, he seems to have no particular interest in Zen and the East, and despite his use of drug-world argot and political invective, his poetry is decidedly more tempered, more detached, more humorous than that of, say, Allen Ginsberg. Finally, and most important, Dorn, as he himself insists, is a narrative poet—an unusual condition today when the norm tends to be the fragmented lyric or open-ended sequence.

What, then, is Dorn's poetry like? "The Rick of Green Wood" (1956), which opens *The Collected Poems*, contains most of Dorn's typical stylistic traits. It begins:

> In the woodyard were green and dry
> woods fanning out, behind
>   a valley below
> a pleasure for the eye to go.
>
> Woodpile by the buzzsaw. I heard
> the woodsman down in the thicket. I don't
> want a rick of green wood, I told him
> I want cherry or alder or something
>   strong
> and thin, or thick if dry, but I don't
> want the green wood, my wife would die
>
> Her back is slender
> and the wood I get must not
> bend her too much through the day.
>
> Aye, the wood is some green
> and some dry, the cherry thin of bark
> cut in July.
>
> My name is Burlingame
> said the woodcutter.
> My name is Dorn, I said.
> I buzz on Friday if the weather cools
> said Burlingame, enough of names.

Compare this to Frost's famed "The Woodpile" and Dorn's originality becomes apparent. What begins in low key as a narrative about the purchases of some firewood is made new by Dorn's idiosyncratic syntax and lineation, his offbeat rhymes, his peculiar mixture of high and low styles, of realism and fantasy. It makes no sense, for example, for the poet to say, "I don't / want the green wood, my wife would die," especially since he is himself obviously drawn to it. But the non sequitur underscores Dorn's theme, which is the "pied beauty" and fragility of this special moment in November, before the cold sets in, before things "bend." And so Dorn's pastoral emphasizes uncertainty. The preposition "behind" in line 2 is oddly ambiguous: does it refer to the "woods fanning out" or to "the valley below"? This construction is followed by the phrase, "a pleasure for the eye to go," where we would expect the verb "to see"; and the laconic free verse pattern of the opening line is broken by the exact rhyme "below" / "go." Dorn has a habit of introducing rhymes where we least expect them; note the buried internal rhymes, "dry" / "die" / "July"; "slender" / "bend her"; "Burlingame" / "names." Especially interesting is the abrupt shift from shorthand sentences like "Woodpile by the buzzsaw," to the lyric archaism of "Aye, the wood is some green / and some dry," to the down-to-earth colloquial tone of the Burlingame passage, which modulates, in turn, into the high lyric mode of the poem's conclusion, with its slow stately rhythms and verbal repetitions:

> Out of the thicket my daughter was walking
>   singing—
> backtracking the horse hoof
> gone in earlier this morning, the woodcutter's horse
> pulling the alder, the fir, the
> hemlock
> above the valley
>   in the november
> air, in the world, that was getting colder
> as we stood there in the woodyard
> talking
> pleasantly, of the green wood and the dry.

The one Dorn "signature" absent from "The Rick of Green Wood" but very important in the poetry is his wonderful sense of humor, sometimes black as in "The Hide of my Mother," sometimes delicate irony as in "Time to Burn," a witty account of the morning-after-the-night-before, when the poet's girl is making up to the local swell in a small-town bar, and he must mark time in what seems

like "3 days to midnight." Dorn's sense of the comic absurdity of ordinary situations is nowhere more evident than in "The First Note (From London)," which
describes the reaction of the poet and his wife to the peculiar intimacy and sense
of enclosure of British trains:

> We got into one of those old
>   coaches
>   which has no access
> forward or back but is self contained
> and it was strained being so enclosed and
>   locked off
> by the speed of passage, alone
> and even though
> she was my wife we flirted
> almost, we were almost in our confusion
>   shy
> scarcely believing our situation so sealed
>   off.
>
> We considered of course making it then
>   and there
> while moving
>
>   but settled for a quiet kiss when
>   halfway through it
> abruptly and to our amazement
> we found ourselves in some small station
>   smiling
> into the equally smiling face
> of a railway man idling
> on that minor and unremembered
>   platform, nonetheless
> we were sober and chaste
> and slightly disappointed
> from thence to Croyden.

Here the effect of geography on human behavior is rendered with delicate
irony. The American husband and wife, unfamiliar with the custom of the country, and not quite knowing whether to take advantage of "a situation so sealed

off," ultimately become as "sober and chaste and slightly disappointed" as the landscape through which they travel. Smiling into the "equally smiling face" of the railway man, they blend into the topography.

Dorn is less successful when he tries to incorporate history into his poems. "The Land Below," for example, contains fine passages anatomizing the landscape of Taos, with its Fourth of July picnic in the Plaza, its tourist carrying travel kits bearing Christ's image and jostling with the native Indians. But when Dorn tries to relate this landscape to Schliemann's Troy, the Troy of Hector, the results are not happy, for Dorn lacks Pound's ability to revivify historical material, to make it part of the ongoing present. His is the lyric of geography, not of history. Accordingly, his overtly political poems are often simplistic and one-dimensional: "Whit Sunday," which begins with the lines, "England beware / the cliff of 1945 / turns a natural insularity / into a late, and out of joint / naturalism of inbred / industrial indecision," is invective rather than poetry.

Yet in the same years that Dorn was writing such angry political poems, he also composed some of the freshest, most natural love poems of our time—lyrics full of warmth, wit, and gentle self-deprecation. In "Song" (1967), he recalls a girl met only once in England and realizes wistfully that although he was no more than "An occupier / Of one of the waves of her intensity," his wrist still bears "The banding of her slightsmiling lassitude." "Slightsmiling lassitude" neatly sums up the comic futility of the poet's love. The twenty-four "Love Songs" of 1969, which must be read as a sequence, are full of such witty wordplay and nuance.

But charming as Dorn's short lyrics are, in terms of scope and accomplishment, they must take second place to *Slinger*, Dorn's four-part epic poem begun in 1968, which is, I believe, one of the masterpieces of contemporary poetry. In the little New Mexico town of Mesilla, the narrator ("I") meets "The Cautious Gunslinger / of impeccable personal smoothness / and slender leather encased hands / folded casually / to make his knock." "I" sets out on a quest, ostensibly for "Hughes / Howard" but actually for something nameless, with this mysterious sharpshooter, his talking horse, his sometime mistress, the whorehouse madam, Lil, and a traveling bard known only as "The Poet." Other characters appear and disappear, but plot and characterization are subordinated throughout to Dorn's theme, which is the opaqueness of language, the mystery of human identity, the impossibility of getting meaningful answers to one's questions. At one point, "I" asks Gunslinger: "What does the foregoing mean?" To which Slinger replies, "*Mean*? / Questioner, you got some strange / obsessions, you want to know / what something *means* after you've seen it, after you've been there / or were you *out* during / That time? No. / and you want some *reason*."

To *mean*, in Gunslinger's world, is "a mortal sin," and "I" is always getting into trouble because he is "constructed of questions," wanting to know who's who, what's happening, and why. Gunslinger won't have it: "The mortal can be described," he insists, "That's all mortality is / in fact." There are no laws governing the universe, no abstract principles: "never mind he said, are these / men men. . . . Is my horse a horse?" And indeed, how can one tell? For when, in a wonderfully absurd sequence, the horse gets stoned, he turns into Claude Lévi-Strauss and informs the perplexed narrator that he studies "the savage mind." "The Horse," says Slinger wryly, "is a double agent."

If Book 1 were just a clever attack on current hermeneutic theories, it would soon become tiresome, but Dorn's feat is that he incorporates his phenomenological esthetic into the frame of the familiar Western. The "STRUM" of the guitar punctuates all events and movements, and the characters perform ordinary human functions just when we least expect it. In Book 1, for example, Slinger announces loftily, "Time is more fundamental than space" and then "goes into the desert to pee." "*Yes*, he reflected / when he returned, that's less." The poem accommodates both the realistic low-class conversation of Lil ("*Shit, Slinger! you still got that / marvelous creature, and who is this / funny talker, you pick him up / in some sludgy seat of higher / learnin, Creeps! You always did / hang out with some curious refugees*" and the mock-heroic Houyhnhnm—like talk of Horse, who rebukes the narrator with the words, "Mortal, what do you mean . . .?" It also contains a number of parody Western ballads like the Poet's "Song about a Woman":

> On a plane of this plane
> stood a dark colonnade
> which cast its black shadows
> in the form of a conception made
> where I first saw your love
> her elbows at angles
>
> her elbows at black angles
>
> her mouth
> a disturbed tanager, and
> in her hand an empty dmajuana
> on her arm an emotion
> on her ankle a band
> a slender ampersand.

Homonyms, puns, nonsense words, coinages, archaisms, jingly rhymes,

ballad tunes, guitar notes, abstract nouns embedded in prepositional phrases—
Gunslinger is a collage of all these things. The epigraph for Book 3 is "The inside
real / and the outside-real"; and when Gunslinger regards "the stereoscopic
world," he is "astoned," while Lil rebukes him for his "hostile talk." The poem's
form perfectly embodies Dorn's theme that nothing is what it seems to be: "only
appearance. Perceive / not know." Indeed, one cannot *know* anyone else because,
as Dorn explains in the interview, today "the ego is pretty obviously dead." Names
like "Heidegger" are not used referentially; rather, they function as "widely understood and widely evocable intellectual signs" that "don't really mean anything."

In Book 2, the Poet announces that "I is dead." "I" must disappear because he
is too rational, too logical and human to participate in Gunslinger's bizarre quest
journey. But even this disappearance is not meant to be taken too seriously. Lil's
only response to the news is "That ain't grammatical, poet." And in Book 3 "I" is
allowed to return "from the cultural collective," purged of his questioning spirit.
He "comes through the door" of the Café Sahagun in downtown Cortez, Colo-
rado, "twirling his psychognosis / in his fingers / and throws it at effective intervals / into the air / like a texas cheerleader."

The quest, not surprisingly, leads nowhere. In an unnamed desert, the pil-
grims part company. Slinger (now Zlinger) addresses his friends in a marvelous
parody of English poets, beginning with Keats:

> Keen, fitful gusts are whispering here and there
> The mesas quiver above the withdrawing sunne
> Among the bushes half leafless and dry
> The smallest things now have their time
> The stars look very cold about the sky
> And I have grown to love your local star
> But now niños, it is time for me to go inside
> I must catch the timetrain
> The parabolas are in sympathy.

Lil ("Dear Lillian") goes back to Wyoming; the Poet announces that he is "Moving to Montana soon / going to be a nose spray tycoon"; and "I" is given a last
warning by Slinger:

> Goodbye I, keep your eye
> on the local species
> they're nothing
> but a warehouse full of peanuts

Slinger runs to more than two hundred pages (maddeningly unnumbered!), and there are inevitably some dull stretches, particularly in "The Cycle" (Book 3), which often seems too abstract, too clever in its parodies of Blake, and its allusions to modern physics and Parmenides. Dorn himself recognizes that the later books are more abstract than the first, which is filmlike in its intensity. But *Slinger* is surely one of the most ambitious and interesting long poems of our time, a truly original cowboy-and-Indian saga, rendered in the most ingenious mix of scientific jargon, Structuralist terminology, junkie slang, Elizabethan sonneteering, Western dialect, and tough talk about kicking "a gorilla in the balls." Indeed, the real hero of *Slinger* is neither Gunslinger nor the curious "I" but language itself, the language of our time, refracted, distorted, heightened, but always recognizable as the jumble of speech we hear around us and see in print. When, at the end of the poem, Slinger announces his departure:

> But it grieves me in some slight way
> because this has been such fine play
> and I'll miss this marvelous accidentalism

The reader can only agree. The "fine play" of *Slinger*—its "marvelous accidentalism"—is quite literally *horse play*, but horse play so learned and witty that it makes most of our long poetic sequences, with their obsessive confessional momentum, look like child's play. In Book 2, Gunslinger and his party come across an ingenious machine called a *Literate Projector*, which turns 35 mm film into script rather than vice-versa. Like this *Literate Projector*, Dorn's comic epic "will Invent a whole new literachure / which was Already There."

CHAPTER 13

Robert Lowell in Search of Himself

Three decades ago, the young Robert Lowell, on the threshold of his own poetic career, wrote a fascinating review of Dylan Thomas's *Selected Works*, in which he complained of Thomas's unfortunate tendency to introduce symbols unsupported by their context or "rewrite with . . . same symbols and language a poem that . . . had already written." "Few poets," Lowell remarks, "have wasted so many fine lines on unsuccessful poems . . . If Thomas kept his eye on his object and depended less on his rhetoric, his poems would be better organized and have more to say."

The same strictures can be applied to much of Lowell's own poetry; and it is the great merit of this selection, made by the poet himself, that he has been the severest self-critic, the most rigorous of editors, disregarding most of his own "unsuccessful poems" as well as the slacker portions of the longer sequences. This is especially true of the first half of *Selected Poems*, which covers Lowell's work through *Near the Ocean* (1967). The early elegy, "In Memory of Arthur Winslow (*Death From Cancer*)," for example, originally had four parts, containing much bombast, invective, and a rather shrill pseudo-Catholicism; witness the following unfortunate mixed metaphor:

> O Mother, I implore
> Your scorched, blue thunderbreasts of love to pour
> Buckets of blessings on my burning head . . .

In *Selected Poems*, Lowell includes only part 1 of the elegy, which is a sympathetic and touching portrait of an old man dying from cancer and uncertain

Review of *Selected Poems* (Farrar, Strauss), by Robert Lowell. *Washington Post Book World* 4, July 1975, H7–8.

about the afterlife. Again, the later "Fourth of July in Maine," a poem I myself have always regarded as an uneasy blend of elegy and satire, is now called "Night in Maine"; thirteen of the original nineteen stanzas have been removed, thus freeing the poem of its topical political allusions and somewhat facile sarcasm, and turning it into an intimate elegy for the poet's cousin Harriet Winslow as well as for his own youth and love: "we turn / our backs, and feel the whiskey burn."

The Mills of the Kavanaughs (1951) and *Near the Ocean* (1967) have generally been considered problematic transitional volumes, and Lowell discerningly cuts down both to manageable proportions. Thus, *Selected Poems* includes only the last five verse paragraphs (roughly one-tenth) of the title poem of *Mills*, the poet evidently sensing that the long dramatic monologue, which attempts to fuse topical realism with liturgical and classical symbols, was not his metier. Similarly, he condenses the longer poems of *Near the Ocean* and omits all the translations, including the long "Vanity of Human Wishes." Happily, the marvelous title poem, which uses the myths of Perseus and Medusa and of the *Oresteia* to dramatize the troubled relationship between the poet and his wife, is kept intact.

I think it was especially wise of Lowell not to include his translations in *Selected Poems*. *Imitations* (1961) has its staunch defenders who argue that, however erratic Lowell's translations may be as translations, the book has a careful formal design, expressing the poet's own vision rather than those of the poets he translates. This may or may not be the case, but a selection from *Imitations* would merely have emphasized the opposite: the frequent laxity and the impropriety of idiom and phrasing, as when Baudelaire's lines, "Je pense a mon grand cygne, avec ses gestes fous, / Comme les exiles, ridicule et sublime, / Et rongé d'un désir sans trêve!" become "I think of the great swan hurled from the blue, / heroic silly—like a refugee / dogged by its griping angst. . ."

So much for omissions. The selection from Lowell's first major volume, *Lord Weary's Castle* (1946) is rigorous (fifteen out of forty-two poems) but almost invariably right; the great poems in this book—"Colloquy in Black Rock," "The Quaker Graveyard in Nantucket," "At the Indian Killer's Grave," "Mr. Edwards and the Spider," "Between the Porch and the Altar"—are all here. I wish there had been room for that astonishing war poem "Christmas Eve Under Hooker's Statue" ("Tonight a blackout. Twenty years ago / I hung my stocking on the tree"), and for "Buttercups" and "Rebellion," which prefigure Lowell's later personal mode. But these are minor quibbles. *Life Studies* (1959), the sequence that inaugurated the so-called confessional movement, is to my mind Lowell's greatest book, his unique contribution to modern poetry: Lowell evidently thinks so too, for he includes the entire volume, omitting only the prose memoir

"91 Revere Street" and "The Banker's Daughter," an ironic portrait of Marie de Medici, which has no real place in this autobiographical sequence of lyrics. Again, the sampling from *For the Union Dead* (1964), essentially a sequel to *Life Studies*, is generous: twenty-three of the original thirty-five poems are reprinted, including such masterpieces as "The Old Flame," "Night Sweat," and the title poem.

The result of this selection process is that the reader is dazzled, all over again, by the sheer force, energy, and intensity of Lowell's poetry. From the opening poem of *Lord Weary's Castle*, with its graphic images of decay:

> There mounts in squalls a sort of rusty mire,
> Not ice, not snow; to leaguer the Hôtel
> De Ville, where braced pig-iron dragons grip
> The blizzard to their rigor mortis
> ("The Exile's Return")

to the frightening conclusion of "For the Union Dead":

> The Aquarium is gone. Everywhere,
> giant finned cars nose forward like fish;
> a savage servility
> slides by on grease.

Lowell presents us with a phalanx of sharply etched particulars. His is the "unforgivable landscape" of postwar New England, whose center is Beacon Hill, and whose circumference includes the Quaker Graveyard in Nantucket and the Windsor Marsh of Jonathan Edwards to the North; the claustrophobic skyscrapers of New York's West Side to the south. This alien and glacial world ("In Boston serpents whistle at the cold") is redeemed, if only on occasion, by the possibilities of friendship and love, the pleasures of art, and especially the poet's ability to laugh at his own foibles, as in such poems as "To Delmore Schwartz," "Waking in the Blue," or "Eye and Tooth."

Such autobiographical poems as "Grandparents" and "Skunk Hour" have influenced a whole generation of poets. In *The Poetic Art of Robert Lowell*, I have argued that a poem like "Waking in the Blue" gave rise to an essentially new genre that we may call "the mental hospital poem"; in a similar vein, the famous "Man and Wife," with its arresting opening ("Tamed by *Miltown*, we lie on Mother's bed") can now be seen as the progenitor of the currently popular genre of "failed marriage poems." It is especially good, then to have all these poems reprinted in one volume. But the second half of the *Selected Poems* is devoted to Lowell's most recent work—*History, For Lizzie and Harriet* and *The Dolphin*—all published in 1973. And here I wish Lowell had chosen to include fewer poems, and often in different sequence.

Lowell's latest volumes are, as is well known, reworkings of *Notebook 1967– 68*, which appeared in 1969, and the second enlarged *Notebook* of 1970. All the poems in *For Lizzie and Harriet* originally appeared in *Notebook*, as did all but 80 of the 368 sonnets in *History*. *The Dolphin*, on the other hand, is an entirely new sonnet sequence. Although only 29 of the 108 *Dolphin* sonnets are included in *Selected Poems*, even this number seems excessive, for I regard *The Dolphin* as the low point of Lowell's career, a brief excursus into the world of straight-forward confessionalism and soap opera, a sequence that may well be "true to life" (too true!), but which is largely devoid of the thematic density and tonal complexity of the earlier autobiographical poems.

The sequences from *History* and *For Lizzie and Harriet* are much more success-ful, but Lowell's reshufflings of individual poems are puzzling. In organizing his new sequences, the poet has provided a much more coherent plot (with begin-ning, middle, and end), but in so doing, he loses the advantages of the diary mode that informed the first *Notebook*. "My plot," Lowell said in the afterword to that volume, "rolls with the seasons." "The time is a summer, an autumn, a winter, a spring, another summer." The seasonal cycle is a very effective device because as one reads through *Notebook*, one comes to participate in the poet's private life, his shifts in mood, his nagging concerns and self-doubts. But when the individual sonnets are regrouped, as they now are, in chronological or thematic units, the sense of spontaneity and intimacy characteristic of *Notebook* is largely lost.

The first *Notebook*, for example, contained a series of fourteen sonnets called *Long Summer*, recording, in oblique fashion, the poet's gradual coming to aware-ness, during one hot summer in Maine, that something is seriously wrong with his marriage, indeed with his whole mode of living. Anxiety is the keynote. The opening poem, which begins, "At dawn, the crisp goodbye of friends; at night, / enemies reunited, who tread, unmoving, / like circus poodles dancing on a ball," turns up in *Selected Poems* in the section called "From *For Lizzie and Harriet*," although, oddly enough, it does not appear in that volume at all. But the third poem of *Long Summer* ("Months of it, and the inarticulate mist so thick / we turned invisible to one another / across the room") found its way into *History* as no. 6 of a new sequence called *1930s* and is now reprinted in the *Selected Poems*. "Nineteen Thirties" becomes a self-contained unit, in which the central empha-sis is placed on nostalgia for the Maine of the poet's boyhood. As such, the son-net takes on an equivocal meaning, and the original focus is blurred.

In *History*, Lowell rearranged a series of *Notebook* sonnets so as to create an orderly progression from prehistoric times to the present. In the group included in *Selected Poems*, we move from Alexander to Eugene McCarthy, meeting, along the way, such figures as Cato, Cicero, Attila, Mohammed, Roland, Louis IX, Saint-Just, Napoleon, Margaret Fuller, Lincoln, and finally, Stalin, Martin Luther King, and Robert Kennedy. For those fond of neat chronology, such development may look impressive, but I would argue that order is now superimposed at the expense of immediacy. The desire to supply range, moreover, tempts Lowell to include such already dated poems as "For Robert Kennedy 1925–68," which contains the following passage:

> Doom was woven into your nerves, your shirt,
> woven into the great clan; they too were loyal
> and you too were loyal to them, to death.
> For them like a prince, you daily left your tower
> to walk through dirt in your best cloth.

After Watergate, after the gradual debunking of the Kennedys that we have witnessed in recent years, these lines seem oddly beside the point.

But these are minor cavils about an important book. *Selected Poems* provides the best possible entry into the imaginative universe of Robert Lowell. Reduced in bulk, *History*, *For Lizzie and Harriet*, and even *The Dolphin* seem more interesting than in their longer versions. As for the earlier volumes, Lowell's autobiographical-historical poems now look better than ever, especially when we compare his craftsmanship and tact, his sense of history and geography, and his command of convention and genre to the drearily simplistic revelations turned out en masse by neoconfessional poets writing today. Those who have not followed Lowell's career volume by volume now have a chance to come to terms with one of our major poets.

CHAPTER 14
Talking at the Boundaries

> i had always had mixed feelings
> about being considered a poet   "if robert Lowell is a
> poet i dont want to be a poet   if robert frost was a
> poet i dont want to be a poet   if socrates was a poet
> ill consider it"

For the past few years, David Antin, who has been, at various times, an engineer, a linguist, and a poet, and who is currently professor of Visual Arts at the University of California, San Diego, has been performing spontaneous "talk poems," improvisations made for particular occasions in particular places and then recorded on tape and transcribed on the typewriter. At first, Antin thought of these improvisations as "lectures" or "talks," but one time, when he and his wife, the painter Eleonor Antin, were driving back from Pomona College in LA to their home in Solana Beach, they decided to listen to the tape of the Pomona talk, and Eleanor said, "My God, it's a poem." Her husband agreed: "because i see all poetry as some kind of talking . . . and because ive never liked the idea of going into a closet to address myself over a typewriter." "I see my talking pieces," says Antin, "as philosophical inquiries to which I try to bring the resources of language, not only my own language, but natural language in its natural setting." He is careful to insist that such a "talk poem" is not prose, for prose is "an image of the authority of 'right thinking' conveyed primarily through 'right printing'— justified margins, conventional punctuation, and regularized spelling." Indeed, when *boundary 2: Journal of Postmodern Literature* was preparing the galleys of Antin's first "talking piece," "what am i doing here?" he insisted that the entire "poem" be reset because the typesetter had inadvertently set it up as prose with

Review of *Talking at the Boundaries*, by David Antin. *The New Republic*, March 5, 1977, 33–35.

the "straight jacket" of left and right margins, thus obscuring the central fact that "these texts are the notations or scores of oral poems."

Is this all pretentious nonsense? Anyone interested in the "boundaries" of contemporary "poetry" should begin by reading the heated exchange between William Spanos and Robert Kroetsch, the editors of *boundary 2*, as to whether "what am i doing here?" deserved publication (see Spring 1973 issue). Kroetsch takes the conservative position: he argues that Antin's talk-poem assumes that "to write at all is somehow to create art"; that a talk-poem "becomes poem as pure content . . . an avoidance of the problem of form," and that it is "naive in its avoidance of selection." Spanos, on the other hand, admires the poem's "structural rhythm—an interspersion of 'story' and speculation," its "rhythm of an intelligent and sensitive speaking voice, which probably accounts for the sense of exploration it generates." He argues that Antin's text "*reverberates* with echoes of the past (the oral poetry of Homer, Plato's Dialogues, the whole Parry and Lord *Singer of Tales* context) and is at the same time utterly *situated* in the present: McLuhan, the French "*parole*" rather than "*ecriture.*"

The Antin talk-poem is not, perhaps, a useful model for other poets; in the hands of a lesser master, it might easily become, in Kroetsch's words, "pure content," "naive in its avoidance of selection." But then, as David Bromige puts it, "Who talks like David Antin?" And this brings us to the positive dimension of *talking at the boundaries*. Antin is surely one of the wisest, wittiest, most perceptive, and human "talkers" we have, and whatever the value of the genre in the abstract, *his* talk poems do have what Spanos calls "structural rhythm." In the first place, the reader must not be fooled by Antin's naive stance, his seemingly flat empiricism, his air of being no more than a casual "talker." Antin is never merely a camera. Each of these eight pieces is organized around a central theme or image: it may be the nature of memory and identity ("what am i doing here?") or the question of mimesis ("remembering / recording / representing") or the meaning of marriage ("a private occasion in a public place"). Each talk-poem seems to move forward by purely random means when, in fact, the words continually loop back to a limited set of variables providing at the beginning of each "talk." Antin's most notable influence is Gertrude Stein, the Stein of "Composition as Explanation" and *The Making of Americans*. Take the second poem, "is this the right place?" delivered at the Moore College of Art in Philadelphia in lieu of an anticipated "lecture" on Marcel Duchamp. It begins:

> when i was asked what i wanted to talk about   before i came here
>   i picked up the telephone   in san diego and   bill miller
> from the philadelphia art museum   spoke to me on the phone

> said "what are you going to talk about?"   and   i had
> about   five seconds   to decide   and in the five seconds
>   i realized   that theres something peculiar about talking on a
> telephone   when youre three thousand five hundred miles away
>   which is approximately the distance   long winded crows
>   take when they go directly from san diego   to philadelphia
>   and i remembered philadelphia very vaguely   as i kept trying
> to think of   philadelphia   im an old new yorker as youll prob-
>   ably recognize from my accent   which is fairly marked   and
>   i thought of philadelphia "what does philadelphia have?"

This "overture" immediately introduces the notion of *space* (or sense of place) and sets the stage for the witty exploration that follows. The telephone can seemingly bridge space, yet Philadelphia and California retain their separate identities. The word "philadelphia" appears six times in these thirteen lines (five times in the last five lines), each time in a slightly altered context, as if the speaker were trying to come to terms with the reality behind the name.

Once Antin has set up his key words and phrases—*telephone, five seconds, philadelphia, ninety-mile drive, California*—the rest follows with great comic gusto. The central question: "is this the right place?" initially produces a hilarious account of cross-country plane travel (on the top of page 28 the word "plane" and its cognates occur in almost every line). For Antin, the West–East plane trip with its inevitable loss of three hours of daylight becomes a journey "into the past," "into some time thats anterior to your own time," and he describes with deadpan literalism how one tries to occupy oneself on such a journey so as to avoid the frightening sense of being swallowed up by time. After the bloody mary (consumed somehow much too early in the day) and the earphones and the tasteless food and the radio news, the movie begins:

>   and then they put on a movie   and you don't really
> want to hear the movie   because there is a movie about a rodeo
>   clown   you know this   because you see his face and its all white
> and somebody is beating him up and   you dont know why and
> you dont really care   but you watch it and   people come by
>   and someone is computing his expense account next to you
>   and you say to yourself "what place is this?"   "is this a right
> place?"   and   "where am i going in this right place?"   somehow
> im over kansas   and you look down and you say "this must be
> kansas because thats how long ive been travelling"   but you cant

see kansas   what you see are rifts in clouds and you wonder
"what place is that under there?"

Here the effect of verbal and phrasal repetition is to disorient both speaker
and audience. What is a "right place" and what does it prepare you for? "ive
always had this fear," Antin notes, "that experience prepares you for what will
never happen again." And he introduces a new key word—"worth." What is college worth? What is "this place" worth? Antin now has us in the palm of his
hand and so he stops to tell a story. The "interspersion of 'story' and speculation"
is, as William Spanos notes, one of the central features of Antin's talk-poems; in
bringing narrative back into poetry he does enlarge the horizons of the closed
lyric, bringing it closer to the oral tradition. In his laconic account of why and
how he left the New York art world for the California art world, Antin provides
a marvelous image of the fortuitousness, irrationality, and pleasurable confusion
of contemporary American life. He recalls that he took the San Diego job by
"accident," but once he set out for the West, he seemed to be living in a comic
surrealistic nightmare. In a Phoenix motel, he accidentally heard the news that
Andy Warhol had been shot back East; later, his sick child needed a doctor, but
the "medical centers" of Southern California seem to have no doctors, at least
not during lunch hour: "medical centers" in Southern California are beautifully
designed and covered with ice plant. There are no doctors but too many dentists,
and we hear anecdotes about one or two of these citizens. Trying to make his
way in the New West, Antin developed the nagging conviction that "this culture
develops feeling   in one or in ones life   that this is not   the   right place   no
matter where you are   it isnt the right place   because its not the right time."

And so it goes. Antin is not bitter about these problems; his stance is amused,
bemused, detached, skeptical. Life, after all, is like that. Thoughts circle back
to his own "college" days, City College having been the "place" Antin attended
after a stint in a bubble-gum factory. Was this the right place? After majoring "in
about eighteen different things," the poet felt wholly unprepared for "life." But
the system would not allow such deviation:

                              and i walked in with my program for a physio-
logical psychological major or whatever it was and they said to me
"you have graduated?"   and i said "I have graduated?   how
could i have graduated?   i didnt take hygiene 71" they said
"you have graduated   graduated"   and i said "graduated?"
          they said "yes   we will take   we will accept zoology 32
          as hygiene 71"   i said "but it isnt   i dont know all about

those sex practices you describe in hygiene 71   ill never know
and ill be sent out into the world   whereas all ill know about will
   be the various nervous systems of the vertebrates"   and they
   said "no   no   no   youve graduated"   i said "i havent
had math 61"   and they said "math 61 is elementary mathematics
         youve had the theory of complex functions   out!"   and
there i was   not that i couldnt support myself   id been sup-
   porting myself since i was sixteen   but i wasnt prepared for being
   issued forth from this   preparational device   this institutional
preparation device   i really wasnt ready for it   i didnt know
what i was going to do what was i going to do with my life?

In this passage, one should note the brilliant variations on the word "graduated," and the subtle progression from "i didnt," "i havent" "i dont know" to "i
couldnt" "i wasnt prepared," "i really wasnt ready." By the time we come to the
end of this section, we know, of course, that Antin was "prepared," that he was
"doing it all along," that indeed, "i could do anything i wanted." Well, then, is
this the right place? In the poem's conclusion, a kind of anticrescendo, Antin
declares: "ive never had the sense of being adequately prepared for it   its always
arrived too early   it should have arrived later." But "accident" is the secret of art
as well as of life:

         how do you know when youre through with some-
thing?   you know because the phone rang   as somebody once
pointed out   and then you cant ever get back to it again and its
as ready as it will ever be   because theres no reason to go on
         the telephone rang   why not?   now i might say   of
this particular disclosure   that theres no place at which i can end
 it   without producing a kind of profoundly pornographic poetic
 effect   which i assure you i can do   i could produce a vast
symphonic conclusion   and you might walk out feeling benefited
         but i wont do it

Not that this disclaimer is a sleight of hand. Antin has "done it," although in a
wholly nontraditional way. The strictest Formalist would have to admire the
orderly structure of "is this the right place?," which begins with a ringing telephone and ends with "the telephone rang," which starts with one of the central
human questions and demonstrates that "it" ("any place") is and is not the right

place, depending on our angle of vision, our mood, the time of day, and a hundred other contingencies.

Despite his protestations to the contrary, then, Antin does rely upon a principle of selection. "Poetry," as he puts it in one of the later pieces, is not just "talk" but "improved talk." Whether "poetry" is the best term for the sort of "improved talk" Antin gives us is another question. His improvisational technique resembles what Lévi-Strauss has called *bricolage*; "is this the right place?" sounds as if Gertrude Stein had collaborated with Mark Twain, injecting his humor, his dialect, and especially his version of the tall tale into her austere and immaculate verbal compositions. But whatever we choose to call Antin's texts, their ingenious network of repetition, their interweaving of narrative and rumination, their presentational immediacy and speculative complexity make *talking at the boundaries* one of the most challenging "art works" of the mid-1970s.

CHAPTER 15

Houseboat Days

The popular success of John Ashbery's *Self-Portrait in a Convex Mirror* in 1975 (it won a Pulitzer Prize, a National Book Award, and a National Book Critics Circle Award and has sold some 20,000 copies) had less to do with that book's special qualities—qualities that had been present in Ashbery's work all along—than with shifting tastes.

Ashbery's poems have always had a sense of doubleness: an extraordinary transparency coupled with an equally extraordinary mysteriousness. From the opening page of *Some Trees* (1956), with its "laughing cadets" announcing, "Everything has a schedule, if you can find out what it is," to the sinister dream sequences of *The Tennis Court Oath* (1962) and the "lacustrine cities" of *Rivers and Mountains* (1966), Ashbery was continuously struggling to invent a language freed from what he once called "the mania of over-interpretation," the disease of "objective correlativitis." His verbal strategies, so different not only from those of the established poets of the fifties and sixties but also from the "personism," to use Frank O'Hara's phrase, of his fellow "New York Poets," have been largely misunderstood until quite recently. Ashbery has long held that "you can't say it that way any more," and a public that would flock to a major Duchamp retrospective was ready to give assent to his conviction.

Houseboat Days, already into its second hardcover printing, marks a decisive advance over the earlier books, even over *Self-Portrait*, for Ashbery now interlaces his familiar "prosaic inflections" with the most racy and resonant particulars. It is like throwing a pebble in a pool and making countless ripples. The

Review of *Houseboat Days*, by John Ashbery. *Washington Post*, October 30, 1977.

best entry into the enchanting world of *Houseboat Days* is provided by Ashbery himself in an essay he wrote some twenty years ago on Gertrude Stein:

> *Stanzas in Meditation* gives one the feeling of time passing, of things happening, of a "plot," though it would be difficult to say precisely what is going on. Sometimes the story has the logic of a dream . . . at other times it becomes startlingly clear for a moment, as though a change in wind had suddenly enabled us to hear a conversation that was taking place some distance away. . . . But it is usually not events which interest Miss Stein, rather it is their "way of happening," and the story of *Stanzas in Meditation* is a general, all-purpose model which each reader can adapt to fit his own set of particulars: The poem is a hymn to possibility.

Houseboat Days is full of such "hymns to possibility." Typically, Ashbery's new poems begin as narratives:

> They all came, some wore sentiments
> Emblazoned on T-shirts.
> ("The Other Tradition")

> At the sign "Fred Muffin's Antiques" they
> turned off the
> road into a narrow lane lined with shabby houses.
> ("On the Towpath")

> A little girl with scarlet enameled fingernails
> Asks me what time it is.
> ("Melodic Trains")

But no sooner is such a bit of "plot" given than the mirror clouds over and it becomes impossible to say, "What is going on?" In "Street Musicians," the "One" who "died" oddly reappears, nine lines later, snatching "Glimpses of what the other was up to," and we learn that "So they grew to hate and forget each other." The narrative presented between these two points in the poem has "the logic of a dream": the "other" street musician, having lost his soul, walks the streets "through increasingly suburban airs and ways."

Next, we hear of "The plush leaves the chattels in barrels / Of an obscure family being evicted / Into the way it was, and is." What obscure family? What is "the way it was, and is"? And is "leaves" a noun in apposition to "chattels" or a verb whose subject is "plush"? One cannot, indeed one should not answer these questions. For Ashbery purposely shifts ground, moving from one kind of diction or one pronoun to another, so as to present us with a haunting and hallucinatory image of absence, of separation and loss.

In the second stanza, the narrative dissolves completely as the poet appears in his own person: "So I cradle this average violin that knows / Only forgotten showtunes, but argues / The possibility of free declamation anchored / To a dull refrain." The season, as in the first stanza, is autumn: "November, with the spaces among the days / More literal"; the violin suggests that the poet is himself one of the street musicians of the title, but which one? And now the poem rounds to its extraordinary conclusion:

> Our question of a place of origin hangs
> Like smoke: how we picnicked in pine forests,
> In coves with the water always seeping up, and left
> Our trash, sperm and excrement everywhere, smeared
> On the landscape, to make of us what we could.

"Street Musicians" recalls Wallace Stevens's "Peter Quince at the Clavier"; both poems are music-inspired meditations on lost love, on the meaning of endings. But in Ashbery's convex mirror, Stevens's coherent meditative moment gives way to fracture. The poem's images are vivid and concrete, but they are peculiarly emptied of "content." Thus its plot becomes an "all-purpose model which each reader can adapt to fit his own set of particulars." Think of the possible "stories" contained in these two stanzas, stories of love, desertion, eviction, betrayal. Or again, there may be no story at all; the poet may be talking to himself, rejecting a former identity that no longer suits him.

The journey motif found in "Daffy Duck in Hollywood," with its "comings and goings" on an "emerald traffic-island," turns up in poem after poem. To make a pilgrimage, whether "*en bateau*" or in "boxcars" or on "Melodic Trains," is to be, paradoxically, at home. Hence the "Houseboat Days" of the title poem are happy days, and this is Ashbery's most erotic, his happiest book. Nature, no longer Emersonian, has been domesticated, and artifice wins the day.

Everywhere we meet stylized paradigms of Renaissance England ("Fantasia on 'The Nut-Brown Maid'"), Second Empire Paris ("On the Tow Path"), fin-de-siecle London. Thus "Valentine" begins with a parody Elizabethan sonnet in which the lover appears as his own best enemy:

Like a serpent among roses, like an asp
Among withered thornapples, I coil to
And at you. The name of the castle is you,
El Rey. It is an all-night truck-stop
Offering the best coffee and hamburgers
in Utah.

The prose sections that follow play ingenious variations on this foolish metaphor. First, the seven-story castle turns into a drab house in Hampstead, "the brick one in the middle of the block," as seen in an Arthur Rackham fairy-tale book. In the "bearded twilight," this Victorian picture takes on Surrealist coloring:

The wallpaper is a conventionalized pattern, the sliced okra and star-anise one, held together with crudely gummed links of different colored paper, among which purple predominates, stamped over a flocked background of grisaille shepherdesses and dogs urinating against fire hydrants.

So much for valentines that portray lovers as "aristocratic bisque figures, a boy in delicate cerise and a girl in cornflower blue." The dramatic monologue that follows is, by contrast, a love song à la Nabokov, but the Disneyesque Bloomsbury of "Irina," whose "beloved articles" are accused of being "a bit too / Advanced by present-day standards," has no more staying power than the Rackham fairy tale. Abruptly, the monologue breaks off and a new voice, serious and intense, speaks:

These things I write for you and you only.
Do not judge them too harshly.

If the "castle" of the beloved turns out to be a "house of cards . . . built on / Shifting sands," the poet himself is discovered to be "the inhabitable one":

But my back is a door to you, now open, now shut,
And your kisses are as dreams, or an elixir
Of radium, or flowers of some kind.
Remember about what I told you.

This quiet conclusion seems utterly right, a momentary breakthrough into a world where love is possible. Ashbery has prepared us for it through a dazzling series of crosscuts and dissolves; his strategy is, in Charles Olson's words, to "keep it moving"; he never allows the poem to yield up a paraphraseable statement or to come to a point of rest before the end. Image after image, aphorism after aphorism is introduced, inspected, knocked down, recycled. Nothing is what it seems to be. And yet everything IS. In *Houseboat Days*, Ashbery has gone further than ever before in creating what he called, with reference to the French Surrealist Reverdy, a poetry of "transparency" in which images have no "symbolic signification," a poetry of *presence*.

> You turn
> To speak to someone beside the dock and the lighthouse
> Shines like garnets.

This is the most exciting, the most original book of poems to have appeared in America in the 1970s.

CHAPTER 16

Charles Olson in Connecticut

I n the early 1960s, when Olson was teaching his now legendary poetry courses at Buffalo, Charles Boer was one of his most ardent student disciples. Later, when Boer became a member of the English department at the University of Connecticut, he frequently invited Olson, who had returned to his native Gloucester, down for a visit, but "it was like inviting the Pope. I never really expected [him] to come." In December 1969, however, Olson not only came; like the Man Who Came To Dinner, he stayed for more than three months, first at Boer's house (until the latter nearly broke down from the strain of hosting his gargantuan guest) and then at a nearby hotel. For a time, he taught at the university, where he typically enchanted a select group of students and alienated most of his colleagues. But in December Olson contracted a fatal cancer of the liver, and he died in January of 1970.

Charles Olson in Connecticut is Boer's intimate record (written in the second person as a tribute to Charles) of these last months. Although he frequently refers to Olson's past and provides vivid anecdotes about the poet's youth in Gloucester or his later misadventures in the Washington bureaucracy of the 1940s, he modestly disavows any intention of writing a "definitive biography." His is a highly personal portrait and, as such, one's response to it is naturally colored by one's own view of Olson. For Boer himself never questions Olson's status as Great Poet; both literally (he measured six feet eight inches and weighed 255 pounds) and figuratively a "Gulliver in Lilliput." Thus, although the memoir makes no bones about Olson's megalomania and egocentricity, his erratic behavior, his rudeness and crudeness, Boer implies that such faults are to be viewed as the

Review of *Charles Olson in Connecticut*, by Charles Boer. *Yearbook of English Studies* 8 (1978): 295–98.

charming eccentricities of a genius. Poets, it seems, are exempt from the laws that govern the lives of ordinary people.

The reader who shares this view of artists in general, and Olson in particular, will undoubtedly find this memoir witty and warm, humane and touching. But if one happens, as I do, to take a less positive view of Olson's achievement, one finds oneself all too frequently exasperated by Olson's behavior as well as by Charles Boer's tolerance of it.

For one thing, nothing in this book convinces us that Charles Olson (especially in his final phase) had a great mind. He may have had much random knowledge of Anatolian artifacts and Mayan hieroglyphs, but it is not clear to what use he actually put these materials. As a philosopher, he was given to pseudo-profundities: myth, for example, was to be divided into "three proper areas: *initiatic cosmos, the world of nature,* and *the celestial world.*" Of Whitehead, his favorite philosopher, he could write: "The spiritual is all in Whitehead's simplest of all statements: Measurement is most possible throughout the system. That is what I mean. That is what I feel all inside. That is what I love." And although he dismissed most of his fellow poets as ignorant bores, toward the end, he himself was writing poems like the following:

> the Blow is Creation
> and the Twist the Nasturtium
> is any one of Ourselves
> And the place of it all?
>   Mother Earth alone
>
> I prefer an earlier America. I didn't
> know what I wd. (p. 70)

This is not exactly Making it New.

But what about Olson's fabled powers as a conversationalist? "There was not a sane man," Boer reports, "who could match Olson as a talker. Your conversation was overwhelming":

> It would be a two-way exchange, fast and easy, for the first few hours. Then, as my energy started to droop, you would actually pick up the pace, getting more and more intense as you saw me flagging. After several hours of listening to you talk in an increasingly booming voice about everything from poetry to cigars, I was exhausted. . . . Sometimes you would talk for nine or ten hours straight. At first it was marvelous. I felt privileged to have the

Olson genius all to myself at my table. But as the hours went on, and the days too, I couldn't keep it up.

The author consistently takes this apologetic line. When a week's supply of dirty dishes had piled up in the sink, he "formally" asked Olson's "permission" to wash up, making sure he played Stravinsky and Dylan records the Great Man would enjoy so that he would not be bored while his host worked. When the phone rang for "Cholly," Olson would hang up on the caller. When friends came to visit, Olson told them, "Boer's busy and won't be able to see you for a few weeks." At a dinner party given by Charles Brover, another former Buffalo student now teaching at Connecticut, Olson excitedly slammed his fist on the glass-top coffee table, smashing it to bits. What was his reaction to his accident? "You quickly said you were sorry, offered to pay for it, then went right on talking." On the way home, "you kept grumbling . . . about Brover's politics" and criticizing his guests. At the same time, though, Brover told me that you called him afterward, to thank him for the dinner, and also to tell him, 'There's just the three of us, Brover, just the three of us: you, me, and John Wieners.'"

Delightfully eccentric? Or callous and hypocritical? When William Moynihan, the chairman of the English department, arranged, against all odds, to get Olson a teaching appointment in the middle of the term, the poet remained unimpressed, implying that such favors were, after all, no more than he deserved. On his first day of class, arriving with his wicker baskets filled with Keebler cookies and books stuffed with toilet-paper book markers, he greeted his audience "with a long blast of the foulest language [he] could muster," hoping to scare away the more timid students, especially the women. "This," Mr. Boer fondly recalls, "was a tactic you had used effectively at Buffalo."

I find nothing endearing or charming about this anecdote. Even more irritating is the account of Charles Boer's near breakdown as a result of Olson's endless talk-and-drink marathons, and the impossibility of convincing Olson to move out. "I told you," Boer recalls, "that if you didn't go, I was going to go. You said that was *fine*, that I *should* go." Later, when Olson finally moved to the Altaveigh Hotel, Boer continued to play the role of adoring slave. One evening, ill with a high fever, he actually tried to cancel a dinner engagement with Olson. In a fury, the poet summoned him to the hotel. Sweating and shivering, Boer arrived at the appointed hour.

One can argue, of course, that as an aspiring poet, Boer could put up with a great deal of bullying from his mentor in return for the privilege of daily contact with genius. Certainly he gained as much as he lost from the intense relationship. But what about Olson's attitude toward ordinary people? Mr. Boer suggests that working people, waitresses, janitors, shoemakers, adored Olson and catered to his every whim. Yet he could be brutal. One anecdote should suffice. When admitted to the hospital, Olson had to share a room with a bourgeois type who was suffering from an inflamed testicle. This man, whose family generally sat in silence by the bedside, was overwhelmed by the "boisterous giant" in the neighboring bed, not to mention his boisterous visitors, and complained to the nurses that his roommate was crazy. Incensed, Olson told him one night: "'Listen, McCormack, if you don't shut up and stop telling the nurse that I'm crazy, I'm going to get up out of this bed and come over and squeeze you know what!'" After a few such threats, McCormack became so terrified that "he started screaming for help and they had to take him out and give him another room." Olson and Boer were jubilant: "You finally had a room to yourself!"

I suppose that Olson's admirers will regard this as an exemplary tale, illustrating the triumph of artistic genius over Babbitry. And his genius, Mr. Boer believes, was never more in evidence that during the grueling ride to New York Hospital where the dying poet spent his last painful days. En route, Olson recited the "Poor naked wretches" speech from *Lear*. Mr. Boer comments, "I could only marvel, Charles, at the greatness of your heart that you should come up with that speech from that play on this coldest of winter days in an ambulance now drifting into the gloom of New York where you must certainly have realized your life would soon end."

Great poet or great poseur? Whatever we make of it, there is no doubt that Olson himself was convinced of his greatness. When Boer, who was covering his classes, asked him what the topic of discussion should be, Olson replied, "Tell them about me . . . Tell them who I am" (p. 117). When asked what kind of funeral ceremony he wanted, he said, "Just have all my friends stand around and talk about me." And even his carcinoma of the liver could be assimilated into the Great Olson Myth: "I'm Prometheus," he announced one day, "because Prometheus got it in the liver!"

Boer's record of what Olson said and did is consistently lively and compelling; he is particularly good at defining the tensions and contradictions in Olson's amazing personality. But ultimately, he loves the great Charles too much to be able to evaluate his accomplishment or to place it in a larger context. A later generation, however, will judge it, and I think the verdict will be less than happy. One would think that the Pound case had taught us, once and for all, that the Nietzschean view of the Poet as Superman, above and beyond all law, is a very dangerous one. Bullying nurses and fellow patients who happen to be ordinary middle-class citizens is, to my mind, neither brave nor endearing; it is merely offensive. Again, I find Olson's disparagement of the

Academy and his contempt for his colleagues irritating because it is precisely the Academy that launched his career in the first place, and it has continued to be the Academy (whether Black Mountain, Buffalo, or Berkeley) that has credited him with the title of "Major Poet."

Charles Olson in Connecticut reminds us what a good thing it is that in our society poets and philosophers do *not* become kings. Having spent so much time imaginatively dwelling in the world of the Second Millennium BC, Olson seemed finally to have forgotten what *civilization* is.

CHAPTER 17

The Greening of Charles Olson

This is, everyone has remarked, a vintage year for Charles Olson studies; aside from the three books under review, there is George Butterick's monumental *Guide to the Maximus Poems* (University of California Press, 1978). Four scholarly books, then, on a poet some believe to be, as does Sherman Paul, the central poet of his time, the rightful heir of Emerson and Whitman, while others, like Harold Bloom, have given Wallace Stevens, a poet as antithetical as possible to Olson, the very same title. Still others, most notably the post-Structuralists, whose eye is turned not to Emerson but to the continent, barely seem to know of Olson's existence. We thus have a peculiar anomaly. A byword in the pages of *boundary 2, a Journal of Postmodern Literature*, Olson's name does not so much as appear in the index to Matei Calinescu's recent *Avant-Garde, Decadence, and Kitsch* (Indiana University Press, 1978), a book that is also about postmodernism. Whose postmodernism is the real thing? Is there a real thing? Olson's poetry and poetics raise some of the most interesting theoretical issues confronting us today and it is these issues, rather than the specific interpretations of Olson texts found in the three books under review, that I wish to discuss here.

Paul Christensen's stated premise is that "the essential Olson lies somewhere in a momentous rejection of a culture, a civilization, the values and philosophy of which have gradually diminished the unruly vitality of human awareness. Everything Olson wrote—the essays, the poems, the rambling harangues—speak to this one concern: how to restore to human beings their own primal energies." The same prophetic thrust is admired by Sherman Paul:

Review of *Charles Olson: Call Him Ishmael*, by Paul Christensen; *Charles Olson: The Scholar's Art*, by Robert von Hallberg; and *Olson's Push: Origin, Black Mountain and Recent American Poetry*, by Sherman Paul. *Criticism* 21, no. 3 (Summer 1979): 251–60.

There was a hiatus between the wars and the advances of innovators, especially Pound and Williams, were not carried forward until Olson and the writers of his generation recovered that ground and began to build on it. The recovery and redirection of the poetic tradition—and it reaches back beyond Pound and Williams to Emerson and Whitman—is one measure of the importance of Olson's work. It is part of a new sally of the human spirit.

Projective verse, as Olson conceived of it, is, for Paul, as for Christensen, "a poetics of present experience, of enactment. It replaces spectatorism with participation, and brings the whole self—the single intelligence: body, mind, soul—to the activity of creation."

Robert von Hallberg, whose book is the most challenging of the three, is more cautious about the Great Tradition: "The premise of this book is that Olson deserves close attention precisely because his poems do not conform to what modern critics have argued is essentially poetic." Olson's is an expository poetry, designed less to delight than to teach; it is "offered as explanation and understanding, not as expression." Accordingly, there is no point in submitting this poetry to formal verbal analysis, to look for "delicate shades of irony," metrical niceties, or constitutive image patterns. Like Hesiod, whose *Works and Days* and *Theogeny* stand squarely behind Olson's work, he regards his role as essentially didactic.

Both von Hallberg and Christensen trace Olson's origins as a poet back to his withdrawal from government service at the end of World War II, a withdrawal prompted by his disillusionment with "postwar American imperialism" and "hypocrisy," and his consequent search for a new frontier, first in the American past (See *Call Me Ishmael*, admirably elucidated by Christensen), and then in such historical and cultural outposts as those of the Maya and the pre-Socratics (cf. Pound), is assimilated into the epic of Maximus—postmodern man in search of the new polis in his native Gloucester, Massachusetts. The assimilation of philosophical systems is a major concern of all three studies, and it should be said at once that, despite all their talk of "field composition" and "projective poetics," Christensen and Paul are at least as concerned with content as is von Hallberg. Indeed, all three studies are essentially explicative: they analyze what Olson says, both in his poems and in his difficult prose, and trace the sources of his "philosophy."

To see what such exegesis can and cannot do, let me summarize the three readings of "The Kingfishers," a poem Guy Davenport has called "the most energetically influential text of the last thirty-five years," a text that "divides decisively Modern from Postmodern poetry."[1]

Sherman Paul devotes the better part of his first chapter to "The Kingfish-ers," which he calls "as important to Olson's work as 'The Second Coming' is to Yeats's." In this "Poundian poem," collage is the structural principle, and so "we should no more be surprised to find a transposition from the article on kingfishers in the *Encyclopedia Britannica* (eleventh edition) than to find Mao's words" ("The light of the dawn is before us").[2] But, unlike Pound, Olson stresses movement:

> "What does not change / is the will to change" becomes "When the atten-tions change / the jungle // leaps in"—slight alteration, the break after "jun-gle," owing to Olson's wish to enact the leap.)[3]

Whereas Pound looked to Classical civilization for the sources of renewal, Olson turns to Amerindian and Eastern culture deploying images like the "E on the stone" and the Aztec burial mound so as to show that only by going outside our own civilization can there be hope for renewal. Further, Olson contrasts the evil change embodied in Cortez's conquest of Mexico (or of warfare in general) to change-in-process: Ammonius' speech in Plutarch's "The E at Delphi" that "Into the same river no man steps twice." Ultimately, the poet turns from Pound ("I am no Greek: hath not th'advantage") to Rimbaud:

> Si j'ai du goût, ce n'est guère
> Que pour la terre et les pierres[4]

Paul glosses these lines by a passage from Olson's *The Special View of His-tory*: "It is this which Heraclitus meant when he laid down the law which was vitiated by Socrates and only restored by Rimbaud: that man is estranged from that [with] which he is most familiar. One must learn to be at home in the phys-ical world." And so "The Kingfishers" concludes with the poet hunting among stones, "in order to receive . . . some valuable lessons of renewal."

Paul Christensen's reading of "The Kingfishers" pursues similar themes. After describing the poem's structure as that of "*montage* or *collage*," Christensen observes:

> Each of the three main sections of the poem builds on the accumulation
> of detail which the previous section introduced. . . . The E ("on the stone")
> refers to a cultural order that has disappeared in the historical process:
> reduced, possibly, to a mere character, but expressive of a civilization, a polis
> that had at one time achieved a high level of integrity and etched its mark

upon the center of its defined world, on a navel stone. Mao's words depict
a world fallen into corruption, the state of cultural disintegration from
which he must now rise, looking into the rising sun as a complex symbol of
renewal and illumination.

And the kingfisher itself becomes "the central metaphor of change itself; for its
constancy is composed of the rhythms of renewal and decay." In section 3, the
speaker discovers his kinship to the conquered Aztecs and rejects the Greco-
Roman heritage in favor of the Indian; he rejects "the status quo, which he has
already described as a 'pudor pejorocracy'" in favor of his will to "hunt among
stones." The poem, concludes Christensen, "communicates concretely . . . the
anxiety of the speaker to find a culture in which change is understood, not
fought or ignored to some tragic or brutal end."

Von Hallberg comments chiefly on the function of Mao in the poem and then
argues that "Olson's freedom from history allows him to shift idioms abruptly,
without warning, without explanation:

I am no Greek, hath not th'advantage."

Von Hallberg notes: "The poetic advantages of this posthistorical language are
clear, especially in American poetry: the poet who can go outside his tradition,
without apologies, to get what he wants." But he adds with slight asperity, "The
cost is no less high, however. This hodgepodge of diction can cohere only with
the force of a strong but still individual voice." Presumably the voice of "The
Kingfishers," if not of certain other Olson poems, meets this test. The important
thing, in any case, is the poem's lesson, which is that "change itself is the goal."
Mao, for that matter, functions less as specific Communist revolutionary than as
the incarnation of "the will to change."

There is, one concludes, general agreement as to what "The Kingfishers"
means; on this level, Sherman Paul's careful analysis is especially persuasive. But
Paul and Christensen, and to a lesser extent von Hallberg, regularly jump from
such semantic analysis to conclusions that seem to have less to do with the texts
under discussion than with Olson's repeated insistence, in his essays and interviews, that he was doing something *new*. Indeed, here, as in almost all critical
discussions of Olson by his adherents, an old-fashioned intentionalism clouds
the real issues. Let me elaborate.

(1) It is regularly assumed that "The Kingfishers" marks what Robert Duncan has called "the opening of the field," the move away from "the formalist
(New Critical) closed conception of the poem and with it a cosmology and

epistemology of the kind that underlay symbolism" (Paul, p. xvi). "'The King-fishers,'" says Paul, "is an open form permitting the poet, as Allen Ginsberg says, to score the development of his ideas"; it is "above all . . . an action." Olson's essays make clear, Paul argues, that "true poetry . . . is not symbolist, and he invokes the dance not in the service of the transcendent but of the immanent, as a practical discipline of body consciousness—of proprioception. . . . he speaks always as a participant and not as an observer."

Von Hallberg has a subchapter called "Anti-Symbolism," in which he quotes such famous Olson statements as "It doesn't take much thought over Bill [Williams'] proposition—'Not ideas but in things'—to be sure that any of us intend an image as a 'thing,' never, so far as we know, such a non-animal as symbol."[5] Allegiance to Williams's dictate means "absolute opposition to Eliot, whom Olson recognized to be in the Symbolist tradition" (H, p. 45). For "the Symbolists aspire to an order of reality beyond the mundane experiences of actual people, beyond what Mallarmé calls 'ici-bas.' The function of this nonmimetic art is to express the yearning to transcend. Olson, though, had no desire to write off the mundane and the actual." In the same vein, Christensen sees Olson's poetry as essentially "logopoetic" rather than "Imagistic" and talks of his rejection of Eliot and the Imagist Pound. "'The Kingfishers,'" he writes, "is a model of the projectivist poetic executed successfully," a work that shows "not the image but the forming of the image in the mind of the observer." Like Paul and von Hallberg, Christensen relates this and other poems to the famous manifesto "Projective Verse," with its call for "FIELD COMPOSITION," poetry as "energy discharge," the credo that "ONE PERCEPTION MUST IMMEDIATELY AND DIRECTLY LEAD TO A FURTHER PERCEPTION. . . . get on with it, keep moving . . . USE USE USE the process at all points."[6]

But the readings of "The Kingfishers" I cited above give us little sense of the poem as open field, as process or energy discharge. If the opening line, set off by itself, is, as Paul says, "a text for meditation containing the poem that activity of thought unfolds," one could argue that, Olson's poetics to the contrary, "The Kingfishers" is the perfect example of a closed poem. Olson knows from the beginning precisely where he is going; he marshals his properties—symbolic birds, the "E on the stone," "what Mao said," the Aztec burial mound, the plunder of Cortez, Fernand talking "lispingly of Albers and Angkor Vat"—and orchestrates them so as to create a very definite dialectic. Thus, as Christensen notes, "The loot taken by Cortez in his conquest of Mexico is listed carefully as a preface to the last"; or again, "the feed-back is / the law" (1, 4) leads to the search for a usable past in part 2. Olson, according to von Hallberg, "had no desire to write off the mundane and the actual," but do we in fact find more "mundane" or "actual" images here than in, say, *The Waste Land*? Or, for that matter, in what sense is "The Kingfishers" more of an energy discharge than Eliot's great collage poem with its sudden cuts from "I read much of the night, and go south in the winter" to "What are the roots that clutch, what branches grow / out of this stony rubbish?" or from the "broken fingernails" of the girl "On Margate sands" to the fragment "To Carthage then I came" in "The Fire Sermon"?

Indeed, Olson's poetic father may well have been Eliot rather than those "predecessors" he chose for himself—Pound and Williams. Here Harold Bloom's "anxiety of influence" should be taken into account. Olson, like so many poets of his time, railed long and loud against Eliot. But Sherman Paul himself points out that the kingfisher image echoes *Burn Norton*:

> After the kingfisher's wing
> Has answered light to light, and is silent, the light is still
> At the still point of the turning world.

He rightly observes that Olson inverts Eliot's meaning: his "secular" kingfisher becomes the symbol of change, not of the still point. But the point is surely that in the "postmodern" as in the "Modern" poem, the kingfishers are never primarily "the mundane and the actual"; they are, on the contrary, consistently designated as emblematic. And even Fernand, the lisping Frenchman who talks of "Albers and Angkor Vat," is quite unlike Pound's characters—"Fordie," "Uncle William," "poor old Homer blind as a bat"—characters who are recalled precisely for their individuality. The poet "thought of Fernand" because he must have, at the outset of his poem, a representative of the effete, decadent Europe, a culture that fails to comprehend the significance of the Maya.

Compare "The Kingfishers" to a genuinely postmodern poem like Ashbery's "Pyrography" or to a text like Beckett's "Ping" and the difference becomes clear. Even the allusion to Rimbaud in part 3 betrays Olson's real bent. Rimbaud's "Fêtes de la faim" is not, as Paul, following Olson, seems to think, about anything so simple as the need to return to the earth, to live "the physical life." For Rimbaud, such descent into the earth is always related to thirst: the liquefaction of rock renews the poet's creative force ("la future vigeur"). But Olson's Rimbaud is a symbol of Natural Man as opposed to Cultured Man (the Pound who wants to judge our civilization in terms of Classical models). And Natural Man, in this systematic poem, learn to hunt among stones.

(2) Olson, the inventor of "anti-Symbolist" fields of action: this is one aspect of the myth. A closely related one has to do with Olson the Objectist. The central text here is again "Projective Verse," in which "Objectism" (despite Olson's

protest to the contrary, the term is roughly equivalent to "objectivism" as Zukofsky and his circle understood it) is defined as the "getting rid of the lyrical interference of the individual as ego, of the 'subject' and his soul, that peculiar pre-
sumption by which western man has interposed himself between what he is
a creature of nature . . . and those creations of nature which we may with no
derogation, call objects. For a man is himself an object." And in a related essay,
"Equal, That Is, to the Real Itself," Olson aligns himself with Keats as a poet of
Negative Capability (*Human Universe*, 116).

Taking his lead from Olson, Sherman Paul distinguishes between the Jungian
Self and Ego, as they appear in *The Maximus Poems*: "The self in its own space-
time is the essential formal element of the poems, and its story, the sequence
of its occasions, is the essential narrative. Not the 'EGO AS BEAK.'" But here is
Paul's comment on the passage in "I, Maximus of Gloucester, to You" that culminates in the lines:

> o kill kill kill kill kill
> those
> who advertise you
> out)

> Lear's cry of outrage . . . is the extreme expression of revulsion and identifies
> both an object of hate and a moral direction. . . . They [movies, magazines,
> radio, advertising] are plagues to Maximus . . . because like muzak, they dis-
> tract us, keep us from hearing what we have just head . . . and in his poem
> they name a late stage of capitalism—the consumer he opposes to the early
> productive capitalist of the fishery—and an action . . . which relates our
> estrangement from the familiar world to the misuse of language.

No doubt this is an accurate account of what Olson wants to convey to his reader
in this, his first Maximus poem. But where is the "objectism" he has advocated?
The "interference" of the ego may not be "lyrical"—it is true that Olson is not a
confessional poet—but for pure unadulterated "egotistical sublime," it is hard to
beat this and a hundred similar passages in *Maximus*.

Christensen and von Hallberg are more cautious: they admit that Olson's
poetry does not always embody the Objectist poetic, which both relate quite
rightly to Whitehead, especially to the doctrine that "the things experienced and
the cognisant subject enter into the common world on equal terms." "All actual
things," wrote Whitehead in *Process and Reality*, "are subjects, each prehending
the universe from which it arises." Olson scribbled in the margin of his copy:

"the End of the Subject-object thing—wow!" (see von Hallberg, 113). But despite that "wow!" it is not clear to me how subject and object enter into the common world on equal terms in, for example, "The Librarian," which von Hallberg cites as an instance of successful "objectism." It is true that in the course of this, one of Olson's finest poems, Gloucester may be said to enter the poet's mind:

> Where is
> Bristow? when does I-A
> get me home? I am caught
> in Gloucester. (SW, 219)

But the process of internalization does not seem essentially different from, say, the movement in Stevens's "The Snow Man" or in Lawrence's "Bat." Again, when Christensen says of *Maximus* that "the desire is to make Gloucester become continuous with himself so that there are no longer barriers of subject and object between them," he is simply accepting Olson's word for it and hence contradicting his own accounts of what that "subject" repeatedly *says about* the "objects" in its field. A page after the previous statement, for example, Christensen writes: "And Maximus regards the people of Gloucester as having been corrupted by the commoditization of all aspects of life":

> love is not easy
> but how shall you know,
> New England, now
> that pejorocracy is here.

Reading such lines, we do know, I think, that the "subject," Olson the Preacher, and the object, the New England "pejorocracy" as seen in the particulars of modern Gloucester, are not one.

(3) Although Paul and Christensen make greater claims for Olson as a poet than does von Hallberg, they agree with him that Olson was perhaps most remarkable as a teacher. Christensen's long chapter on Olson's influence on the Black Mountain poets—an influence stubbornly claimed by Creeley, Duncan, Dorn, Blackburn, and others, even though it is much less evident in their actual poems than in their interviews and statements of poetic—makes the case for the "enormous impact" Olson's doctrines had on younger poets. "For him," says Sherman Paul, "the true relation between people was pedagogic—and it was chiefly in the generous way of his teaching that he gave pleasure and consolation."

What, then, does Olson teach us? Paul sees him as the apostle of Emerson's "Party of Hope," the Party of Nature versus Culture, teaching us that we can fill space with our own projections and rediscover wholeness by our contact with the Great Mother. In mapping the geography and history of Gloucester, "he showed use how to find place . . . because it has a history. . . . We repossess place in repossessing the experience of it. Polis is eyes."

In short, "an ecological vision" as Paul calls it (p. xviii). Christensen puts it a bit differently: "Olson's canon has within it a potent utterance: life is strangled by systems. Existence has an order that cannot be isolated from nature" (p. 212). The poet must be "the measure of awareness . . . that lone human figure thrust deep into the uncertainty of the real, where he lives and expresses himself joyfully and is ultimately joined by others."

No one is likely to quarrel with these generalizations. But in the course of interpreting specific poems, all three critics make us swallow any number of statements that strike a nonmember of the Olson Club as misguided when not downright silly. Here are some random examples:

Olson admired Mao for insisting that the revolution be not just political or economic but above all cultural. In 1952 Olson believed that New England was to be the center of a cultural revolution. (von Hallberg)

What Olson decries is the movement away from labor, the development of capitalism. Parasitic absentee ownership is the source of corruption in Letter 3. (von Hallberg)

At the moment [1951], however, one conclusion was already evident to [Olson]: Mayan art, which had sprung from sources beyond Greco-Roman influence, exposed a more intense human attention to human experience than did Western art. (Christensen)

To sustain, nourish, increase, advance, make daily life a dignity—this is polis . . . The modern hero (post-Dante) lacks the first will to coherence. [In contrast to the Sumerian model described in "Human Universe"] His is a "contrary will" to dispersion, to destruction. . . . his heroism is not defined in terms of cultural achievement but in terms of the spoliation of nature. (Paul)

450 B.C., the only date in the essay ["Human Universe"] . . . locates the advent of the Greek system, the crucial moment when logos displaced "live speech," and discourse itself became an arbitrary, closed universe. (Paul)

Here [Letter 13] indeed is a "dreamless present" of "merchandise men" in which it is impossible to move, in which the truth and promise of the New World has been betrayed by lies, and the Goddess, embalmed, is merely Jean Harlow (the sex symbol of Olson's youth), "As she lies, all / white." (Paul)

Lest I be accused of taking these statements out of context, let me assure the reader that all are paraphrases or explanations of Olson's arguments rather than independent value judgments on the part of the respective critic. But what seems so remarkable is that the commentators consistently refer to these doctrinal statements as if they were (1) original and exciting and (2) true. This is not the place to test Olson's "special view of history" or mythology, but suffice it to say that any intellectual who is not directly involved with the study of Modern American literature would probably find these notions simplistic and banal, if not just plain wrong. How can one take seriously a didactic poet who teaches us that after 450 BC "discourse itself became an arbitrary, closed universe," that the Sumerians or Maya should be our models for behavior, that the Puritans were just competitive capitalists? In discussing Pound, critics generally admit that the treatment of usury as the source of all evil is misguided, but how much more complex or valuable are Olson's economic and historical theories?

Von Hallberg does admit that the later Maximus poems fall apart, that "Olson seems to have resigned himself to teaching by example rather than precept." He concludes:

American literary culture appears to have no way of handling a poet like Olson, committed to a pedagogical and rhetorical poetics, short of labeling him a shaman, and Olson perhaps had no experience at rejecting what was, after all, flattery. If this was the case, it is not hard to see why his later poetry was egocentric, though it is depressing to witness how, almost routinely, contemporary culture can corrupt so ambitious and so American a poet.

It *is* depressing but the problem is larger than von Hallberg suggests. To understand the Olson cult, we must consider the increasing isolation of the poet in postwar America. Anthropologists, archaeologists, historians, political scientists—these are the intellectuals who might shed light on Olson's "causal mythology." But of course they don't read Olson or, for that matter, any contemporary poetry. The literary people who do—mostly in the academy despite the claim of Olsonites to be anti-academic—are unfortunately susceptible to the large doses of antirationalist, primitivist doctrine in the air. It was the Literary Establishment, after all, that hailed Charles Reich as a seminal thinker.

With the demise of the New Criticism, value judgments and literary norms have become increasingly suspect; no one dares to say that a poem *should* have certain qualities or meet certain standards. At the same time, post-Structuralist critics are busy applying increasingly sophisticated analytic tools to what are, in fact, certified texts—Rousseau's *Confessions*, Poe's *Purloined Letter*, Freud's *Interpretation of Dreams*—so that, again, problems of value don't arise. The result, for practical criticism, is defensive exposition. In this sense, the new Olson books are typical: if you already admire Olson, these books will give you reasons to admire him still more and will provide some sturdy support for your enthusiasm. If you don't, they are not likely to change your mind. The notable achievement of von Hallberg's book is that at least it raises the right questions, asking us to consider in what, if any, sense Olson has claims to being a major poet.

In the years to come, we will be rethinking these issues, sorting out the valuable Olson from the "plotions of obfuscatory verbiage," found all too frequently in the later Maximus poems.[7] In the meantime, we have three scholarly and valuable guidebooks that tell us what Olson's difficult poetry is all about and place it in its historical context. As a general introduction, Paul Christensen's *Charles Olson* is especially good; as a commentary on *The Maximus Poems*, Sherman Paul's *Olson's Push* is an indispensable supplement. But both books convince me that Olson was, in fact, less the father of postmodernism than he was the last of the great system builders. Who nowadays tries to write a poetry encompassing ancient history, myth, geography, religion, philosophy, the new mathematics and physics, American politics? Our poetry has become more modest; it tries to define life as it is lived (or invented, or dreamed) rather than the abstract "human universe." Like Eliot's Hieronimo at the close of *The Waste Land*, Olson might have said: "These fragments I have shored against my ruins." But in the "postmodern" universe of 1980, we are perhaps less fearful of fragments. And from this vantage point, a poem like "In Cold Hell, In Thicket" (1951) is beginning to look positively traditional.

Notes

1.   "Scholia and Conjectures for Olson's 'The Kingfishers,'" *Boundary 2*, 2 (1973–1974), 251; "In Gloom on Watch-House Point," *Parnassus: Poetry in Review* 4 (1976), 253.

2.   For the text of "The Kingfishers," see Charles Olson, *The Distances* (New York: Grove Press, 1960), 5–11.

3.   Since Olson frequently uses the slant line (/) within a line, I follow Sherman Paul's practice of marking line breaks by a double slant line (//).

4.   The source is Rimbaud's "Fêtes de la faim"; Wallace Fowlie translates the lines: "If I

have any taste, it is for hardly / Anything but earth and stones." See Wallace Fowlie (trans.), Rimbaud, *Complete Works, Selected Letters* (Chicago: Phoenix Books, 1967), 146–47.

5.   See "On Poets and Poetry," *Human Universe and Other Essays*, ed. Donald Allen (New York: Grove Press, 1967), 65. Subsequently cited as HU. Note that Olson misquotes Williams's famous "Not ideas but in things!"

6.   See "Projective Verse," *Selected Writings of Charles Olson*, ed. Robert Creeley (New York: New Directions, 1966), 16–17. This text is subsequently cited as SW.

7.   The phrase is Hugh Kenner's; see *A Homemade World* (New York: Alfred A. Knopf, 1975), 182.

CHAPTER 18

Poetic Artifice

The author of this book died in 1975 at the age of twenty-seven. At the time of her death, she had already published two volumes of poems and a number of important essays on avant-garde poetry; she had also completed the ambitious study under review here. To call Veronica Forrest-Thomson a gifted young critic would be an understatement; her ability to discern value and its absence in the work of her contemporaries is, as I shall argue, often quite startling. Nevertheless, *Poetic Artifice* is not quite a satisfactory book; it suffers from an unnecessarily rigid theoretical frame, a frame, one suspects, that Forrest-Thomson adopts, consciously or unconsciously, as a defense of the Neo-Dada enigma poetry she and such kindred spirits as John Ashbery and J. H. Prynne were writing in the late sixties. Let us begin with the theory. Here is Forrest-Thomson's opening paragraph:

> This book is an attempt to talk about the most distinctive yet elusive features of poetry: all the rhythmic, phonetic, verbal, and logical devices which make poetry different from prose and which we may group together under the heading of poetic artifice. If prose often resembles the "natural" language of ordinary speech, poetry is resolutely artificial, even when it tries to imitate the diction and cadences of ordinary speech. The poem is always different from the utterances it includes or imitates; if it were not different there would be no point in setting down these utterances or writing these sentences as a poem. Not only does poetry use techniques which would be strange or out of place in prose; it depends on a host of conventions which we apply only in reading and writing poems.

Review of *Poetic Artifice: A Theory of Twentieth Century Poetry*, by Veronica Forrest-Thomson. *Contemporary Literature* 21 (Spring 1980): 291–96.

Here Forrest-Thomson writes as if there had never been a controversy about "literary" versus "ordinary" language, as if no one had ever questioned what Stanley Fish has termed "deviation theories" of style. More important, even the Formalist, who would agree with the author's distinction between poetic and ordinary language, would question the rigid bifurcation between poetry and prose: is it really true that "poetry depends on a host of conventions which we apply only in reading and writing poems"? Given the current state of the arts, the dissolution of boundaries between, say, a "prose narrative" by Guy Davenport and a "prose poem" by W. S. Merwin, Forrest-Thomson's insistence that poetry is always "unique" and "different" seems questionable.

Still, we should grant Forrest-Thomson her strict Formalist-Structuralist donnée because it enables her to come to terms with what continues to be the central weakness of practical criticism vis-à-vis poetry: its focus on "a thematic synthesis stated in terms of the external world" (p. xi), or, as the Russian Formalists put it, its orientation toward the message. Forrest-Thomson argues, convincingly, I think, that British poetry of the fifties and sixties has itself suffered from this critical stance, for "Whatever technical innovation [the poets] display is swiftly taken up and smothered by a critical reading anxious to convert all verbal organization into extended meaning—to transform pattern into theme." The result of such thematically oriented criticism is that poets like Anne Sexton and Ted Hughes have been foolishly overpraised "for opening up new depths of psychological insights," while the real innovators have been largely ignored or misunderstood.

So far, so good. Forrest-Thomson takes as her motto Wittgenstein's famous precept: "Do not forget that a poem, even though it is composed in the language of information is not used in the language-game of giving information." But in making a case for the precedence of poetic structure over poetic content, Forrest-Thomson invents a fussy and cumbersome terminology that often confuses the issues. Her key terms are: Naturalization—the "attempt to reduce the strangeness of poetic language and poetic organisation by making it intelligible, by translating it into a statement about the non-verbal external world, by making the Artifice appear natural." There are two kinds of Naturalization: external (later defined as "bad") and internal (or "good"). External Naturalization, in turn, involves two complementary processes: (1) External Expansion—the naturalization of details "by expanding them into the external world, as a comment upon it"; and (2) External Limitation—"the limitation imposed by external expansion on the formal features which we can take account of in our interpretation." Correspondingly, Internal Naturalization involves (1) Internal Expansion—expansion that takes place "within the limits imposed by the poem's style, as we try to take account of any formal features we can identify"; and (2) Internal Limitation—"the limitation of the external contexts that are brought on according to the needs of external expansion." There is also something called Suspended Naturalization; it occurs when "we know that we cannot create a thematic synthesis in terms of the external world but we can still observe the interaction and mutual reinforcement of the various types of pattern in the poem." The poetry of J. H. Prynne is a case in point.

Whatever the naturalization process in which we are engaged, Forrest-Thomson posits, "We are bringing together levels of poetic organisation and moving toward some new kind of organisation." In so doing, we are guided by the Image Complex, "a level of coherence which helps us to assimilate features of various kinds, to distinguish the relevant from the irrelevant, and to control the importation of external contexts." What Forrest-Thomson means by the term "image complex" is never made clearer than this; one gathers that "image complex" is something like Reuben Brower's "key design," or Roman Jakobson's "dominant," the focusing component of the poem that guarantees the integrity of structure. But it is an unfortunate term for it implies that "structure" has to do with "imagery"—an equation Forrest-Thomson, who talks of the phonetic image complexes in Shakespeare's sonnets, does not really intend to make. Our perplexity is further compounded when we learn in chapter 3 that Pound and Eliot were masters of the "disconnected image complex."

Ironically, all this terminology could be scrapped, for what Forrest-Thomson is really after is a way of reading poems that will take into account the interrelationship of the various levels of poetic discourse: the phonological and the syntactic as well as the semantic; like the Formalists, she regards meaning as an internalized component of poetic structure. Consider her treatment of Ezra Pound's "Homage to Sextus Propertius," a poem, so Forrest-Thomson believes, that is almost always subjected to "bad Naturalisation." Here is the author's pastiche of what such Naturalization yields:

We know that Ezra Pound was an expatriate American poet and that the poem is dated 1917, at which time he was living in London; we know that Sextus Propertius was a Latin poet living in Rome and writing in the first century A. D. These facts make an external context. . . . Official and respected poets are mocked along with their patrons . . . the reason for this is plain when one recalls the fact that both Pound and Propertius were relatively unknown and unpatronised. Both were better poets than those who were so belauded, and they felt this was the fault of society for wanting "a worn-out poetical fashion." . . . What of the style of the lines? They are obviously rather loose free verse and that is explained by the fact that Pound/Propertius' grievance was caused partly by their attempt to write in new and experimental ways. That is all we need to know about the style, and we can move straight on to our external thematic interpretation. Pound expresses his bitterness toward his society by an "imitation" of an earlier author who also wrote obscurely and expressed bitterness at his society. Pound was quite right, because pre-war England was very like Rome in the last days of the Republic and the beginnings of the Empire.

No doubt, Forrest-Thomson is right to assume that this is the sort of reading given to the "Homage" in standard undergraduate courses. How, then, does she avoid "external Naturalisation"? First, she argues that it is not important whether anything in prewar Britain corresponds to Propertius's Rome. Rather, the "Homage" asserts both at the conventional and the stylistic levels "a poetic ancestry with a technical forbear." Pound's artifice is itself an homage to a poetic predecessor; his "crabbed style" alludes to the Alexandrianism of the Roman poet. Again, the pronouns shift categories, creating "a whole class of 'poetic voices." The "I" thus becomes "any poetic voice which ranges itself against the other forms of verse displayed and parodied here." The effect of the poem's various tensions—between an authoritative end-stopped line and the slangy language that line contains, between unofficial "asides" and official statement—is to distance and fictionalize the situation: "Pound/Propertius" becomes a "mythical figure" who "can only exist within the realm of artifice" (p. 36), that is to say, in the words on the page.

The analysis of Pound's parodic style is excellent, but I wonder if Forrest-Thomson's rigid refusal to say anything about Pound's actual view of Propertius and his milieu is not as extreme a position as the one she attacks. Indeed, what she calls a "bad Naturalisation" would, in this case, support her own "internal expansion" and "limitation," for it is, after all, Pound's choice of Propertius that generates the very stylistic features she talks of. For a sensible combination of the two approaches, one may consult Donald Davie's two books on Pound.

Veronica Forrest-Thomson is at her best when she turns to contemporary poetry. She is able to show that a poem like Philip Larkin's "Mr. Bleaney" can only be read by means of external naturalization: the fate of the ordinary man who dwells in his pathetic little bed-sitting room has no meaning unless we can compare his way of life to others that we know. Indeed, we feel that Mr. Bleaney's life has been pathetic and tawdry only because we presumably know better. Thus the hard-boiled but sensitive narrator who tells Mr. Bleaney's story obviously uses the world beyond the poem as his norm, even though he characteristically abjures his own insight into the case in his final "I don't know." The poem, Forrest-Thomson argues, "fulfills the reader's expectations, leading him out toward the world and inviting him to think of it once more. But it does no more than that."

Such poems are, of course, instantly popular. A related case is that of Ted Hughes, about whom Forrest-Thomson writes both bravely and harshly. In a volume like *Crow*, she argues, Hughes takes a perfectly predictable symbol and makes what seem at first reading "daring" metaphysical statements about the universe. At the same time, "there is not sufficient use of the non-semantic levels to allow the reader to perceive a formal pattern." The dislocation of the universe, which is Hughes's theme, is nowhere associated with dislocation on the syntactic or prosodic level. Rather, the simple declarative sentences are spun out in flat and repetitive free verse lines, one rather like the next. What is the function of repetition in this context? There is none, no relationship between form and theme; the imagery, not grounded in a formal complex, becomes merely stagy. Hughes "wants to be mysterious thematically without letting it affect his technique."

Forrest-Thomson quite rightly distinguishes between Hughes's frequent poetic posturing and the more integral visionary poetry of Sylvia Plath, although I think she overrates Plath in the process. More interesting is her distinction between Ted Hughes and John Ashbery. Her analysis of "'They Dream Only in America,'" written before *Self-Portrait in a Convex Mirror* (1975) finally brought Ashbery fame, is very acute. She understands as have few commentators, including Harold Bloom who found *The Tennis Court Oath* (in which "The Dream" appeared) a "fearful disaster," that Ashbery's poem must be regarded as a "dream landscape." This is not to say that it is merely impenetrable. Whereas the neo-Surrealist poems of David Gascoyne and Andrew Crozier are characterized by total unintelligibility (reading them, says Forrest-Thomson, is like finding the telephone off the hook), Ashbery's syntax always provides some kind of opening even though the opening leads to no formulation of meaning. "'They Dream Only of America'" disrupts the chain of cause and effect; it is impossible to know who "they" are and what it means "to be lost among the thirteen million pillars of grass." But the promise of meaning hovers in the air. The key "image complex," in this case, is the word "America": "The poem works on the assumption that, at first, the reader will take 'America' for granted. Whatever other external references are suspended, we know about America; it is the continent across the Atlantic which has properties in our minds, of affluence, materialism, success—Whitman's American dream and also Norman Mailer's." But, and this is the special artifice of the poem, after the eighth line, we cannot take even these attitudes to America for granted. The phonetic solidarity of this line ["The *lake* a *lilac* cube"] "asserts the dominance of a formal order, its block-like resistance to empirical contexts." And from this point on, the conventions of the detective story are parodied just as the poem parodies the reader's presuppositions about America. Each line seems to promise a connection that is subsequently eroded. Disclosure of meaning is always imminent, but it never comes. The triumph of Ashbery's artifice is to keep us on our toes, waiting to learn what it was that happened "behind barns," or what door the mysterious "key" will open.

Within the context of postmodernism, Forrest-Thomson's stress on "artifice" thus makes good sense. When, on the other hand, she discusses the phonological and metaphorical image complex found in the words "as stone" in line 4 of Shakespeare's Sonnet 94, or when she contrasts Eliot's "suspended naturalisation" to that of Stevens, her stress on stylistic device often seems excessive. *Poetic Artifice* is subtitled "A Theory of Twentieth-Century Poetry," but its value is less theoretical than historical. It is an eloquent defense of what we might call the New Anglo-American Poetry.

CHAPTER 19

The Vendler Factor

This collection of Helen Vendler's essays and reviews on modern American poets, written over the past decade chiefly for the *New York Times Book Review*, the *New York Review of Books*, and the *New Yorker*, has already received, deservedly, I think, its own rave reviews from a galaxy of critics, among them Irvin Ehrenpreis, William S. Pritchard, and Monroe Spears. The energy and brilliance of Vendler's writing, her sympathy and tact in bringing to the reader's attention the particular qualities that make a given poem memorable, her affinities with Randall Jarrell and R. P. Blackmur—these have been remarked upon. Some, like Denis Donohue, have taken issue with Vendler's peremptory dismissal of the later Eliot (of *Four Quartets*, she remarks, "Can nervousness be cured by ethics?"); others, like Donald Hall, have questioned her adulation of Lowell's last book, *Day by Day*. I do not propose here to debate these particular issues or others like them once again. It is perhaps more important, at this stage, to try to define what are, beneath the glitter of the individual essays, Vendler's central critical assumptions, assumptions that are not only unstated but perhaps largely unconscious.

Helen Vendler has always avoided theory. What she says of Randall Jarrell could just as well be said of her: "He was, for better or worse, a member of no school of criticism; he was no theorist; he felt happier writing about the nineteenth and twentieth century than about earlier periods where what you see in what you read depends radically on historical information; he wrote always 'to show to others' and not to muse to himself. He was not, in short, a Frye, an Auerbach, a Blackmur, an Auden." And further, "Jarrell, in his criticism had three special talents. He thought naturally in metaphor. . . . he wrote, in almost

Review of *Part of Nature, Part of Us*, by Helen Vendler. *Contemporary Literature* 22 (Winter 1980–1981): 96–103.

every account, an implicit suspense story; and he saw books constantly as stories about human beings." This deftly defines Vendler's own way of looking at contemporary poetry. An impatience with history as well as with theory, a natural gift for metaphor that makes Vendler herself something of a poet ("Ginsberg's avalanche of detail is like the rain of dust and lava that preserved Pompeii—here lies America, in literally thousands of its emanations"; or again, with reference to Merwin's *The Miner's Pale Children*, "Is it ill-will in a reader to want to force-feed these pale children till they, when cut, will bleed?"); and above all, a concern for poems as "stories about human beings."

What kind of stories? Vendler likes them best when they are, in the words of one of her titles, "Apollo's Harsher Songs." Thus she says of Stevens:

> Many of Stevens' poems—read from one angle, most of the best poems—spring from catastrophic disappointment, bitter solitude, or personal sadness. It is understandable that Stevens, a man of chilling reticence, should illustrate his suffering in its largest possible terms. That practice does not obscure the nature of the suffering, which concerns the collapse of early hopeful fantasies of love, companionship, success, and self-transformation. As self and beloved alike become, with greater or lesser velocity, the final dwarfs of themselves, and as social awareness diminishes dreams of self-transcendence, the poet sees dream, hope, love, and trust—those activities of the most august imagination—crippled, contradicted, dissolved, called into question, embittered. This history is the history of every intelligent and receptive human creature, as the illimitable claims on existence made by each one of us are checked, baffled, frustrated and reproved—whether by our subsequent perceptions of their impossible grandiosity, or by the accidents of fate and chance, or by our betrayal of others, or by old age and its failures of capacity.

The shift, in the last sentence, from third to first person, from the particular "I" of Stevens's late poems to the generalized "we" who read them, quite takes one's breath away. The implicit moral judgment, the concern that the poet's values are also the critic's is profound. Many of us will agree that the late poems do call into question the poet's dream of love and self-transformation, but does it really follow that Stevens's history is "the history of every intelligent and receptive human creature"? Do we all live to see our "early hopeful fantasies" "crippled" and "contradicted"? It is an assumption that Vendler makes again and again. Here she is on Lowell: "Lowell's late practice is profoundly irreligious, reality-bound, ordered not by any structural teleology but by a confidence in free association, addressed not homiletically to an audience, but painfully to the self, private rather than public, closer to the epistolary than to the oratorical, as various as conversation in its tonal liberty, free to seem desultory and uncomposed, and, above all, exempt from the tyranny of the well-made." Such poetry, says Vendler, is not "comfortable," but "it has the solace of truth in its picture of the misery, sense of stoppage, and perplexed desultoriness of middle age." If it cannot quite speak to the young, "it sums up another phase of life, no less valuable, no less moving, no less true."

Or again, here is Merrill, whom Vendler calls "one of our indispensable poets": "What is in the American mind these days—the detritus of past belief, a hodge-podge of Western science and culture, a firm belief in the worth of the private self and in the holiness of the heart's affections, a sense of time and space beyond the immediate is here displayed for judgment." Merrill is further praised for "locat[ing] value in the human and everyday rather than in the transcendent." Such concern for the human with the attendant realization that transcendence is not possible is also a theme in Vendler's essay on Adrienne Rich. Of "Trying to Talk with a Man" (it begins "What we've had to give up to get here— / whole LP collections, films we starred in"), Vendler writes: "Which of us, at forty, will not wince at the fluoroscopic truth of that list: we can name our own LP's, our fantasy PTA neighborhood self-projections, our parents' cookie jars, our dramas of love and self-pity, our slides into regressive and delusory role-playing. Critics who represent Rich's recent poetry as the utterance of exaggerated feminism alone seem not to have read these plainspoken passages, returning throughout this book, passages showing (in the jargon of today) where we are all at."

But suppose "we" do not feel that this is "where we are all at"? Suppose we cannot quite identify with what Vendler calls "the whole long trip that has brought them (Rich and her husband and, by extension, Everywoman and Everyman) to this ghost town"? What then? Is the poem still an important one? Is Rich still an important poet? Or, to put it another way, is the moral value of the poem its aesthetic value as well?

Vendler is nothing if not sensitive to the language of poetry, but the fact is that her first concern is always with the moral imperative. Accordingly, if one doesn't happen to share her particular values, to sympathize, for example, with the plight of the married woman who is "Trying to Talk with a Man"—it is difficult to concur with many of the judgments made in the course of these reviews. For Vendler's particular moral norms preclude at least the following: (1) religious poetry, the poetry of transcendence, probably Vendler's greatest bugbear: witness her strong dislike of "Ash Wednesday" and *Four Quartets*; (2) poetry of intense erotic celebration, as in the exuberant and mystical lyric of Goethe's

West-Oestlicher Divan; (3) poetry in which the "private self," far from being at the center, becomes just one item in the large mythographic collage of the present; here I am thinking, of course, of Pound's *Cantos*, a text that Vendler has always admittedly avoided; (4) the poetry of play, of intellectual game that values ideas for their own sake as in Auden's late great *paysages moralisés* like "Bucolics" ("Surely," says Vendler in what I take to be a real error in judgment, "the Auden that will last is the prewar Auden—the irreverent, vivid, daring and thoughtful"); and (5) poetry that subordinates the articulation of detachable meaning to the creation of artful structures, that prefers the play of signifiers to the "importance" of the signified; the linguistic construct to whatever truth may lurk behind it; here I would place Gertrude Stein and Williams's *Spring and All*, the Dada and Futurist lyric, or indeed a text like Ashbery's "Litany."

But for Vendler it is the private self that must be squarely at the center of the poem, and that self must come to terms with its past and future, must see, as did Stevens, its "dreams of self-transcendence" crumble, its imaginative activities curtailed and crippled. The demand for suffering leads the critic into certain odd inconsistencies. Thus Lowell's *Day by Day* is praised for being so unabashedly true to life, for its willingness to conclude a poem with the line "Yet why not say what happened?" "Lowell," says Vendler, "to whom every word in the language has by now its distinct musical value, can, with an accuracy to within a feather's weight, 'say what happened.'" Having renounced his "former panoplies," he is left with the quotidian: "a wife, children, the seasons, ill health, acquaintances, friends living and dead, a walk, a photograph, a poetry reading, a dinner out, shaving, making love, insomnia, fishing." Curiously enough, Frank O'Hara is criticized for precisely the same refusal to separate art from life:

> Two aspects of his work tended to do O'Hara in: his radical incapacity for abstraction . . . and his lack of a comfortable form. . . . The longest poems end up simply messy, endless secretions, with a nugget of poetry here and there, slices of life arbitrarily beginning, and ending for no particular reason. "Dear Diary," says O'Hara, and after that anything goes. The perfect freedom any diarist enjoys—to put anything down that happened on a certain day only because at the head of the page there is that hungry date saying June 13, 1960—is what O'Hara claims for himself in his long poems.

I find this very puzzling. Why is Lowell's renunciation of formal constraints so attractive, whereas O'Hara's is a test on "the limited attention span of the poet or his reader"? If Lowell can record, in diary fashion, "what happened," and still maintain fidelity and precision, why can't O'Hara? The answer, I think, is that

Vendler intuitively prefers "what happened" to Lowell to "what happened" to O'Hara; she is deeply moved by Lowell's "heartbreaking" "fragment of an auto-biography," which records "his late, perhaps unwise, third marriage; the birth of a son, the very worst memories suppressed from *Life Studies*, memories of having been an unwanted child and a tormented adolescent; exile in Britain and Ireland; the death of friends; clinical depression and hospitalization, lovemaking and impotence; distress over age; fear of death. Against all this is set the power of writing."

Is the "power of writing" about such suffering innately valuable? In writing of Stevens and Lowell, Bishop and Rich, Vendler implies that it is. Measured against these poets, O'Hara appears too insouciant, although he is, of course, not nearly so jaunty and cheery as Vendler would have us believe, and he too has his depressions and fears of death. But his poetic strategy is to treat feeling with bemused detachment, to refuse to take himself too seriously. His poems sug-gest, at least indirectly, that the "Personism" he seems to dwell on is not perhaps the primary thing. As his friend John Cage put it in an essay on "The Future of Music": "more and more this concern with personal feelings of individuals, even the enlightenment of individuals, will be seen in the larger context of society. We know how to suffer and control our own emotions. If not, advice is available. There is a cure for tragedy. The path to self-knowledge has been mapped out by psychiatry, by oriental philosophy, mythology, occult thought, anthroposophy, and astrology. We know all we need to know about Oedipus, Prometheus, and Hamlet. What we are learning is how to be convivial. 'Here Comes Everybody.'"

I am not saying that Cage is right and Vendler wrong when she declares, in talking of Stevens, that "feeling—to use Wordsworthian terms—is the organiz-ing principle of poetry." But I do think she should perhaps be more aware of the foundations of her own judgments, of why she believes that poem x is "trans-parently beautiful" or poem y "bores." By the same token, the reader should be aware that the map of modern poetry presented in these pages is a highly personal one; its shapes and forms are dictated by a central faith in the holiness of the heart's affections and the maladies of the quotidian. We are not, it seems, meant to be happy except for brief moments. And even these occurred long ago. Life is always a struggle and most of us find it hard to survive.

Given these premises, however, Vendler succeeds time and again in giving her reader the precise graph of a poet's consciousness, his or her successes and failures. I think her finest essays are those on Stevens and Merrill; the latter's sensibility has not been explored by anyone as discerningly as it has by Ven-dler, and she has a wonderful way of explaining the poet's arcane images and allusions, making even the difficult *Mirabell: Book of Numbers* a radiant and reasonable whole. In evaluating Merrill's achievement, Vendler maintains perfect poise and toughness of judgment; she is not swept off her feet.

If her essays on Lowell and Rich are somewhat less successful, it is because here she becomes a shade defensive; she is the one who suffered, she was there. In itself, the essay on Rich is both moving and convincing, but the cited passages never quite live up to Vendler's commentary on them. Thus she says of the following lines:

> but this
> after all
> is the narrows and after
> all we have never entirely
> known what was done to you upstream
> what powers trepanned
> which of your channels diverted
> what rockface leaned to stare
> in your upturned
> defenseless
> face.

"The ending may be sentimental, but the river and the mind to which it corresponds are heavy with truth." I remain unconvinced that the river metaphor can be "heavy" with any truth, and I am even less convinced by what I take to be Vendler's one real lapse in this book: her encomium on Dave Smith. Of a poem called "On a Field Trip at Fredericksburg," Vendler writes, "The poem takes shape, beautifully following the drift of experience and reflection." Then she quotes the entire poem, which begins:

> The big steel tourist shield says maybe
> fifteen thousand got it here. No word
> of either Whitman or one uncle
> I barely remember in the smoke
> that filled his tiny mountain house.
> If each finger were a thousand of them
> I could clasp my hands and be dead
> up to my wrists. It was quick
> though not so fast as we can do it
> now, one bomb, atomic or worse,
> one silly pod slung on wing-tip,

high up, an egg cradled
by some rapacious mockingbird.

Vendler praises Smith's "daring flashes" in this poem, the demotic beginning, modulating first into the "surrealistic fantasy" of lines 6–8 and then into the "dismissive meiosis for the atomic bomb ('one silly pod')." Perhaps it is my own blindness that leads me to regard the beginning of the poem as contrived rather than "demotic" and to dismiss the passage about the atom bomb as the most tired of clichés. There is, of course, no way to prove that Smith's poem is either as good as Vendler thinks it is or as bad as I take it to be. It is the nature of subjective criticism to make such proof impossible, indeed undesirable. Vendler cites Jarrell's definition of the critic as "an extremely good reader—one who has learned to show to others what he saw in what he read." It is in this sense that Vendler is an exciting—if sometimes irritating—critic; she does show to others, with astonishing economy, vigor, vividness, and penetration, what she has seen in the poems she has read. *Part of Nature, Part of Us* is certainly a remarkable achievement, even if there are those of us who will wonder whether the Arnoldian—and ultimately Romantic—norms implicitly governing Vendler's evaluations (and even the selection of poets she discusses) still make sense as we approach the fin de siècle of our own postmodern age.

CHAPTER 20

The Dice Cup

I met Max Jacob. Fernande and he were very funny together. They felt
themselves to be a courtly couple of the first empire, he being le vieux marquis
and kissing her hand and paying compliments and she the Empress Josephine
receiving them. It was a caricature but a rather wonderful one.
—GERTRUDE STEIN, *The Autobiography of Alice B. Toklas*

Max Jacob does discover everybody before anybody does that is quite certain.
Everybody comes to him he is always there and so they always see him.
—GERTRUDE STEIN, *Everybody's Autobiography*

The "rather wonderful" caricaturist who could entertain Picasso's mistress,
the "ami de la maison" who was "always there" and "discovered everybody"
is likely to be the only Max Jacob known to most American readers. Apollinaire,
Pierre Reverdy, Blaise Cendrars—these contemporaries of Jacob have long been
available in New Directions editions as well as in expensive bilingual texts published by university presses (witness the recent scholarly edition of Apollinaire's
Calligrammes by California). But Jacob has been curiously neglected by American critics, if not by the poets of our own avant-garde: six of the latter—John
Ashbery, David Ball, Michael Brownstein, Ron Padgett, Zack Rogow, and Bill
Zavatsky—have now collaborated on an edition of *Le Cornet à dés* (The Dice
Cup), bringing together for the first time in English a large selection of the prose
poems contained in the 1917 text. Anyone interested in what is happening in
poetry and poetics today will be grateful to Sun Press and to Michael Brownstein for editing this book.

Review of *The Dice Cup*, by Max Jacob, ed. Michael Brownstein. *Sulfur* 6 (1983): 172–79.

Why has Jacob received so little attention in America? His hermeticism is often cited as a reason, but surely *Le Cornet à dés* is no more difficult than, say, Mallarmé's "Un coup de dés," now a fashionable seminar text. No, I think that Jacob stands somewhere outside the canon, despite his close association with Picasso and Apollinaire, because of his antilyrical stance, his preference for a poetry of wit and intellect to one of emotion recollected in tranquility. Perhaps Romanticism, ever more "belated" and trivialized, has had to run its course before we could appreciate the tough-mindedness of a poem like the following:

Mutuel Mépris des Castes

Pas ailleurs que chez ce dompteur de bêtes! dans l'antichambre pleine de boîtes à chaussures en carton, lui-même parut ou plutôt ce fut son propre portrait par Van Dongen: un costume à carreaux noirs et blancs dont les cuirs étaient d'un brun doré. Son oeil mal indiqué était gros et ses cheveux pendaient comme des ailes de chocarneau (c'est un oiseau au plumage frisé). Le dompteur m'offrit du tabac et me recommanda à sa femme, une blonde effacée: "Vous n'êtes jamais entrée dans une cage?—Si, comme bête!" me dit-elle. Je ne compris pas; elle m'expliqua qu'ils louaient un grand apparte-ment meublé pour pouvoir dépenser les cinq cents francs qu'ils gagnaient quotidiennement: "Nous n'avons rien à nous, rien! regardez! ces chauss-ures! quelques livres et voilà! C'est pourquoi nous ne vous retiendrons pas à dîner." Le dompteur de bêtes fauves revint et fut surpris de ma présence. Je crois qu'il était aussi dentiste pour animaux.
—*Le Cornet à dés* (Paris: Gallimard, 1945), p. 141

Mutual Contempt of the Castes

Where else but in the animal tamer's house! In the ante-room full of card-board shoe-boxes, he himself appeared or rather it was his own portrait by Van Dongen: black-and-white checked suit whose leather parts were a golden brown. His poorly drawn eye was big and his hair hung down like the wings of the *chocarneau* (a bird with curly plumage). He offered me some tobacco and commended me to his wife, a mousy blonde. "You have never been inside a cage?" "Yes, as an animal!" she said. I didn't understand; she explained that they rented a large furnished apartment in each city so as to be able to spend the five hundred francs they earned every day: "We have nothing of our own, nothing! Look—those shoes, a few books, and that's it! That's why we can't invite you to stay for dinner." The animal tamer returned and was surprised to see me there. I think he was also an animal dentist.
—translated by John Ashbery, p. 58

Here the layers of parody are very complex. The kernel of the text is classic La Fontaine beast fable, meant to teach us some sort of moral lesson about snobbery and class consciousness. But the fable is wittily inverted: here the animal and the animal tamer are one and the same, with the further comic twist that the animal the tamer resembles, far from being a "fauve" (Ashbery's translation does not give us the force of "Le dompteur de bêtes fauves") is the foolish "*chocarneau* (a bird with curly plumage)." In this context, the narrator's question to the animal tamer's wife, "You have never been inside a cage?" and her response, "Yes, as an animal" seems wholly reasonable. Ashbery's epithet "mousy blonde"—the original has the more neutral "une blonde effacée"—playfully contributes to the beast fable.

But Jacob is not saying anything as trite as that human beings are really animals. For, as the narrative makes clear, human beings are indefinable in the first place. The animal tamer is not a person at all; he is "his own portrait by Van Dongen," a carelessly constructed painting (like all Fauve paintings, Jacob implies) in which the "black-and-white checked suit" has "leather parts" and the single eye seen in profile is "poorly drawn." Indeed, the whole text is a satiric portrait of the Fauve artist, whose pretensions to savage grandeur are beautifully deflated in the final image of the animal tamer as "also an animal dentist." The Fauves have, in other words, taken the bite out of art.

But again, Jacob's little fable is not just an attack on what were, from his Cubist perspective, a group of rival painters. Beyond the local satire, we find a serious examination of the vanity of human wishes, the bourgeois desire to have something to show for one's earnings ("a large furnished apartment in each city" with its "ante-room full of cardboard shoe-boxes"), a desire bound to be rebuffed: "We have nothing of our own, nothing. Look—those shoes, a few books, and that's it. That's why we can't invite you to stay for dinner." Ultimately, then, this *is* a fable and it does have the moral announced in the title: the mutual contempt of the castes is the rivalry between Fauves and Cubists (Jacob himself), the bourgeois (animal tamer) and the artist (the man who can't be invited to dinner). From this perspective, we can now understand the first sentence: "Where else but in the animal tamer's house"—a house that is really a cage with the tamer and his wife inside it—would one learn this lesson? And what would it mean to dine with an animal dentist?

To say, as have various commentators, that a prose poem like this one is "dislocated" or "Surrealist" or engages in "complex wordplay" does not really tell us very much. Jacob's dream narratives superficially resemble Rimbaud's ("War," for example, contains echoes of "Parade" with its "drôles très solides"), but their real affinity is less with Rimbaud or the Surrealists (or, for that matter, with the

Cubist painters) than with an exact contemporary whose work Jacob could not have known at the time he wrote the poems collected in *The Dice Cup* (1903–1910) but whose role as Jewish outsider and victim curiously parallels his own. I am thinking of course of Kafka: here is "The Aunt, the Tart, and the Hat" (La Tante, la tarte, et le chapeau) in Ashbery's translation:

> When I was a business employee I shared a small three-room apartment with a colleague. We didn't quarrel, because we were always very tired, but we spent a great deal of time identifying various pieces of clothing: a pair of trousers had been left in the living room: its ownership was established. One day at the shop an event occurred: my friend had had part of his beard shaved off. That same day he was supposed to carry a package to a district where I had to go on an errand. I took the package not without having reflected a long time. There was a great deal of talk about which metro line I ought to take and the question of the three pennies was an agitated one. That very evening at the shop, my friend invited us to lunch at his aunt's. The aunt was a former actress, almost very old, very tightly laced in her corset and who, once a year, made herself a little hat in the form of a tart which she rushed to put on when she was asked to sing. She sang the repertory of Thérésa. As a joke, we were served a tart in the form of a little hat. At table, there were two lovers: "I know all about that," said the old lady, "but you, my pretty child, do you realize what you are exposing yourself to?" The pretty child was at least forty years old. She replied that she had a grown son and a grown daughter and that she liked young men.

Here, as in Kafka, the plot line seems at first perfectly orderly and sensible: this happened, and then this, and then something else. "When I was a business employee I shared a small three-room apartment with a colleague." What could be more straightforward and simple? Throughout the text, Jacob provides a great deal of specification: "One day at the shop an event occurred," "That same day," "the three pennies," "That very evening at the shop," "At table, there were two lovers," and so on. But the temporal and spatial expectations set up by these phrases are never met for the events that unfold are seemingly quite unrelated. The establishment of ownership of "various pieces of clothing," for example, has no connection to the shaving off the beard. The shaving incident, moreover (is the "friend" in question the same person as the "colleague" or not?), seems to have nothing to do with the errand to the outlying district, the carrying of the package, and the question which metro line to take. We only know that somehow it leads to the invitation to lunch by the friend's aunt who makes hats in the forms of tarts and vice versa. (The punning on *tarte* and *tante* is, of course, lost in the English but the near-rhyme of "aunt"/"tart"/"hat" is a respectable substitute.)

The *dejeuner* itself is absurd. The pretty child (a "belle enfant" of "at least forty") whom the aunt warns of indecent exposure and who responds that "she had a grown son and a grown daughter and that she liked young men," may be referring to the narrator and his colleague (are they the "two lovers" at the table?) or to someone else. We have, in any case, a seemingly "normal" anecdote transformed into what Ashbery himself has called "an open field of narrative possibilities." For we can invent all sorts of stories that "fit" this particular frame. First, there is clearly some reference to a homosexual love affair. But then, who are the three men referred to in the phrase "My friend invited us to lunch at his aunt's"? Again, there is some sort of satire directed against no-longer-young bourgeois ladies with particular pretensions, here summed up in the tart-hat identification and the tante-tarte identity, with its pun on *tart*. Indeed, identity is in question throughout the poem for it is never clear who's who and what the relationship between the various characters signify. The characters are, moreover, nameless and faceless: the aunt, the pretty child, my friend, my colleague, us, them. The poem thus questions, as do so many of Jacob's texts, the very meaning of identity as well as the "normalcy" of everyday life, the work and eating rituals of bourgeois family culture, the value of reasoned action ("I took the package not without having reflected a long time").

The mode of "The Aunt, the Tart, and the Hat" thus looks ahead to some of Ashbery's own narrative poems (e.g., "The Wrong Kind of Insurance"), as well as to the Zen stories in John Cage's *Silence* or the comic anecdotes that weave in and out of David Antin's talk pieces. In such texts, the individual clause or sentence is usually perfectly intelligible but the sentences fail to add up, their absurd conjunctions pointing toward the confusion between illusion and reality, between the attempt to set down what happened and the actual ways in which poetic creation takes place.

No translation can, of course, do justice to Jacob's poetic language, which relies heavily on punning and sound play. Bill Zavatsky valiantly renders the famous epigram from "Le Coq et la perle":

> Comme un bateau est le poète âgé
> ainsi qu'un dahlia, le poème étagé
> Dahlia! Dahlia! que Dalila lia

as

> Like a ship is the agéd poet
> Like a dahlia, the terraced poem
> Dahlia! Dahlia tied by Dahlia!

Here the last line is a fair facsimile of the original, but Jacob's sly reference to Rimbaud's "Bateau ivre" involves a play on "poète âgé"—"étagé," which is wholly lost in the translation. Again, consider what happens to "Le brazero, zéro!":

> Le brazero, zéro! il s'exaspère de n'être pas un triangle muni d'ailes noires. Il se mord la queue, il est traversé de rails bleus qui se rallient, le raient et le raillent.

Zavatsky renders this:

> The brazier, zero! it's exasperated at not being a triangle fitted with black wings. It bites its own tail, it's crisscrossed with blue rails that rail, raze, and roil at it.

The design is to preserve Jacob's alliteration and onomatopoeia but the effect is somewhat self-conscious because "rail, raze, and roil" does not re-create Jacob's comic use of three words that sound almost identical but mean entirely different things: "se rallient" (rally), "raient" (part, as in to part one's hair), and "raillent" (mock or make fun of).

In some cases, the translator's task is made virtually impossible. Here is a third fragment from "Le Coq et la perle":

> Cet Allemand était fou d'art, de foulards et de poulardes. Dans son pays, la reine-Claude est peintre sur les foulards; à table, on en sait aussi rôdent aut- our des poulardes.

Here "fou d'art"—"foularde"—"poularde" function as what Raymond Roussel called "rimes de faits," that is, rhymes for events in the sense that sound itself controls the direction of the narrative. The English rendition—"mad about art"—"silk scarves"—"big fat hens"—is not likely to help the reader understand Jacob's complex phonemic play.

On the whole, however, the poet-translators succeed in capturing Jacob's peculiarly mordant tone, especially in the case of the longer narrative pieces. *The*

Dice Cup provides us with a good selection from *Le Cornet à dés* but includes less than half of its prose poems. Let us hope that Brownstein and his collaborators will decide to do the entire 1917 text as well as a selection from Jacob's verse poems, especially *Saint Matorel* (1911). Surely there would be today an enthusiastic audience for a poet who declares, with such curiously postmodern inflections:

> When one paints a picture, it changes completely with each touch, it turns like a cylinder and is almost endless. When it stops turning, that's because it's finished. My last one showed a tower of Babel in lighted candles.

A tower of Babel in lighted candles. The process of creation, in other words, can never produce "finish" or stasis. The gap between conception and achievement remains open; its mysteries provide us with continuing delight.

CHAPTER 21

The Challenge of German Lyric

Goethe and Heine in Translation

"Let the candidate," declared Ezra Pound in 1918, "fill his mind with the finest cadences he can discover, preferably in a foreign language, so that the meaning of the words may be less likely to divert his attention from the movement. . . . Let him dissect the lyrics of Goethe coldly into their component sound values, syllables long and short, stressed and unstressed, into vowels and consonants."[1]

The "candidates," of course, have done no such thing. For one thing, German is no longer a language with which the contemporary poet is likely to be familiar. For another, the lyric of Goethe, like that of Heine or, for that matter, that of a great Modernist poet like Brecht, is notoriously difficult to translate, *melopoeia*, to use Pound's term, being so centrally important. Confronted by a quatrain like:

> *Es schlug mein Herz, geschwind zu Pferde!*
> *Es war getan fast eh gedacht.*
> *Der Abend wiegte schon die Erde,*
> *Und an den Bergen hing die Nacht.* (Goethe)

the translator is caught between the Scylla of literal translation:

> My heart pounded. Quickly, to horse!
> No sooner was it thought than done.

Review of *Selected Poems*, by Goethe, ed. and trans. Christopher Middleton; and *The Complete Poems of Heinrich Heine*, by Hal Draper. *American Poetry Review* 12, no 5 (September–October 1983): 10–17.

Evening was already cradling the earth,
And on the mountains hung the night. (my translation)

and the Charybdis of imitating Goethe's meter and rhyme scheme:

My heart beat fast, a horse! away!
Quicker than thought I am astride,
Earth now lulled by end of day,
Night hovering on the mountainside. (Middleton)

Christopher Middleton reproduces the *abab* rhyme at the expense of Goethe's tone: line 2, with its intricate assonance of *e* and *a* sounds, stresses action, an action that evaporates in the clumsy and faintly archaic "I am astride." Again, the transitive force of lines 3–4 is lost by turning Goethe's subject-verb-object clauses into noun phrases; the word "mountainside," moreover, diffuses the force of the plural, "Bergen." But most important, here the attempt to capture the melopoeia of the original destroys its phanopoeia: for Goethe, nature is alive; hence the evening can cradle or rock the earth and night hang on the mountain. Middleton's passive constructions, his choice of "lulled" and "hovering," thus neutralize Goethe's meanings, his expression of animistic faith.

But surely, the reader will object at this point, there is a middle course between literal word-for-word translation and the sort of phonemic equivalence Middleton aims for. Why not, for instance, follow the example of Richard Howard's recent (and already celebrated) translation of Baudelaire's *Les Fleurs du Mal*, which, by Howard's own account, compensates for the loss of rhyme by finding "other means of getting the wire into the air. . . . other tactics for keeping the poem suspended."[2] This sounds reasonable enough when one remembers that French, being a highly inflected language, rhymes almost effortlessly—"fl*euve*"/"v*euve*"; "resplen*dit*"/"gran*dit*," to take the first quatrain of Baudelaire's "Le Cygne," not to mention the countless rhymes on final *é* as in "peché"/"volupté." Accordingly, rhyme is less prominent in French than in a less inflected language like German, whose rhymes are rarely vowel rhymes. Again, like English and unlike French, German is a stress language so that the rhyming syllables are sharply foregrounded ("ged*ácht*"/"N*ácht*"). This is not to say that rhyme counts for nothing in a poet like Baudelaire: take the first stanza of "Le Voyage":

Pour l'enfant, amoureux de cartes et d'éstampes,
L'univers est égal à son vaste appetit.

Ah! que le monde est grand à la carté des lampes!
Aux yeux du souvenir que le monde est petit!

When Howard renders Baudelaire's rhyming alexandrines in blank verse, thus eliminating the closure, the click of the spring, as it were, created by the chiasmus of lines 3–4, which culminates in the final rhyme, something central has obviously been lost:

> The child enthralled by lithographs and maps
> can satisfy his hunger for the world:
> how limitless it is beneath the lamp,
> and how it shrinks in the eyes of memory!

Still, Baudelaire's sardonic awareness of the gulf between desire and its object comes through Howard's "cool" rendition. But when as in the case of Goethe's and Heine's ballad stanzas and octaves, rhyme virtually controls verse structure and creates semantic density, the translator's role becomes more problematic.

I raise this issue because it may help us to understand the curious neglect the great German poets have suffered, not, of course, among scholars, but certainly among poets. Check the annual *MLA Bibliography* and you will find roughly one hundred entries under the name Goethe or Heine; check the index of *Poetry* or *The Yale Review* or *Parnassus* or, for that matter, *American Poetry Review*, and these poets might as well not exist. Rilke is the notable German exception, the darling of poets as diverse as Robert Bly or A. J. Poulin Jr., or Stephen Mitchell (see *APR*, January–February 1982). But then Rilke is primarily a poet of logopoeia: translators of the *Duino Elegies* or the *Sonnets to Orpheus* are interested in his complex meditative structures; they want to re-create the dialectical thought patterns that make these poems unique. But what of those poets who, in Eliot's words on the metaphysical poets, "feel their thought as immediately as the odour of a rose"? In the same year that Richard Howard's translation of Baudelaire has been discussed in virtually every major newspaper, magazine, and critical journal (and for this reason I shall not take it up in my French column), Hal Draper's monumental and magnificent *Complete Poems of Heine* has barely received notice. Granted that Howard is well known as a poet in his own right and Hal Draper is not; granted that *Les Fleurs du Mal* is a volume centrally important to the whole Modernist enterprise in Anglo-America—still, something seems very wrong. For who could be more "modern" than the quixotic Heine, the baptized Jew from provincial Germany, self-exiled in the Paris of the Second Republic; the student of Hegel and forerunner of Nietzsche, whose "simple" ballads like

"Die Lorelei" and "Die Grenadiere" every German schoolchild can recite; the poet of endless Sehnsucht for his beloved who came to cast a cynical eye on the pleasure of eros; the friend of Marx and Saint-Simon who, in his last years, espoused the cause of monarchy; the author of devastating critiques of Christianity, whose lyric is full of references to the supernatural?

Why, then, is Heine's poetry so inaccessible to American readers? Why, at a time when German philosophy from Kant to Hegel to Heidegger and Gadamer is more popular than ever, when the Nietzsche cult dominates Humanities Departments in the universities, when the New German Film and the New (i.e., neoexpressionist) Painting is making such waves, is German poetry so unknown? The answer, I think, has to do precisely with the problem of sound in poetry, and specifically with the differences between German and English metrics. In our own highly uninflected language, the average number of words to any given rhyme sound is less than three.[3] As such, it is surely no accident that our dominant verse form from Elizabethan drama down to Wallace Stevens's "Sunday Morning" has been blank verse. Unrhymed iambic pentameter, as John Thompson notes, has no inherent tone:

> Except for free verse [which has replaced it in the twentieth century], it is the form closest to the form of our speech. Its stresses alternate as our English speech stresses tend to do and its measure of 5 strong stresses marked by the juncture of the line end, a measure readingly apprehended without counting, both stimulates and accommodates the way we make phrases and clauses as we speak.[4]

Blank verse is the form of *Paradise Lost*, of Wordsworth's *Prelude* and Browning's *The Ring and the Book*. Rhyme, on the other hand, has tended to be reserved for the smaller forms—sonnet, ballad, satire. (Two notable exceptions are Byron and Yeats, both, interestingly, great admirers of Goethe.) Once free verse became the dominant form, as it has in our century, the question of rhyme no longer seems urgent. But in the case of translation, especially from the German, we cannot very well ignore this and related questions about sound structure. The new translations of Goethe by Christopher Middleton and of Heine by Hal Draper provide us with an occasion to think about these matters.

I

Christopher Middleton is himself a very sophisticated and accomplished poet; his roots are in Dada and Surrealism, but his Dada has, so to speak, a

tough-minded British hard edge; his experiments with language include concrete and found poems, collage texts, prose fables as in *Pataxanadu* (1977), and
the extensive use of punning and wordplay in the tradition of the Russian Futur-
ists. His translations from the German include such diverse poets as Hölderlin
and Hoffmansthal, Benn and Trakl, Celan and Grass; he has also translated novels (Christa Wolf's *The Quest of Christa T.*) and the *Selected Letters* of Nietzsche.
Given this background, he seems a very logical choice as a translator of the
Selected Poems, the first of the projected twelve-volume edition of Goethe's *Collected Works in English* underway by Suhrkamp/Insel. The bilingual text is hand-
somely produced; the choice of poems on the whole quite sensible (no phase
of Goethe's career is ignored), and the notes adequate for the general reader. It
is a volume ideally designed for those who know just a little German, but not
enough to read Goethe on their own.

I say "a little German" because I am not sure that the English versions alone
will convince the reader of Goethe's lyric genius. In his excellent introduction,
Middleton raises some of the central issues:

> Translating a poem is not quite the imaginative act of writing one. All the
> same, the synthesis of possibilities for which a translator settles is derived
> from his judgment as a feature of his linguistic imagination. He tries to
> weigh each value singly against all the others, grading also each to each as
> functions of a whole consortium, much as Kurt Schwitters required of the
> Merz artist. In Goethe's poems, rhyme belongs somehow with linearity, and
> linearity somehow belongs with a fluid resolution of a stark-edged form.
> Rhyme belongs also with an air of improvisation in so far as the lyrical
> speech-act flows, to all appearances, straight from a perception of circum-
> stance (or an "occasion"). At the same time, his poems always have a high
> finish.

The "fluid resolution of stark-edged form," the improvisatory air coupled with
"high finish"—these are indeed distinctive features of Goethean lyric. Middleton also recognizes the difficulty these features raise for the English translator:

> How can one invent in rhyme a "believable modern bold English idiom"?
> . . . A tacit faith in the cosmic harmony might seem to underlie the ability of
> older poets—think of Keats, of Byron—to rhyme with great zest and no effort.
> Rhyme was closure, proof of the veracity of the lyrical disclosure. It was also
> secretly linked with the onward thrusting of (apparent) extempore, with the
> crisp definition and suavity proper to any style. . . . Rhyme in translation,

however is, likely to coarsen the effect, to smell of the lamp. There is, then a general problem: how to make rhyme sound as unprompted and as interesting as possible. This can be done, if coupled or alternate lines have sufficient flow and consonance in other phases, not over the line-breaks only, but in larger syntactical units, and in variant kinds of sound-patterning, such as assonance, whether final or inside the lines. . . . The point is, of course, to rhyme not because the original does, but because rhyming is proper to this English tonal mimesis of the original poem's *decorum.*

Again, this is eminently sensible and well argued. Middleton also discusses the importance of linearity for Goethe, as well as the marvelous "balance between linearity and undulance," the "dialectic of closure and disclosure" achieved in his poems. "A line begins, opens up, closes (with or without rhyme); but no sooner has it closed than it is opening into the next line, in a fugitive instant, a pure transition." Middleton calls this effect "shutterflutter," and the translator's role, as he sees it, is to capture Goethe's "urgent forward motion" by finding a contemporary idiom free from the archaisms and poeticisms usually found in Goethe translations. The classics, he remarks wryly, tend to get translated in what stimulates the appropriate period style: in Goethe's case, such "antiquing" is particularly foolish since his language, like Wordsworth's, was intentionally designed to subvert eighteenth-century artifice. Unlike, say, Hölderlin, whose "intellectualism has a rigorous dialectical character, even when it is rhapsodic," Goethe is essentially a "sensuous, demonstrative, exploratory, divinatory poet"— accessible to the Volk even as he moves easily into the Orphic, the Sublime. It is Goethe's "totalization," Middleton posits, his belief that the poet can fill his entire world with metaphors and analogies so as to create a living texture of meaning, a presence, that seems alien to contemporary readers: "[Goethe] was one of the last poets of the old projective imagination. . . . Soon after Goethe, all such totalizations were to become suspect." The increasing role of irony and equivocation in Heine's work is a case in point.

Given these fine insights about Goethe's poetry, I find Middleton's actual translations curiously disappointing. The poet who writes so intelligently about the need "to rhyme interestingly on different parts of speech" and to avoid the "*antiquing*" of Goethe's diction, inexplicably translates a quatrain like the following:

> *Wie herrlich leuchtet*
> *Mir die Natur!*
> *Wie glänzt die Sonne!*
> *Wie lacht die Flur!* ("Mailied," 1771)

as a kind of nursery rhyme:

> Marvellous Nature
> Shining on me!
> Glorious sunlight
> Field shaking with Glee!

Here Goethe's naturalness gives way to a formulaic diction—"Marvellous nature," "shaking with glee"—that overstates the case: the poet is not claiming that Nature shines on him; he is simply remarking that the natural world seems to be lighting up from within; the fields, accordingly, are laughing. John Frederick Nims's version, which Middleton gives as an alternate, is much more effective in this regard:

> How fine a light on
> Nature today!
> The sun's in glory!
> The fields at play! (p. 11)

Or, to take a more egregious case, consider what happens to Goethe's famous "Wandrer's Nachtlied" (Wanderer's night song):

> *Über allen Gipfeln*
> *Ist Ruh,*
> *In allen Wipfeln*
> *Spürest du*
> *Kaum einen Hauch;*
> *Die Vögelein schweigen im Walde.*
> *Warte nur, balde*
> *Ruhest du auch.*

A literal translation would give us something like the following:

> Above the mountain peaks
> It is quiet,
> In all the tree tops
> You feel
> Barely a breath;
> The little birds are silent in the forest.

Just wait, soon
You will rest too.

Here is Middleton:

Over mountains yonder,
　　　A stillness;
Scarce any breath, you wonder
　　　Touches
The tops of all the trees.
　　　No forest birds now sing;
A moment, waiting—
　　　Then take, you too, your ease.

To see what has gone wrong here, we must look closely at Goethe's eight-line stanza, whose rhyme scheme is *ababcddc*. The first thing to notice is that the line lengths are uneven and that meaning is created by the disjunction of syntax and meter. Thus the falling rhythm of the first line (three trochees) culminates in the single iamb of the end-stopped second line, "Ist Rúh." Line 3 begins as if it were to be an echo of line 1 although the first foot is foreshortened—"In állen Wípfeln"—but there is a sudden turn as the fourth line fails to fulfill the pattern, substituting verb and subject pronoun for predication. Again, since the line is run-over, we read on breathlessly to the end of the next line, a choriamb ending on a new rhyme sound

　　　/　　x　x　　/
　　Kaum einen Hauch

where the stress pattern is reinforced by assonance. The predominance in these lines of low vowels—*u*, *ü*, and *au*—and the rhyme on the guttural *ch* (the phoneme *AX*) creates a sound pattern that enacts precisely what the poem is saying: silence is about to fall. Now Goethe introduces a long (9 syllable, 3 stress) line made up of dactyls ever so lightly stressed, with short vowel sounds and liquids predominating. This line in turn receives an echo from the foreshortened seventh line: "Wálde: is picked up by "Wárte," there is a pause after "nur," and then the feminine rhyme "bálde" accentuates the fall into silence. Finally, the eight line centers our attention on the poet-wanderer himself; we realize that this is a poem about *his* need for rest and *his* oneness with nature. So the final line introduces a new idea even as it takes us back to line 5 via rhyme and rhythm (/ x x /)

and back to line 2, "Ruhest" echoing "Ruh." The mirroring effect (as within, so without) is anticipated by the muted anthropomorphism of the verb "Schwei-gen" (line 6), a verb conventionally referring to the silence, not of birds but of persons. The vocalic structure of line 8:

> / x   x   /
> *Ruhest du auch*

and the *h–ch* alliteration creates what can best be called a final exhalation of breath. The song is over.

Can such a poem be translated at all? Longfellow, whose translation Middle-ton reprints next to his own, did it this way:

> O'er all the hill-tops
> > Is quiet now,
> In all the tree-tops
> > Hearest thou
> Hardly a breath,
> > The birds are asleep in the trees:
> Wait, soon like these
> > Thou, too, shalt rest.

I find this version somewhat preferable to Middleton's because at least Longfel-low has the basic rhythm right (note the choriambic fifth line followed by the long sixth), and he preserves Goethe's syntax. But his rhymes are leaden ("hill-tops"/"tree-tops"; "trees"/"these"), and he must resort to filler to get even these rhymes. Goethe's mood of hush, of threshold experience, does come through, at least in the middle lines, which is more than one can say for the Middleton version with its "yonder"/"wonder" rhymes and its stilted conclusion. "Then take, you too your ease," an example of the very antiquing Middleton wants to avoid. What happens when the figure of sound disappears is that the *Night Song* becomes merely trivial, a nice little mood piece. For its theme—the reciprocity of the natural and the human—is lost in translation: note, for example, that Mid-dleton's line, "No forest birds now sing," is quite different from the reference to the birds' "schweigen." Again, the phrase "A moment, waiting" strikes me as all wrong, for in the moment of observation, the wanderer does not perceive the moment as such.

If we compare this translation to Middleton's own poems, for example those collected in *Carminalenia* (Carcanet Press, 1980), we may well wish that he had not worried about rhyme and meter at all, and had recast the "Wanderer's Night Song" in the free-verse mode of such poems as "How to Watch Birds":

Nothing to it. Live your way
Into the magnitudes of
Their bodies. Breathe your way
Into their disappearing

Flight. Be
Silent, go with them, strip off
Opaque muscle, breakable
Bone. Unframe

Your speech, be tree, air, without
Winking fly
Clean through your eyeballs. Or slit-eyed
Glancing sideways

Catch them on the hop. Soon
Sleep with them, a branch
Will shape your claws,
Grip it.

No forest birds, these; no ease, moreover, for the poet who must learn to "Breathe [his] way / Into their disappearing / Flight," to "shape [his] claws" on a branch so as to enter their alien world. The four-line stanzas rely on complex alliteration and internal rhyme, as in "*Opaque* mus*c*le, *breaka*ble / *B*one. Un*frame*," to give them structure; the lines, heavily enjambed and broken within, have a harsh urgency that conveys the poet's lesson. The cut, for example, between "Be" and "silent"—this is Middleton speaking in his own voice, a voice that is not at home with a line like "Then take, you too, your ease." Perhaps, then, it would have been better for Middleton to take the Poundian approach to translation, to use Goethe's poem merely as a starting point for his own invention. But then the publisher, who has, after all, commissioned a *Selected Poems* of Goethe, not of Middleton, might have been less than pleased. There is no easy solution to this dilemma.

A poet who almost always uses free verse or prose, Middleton is, not surprisingly, much more successful with Goethe's poems in free rhythms, for example "Harzreise im Winter" (A Winter Journey in the Harz), evidently composed on horseback during a prospecting expedition for minerals in 1777. Here is the Pindaric opening:

> *Dem Geier gleich*
> *Der auf schweren Morgenwolken*
> *Mit sanftem Fittich ruhend*
> *Nach Beute schaut,*
> *Schwebe mein Lied.*

> As the buzzard aloft
> On heavy daybreak cloud
> With easy pinion rests
> Searching for prey,
> May my song hover.

Here, despite the loss of the harsh sounds in line 1 (alliteration of hard *g*'s, assonance of *ei*), Goethe's suspended syntax, a single sentence draped over five lines with verb and subject coming only in the fifth, is re-created by Middleton in lines tightly woven to match the forward motion of the original. Again, the metaphor remains intact: the song, hovering in the air and waiting to complete itself even as the buzzard hovers, waiting for his prey. From this arresting opening, the poem moves relentlessly to its climax, its invocation to the Power that animates both the buzzard's world and the poet's.

Even more successful are Middleton's versions of the *Römische Elegien* (Roman Elegies), the openly erotic, secular, somewhat cynical poems of a Catullian or Propertian cast, written during Goethe's stay in Rome, where he first tasted the pleasure of sexual passion undisguised by the spiritual and ethical claims that had governed his liaison with Charlotte von Stein in the preceding Weimar years. In the "Second Elegy," for example, the poet thanks Amor (Cupid) for finding him a girl of humble origins whom he can enjoy without the fanfare—dinners, dances, parties, fancy clothes—associated with the courtship of society ladies:

> *Ekel bleibt mir Gezier und Putz, und hebet am Ende*
> *Sich ein brokatener Rock nicht wie ein wollener auf?*
> *Oder will sie bequem den Freund im busen verbergen,*
> *Wünscht er von alle dem Schmuck nicht schon behend sie befreit?*
> *Müssen nicht jene Juwelen und Spitzen, Polster und Fischbein*
> *Alle zusammen herab, eh er die Liebliche fühlt?*

Airs and finery bore me; when all's said and done, it's the same thing
   Whether the skirt you lift is of brocade or of wool.
Or if the wish of a girl is to pillow her lover in comfort,
   Wouldn't he first have her put all those sharp trinkets away?
All those jewels and pads, and the lace that surrounds her, the whalebone,
   Don't they all have to go, if he's to feel his beloved?

Here the effect depends largely on the tension between homely images (the bro-cade skirt versus the woolen one, the lace and whalebone undergarments) and the highly formalized verse structure of the elegiac distych (two unrhymed dac-tylic hexameters, the first, of 14 syllables, with a feminine ending, the second, of 13, with a caesura after the third stress [/ x / || / x x /] and masculine ending).

Middleton's version is somewhat more evasive than Goethe's (e.g., line 3 literally means "or if she wants to be free to bury her lover in her breast" rather than the euphemistic "pillow . . . in comfort"), but on the whole he skillfully re-creates the tone of Rococo artifice of the original, playing off the formal couplet against the colloquial force of a speaking voice that exhorts, ques-tions, and exclaims as it weighs its case in mock seriousness. No doubt, the secular playfulness of the *Roman Elegies* is more congenial to Middleton than are Goethe's more rapturous nature hymns, or again, his profoundly serious meditations on love like "To Charlotte von Stein" or the "Trilogy of Passion." And since Middleton's preference may well reflect that of most readers of the 1980s, his translations of the so-called classical poetry (see pp. 98–199) should find an enthusiastic audience in Anglo-America.

II

Hal Draper's English version of *The Complete Poems of Heine* is an altogether larger affair. The book blurb cryptically tells us that "Hal Draper is an inde-pendent writer now living in the San Francisco Bay Area. He began working on his translation of Heine's poetry in 1948 and completed the project in the mid-seventies." A quarter century of work, yet the author's own acknowledge-ments—to various friends and Heine experts—tell us little about the evolution of this labor of love. In his short introduction, Draper primarily explains why his edition, unlike, say Middleton's, is not bilingual. "My Heine," he says, "is intended for English-speaking readers, not for students of German literature. . . . The reader is invited to approach Heine as an experience in English."

This may or may not be a good idea. By omitting the German, Draper forces the reader to take the plunge into the whole poetic oeuvre without too much questioning; again, by omitting the German, he is able to include more: Heine's verse tragedies *Alamansor* and *William Ratcliff*, the Porg satires, *Atta Troll* and *Germany*, and many previously uncollected and unpublished poems. As such, Draper's Heine obviously marks an advance over what is, by Draper's own admission, "one of the great verse translations in English literature," namely, Louis Untermeyer's 1937 translation of the lyric poems. On the other hand, in making verse his principle of inclusion, Draper leaves out such important works as *The Harz Journey*, a so-called travel sketch that juxtaposes verse and prose passages, anecdote and dream sequence, political commentary and lyric effusion, in what is a curiously modern collage form. It might have been more interesting for the contemporary reader if Draper had included works like this one as well as such political texts as *Lutetia* rather than giving us still more folk ballads and songs of unrequited love.

But these are minor cavils. The strength of Draper's translation is, ironically, Middleton's weak point—the handling of stanzaic structure. Like Middleton, Draper chooses to follow the original:

Take the ancient problem of meter and rhyme: I confess that I have fallen in with those who tend to get fetishistic about these matters of form, and I have insisted on adhering to Heine's own rhyming and metrical patterns. . . . Justification? Perhaps it is the challenge. Perhaps one has the right to assume that there was good reason in the poet's art.

Does it work? Does Draper manage to convey the seeming ease and naturalness of the Heine lyric, its subtle shifting from "elevated" diction to colloquialism? Draper makes the analogy between his English version and the modern "art book":

The most expansively printed books with plates of great paintings by Veronese or Van Gogh or Vermeer, can only disappoint if you put the reproduction alongside the original. Yet they can give a great deal, if the original had a great deal to give in the first place.

And so Draper exhorts us to "take *this* Heine on his own terms: posing, declaiming, miming, complaining, accusing, lying, loving, lusting, hating, defaming, begging, horrifying, delighting—in other words, busy being Heine."

This is all very well but one could argue that, just as the art historian reviewing a book of Vermeer plates, can only assess their quality by comparing them to the actual paintings, so the critic had best begin by reading Draper's English version of Heine intertextually—that is, alongside its German source. To do this is to realize that, Draper's comments notwithstanding, his are not at all Poundian free renderings—poems to be read primarily in their own right—but, ironically, close line-by-line translations of the originals.

Heine's first major collection, *Das Buch der Lieder* (The Book of Songs) of 1827 was, by the time of the author's death in 1856, the most widely read book of poetry in world literature. Its seemingly simple folk songs, so many of which have been set to music, are actually highly complicated with respect to phrasing and rhythm; as in the case of Goethe, melopoeia dominates this poetry although Heine's structures are less elaborate than Goethe's, his favorite form being the four-line ballad stanza (alternating tetrameter and trimeter) rhyming *abab* or *abcb*. The imagery in these little poems is often quite tricky. Take the following:

> The lotus flower is drooping
> In the sun's majestic light,
> With lowered languid forehead
> Dreaming she waits for the night.
>
> The moon he is her lover;
> She wakes in his beams' embrace,
> To her lover alone unveiling
> The innocent flower of her face.
>
> She beams and gleams and glistens
> And gazes mutely above;
> She weeps scented tears and trembles
> With love and the pain of love.
> (*Lyrical Intermezzo*, No. 10)

> *Die Lotosblume ängstigt*
> *Sich von der Sonne Pracht,*
> *Und mit gesenktem Haupte*
> *Erwartet sie träumend die Nacht.*
>
> *Der Mond, der ist ihr Buhle,*
> *Er weckt sie mit seinem Licht,*
> *Und ihm entschleiert sie freundlich*
> *Ihr frommes Blumengesicht.*

> *Sie blüht und glüht und leuchtet*
> *Und starret stumm in die Höh;*
> *Sie duftet and weinet und zittert*
> *Vor Liebe und Liebesweh.*[5]

Syntactically, "The Lotus Flower" consists of a series of short declarative sentences; the poem has none of the suspension that makes Goethe's sentences, often draped over five or six lines, so difficult to translate. Again, each stanza has only one rhyme (lines 2 and 4); the rhymes, moreover, are semantically and syntactically unexceptional (a noun rhyming with a similar noun as in the case of "Nacht"/"Pracht"), in keeping with the tradition of folk song. Still, it is remarkable to what extent Draper has re-created the simplicity and subtlety of the original. Heine's poems seem to be based on no more than a botanical observation: the lotus reverses the rhythm of the normal flower, closing to the sun and opening only in the dark. But the poem ironizes this state of affairs, for the lotus is endowed with peculiar feelings of her own. In the first stanza, she is shown as shying away from the sunlight ("drooping" does not quite convey the force of "ängstigt sich") and anxiously awaiting the night. For the moon, her lover who arouses her, she unveils her "innocent" ("fromm" means "pious" and "devout" rather than merely "innocent") face, but then, in the third stanza, there is an odd shift. The innocent lotus flower becomes the aggressor, beaming and gleaming and glistening, weeping and trembling "With love and the pain of love." The poet has, in other words, projected onto the female flower his own sense of frustration and unrequited love. He is, in one sense, the sun spurned in stanza 1; he would like to be the moon that entices the maiden of stanza 2; he would like, moreover, to have the woman be the one who suffers. But all this is presented so delicately and economically that one barely notices the turn in stanza 3, in which the "simple" little nature poem takes on a slight edge of sadomasochism. Draper's version certainly conveys this delicate shift although not perhaps as fully as the original, whose final rhyme is approximate ("Höh"/"Liebesweh") as if to warn the reader that the ballad form, just like the natural communion described, fails to meet the expectations it arouses.

> A pine is standing lonely
> In the North on a bare plateau.
> He sleeps; a bright white blanket
> Enshrouds him in ice and snow.

He's dreaming of a palm tree
Far away in Eastern land
Lonely and silently mourning
On a sunburnt rocky strand.
(*Lyrical Intermezzo*, No. 33)

Ein Fichtenbaum steht einsam
Im Norden auf kahler Höh.
Ihm schläfert; mit weisser Decke
Umhüllen ihn Eis und Schnee.

Er träumt von einer Palme,
Die, fern im Morgenland,
Einsam und schweigend trauert
Auf brennender Felsenwand.

Like the lotus poem, this lyric begins on a narrative note: the poet is telling us a little story about a pine tree. But the fairy-tale rhythms and diction are deceptive: the vision embodied in the text is that of a universe in which desire, never to be satisfied, reigns supreme. For what does the little pine tree, buried in the northern snow, want but the one thing it can't have—its very opposite, the Southern palm? The poem juxtaposes North and South, ice and fire, dark and light, even as, paradoxically, both pine tree and palm tree are rooted in the same place—the pine "auf kahler Höh" (on a barren height or cliff), the palm "Auf brennender Felsenwand" (on a burning, and hence bare, wall of rock). Perhaps, in other words, desire and its object are really one and the same.

Here Draper's version falls short: to translate "brennender Felsenwand" as "sunburnt rocky strand," evidently for the sake of rhyme, is to do away with the paradoxical status of pine and palm. But the very change alerts us to something interesting: it makes us see, even more clearly than if we just read the poem in German, the economy of Heine's lyric, the slender means rigorously chosen so as to create the desired effect. Add or subtract a single word—in this case, the addition of "rocky strand"—and a central nuance will be lost.

Between the publication of *The Book of Songs* and *New Poems* (1844), Heine worked as dramatist, journalist, literary critic, pamphleteer. These varied interests had a decisive influence on the poetry: the new Paris lyric, especially the cycle *Sundry Women* (Verschiedene) is much more openly erotic, more cynical:

>The maid looked over the ocean
>And sighed with a worried frown;
>She sighed with deep emotion
>Because the sun went down.
>
>Dear girl, don't let it grieve you,
>It's an old trick, you will find;
>In front he sinks, to leave you
>And come again from behind. (p. 334)

Or, in a more comic vein:

>How shamefully you acted
>I've told no man—don't doubt it.
>I went instead out over the sea
>And told the fishes about it.
>
>On solid land, there only
>I've left you a reputation;
>But over the whole wide sea your shame's
>The topic of conversation. (p. 334)

Here the second stanza does not have the punch of the original, in which the subject, "deiner Schande" (your shame or your disgrace) is left for the final rhyme:

>*Ich lass dir den guten Namen*
>*Nur auf dem festen Lande;*
>*Aber im ganzen Ozean*
>*Weiss man von deiner Schande.*

Such twists of the knife often disappear in translation, but if we read "Seraphine," "Clarisse," "Diana," and the others in sequence, we will be struck by Heine's peculiarly modern eye for the sordid detail, the unpleasant truth behind the accepted convention. In "Yolande and Marie," for example, the poet presents himself ironically as torn between "love" for a mother and her daughter:

Now which one should I fall in love with?
Both keep me thoroughly beguiled.
The mother's still a lovely woman,
The daughter is a lovely child.

Pale face and inexperienced body—
They touch my heart, just to be seen!
Yet wiser eyes excite me also:
They know what tenderness can mean.

Here the language of romantic love—"fall in love," "beguiled," "touch my heart," "tenderness"—is exploded by the final metaphor:

My heart is like our friend the jackass
Who stood between two bales of hay
And vainly racked his brains debating
Which way the tastier fodder lay.

An adequate, if not wholly satisfactory, rendering of the German, in which the jackass is not named (Heine refers only to "the gray friend"), and the meaning is suspended until the last line:

Es gleicht mein Herz dem grauen Freunde,
Der zwischen zwei gebündel Heu
Nachsinnlich grübelt, welch von beiden
Das allerbeste Futter sei.

The lyrics of *Sundry Women* are, in any case, daring variations on the theme of sexuality as commodity; not surprisingly, they were spurned in the poet's native country as horribly immoral. In January 1844, four years before the Revolution of 1848, which was to play such a large part in his friend Karl Marx's thinking, as in his own, Heine wrote his great satiric poem *Germany, A Winter's Tale* (Deutschland, Ein Wintermärchen). A few months earlier, he had dared to return to Germany for a few weeks even though the Prussian authorities had issued a warrant for his arrest. Within six weeks after his return to Paris, he had completed his mock-epic, based on his journey from town to town. *Germany* has twenty-seven cantos ("caputs"), written in ballad quatrain; its main target is the reactionary sensibility of the Prussians, their apathy, servility, narrowness. The technique is ironic juxtaposition, as in:

> While the little girl warbled of heavenly joy
> In accents so uplifting,
> The Prussian customs men gave my bags
> A thorough searching and sifting. (p. 485)

Or comic simile, as in this stanza about the military:

> They still stalk about as straight as poles,
> And stiffly turned out you meet them,
> As if they just had swallowed the stick
> That once was used to beat them. (p. 487)

Throughout the poem, realism is laced with fantasy, myth, and legend, political allusion with sardonic accounts of the meal his mother serves him, an evening with old friends at the Café Lorenz in Hamburg, a night in a filthy featherbed at a provincial inn, and so on. But the poem is finally quite serious in its condemnation of a world where

> There are hells from which there is
> No possible liberation,
> Where neither the Saviour's pardon nor
> Any prayers can bring salvation. (p. 536)

Political change, not the yearning for deliverance, must finally provide an answer.

For the contemporary reader, Heine's mock-epic journey poem has a particular interest. The strict verse form may initially be off-putting, a violation of the postmodern drive toward open form and process poetics, the Olson-Creeley insistence that FORM IS NEVER MORE THAN THE EXTENSION OF CONTENT. But suppose we consider the ballad stanza used in *Germany* as a variant on the rule—any rule—poets like Jackson MacLow and John Cage are currently imposing on their work—say, so many characters per line or so many words containing a particular letter, and so on. The trick, in such cases, is to observe the rule even as one undermines it at every turn. So Heine introduces comic rhymes, extra stresses, verbal dissonances, digressions, dream sequences—all the stock-in-trade, in fact, of the *improvissatore* creating what has been called unforeseen discourse. Byron's *Don Juan* is a close analog but so, for that matter, are Pound's *Cantos* and, in a different way, James Merrill's *The Changing Light at Sandover*. Indeed, what Heine's satiric mode can teach us is that political poetry doesn't need to be, as some of our younger poets seem to think, endlessly high-minded, self-righteous, and outraged by the Tragedy-Of-It-All. The political life, even in El Salvador, is, as Eliot Weinberger has recently argued in a brilliant essay,[6] both compromised and complicated.

What makes Heine seem so oddly contemporary is his sensibility—his nervous energy, his candor, his ambivalence about radical politics, sexuality, family, nation—even about the afterlife. Like his own Ponce de Leon in the late great poem "Bimini," he yearns for the fountain of youth only to find that that fountain is also the river of death:

> Splendid waters! splendid land!
> Whosoever gets there never,
> Never leaves it—for this land
> Is the real Bimini.

A political radical who condemned the life of the German (as well as the French) bourgeoisie, Heine is also the poet who discovered, from the "mattress grave" where he spent the last eight years of his life, that *life*—any life at all—is infinitely precious. Like Goethe before him, he was at once *disenchanted* and yet wholly *engaged*. Hal Draper's translations give us a clear idea of Heine's broad range of interests as well as of his directness and concretion. "After Villon," said Pound, "[Heine is] the next poet for an absolutely clear palette."[7] A reproduction of that palette—like a plate in a good art book—is now before us, challenging us to visit the museum and see for ourselves.

Notes

1. "A Retrospect," in *Literary Essay of Ezra Pound*, ed. T. S. Eliot (London: Faber and Faber, 1954), 5.

2. "Foreword," Charles Baudelaire, *Les Fleurs du Mal: The Complete Text of The Flowers of Evil*, trans. Richard Howard (Boston: David R. Godine, 1982), xx.

3. I owe this information to Arthur Melville Clark, "Rhyme," in *Princeton Encyclopedia of Poetry and Poetics*, ed. Alex Preminger, enlarged ed. (Princeton, NJ: Princeton University Press, 1974), 707.

4. "Blank Verse," in *Princeton Encyclopedia of Poetry and Poetics*, p. 78.

5. The edition used is Heinrich Heine, *Sämtliche Werke* (Leipzig: Insel Verlag, 1911); despite its date, many scholars still regard this as the definitive edition. The poem in question appears in vol. 1, 74–75. All subsequent references are to this edition, designated SW; the roman numeral refers to the volume number.

6. Review of Carolyn Forché, *The Country Between Us*, in *Sulfur*, 6 (1983): 158–64.

7. "The Renaissance" (1914), in *Literary Essays of Ezra Pound*, 216.

CHAPTER 22
The French Connection

The introduction to the truly exemplary anthology of twentieth-century French poetry that Paul Auster has put together for Random House has as its epigraph Wallace Stevens' aphorism, "French and English constitute a single language." As Auster explains it:

> If not for the arrival of William and his armies on English soil in 1066, the English language as we know it would never have come into being. For the next three hundred years French was the language spoken at the English court, and it was not until the end of the Hundred Years' War that it became clear, once and for all, that France must be considered an "influence" on the development of English language and literature; French is a part of English, an irreducible element of its genetic make-up.

True enough, but the current French-translation fever testifies less to what Auster calls the "symbiosis" of French and English than to the sad fact that, after nine centuries, that symbiosis is being rapidly eroded. When Eliot wrote his French poems like "Lune de miel" and Pound translated Rimbaud, when Stevens included a French line in every section of "Sea Surface Full of Clouds," educated men and women still spoke and read French as a matter of course. Today, the situation is quite different: on the one hand, French critical theory dominates the universities but, as any check of college bookstores or reading lists would make amply clear, Derrida, Foucault, Paul Ricoeur, Jean-François

Review of *The Random House Book of Twentieth-Century French Poetry*, ed. Paul Auster; *A Tomb for Anatole*, by Stephane Mallarmé; *Poems of André Breton*, ed. and trans. Jean-Pierre Cauvin and Mary Ann Caws; *The Making of the Pré*, by Francis Ponge, trans. Lee Fahnenstock; and *The Collected Poetry*, by Aimé Césaire. *American Poetry Review* 13 (January–February 1984), 40–45.

Lyotard, and the rest are read almost exclusively in translation. Roland Barthes, for example, is, from the point of view of Americans, Richard Howard's Barthes, conveniently available in an ever-growing series of Noonday (Farrar Straus) paperbacks. Indeed the economics of the situation is, of course, wholly on the side of translation: in 1978, I purchased for $12.00 the Seuil edition of Derrida's *L'écriture et la différance*. The Phoenix (University of Chicago Press) translation by Alan Bass costs $6.95.

In a climate in which even French is coming to be regarded as the Exotic Other, we are beginning to see a number of collaborative translations in which an American poet works with a French scholar, as is the case with Clayton Eshleman and Annette Smith's *Aimé Césaire*. We have long accepted this situation when it comes to, say, Arabic or Hungarian (although even in the case of these languages, one wonders what it means to have A. furnish literal glosses that B. then renders "poetic"), but when the poetry to be translated is in French, it may strike us as problematic. Still, such joint translations, sponsored by major university presses, are probably the wave of the future.

Given our increasing monolingualism, it is all the more remarkable that a large commercial press like Random House would publish Paul Auster's anthology of twentieth-century French poetry. For the great thing about this anthology is that it presents us with its poets (from Apollinaire to the present, the cut-off date of birth being 1876) in the translations of precisely those British or American poets who have been most obviously and fruitfully drawn to them. As Auster explains:

> I have used already existing translations whenever possible. My motive has been to underscore the involvement, over the past fifty years, of American and British poets in the work of their French counterparts, and since there is abundant material to choose from (some of it hidden away in old magazines and out-of-print books, some of it readily available), there seemed to be no need to begin my search elsewhere. . . . Only in cases where translations did not exist or where the available translations seemed inadequate did I commission fresh translations. I have tried to arrange the marriage with care. My aim was to bring together compatible poets.

The result of this "matchmaking," as Auster calls it, is that *The Random House Book of Twentieth-Century French Poetry* becomes, among other things, a history of our own poetry. For to trace the lines of influence that connect, say, a Pierre Reverdy to a Kenneth Rexroth on the one hand and to a John Ashbery on the other is to learn much about the mainsprings of postmodernism. I use the latter term advisedly because, as Auster's selection makes abundantly clear, the great French poets of the early decades of the century—Apollinaire, Cendrars, Jacob, Reverdy, Éluard—become part of our own poetic landscape only after World War II. Auster's anthology also suggests that the time lag between French "Modernism" and its Anglo-American versions ceases to exist at some point in the early 1960s. Indeed, by the early 1980s, when a poet like Michael Palmer is translating Emmanuel Hocquard, and Paul Auster himself, Philippe Denis, the energy may well be flowing the other way: certainly the "Language Movement" is influencing French poets rather than vice-versa. It may of course be that the contemporary poets included by Auster—Jean Daive, Alain Delahaye, Anne-Marie Albiach—are not the ones a later generation will judge to be the central ones. Or again, it may be that the best French writers are currently working in modes other than lyric poetry. Whatever the answer, it seems safe to say that the last hundred pages or so of the *Random House Book* have less broad appeal than what precedes them.

Auster's book opens, appropriately enough, with Apollinaire's pivotal voyage poem "Zone," translated by Samuel Beckett. I have written of this translation elsewhere,[1] but let me just say here that what Beckett has done is to give us a kind of black-and-white version of Apollinaire's technicolor narrative, toning down its exuberance, eliminating its rhymes and onomatopoeia, and heightening its sense of anxiety:

> *Aujourd'hui tu marches dans Paris les femmes sont ensanglantés*
> *C'était et je voudrais ne pas m'en souvenir c'était au déclin*
> *de la beauté.*

> Today you walk in Paris the women are bloodred
> It was and would I forget it was at beauty's ebb.

The Apollinaire section also contains Richard Wilbur's verse rendition of "Le Pont Mirabeau," especially commissioned by Auster, who calls it "the first acceptable version of this important poem we have had in English." He may well be right: Wilbur gives us a very close approximation of the particular blend of childlike lyricism and nervous dissonance that characterizes the early Apollinaire:

> *L'amour s'en va comme cette eau courante*
> *L'amour s'en va*
> *Comme la vie est lente*
> *Et comme l'Espérance est violente*

Vienne la nuit sonne l'heure
Les jours s'en vont je demeure

All love goes by as water to the sea
All love goes by
How slow life seems to me
How violent the hope of love can be

Let night come on bells end the day
The days go by me still I stay

Equally remarkable are Paul Blackburn's hitherto unpublished versions of "Automne malade" and "Cors de chasse." The ending of the former posed a formidable problem Blackburn solves nicely. For the intricate sound echoes of the original:

Toutes leur larmes en automne feuille à feuille
Les feuilles
Qu'on foule
Un train
Qui roule
La vie
S'écoule

he substitutes visual patterning:

tears in the fall, leaf by leaf
The leaves
one tramples
underfoot
A train
rolls on
The life that
runs
out

What Blackburn understood is that the poem's sense of autumnal hush of muted grief could not be conveyed in English by replicating Apollinaire's rhymes ("foule"/"roule"/"s'écoule"), that in English rhyme in alternating two-stress lines would be excessively prominent, indeed almost comic. Accordingly, he chose the Imagist solution, letting word choice and placement on the page approximate the poem's dying fall.

Blackburn's and Wilbur's may well be isolated successes; the case of Ron Padgett's version of Apollinaire's "La Petite Auto" is different, for this *calligramme* is easily seen as a precursor of Frank O'Hara's "I do this, I do that" poems as well as of Padgett's own buoyant lyric. It begins:

> *Le 31 du mois d'août 1914*
> *Je partis de Deauville un peu avant minuit*
> *Dans la petite auto de Rouveyre*
>
> *Avec son chauffeur nous étions trois*
>
> *Nous dîmes adieu à toute une époque*
> *Des géants furieux se dressaient sur l'Europe*
> *Les aigles quittaient leur aire en attendant le soleil*
> *Les poissons voraces montaient des abîmes*
> *Les peuples accouraient pour se connaître à fond*
> *Les morts tremblaient de peur dans leurs sombres demeures*

which Padgett translates:

> The 31st day of August 1914
> I left Deauville a little before midnight
> In Rouveyre's little car
>
> With his driver there were three of us
>
> We said goodbye to an entire epoch
> Furious giants were rising over Europe
> The eagles were leaving their aeries expecting the sun
> The voracious fish were rising from the depths
> The masses were rushing toward some deeper understanding
> The dead were trembling with fear in their dark dwellings

This has a colloquial force and energy often absent from the more scholarly translations of Apollinaire. In her definitive bilingual edition of the *Calligrammes* (University of California Press, 1980), Anne Hyde Greet translates lines 7–10 as follows:

Eagles flew from their eyrie to wait for the sun
Voracious fish ascended from abysses
Nations hurled together so they might learn to know one another
The dead trembled fearfully in their dark dwellings

Padgett's version has the advantage of immediacy; the verb forms ("were leaving," "were rising"), for example, give the reader the sense that these things were happening at the very moment (the crucial August 31, 1914, a little before midnight), on the eve of the Great War. Greet's translation of line 9 may be more literal than Padgett's, but his elicits from the text a meaning central to the whole poem: the poignant and mistaken faith that the war could somehow be a threshold to a new knowledge of reality. As for the picture-poem itself, the headline "MARÉCHAUX-FERRANTS RAPPELÉS" is nicely translated by Padgett as "BLACKSMITHS CALLED UP," a phrase I find more appropriate in the context than Greet's "FARRIERS SUMMONED." Altogether, Padgett succeeds in giving us a racy, colloquial poem that can be understood quite independently of the parent text even as it stays very close to the spirit of Apollinaire.

The standard set by the Apollinaire section is maintained in the selections that follow. It is, for instance, a special pleasure to read Max Jacob's prose poems in the versions of John Ashbery and Jerome Rothenberg, for it makes us realize how closely Jacob's black humor and dislocated narrative prefigure elements in their work. And further: just as Jacob looks ahead to poets as different from one another as Ashbery and Rothenberg, so Léon-Paul Fargue's late Symbolist city-scapes strike a responsive chord in a contemporary prose poet like Lydia Davis even as they appealed, on very different grounds, to Wallace Stevens. When Stevens originally read his "Paraphrases" (actually quite literal translations) of Fargue at the Poetry Center in New York in 1951,[2] he remarked on Fargue's affinities to Mallarmé and Valéry. But more interesting for us than this obvious connection is the link to Stevens's own poetry: here, for example, is his version of Fargue's "Une Odeur nocturne":

The lamp sings its slight song quietly, subdued as the song one hears in a shell. The lamp reaches out its placating hands. In its aureole, I hear the litanies, the choruses and the responses of flies. It lights up the flowers at the edge of the terrace. The nearest ones come forward timidly to see me, like a troop of dwarfs that discover an ogre.

Fargue's imagery turns up in the "barely lit" landscape of Stevens's "A Quiet Normal Life":

Here in his house and in his room,
In his chair, the most tranquil thoughts grew peaked.

And the oldest and warmest heart was cut
By gallant notions on the part of night—
Both late and alone, above the crickets' chords,
Babbling, each one, the uniqueness of its sound.
There was no fury in transcendent forms.
But his actual candle blazed with artifice.[3]

But note that Stevens tempers Fargue's lyricism and brings out the irony of the "gallant notions" of his winter scene. Lydia Davis, on the other hand, seems to be interested in Fargue's quasi-Objectivist concentration on *things*, on objects: "A crooked Argand lamp, the color of burnt onion. Its thin arm. Its tinkling kindles it."

As we make our way through the Auster anthology—and there is no way to do it justice here—certain patterns begin to manifest themselves. Beckett, as his translation of Breton and Éluard suggest, has a taste for Surrealism; it would be interesting to explore this taste further and look at Beckett's own early work from a Surrealist perspective. Ashbery's predilections are alternately for the fantastic, as in Jacob, or the austere, minimal mode of Reverdy and later, of Marcelyn Pleynet, the poet of *Tel Quel* who has, like Ashbery, written a good deal of art criticism. Galway Kinnell, not surprisingly, translates Yves Bonnefoy, whose use of hallucinatory dream imagery in straightforward syntactic structures (strings of noun phrases or of simple declarative sentences) parallel his own:

Je nommerai désert ce château que tu fus,
Nuit cette voix, absence ton visage,
Et quand tu tomberas dans la terre stérile
Je nommerai néant l'éclair qui t'a porté.

I will name wilderness the castle which you were,
Night your voice, absence your face,
And when you fall back into sterile earth
I will name nothingness the lightning which bore you.
("Vrai Nom")

A comparable symbiosis takes place between René Char and W. S. Merwin, poets both drawn to the isolated mysterious image, an image that resonates with possible significations. Indeed, Merwin, whose own poetry sometimes seems too easy, too willing to settle for a vague mysteriousness rather than a genuine mystery, is at his best when presented by the challenge of such structures as Char's "Victoire éclair," which begins on the arresting note:

L'oiseau bêche la terre,
Le serpent sème.

The bird tills the soil,
The serpent sows.

and tries to come to terms with the spiritual conversion in which "Avec la lente neige descendent les lépreux" (The lepers come down with the slow snow) and the poet nevertheless experiences "l'amour, l'égal de la terreur" (love, the equal of terror), in the form of a hand he has never seen that puts out the fire and "straightens" the sun. Merwin's version of Char's poem strikes me as virtually a model of what translation should be: even the assonance of "Avec la lente neige descendent les lepreux" is replicated in Merwin's "slow snow."

Another especially successful act of "matchmaking" is that between André Breton and his poet-translators from Edouard Roditi to David Antin. Austin's selection can be usefully compared to Jean-Pierre Cauvin and Mary Ann Caws's new bilingual anthology, *Poems of André Breton*. This book serves an important need, for Breton continues to be known to English-speaking audiences chiefly as the author of the *Manifestos of Surrealism* and possibly the novel *Nadja* even as his arcane poetry has remained inaccessible. Caws's excellent preface and Cauvin's fine critical essay, "The Poethics of André Breton," which serves as an introduction to the volume, should help readers to familiarize themselves with such Bretonian notions as *dépaysement* ("the sense of being out of one's element, of being disoriented in the presence of the uncanny"), *disponibilité* (the "constant receptivity to revelatory signs and events" as well as the "eagerness to invite the occurrence of such phenomena"), and *le hasard objectif* (objective chance). Cauvin is especially good at defining Breton's dialectic (the interplay of masculine and feminine images) and the poet's highly disjunctive, centrifugal syntax. Thus he usually lists and exemplifies for us the syntactic features of automatic writing à la Breton: (1) "Interruption and resumption," (2) "Abrupt shifts in registers of language," (3) "Ambiguity and disjunction by syntactical rearrangement, scrambling, or inversion"; (4) "Abrupt shifts by ellipsis or grammatical shortcutting"; (5) "Hinge words—words straddling two otherwise unrelated words or phrases, thereby conjoining them into word play"; and (6) "the frequent use of certain prepositions, chiefly *à* and *de*, notable for their versatility . . . their agglutinative virtue" (pp. xxxi–xxxv). According to Cauvin:

> The most striking example [of these prepositions] is found in the aptly titled *L'Union libre* [Free Union]. Perhaps Breton's best-known poem, whose 60 lines emblazoning the female body are constructed entirely by means of images introduced by *à* (52 times) and fused by *de* (108 times). . . . The poem is a dazzling litany of surrealist love images connected by repetition alone, without the aid of conjunctions or main-clause verbs.

Given this interesting account of Breton's style, the actual translation of "L'Union libre" is a bit stiff. Breton's opening:

> *Ma femme à la chevelure de feu de bois*
> *Aux pensées d'éclairs de chaleur*
> *A la taille de sablier*
> *Ma femme à la taille de loutre entre les dents du tigre*
> *Ma femme à la bouche de cocarde et de bouquet d'étoiles de*
> > *dernière grandeur.*

is translated by Caws and Cauvin as follows:

> Woman of mine with woodfire hair
> With thoughts like flashes of heat lightning
> With an hourglass waist
> Whose waist is the waist of an otter caught in the teeth of a tiger's teeth
> Woman of mine with a rosette mouth like a posy of stars of
> > ultimate magnitude.

Compare this to David Antin's version:

> My wife whose hair is a brush fire
> Whose thoughts are summer lightning
> Whose waist is an hourglass
> Whose waist is the waist of an otter caught in the teeth of a tiger
> Whose mouth is a bright cockade with the fragrance of a star of
> > the first magnitude. (Auster, 153)

The French language doesn't distinguish between "woman" and "wife" (Ma femme), but, whichever way we take it, "Woman of mine" seems unnecessarily labored. Antin, who settles for "My wife," leaves himself room to spin out the rest with a series of "Whose . . ." clauses whereas the Caws-Cauvin text insists on the repetition "Woman of mine." Again, Antin renders Breton in American syntax:

Whose waist is the waist of an otter caught in the teeth of a tiger

rather than the literal "Woman of mine with an otterlike waist" and the liberties he takes with line 5 seem to me to give us the perfect counterpart of Bretonian dépaysement. Equally brilliant, I think, is Antin's translation of "Une Branche d'ortie entre par la fenêtre," which begins:

> La femme au corps de papier peint
> La tanche rouge des cheminées
> Dont la mémoire est faite d'une multitude de petits abreuvoirs
>   Pour les navires au loin.

> The woman with the crepe paper body
> The red fish in the fireplace
> Whose memory is pieced together from a multitude of small
>   watering places for distant ships.

Compare this to the more literal translation by Caws and Cauvin:

> The woman with the wallpaper body
> The red tench of chimneys
> Whose memory is made up of a multitude of small drinking
>   troughs
> For faraway ships.

"Papier peint" does mean "wallpaper": "tench," Cauvin's note tells us, is "a European fresh-water cyprinoid fish." All well and good, but the Bretonian erotic "frisson" is conveyed, much more graphically, I think, by Antin's reference to a "crepe paper body" and to a "red fish" (never mind what species) "in the fire-place" (quite correct for "des cheminées") rather than "of chimneys." Again, in line 3, it makes more sense to translate "abreuvoirs" as "watering places" (one of its dictionary meanings) rather than "drinking troughs"—a phrase that under-mines rather than enhances the mood of sexual arousal.

I don't wish to carp excessively on what strike me as occasionally awkward locutions in the Cauvin-Caws translation, for we are, I think, fortunate to have before us a volume containing for the first time such a large selection of Breton's difficult poems, as well as much useful scholarly apparatus. Success in translation is, of course, relative, and the David Antin versions of Breton are characterized by the special empathy of one poet for another whose sense of fantasy is akin to his own. It is Auster's particular matchmaking genius—his ability, say, to recognize that Cendrars should be read in the now fifty-year-old translations of Dos Passos or Éluard in those of Beckett, whereas Breton is most accessible in the contemporary translations of a David Antin or a Michael Benedikt, that makes *The Random House Book of Twentieth-Century French Poetry* such a genuinely poetic event. My only reservation—and it is a very minor one—is that I wish Auster's bibliographical aids were fuller. The dates of first publication, for example, might well have been supplied after each poem: surely, especially in the case of poets like Ponge and Char whose work spans many decades, it would be helpful to know when a particular poem was written or first published. The date of translation should also be entered. Perhaps, in a second edition, these omissions can be rectified.

II

This has been a prolific year for Paul Auster. North Point has just published his translation of Mallarmé's *Pour un tombeau d'Anatole*, the 202 fragmentary notebook entries made by the poet during the terrible illness of his eight-year-old son Anatole in the spring and autumn of 1879, an illness that led to the boy's death on October 6. The intensely private fragments, jotted down at odd moments, were not intended for publication; they were preserved by Mallarmé's heir, Mme. E. Bonniot, who delivered them in a soft red box to the critic Jean-Pierre Richard. The latter deciphered, edited, and published them in a scholarly edition in 1961. As Auster explains it, Richard was of two minds about the notes:

On the one hand: wariness. Although he was deeply moved by the fragments, he was uncertain whether publication was appropriate, given the intensely private nature of the work. He concluded, however, that anything that could enhance our understanding of Mallarmé would be valuable.

Then, too, Richard argued—and Auster agrees—that the fragments testify to Mallarmé's "very vivid sensibility" beneath the carefully composed mask of serenity and objectivity.

The publication of *A Tomb for Anatole* raises interesting questions about the nature of poetic fragmentation. Auster comments:

> As they stand now, the notes are a kind of ur-text, the raw data of the poetic process. Although they seem to resemble poems on the page, they should not be confused with poetry per se. Nevertheless, more than one hundred years after they were written, they are perhaps closer to what we today consider possible in poetry than at the time of their composition. For here we find a language of immediate contact, a syntax of abrupt, lightning shifts that still manages to maintain a sense, and in their brevity, the sparse presence of their words, we are given a rare and early example of isolate words able to span the enormous mental spaces that lie between them. . . . Unlike Mallarmé's finished poems, these fragments have a startlingly unmediated quality. . . . in spite of everything, the Anatole notes do carry the force of poetry.

"The language of immediate contact," a "syntax of abrupt lightning shifts," a "startlingly unmediated quality"—one expects a series of elusive, enigmatic fragments on the order of Ashbery's *The Tennis Court Oath* or perhaps John Cage's *Theme & Variations*. But the characteristic fragment in *A Tomb for Anatole* reads as follows:

> *famille parfaite*
> *equilibre*
> > *père fils*
> > *mère fille*

> *rompu—*
> *trois, un vide*
> *entre nous,*
> > *cherchant.*

> family perfect
> balance
> > father son
> > mother daughter
> broken—
> three, a void
> among us,
> > searching. (#76)

"Fragmentation," says the editor of a new collection of essays on the subject, "implies breakage (*frangere*), a part detached, separated, or isolated from a whole—an incomplete work or a portion of writing or a composition that appears to be disconnected or disjointed, an interruption of the so-called aesthetic unity of an artefact."[4] By this definition, Mallarmé's notebook entries are not in fact fragments: far from being disjunct parts, juxtaposed to one another in a new collage structure, they are synecdochic, the part standing, as in the sample above, for the whole. Thus "famille parfaite" is a perfectly coherent shorthand statement: one need only fill in the blanks to get the following: "Our family was perfect when it had the proper balance: father, son, mother and daughter. Now this balance has been broken. There are only three and hence a void among us, us who keep searching for." A similar shorthand occurs again and again, as, for example, in #96:

> mother's fears
>   —he stopped
>   playing
>   today
>
> father listens—sees
>   the mother's eyes
>   —allows to be cared for
> and dreams

III

Poignant as such notebook entries are, I do not myself see how they "carry the force of poetry," as Auster argues. If, for that matter, we compare the "Anatole notes" to the poetic fragments to be found in Ponge's *The Making of the Pré*, the difference becomes clear.

La Fabrique du Pré was first published by Skira in 1971 as part of a series exploring relationships between literature and art. It is a prose meditation in diary form (the entries range from 1960 to 1964) on the gradual creation of the poem "Le Pré" (The meadow), published separately in 1964. The French edition includes illustrations that repeat the productive milieu of the text, images that were in Ponge's mind during the writing and occasionally noted in the text. Chagall's *pré*, for example, faces the margin note that cites it, and an aerial photograph shows Virgil's Lombardy plain, so often evoked in "Sat prata biberunt" (The meadows have drunk their fill).

In the English version, the translator Lee Fahnenstock includes these illustrations, the first being a color photograph of the meadow itself, a particular *pré* at Chambon-sur-Lignon. The book presents, on facing pages, reproductions of Ponge's manuscript (on the left) and on the right an English-language replica of the manuscript in print. We can thus follow, step by step, what Fahnenstock calls Ponge's "love affair with language"—his phonic, semantic, syntactic, and graphic variations on the pré. As Ponge remarks in the entry for October 15, 1960:

> *Le pré est le bien de la decision. pré*
> *Tout y est prêt pour cela. La nature l'a prêté, apprêté pour*
> *cela, tout ye est preparé. . . . Il est rasé au plus près . . .*
> *C'est le bien de la dispute des clercs.*
> *Le lieu du combat bref.*

> The pré is the field of decision. *pré*
> Everything there is ready for it, prêt. Nature has loaned it,
> *prêté*, readied for it, *apprêté*, everything there is
> prepared. . . . It is most closely shaven, au *plus prèsi* . . .
> It is the place of dispute for the scholars
> The field of brief combat.

In subsequent entries, Ponge explores the relationship of *pré* to such cognates as *proche* and *proximité*; indeed, in the course of the meditation, the meadow becomes the language "field" itself; the object of vision is carefully unlayered:

> green
>   A bird there scratches the sky with an acute accent, in
> inverse direction, therefore, to writing.
>   The bird with his acute accent scratches the sky there in
> the sense inverse to writing (and thus of signification).
> Recalling the concrete, reawakens the memory, rends the meaning.

This fragmentary bird image gives way, on the next page, to a series of aphorisms about the relation of painting to "reality" that recalls Magritte's "Ceci n'est pas une pipe":

> To take a tube of green, and spread it on the page, that does
> not make a pré.

They are born otherwise.
They well up from the page
And besides, the page must be brown.

Finally, when we have all but lost sight of the originating impulse of Ponge's meditation, we come to the heavy buff paper on which the poem itself is printed both in English and in French. Lee Fahnenstock's translation of Ponge's free verse, as of his fragmentary prose, is remarkably successful; consider the following:

Fragile, mais non frangible,
La terre vegétale y reprend parfois le dessus
Où les petits sabots du poulain qui y galopa le marquèrent,
Où le piétinement vers l'abreauvoir des bestiaux qui lentement
S'y préciptèrent.

Fragile but not frangible,
The vegetal earth at times takes over again
Where the little hooves of a galloping colt have scarred it,
Or the trampling of the cattle in their lumbering haste
Toward the watering place.

It is true that Ponge's free-verse line, with its concrete, literal images and relatively straightforward syntax, presents the translator with fewer problems than, say, the Surrealist fantasies of Breton; still, Fahnenstock must be commended for her attention to nuance: notice, for example, the slight semantic shift created by translating "le marquerent" as "have scarred it"—a shift that effectively creates alliteration of *r*'s that matches that of the original ("terre—marquèrent").

IV

I turn finally to what will surely be considered one of the most important translations from the French in 1973—Clayton Eshleman and Annette Smith's *Collected Poetry of Aimé Césaire*. A number of these translations had already appeared in Paul Auster's anthology, but it takes more than a handful of short poems to give the reader a sense of Césaire's astonishing poetic power, and the new California bilingual edition puts the entire lyric corpus before us for the first time.

The Afro-Caribbean poet Aimé Césaire was born in 1913 in the then French colony Martinique. Creole was the first language of all black Martinicans, but

Césaire's lower-middle-class parents made strenuous efforts to secure their son the best French education possible: at eighteen, he won a scholarship to the famous Lycée Louis-le-Grand in Paris which, in turn, paved the way for his entrance to the École Normale. In the Paris of the 1930s, two influences converged to shape Césaire's future poetry: the Surrealism of André Breton and his circle, and the new interest in African ethnography, especially the work of Leo Frobenius. As Michael Leiris put it in his 1965 essay "Qui est Aimé Césaire?" (an English translation by A. James Arnold appeared in *Sulfur* 5 [1982]):

> Césaire found in surrealism a way of looking at the world that had to appeal to him. Wasn't surrealism in open revolt against the entire framework of western rationalism, which the European intellectuals assembled around Breton rejected as an intolerable tyranny, less tolerable still for a Black Antillean since that framework is, historically, the one the White *superimposed*, so to speak, on the slaves they imported from Africa and on their descendants?

Together with the African poet and statesman-to-be Léopold Senghor, Césaire developed the concept of *négritude*, which signifies not, as is often thought, "Blackness first," the belief in African superiority, but rather, as Leiris explains, the right to be what one *is*, the right to "remain *different*":

> For Césaire to be conscious of his negritude and to be conscious of it as Martinican demands that he pursue from the start two objectives: politically, to free his country of forms of economic exploitation that condemn the masses to pauperism; culturally, to bring the specifically Antillean element into proper relief, which implies that without underestimating the role of western civilization one must turn toward the African heritage that is so often forgotten or denied by colored Antilleans who want only to be first-class Frenchmen.

These are precisely the themes that find their way into Césaire's first great poem, the long *Cahier d'un retour au pays natal* (Notebook of a Return to the Native Land), published in its first version in 1939, when Césaire returned to Martinique. In the years that followed, Césaire became actively engaged in politics: first as editor of the radical journal *Tropiques*, then as a member of the fledgling Martinican Communist party which, at the end of World War II, elected him mayor of Fort-de-France and the same year as deputy to the Première Assemblée Nationale Constituante in Paris, where he participated in the formation of the new constitution of the Fourth Republic. In the decade that followed, Césaire wrote most of his lyric poetry; he also began to turn away from Communism and officially broke with the party in 1956 when the Soviets invaded Hungary. The precise nature of his Marxist philosophy is, as Smith and Eshleman point out, a complicated question: suffice it to say here that in 1958 he founded the independent socialist Martinican Progressive Party (PPM), which has been returned to the French legislature in every subsequent election. A strong supporter of the Mitterrand government, Césaire continues to write—in the last two decades chiefly drama and essays—and to engage in the cause of Martinican independence.

The appeal of Césaire's poetry depends, I think, on its particular blend of an indigenous vitalism, a violent energy that celebrates the irrational, the strange, even the bestial, with a French sophistication, wit, and learning. If, as Eshleman and Smith note, the poetry is "a perpetual scene of dismemberment and mutilation," if it goes so far as to celebrate cannibalism as that which "symbolically eradicates the distinction between the I and the Other, between human and nonhuman, between what is (anthropologically) edible and what is not, and, finally, between the subject and the object," it is also a self-consciously literary poetry, full of echoes of Rimbaud (especially the Rimbaud of the *Saison en enfer*), Lautrémont, Baudelaire, and Mallarmé. Again, if Césaire's rhythms are influenced by African dances and voodoo rituals, his syntax is so Latinate and his vocabulary so esoteric, that it brings to mind the reference shelf rather than the tribal dance. Jean-Paul Sartre sums it up nicely in a comment cited on the book jacket of the Eshleman-Smith translation:

> In Aimé Césaire the great surrealist tradition draws to a close, achieves its definitive meaning and is destroyed: surrealism, a European movement in poetry is snatched from the Europeans by a black man who turns it against them and assigns a rigorously defined function to it . . . a Césaire poem explodes and whirls about itself like a rocket, suns burst forth whirling and exploding like new suns—it perpetually surpasses itself.

The rocket analogy is a good one: Césaire's is nothing if not an explosive poetry. The *Notebook of a Return to the Native Land*, for example, is a 1,055-line exorcism (part prose, part free verse) of the poet's "civilized" instincts, his lingering shame at belonging to a country and a race so abject, servile, petty, and repressed as his. A paratactic catalog poem that piles up phrase upon phrase, image upon image, in a complex network of repetitions, its thrust is to define the threshold between sleep and waking—the sleep of oppression, the blind acceptance of the status quo, that gives way to rebirth, to a new awareness of what is and may be. Accordingly, it begins with the refrain line, repeated again and again in the first section of the poem, "*Au bout du petit matin*" ("At the end of the earliest morning"—a purposely literal reference to dawn, which Eshleman and Smith awkwardly render as "At the end of the wee hours"), followed by a strophe that characterizes the poet's initial anguish, an anguish always laced with black humor:

Va-t'en, lui disais-je, gueule de flic, gueule de vache, va-t'en je déteste les larbins de l'ordre et les hannetons de l'espérance. Va-t'en mauvais gris-gris, punaise de moinillon. Puis je me tournais vers des paradis pour lui et les siens perdus, plus calme que la face d'une femme qui ment, et là, bercé par les effluves d'une pensée jamais lasse je nourrissais le vent, je délaçais les montres et j'entendais monter de l'autre côté du désastre, un fleuve de tourterelles et de trèfles de la savane que je porte toujours dans mes profondeurs à hauteur inverse du vingtième étage des maisons les plus insolentes et par précaution contre la force putréfiante des ambiances crépusculaires, arpentée nuit et jour d'un sacré soleil vénérien.

Beat it, I said to him, you cop, you lousy pig, beat it, I detest the flunkies of order and the cockchafers of hope. Beat it evil grigri, you bedbug of a petty monk. Then I turned toward paradises lost for him and his kin, calmer than the face of a woman telling lies, and there, rocked by the flux of a never exhausted thought I nourished the wind, I unlaced the monsters and heard rise, from the other side of disaster, a river of turtledoves and savanna clover, which I carry forever in my depths height deep as the twentieth floor of the most arrogant houses and as a guard against the putrefying force of crepuscular surroundings, surveyed night and day by a cursed venereal sun.

Here we have the hallmarks of Césaire's style: impassioned direct address ("Va-t'en"), name-calling ("gueule de flic," "gueule de vache"), parallel constructions that aren't quite parallel ("les larbins de l'orde et les hannetons de l'espérance"), hyperbole ("la force putréfiante des ambiances crépuscalaires"), oxymoron ("dans mes profondeurs à hauteur inverse du vingtième étage des maisons les plus insolent"), violent imagery ("sacré soleil vénérien"), and above all the chantlike rhythm created by the repetition of word and sound, as in "je nourrissais . . . je délaçais . . . j'entendais" or in "de l'autre côté du désastre, un fleuve de tourterelles et de trèfles."

There is really nothing comparable to this mode in American poetry. In the long catalog poems of Allen Ginsberg and Imamu Baraka, we find similarly impassioned repetition, parallelism, hyperbole; again, in a sequence like Galway Kinnell's *The Book of Nightmares*, we meet imagery of perhaps equal violence and stringency. But Césaire's poetry is quite different from Ginsberg's on the one hand or Kinnell's on the other in its curious conjunction of an intense realism (in the course of the *Notebook*, the topography of Martinique, its climate, architecture, and inhabitants are graphically described) with a surrealism that seems so inevitable it may also escape our attention.

Who is it, for instance, that the poet meets "Au bout du petit matin"—a cop or a "bedbug of a petty monk"? Or both? If the former, then the paradise lost he cannot attain is one of a primitive society that had not learned the need for law enforcement. If the latter, the enemy is primarily Christianity. These are, of course, part and parcel of the same complex for Césaire, but the point I am trying to make is that his is a language so violently charged with meaning that each word falls on the ear (or hits the eye) with resounding force. On "the other side of disaster," we read, there is "a river of turtledoves and savanna clover" that the poet carries so deep within himself that it surpasses the height of the most insolent twenty-floor house. But what is the disaster that has occurred? It will take the whole length of the poem to find out. And in the course of the poem, the town, "plate-étalée" (sprawled flat) like Van Gogh's little town in *The Starry Night*, must explode:

> *Elle rampe sur les mains sans jamais aucune envie de vriller le ciel d'une stature de protestation. Les dos des maisons ont peur du ciel truffé de feu, leurs pieds des noyades du sol, elles ont opté de se poser superficielles entre les surprises et les perfidies. Et pourtant elle avance la ville. Même qu'elle paît tous les jours outre sa marée de corridors carrelés, de persiennes pudibondes, de cours gluantes, de peintures qui dégoulinent. Et de petits scandales étouffés, de petites hontes tués, de petites haines immenses pétrissent en bosses et creux les rues étroites où le ruisseau grimace longitudinalement pari l'étron.*

It crawls on its hands without the slightest desire to drill the sky with a stature of protest. The backs of the houses are afraid of the sky truffled with fire, their feet of the drownings of the soil, they chose to perch shallowly between surprises and treacheries. And yet it advances, the town does. It even grazes every day further out into its tide of tiled corridors, prudish shutters, gluey courtyards, dripping paintwork. And petty hushed up scandals, petty unvoiced guilts, petty immense hatreds knead the narrow streets into bumps and potholes where the waste waters grin longitudinally thorough turds.

What strikes me as especially remarkable here and in Césaire's Surrealist lyrics in *Les Armes Miraculeuses* (The Miraculous Weapons) of 1946 is the total absence of sentimentality or self-pity. He can see himself as:

—moi sur une route, enfant, mâchant
une racine de canne à sucre
—trainé hamme sur une route sanglante
une corde au cou
—debout au milieu d'un cirque immense
sur mon front noir une couronne de daturas
voum rooh

—me on a road, a child chewing
sugar cane root
—a dragged man on a blood-spattered road
a rope around his neck
—standing in the center of a huge circus,
on my black forehead a crown of daturas
voum rooh

without casting about for a scapegoat. For, as the "I" comes to realize in the course of the poem, "Nous vomissure de négrier" (We the vomit of slave ships) must exorcise our own cowardice, fear, and hypocrisy before change can take place:

Et voici ceux qui ne se consolent point de n'être pas faits à la ressemblance de Dieu mais du diable, ceux qui considèrent que l'on est nègre comme commis de seconde classe: en attendant mieux et avec possibilité de monter plus haut; ceux qui battent la chamade devant soi-même; ceux qui vivent dans un cul de basse-fosse de soi-même; ceux qui disent à l'Europe: "Voyez, je sais comme vous faire des courbettes, comme vous présenter mes hommages, en somme, je ne suis pas différent de vous; ne faites pas attention à ma peau noire: c'est le soleil qui m'a brûlé."

And there are those who will never get over not being made in the likeness of God but of the devil, those who believe that being a nigger is like being a second-class clerk; waiting for a better deal and upward mobility; those who beat the drum of compromise in front of themselves, those who live in their own dungeon pit; those who say to Europe: "You see, I can bow and scrape, like you I pay my respects, in short, I am no different from you: pay no attention to my black skin: the sun did it."

Césaire, as the classical scholar Gregson Davis, himself a black Caribbean, argued in an essay of 1977, is notoriously difficult to translate. The use of arcane diction, technical vocabulary, Creole and African terms, homonyms, and neologisms, presents the translator with formidable problems, but, what is worse, Césaire's syntax seems to be, in Davis's words, "disordered and lubricious; and the lubricity, real or apparent, is partly a function of the total absence of punctuation."[5] (This is less the case in *Notebook* than in the later work). It is often difficult to know whether a given adjectival modifier belongs to one noun or another; again, so Davis argues, Césaire's "specialized lyric vocabulary," especially his sequences of metaphors, cannot be tampered with without destroying the whole poetic structure. "Interpretation," he insists, "should take into account the total symbolic system of the lyric *oeuvre*."

Eshleman and Smith, who refer to Davis's cautionary statements in their own "Translators' Notes," have clearly taken his lessons to heart. They affirm their desire to preserve Césaire's odd syntax as fully as possible and to reproduce his verbal patterns. Indeed, so careful are they to be literal, that they embed certain of the West Indian or technical terms in the English translation, for example:

Au bout du petit matin, le morne oublié, aublieux de sauter.

At the end of the wee hours, the morne forgotten, forgetful of leaping

where *morne*, so the "Notes" tell us, "is a term used throughout the French West Indies to designate certain altitudes of volcanic origin" and hence "justly applied to the majority of Martinican hills." Or again, we read:

terre grande délire de la mentule de Dieu
earth great delirium of God's mentula (pp. 44–45)

"mentula" being "probably a gallicization of the Latin 'mentula' (penis) based on an Indo-European stem designating a stick agitated to produce fire."

The Eshleman-Smith translation is not always elegant. "Pas un bout de ce monde qui ne porte mon empreinte digitale," which an earlier translator, Emile Snyder, rendered as "not a bit of this earth not smudged by my fingerprint,"[6] becomes "not an inch of this world devoid of my fingerprint," thus erasing the force of the "empreinte digitale" Césaire wishes to convey. Again, it is hard to understand why "Ce qui est à moi / c'est un homme seul emprisonné de / blanc" is translated as "What is mine / a lonely man imprisoned / in whiteness," for an "homme seul" need not be lonely and Césaire's understatement is surely intentional.

"What is desperately needed in an enterprise so important and far-reaching as a translation of Césaire's lyric verse," says Gregson Davis "is an interpreter who has a profound knowledge of Caribbean history and culture, on the one hand, and European literary history, ancient and modern, on the other." Davis is himself such an interpreter and I understand he will soon publish his own translation of Césaire. In the meantime, we have Clayton Eshleman and Annette Smith's brave attempt to come to terms with this difficult and brilliant poet. Smith's scholarship is impressive: the introduction, history of editions, translator's notes, and bibliography are very helpful. Eshleman, who won the National Book Award for his translation with José Rubia Barcia of César Vallejo (1978), seems less at ease with the Surrealist complexities of Césaire than with the more direct emotive thrust of the Peruvian poet. But given the enormous difficulty of translating Césaire for an American readership, it is ungrateful to ask for more than the California translators have given us. It is a genuine gift.

Notes

1.   See *The Poetics of Indeterminacy: Rimbaud to Cage* (Princeton, NJ: Princeton University Press, 1981), 224–29.

2.   See Samuel French Morse, "Introduction," *Opus Posthumous*, by Wallace Stevens (New York: Alfred A. Knopf, 1957), 25.

3.   *The Collected Poems of Wallace Stevens* (New York: Alfred A. Knopf, 1961), 523.

4.   Lawrence D. Kritzman (ed.), *Fragments: Incompletion & Discontinuity* (New York: New York Literary Forum, 1981), vii.

5.   "Towards a 'Non-Vicious Circle': The Lyric of Aimé Césaire in English," *Stanford French Review*, 1 (1977): 136.

6.   Aimé Césaire, *Return to My Native Land* [Cahier d'un retour au pays natal], trans. Emile Snyder (Paris: Presence Africaine, 1971) 66.

CHAPTER 23

The Case of Amy Clampitt

A Reading of "Imago"

Reviewer after reviewer has praised Amy Clampitt's *The Kingfisher* (Alfred A. Knopf, 1983) for its "richness in verbal invention and formal strategies" (Emily Grosholz, *Hudson Review*), its "complex linguistic lyricism" (Peter Stitt, *Georgia Review*), its "intricate patterning" (Joel Conarroe, *Washington Post Book World*), and, above all, its difficulty, in Helen Vendler's words, "A beautiful taxing poetry."[1] "Formal structure," "complex lyricism," difficulty—all these are, of course, New Critical criteria. I want to look closely at the highly praised Clampitt poem "Imago" and then to speculate on what the current wave of Neo–New Critical response to poetry signifies.

> **Imago**
> Sometimes, she remembers, a chipped flint
> would turn up in a furrow,
> pink as a peony (from the iron in it)
> or as the flared throat of a seashell:
> a nomad's artifact fished from the broth,
> half sea half land—hard evidence
> of an unfathomed state of mind.
>
> Nomads. The wagon train that camped
> and left its name on Mormon Ridge.
> The settlers who moved on to California,

Review of *The Kingfisher*, by Amy Clampitt. *Sulfur* 10 (1984): 169–78.

bequeathing a laprobe pieced from the hide
of a dead buffalo, the frail sleigh
that sleeps under the haymow, and a headstone
so small it might be playing house,
for the infant daughter, aged two days,
no name, they also left behind.

Half sea half land: the shirker propped
above her book in a farmhouse parlor
lolls with the merfolk who revert to foam,
eyeing at a distance the lit pavilions
that seduced her, their tailed child,
into the palaces of metamorphosis. She pays
now (though they do not know this)
by treading, at every step she takes,
on a parterre of tomahawks.

A thirst for something definite so dense
it feels like drowning. Grant Wood
turned everything to cauliflower,
the rounded contours of a thunderhead,
flint-hard. He made us proud:
though all those edges might not be quite
the way it was, at least he'd tried.

"But it has no form!" they'd say to
the scribbler whose floundering fragments
kept getting out of hand—and who, either
fed up with or starved out of
her native sloughs, would, stowed aboard
the usual nomadic moving van, trundle her
dismantled sensibility elsewhere.

Europe, that hodgepodge of ancestral
calamities, was hard and handsome, its rubble
confident, not shriveling on the vine,
as here, like an infertile melon—the Virgin
jejune in her grotto of cold plaster, half sick
of that sidelong enclave, the whispered "Cathlick."

Antiquity unshrouds on wimpling canvas,
adjunct of schoolhouse make-believe: the Italy
of urns and cypresses, of stairways
evolving toward a state of mind
not to be found except backstage
among hunchbacks and the miscreants
who control the scenery, flanked
by a pair of masks whose look, at even
this remove, could drill through bone:
the tragic howl, the comic rictus,
eyeholes that stare out of the crypt
of what no grownup is ever heard to speak of
but in a strangled tone whose lexicon
is summed up in one word: Bankrupt.

Bankrupt: the abysm of history,
a slough to be pulled out of
any way you could. Antiquity, the backward
suction of the dark, amounted to a knothole
you plugged with straw, old rags, pages
ripped from last year's Sears Roebuck catalog,
anything, to ward off the blizzard.

Not so, for the born-again, the
shuddering orifices of summer.
On prayer-meeting night, outside
the vestibule among multiple
bell-pulls of Virginia creeper,
the terrible clepsydra of becoming
distils its drop: a luna moth, the emblem
of the born-again, furred like an orchid
behind the ferned antennae, a totem-
garden of lascivious pheromones,
hangs, its glimmering streamers
pierced by the dripstone burin of the eons
with the predatory stare out of the burrow,
those same eyeholes. Imago
of unfathomable evolvings, living
only to copulate and drop its litter,

does it know what it is, what it has been,
what it may or must become?

Amy Clampitt herself, in a curious set of notes at the end of *The Kingfisher*,
supplies us with the meaning of her title. She cites the *American Heritage Dictionary*:

IMAGO. 1. An insect in its sexually mature adult stage after metamorphosis.
2. *Psychoanalysis*. An often idealized image of a person, usually a parent,
formed in childhood and persisting into adulthood.

The "Notes" also tell us that the "merfolk" and "lit pavilions" of the third stanza
refer to Hans Christian Andersen's fairy tale "The Little Mermaid" (which is
evidently Clampitt's favorite fairy tale even as it is mine) and that she connects
this story to the geological fact (read in John McPhee's *Basin and Range* [Farrar
Straus, 1981]) that in past eons the Iowa in which she herself grew up was covered by ocean, a fact that accounts for the land's peculiar sedimentary veneer
and flat contours.

"Imago" is an 83-line poem written in stanzas of irregular length; the verse is,
strictly speaking, "free" although its predominant rhythm is iambic, frequently
even iambic pentameter as in "A thirst for something definite so dense." The
chief sound devices are alliteration and assonance. The syntax is orderly: the first
stanza, for example, is made up of one long sentence, with internal modification,
draped over seven lines. These long-packed sentences, broken by parenthetical
asides like "From the iron in it," recall Elizabeth Bishop or the earlier Robert
Lowell. But the use of the third rather than the first person is a distancing device
these forebears avoided.

The first stanza has two similes—the chipped flint is "pink as poetry," or pink
like "the flared throat of a seashell"—and a metaphor: the flint is "a nomad's arti-
fact fished from the broth, half sea half land." The reference here is to the Iowa of
the poet's childhood, which, as Clampitt's note makes clear, has its characteristic
configurations because it was once under water. The introduction of the seashell,
and the reference to "half sea half land" prefigure, of course, the allusion to "The
Little Mermaid," which becomes explicit in the third stanza. But in case we've
missed the point, the last lines of the stanza spell it out: the remembered flint is
"hard evidence / of an unfathomed state of mind," or, we might say, the mind as
mirror of the unfathomed ocean that is its primeval source.

All the images in the stanza "work," so to speak, and yet I don't quite believe
in them. The "chipped flint," for example, conveniently turns up in the furrow

not because its memory is in any way connected to the poet's situation in the present, but so that the land-sea imagery integral to the poet's theme may be introduced. When images from the past impinge upon our consciousness, we do not, I think, "remember" that A was like an unrelated B, a chipped flint like a pink peony. On the contrary, the comparison is willed, created now, in the act of writing the poem. Indeed, Clampitt does not so much use language to recover a process of experience as she selects carefully those images and metaphors that will work together to make a well-crafted, orchestrated "reconciliation of opposites."

This makes for a good deal of contrivance. Consider the treatment of the land-water tension in the third stanza. The poet refers to her childhood self in the third person as "the shirker." Evidently, in the eyes of others, she was *different*, "propped above her book in a farmhouse parlor." And now the story of the "Little Mermaid "is introduced. In the Andersen fairy tale, we remember, the little mermaid falls in love with a mortal, a handsome prince, and in order to be with him gives up her natural habitat, the water in which she is at home in perfect innocence, to marry him. In order to do so she makes a pact with the devil in the form of a sea witch: she can have her prince only by exchanging her fishtail for legs, but every step she takes will be as painful as if she were walking on knives. At first, the pain seems worth the price, but then the prince begins to neglect the mermaid and falls in love with someone else. The mermaid is totally devastated, languishes, and dies, becoming foam and rejoining the ocean world. It is a tale with all sorts of implications: the clash of innocence and experience, mortal and immortal, and so on.

What does Amy Clampitt do with the mermaid metaphor? Like Andersen's heroine, Clampitt's poet decides to leave the safety of her "merfolk," and head for the "lit pavilions" of the civilization outside her "native sloughs." But the analogy is not convincing because, after all, the Iowa farm family is by definition of the *land* whereas it is the poet who ventures out on the dangerous waters of life. More important, these uneducated and simple farm folk can hardly be expected to see what has happened to their "tailed child" as a seduction to "the lit pavilions" and "the palaces of metamorphosis." Only the poet herself can see it that way. I find the attribution to the "merfolk" of thoughts they can't have irritating, a somewhat self-righteous put-down of these insensitive others who cannot understand her needs.

But neither, for that matter, can the reader. For what are the lit pavilions and palaces of metamorphoses so portentously referred to? In the vocabulary of the New Criticism, which haunts both the writing and the reception of this poem, one would have to say that, alas, these nouns have no objective correlative. Are the "lit pavilions" of the city inevitably treacherous? "She pays now (though they do not know this)," we are told solemnly, but we don't know what she is paying for. Has she run off with a lover? Been seduced by money? Fame? The intellectual life? "She pays now (though they do not know this)" has an aura of self-pity accentuated by the inept metaphor of the final lines, which find the poet "treading, at every step she takes, / on a parterre of tomahawks."

Parterre means (1) the level space in a garden occupied by flowerbeds, or (2) the part of the ground floor of an auditorium or theater that lies under a rear balcony. The second meaning is the more common and is, I think, Clampitt's meaning here. The "mermaid," seduced to the Big City away from her watery primeval Iowa origins, walks forever on a parterre, the polished floor, say, of a theater lobby, feeling every step like the blow of an axe. But here the mermaid metaphor breaks down. In the fairy tale, the mermaid cannot walk without pain because she was not meant to walk at all; the acquisition of legs is unnatural for her. By analogy, Clampitt's mermaid-poet is out of her element in the civilized world of the sophisticated city. What, in this context, do tomahawks have to do with her plight, what, indeed, is the relationship of her sensibility to Native American consciousness?

Cleverness, it seems, is all. The callous Iowa "merfolk"—relatives or schoolteachers—regard the struggling young poet as a "scribbler whose floundering fragments / kept getting out of hand." "Fed up or starved out of her native sloughs," she boards "the usual nomadic moving van" so as to "trundle her / dismantled sensibility elsewhere." It's a familiar story with vaguely Jamesian overtones. Europe, the Great Good Place, turns out to be a "hodgepodge of ancestral / calamities"; "the Italy / of urns and cypresses" (what else?) is no more than a sham: "Bankrupt the abysm of history, a slough to be pulled out of." How or why Europe is thus dismissed is anybody's guess but since we don't know anything about this girl except that she is, of course, sensitive and poetic, there is no way to assess Clampitt's statements about history or about "Antiquity, the backward suction of the dark."

In any case, the painful memories of disillusion—disillusion with the so-called cultured world, whether in America or Europe, lead up to the final image of the luna moth, to the question of what might have happened to the poet had she chosen the sexual life rather than the life of the artist or intellectual. Why these two are necessarily opposites is not made clear. Helen Vendler writes:

In the most hypnotic piece of writing in this strenuously written book, Amy Clampitt looks with a frightening intensity at the sexual evolution of the biological female. Her symbol for this purpose is the imago of the luna

moth emerging from its chrysalis with all its terrifying lurid sexual apparatus of specialized evolution. The moth in its timing obeys the inexorable
water clock, the clepsydra, of the biological imperative. . . . As a poem about
the adolescence of the female, "Imago," with its look at the dreamy girl reading fairy tales leading to its violent stare at sexuality marks a new stage—
speculative, brooding, and powerful—in the poetic mirroring of female
experience.

The question, I suppose, is whether that "violent stare at sexuality" really
takes place here. Vendler admires the rich variety of Clampitt's sources—history
for "clepsydra," Psyche's myth for the moth-as-soul, zoology and botany for fur,
fern, orchid, and antennae, anthropology for totem, the laboratory for pheromones (the substances secreted by insects to attract the opposite sex), and so
on. Yet this glut of allusive properties brings us no nearer to the ostensible subject of the passage: what with the terrible clepsydra of becoming (one can't read
the word "clepsydra" today without thinking of John Ashbery), and the totem
garden of lascivious pheromones (the notes tell us this is a reference to Lewis
Thomas's *Lives of the Cell*), we lose sight of the plight of the mermaid-poet who
has to walk on a parterre of tomahawks. I would argue that what Vendler calls
"the purely biological life" is never a real option: the extremities between which
this woman runs her course are the hardedge Grant Wood farmhouse parlor, on
the one hand, and the unspecified "lit pavilions" on the other. It is all very well
to dredge up out of this glacial drift the symbolic image of the luna moth but
nothing that we know about the poet (and of course we know almost nothing)
relates to that image. We are, in other words, told that the biological imperative
is an alternative of sorts but the preceding stanzas have given us no particular
reason to believe that this is the case.

Clampitt, that is to say, has loaded every rift with ore to the point that the ore
itself becomes self-canceling. We are given so much detail about the sexual evolution of luna moths that we all but lose sight of the central reality of the poet's
own sexuality. To what extent has she become another person? We don't know
because the "she" who is perceived by her people as shirker and scribbler no
more than the stereotypical portrait of the artist as sensitive young girl, alienated
from her uncomprehending Grant Wood family circle. Why "she pays now," why
she must suffer so much, why the "hodgepodge of ancestral / calamities" that is
Europe is no more satisfying than the "native sloughs" of Iowa is not explored.
Nor do we have a vivid sense of what it is this little mermaid wants in life.

Clampitt's, we are told, is a poetry "rich in verbal invention," in "geographical
and literary texture," it is "dense," "metaphysical," "difficult." But this so-called

"difficulty" like the "difficulty" of much late New Critical poetry, is more apparent than real. "Imago," like most of Clampitt's poems has a definite theme alright:
it is "about" the alienation of the poet caught between two worlds, two imagoes.
Thus there is nothing ambivalent about the poet's "merfolk"—callous types who
are given short shrift as just so much Grant Wood hard-edged cauliflower.

The reader's "difficulty," then, can only be one of translation: Question: what
does the luna moth dropping its litter symbolize? Answer: it symbolizes a purely
biological state of being that the poet both envies and knows she can't have.
And so on. Everything here will yield to "translation" provided one uses one's
dictionary and encyclopedia. Given this emphasis on translatability, I take the
Amy Clampitt cult as a sign of our current nostalgia for the good gone days
when POETRY WAS ABOUT SOMETHING, when it conveyed (1) complex
emotions, preferably contradictory; in (2) elegant poetic language, and (3) never
said anything directly that could be said indirectly. Poetic Diction, I'm afraid, is
once again with us as it was in the late eighteenth century and again in the late
nineteenth.

A redolent air of fin de siècle hovers over the poems in *The Kingfisher*, a book
perhaps most clearly understood as a reaction to two prominent strains in postmodern poetry. The first is the "directness" and "spontaneity" of 1960s poetry—
whether Beat, New York School, the San Francisco Renaissance, or the Midwest
Nature poetry of Wright or Bly. *The Natural Words in the Natural Order*—the
Yeatsian dictum of the early century as it was of Wordsworth's "Preface" a century earlier, and as it was at the beginning of the eighteenth century for Swift
and Pope, is now a formula regarded with suspicion: telling it straight is considered the ultimate gaucherie in Clampittland. And second, the cult of Clampitt
is a reaction to the mysteries of John Ashbery, of Neo-Dada and Surrealism, of
concrete poetry and sound poetry, of minimalism and performance art. I am
frequently asked whether I really think that writers like John Cage and David
Antin, whom I included in my book *The Poetics of Indeterminacy*, are poets:
after all, they don't use recognizable verse forms, and worst of all, they seem to
express almost no personal feeling, no attitude, say, to parents or lovers.

Such writing is bound to be disconcerting, especially when it suggests that
we discriminate at our peril between "poetry and "prose," between "lyric" and
"narrative," when it implies that parody and play are just as "valuable" as the
high seriousness of an Amy Clampitt. The Arnoldian need for what Eliot called
"split religion" continues to haunt us.

By now, my own prejudices are obviously showing. I suppose I am finally too
much of a Poundian to appreciate Amy Clampitt's "terrible clepsydra of becoming." I firmly believe that one should not retell in mediocre verse what has already

been done in good prose. Think about this axiom in relation to "Imago": is this particular topos—the alienated bookish childhood, the urge to overcome it, the disillusionment that comes with age—made new by the heavily metaphoric and allusive overlay it is given in Clampitt's poem? Again, as a Poundian, I believe that the poet should use no adjective that does not reveal something. Does it help us to visualize the chipped flint to be told that it is "pink as a peony"?

Perhaps there is finally no substitute for le mot juste. In the opening poem of *The Kingfisher*, we read that the "eiders" (large ducks) "trig / in their white-over-black as they tip / and tuck themselves into the swell, almost as though diving under the eiderdown / in a gemütlich hotel room at Innsbruck." Beautifully descriptive, critics call this sort of thing. I find myself cringing at the last line. Not only because Innsbruck arouses a stock response—a sort of *Sound of Music* lederhosen-cum-yodeling scene in the Austrian alps—but because of the inaccurate usage of the word "gemütlich." Gemütlich happens to be an adverb; the adjective is inflected: *gemütlicher, gemütliche, gemütliches* as in in "Ein gemütliches Zimmer" (room). To put the adverb in front of the noun "hotel room" thus strikes me as a false note, a coy attempt at familiarity as if to say, "Oh, you know about those cozy eiderdowns in those hotel rooms in Innsbruck." As it is, it is merely cute; moreover, it adds nothing to our vision of the ducks diving under the sea swell. In Pound's vocabulary, the image is excessively "viewy." It is not direct treatment of the thing.

But, the reader may well wonder, why do I speak of direct treatment of the thing when I have recently written a book in defense of the Other Tradition, the tradition of undecidability and indeterminacy, of unreal cities? I would say in response that any poem sets up its own network of expectations, its own conventions. In, say, Aimé Césaire's *Notebook of a Return to the Native Land*, we know from the very first refrain line, "Au bout du petit matin," that we are embarked on a hallucinatory journey, that the "real" world must be transformed. But Amy Clampitt's poetry is essentially quite mimetic: it makes statements, applies judgements, displays particular prejudices, all the while pretending that these statements cannot be made plainly. Metaphor, as we learned it at school, is here decorative rather than integral. One could omit "pink as a peony" or "as though diving under the eiderdown / in a gemütlich hotel room at Innsbruck" and still have what is basically the same poem. Try the same exercise on, say, an Ashbery poem and you will see the difference: indeed, you won't be able to determine what images are "more" or "less" important because Ashbery does not hierarchize them; there are no culminating symbols like the luna moth, symbols that claim to center, to ground our experience.

And this is, for me, the heart of the matter. *The Kingfisher* is a book that yearns for origins, for a logocentric universe. Clampitt knows what she wants to *say*, what her heroine (always herself) *feels*, and then goes about the task of find the figurative language to convey it. And she wants her reader to know she has been to Innsbruck and the Italy of "urns and cypresses."

Note

1. *New York Review of Books*, March 3, 1983, p. 19.

CHAPTER 24
"Dirty" Language and Scramble Systems

In one of her captioned photographs (or is it an illustrated poem?), we see blurred cars through a sharply focused, rain-spattered window. The text has no direct connection to the picture: it tells a little anecdote about a woman on her first plane ride, who mistakes the lights from the towns below for stars: "I realized," says the laconic narrator, "She thought we were in Outer Space."

Even a "documentary" photograph, Anderson implies, cannot "capture" a particular experience: written text and photograph remain separate, delimited. Still, the juxtaposition here works because both deal with blurred vision, whether in the form of optical illusion (the photograph) or faulty logic (in the written text). It doesn't matter which came first, the photograph to be captioned or the text to be illustrated, for the "crossing" of the two exemplifies the way things actually happen in our world of communications technology. Such technology, as Craig Owens points out in his essay on Anderson called "Sex and Language: In Between," "is situated in between the emission (or encoding) of messages and their reception (or decoding), and as it has grown it has widened the gap between emission and reception to such an extent that today it is virtually guaranteed that no message will ever reach its destination intact." In such a "scramble system" (Anderson's own term), "communication—a meaningful relationship between speakers—is replaced by the endless, relentless, *circulation* of signs, the circularity of a system closed in upon itself."

Owens's is one of four excellent essays in *Laurie Anderson: Works from 1969 to 1983*, an exhibition organized by Janet Kardon for the University of Pennsylvania's Institute of Contemporary Art (October 15–December 4, 1983). The exhibition was also shown at UCLA's Frederick S. Wight Gallery (January 29–March 4,

Review of *Laurie Anderson, Works from 1969 to 1983*, by Janet Kardon; and *Something (Even Human Voices) in the Foreground, a Lake*, by Kathleen Fraser. *Sulfur* 11 (Fall 1984): 178–83.

1984), where I was one of thousands to see it; it is now at the Contemporary Arts Museum in Houston and concludes at the Queens Museum in Flushing, New York (July 1–September 9). The Anderson retrospective is a show one wishes anyone interested in poetry and the visual arts could see, and the catalog (available from the ICA, Philadelphia, PA 19104) is at least a second-best.

It is impossible to categorize Laurie Anderson's art. She is usually called a "performance artist" (and lately—with some asperity—dismissed by certain artists as a mere "rock star"); her work includes audio and video tapes, multimedia sound and visual room installations, photographs with text, drawings, collage, altered objects, and participatory sound sculpture. In all these works, language plays an important—perhaps the most important—part, her mode being to take absolutely ordinary materials—the photograph, say, of a waitress seen from the angle of the person being waited on in a restaurant, the wholly ritualized discourse of the airline pilot ("Ladies and gentlemen, please fasten your seat belts . . ."), the outgoing and incoming message on the telephone answering machine—and to turn these ordinary language events into sometimes hilarious, sometimes bizarre, sometimes frightening pastiches. In their stubborn dailiness, Anderson's narratives recall John Cage's little Zen stories, but their splicing and collage arrangements are closer to William Burroughs (who appears with Anderson on her new recording, "Sharkey's Day"), and the relation of word to visual image, on the one hand, and to art rock and electronic-organ washes on the other is finally Laurie Anderson's own.

It is impossible here to do more than urge *Sulfur* readers to familiarize themselves with such texts as "Converse Song #5." If this "IT Song" suggests that there is no communication between the sexes (notice that we know nothing about the participants in this dialogue except their gender), the comic twist is that Laurie Anderson, with the help of the synthesizer that disguises her voice, identifies with neither the man nor the woman. She is, as Owens points out, less androgynous (displaying both male and female traits) than situated in a space in-between the two sexes—in a realm, so to speak, of neither/nor. Moreover, in *Americans on the Move*, in which this song appears, Anderson's speech is accompanied by a telling gesture: she extends the violin bow to one side, moving it back and forth like a windshield wiper to form a screen. The "message" is thus intercepted by the process of art; it becomes Anderson's own.

In putting in question the very possibility of language communication, Laurie Anderson clearly has affinities with the Language poets, especially with such women poets as Lydia Davis, Lyn Hejinian, Rae Armantrout, Fanny Howe, and Kathleen Fraser. Fraser has just published a book called *Something (Even Human Voices) in the Foreground, a Lake* (Berkeley: Kelsey St. Press) that takes up some of the same issues we find in Laurie Anderson's performances, but here the mode is less that of collage than of fragmentation and frottage.

In Anderson, we usually know what we are looking at but we don't know what it means. In Fraser's new poems, objects, people, events are decomposed and realigned. The scene is evidently an Italian beach resort (Amalfi coast? Lido? Riviera?); there are at least two couples and an assortment of children; each prose poem has a hint of narrative (e.g., "Covertly, her husband ['s eyes]"). But what happens, what is seen is only partially illusionistic. One thinks of de Kooning or certain Diebenkorns. Here is "Anna ("Are you looking at me?"), if not," a title that challenges us to fill in the gaps:

A lack of confidence stiffening this patch of hand over the body's bronz-
ing, Abbronzato, working at it, and "Do you like it?" Her leg aside his
arm. Arm against friends. Galactic and childish in white while pulling at
hem. Blinking little nipples before the keyhole drift where he lifts a path
of white to display what is his little worry. All your hoarded blemishes
could be big ones gathering a life (subcutaneous) against you. The man
in red bikini buys you houses. You show your present, then he takes it
away under that smile and a change of clothes. Turquoise bikini, rolling
over from the day confirmed as yesterday. Neither headlines, nor even
finer print. Looking for "ponentino" (little Western wind, to us), lifting
your dress for them. She drifts in from bath in Hollywood white satin and
already you are craving it, but you can buy anything and think it doesn't
work. Working-out once, the glaze pulled back its gauzy robe. But you
would not give what was yours much.

Is the "patch of hand" Anna's own or that of her friend or lover? The poem gathers erotic force as "he" (who?) "lifts a patch of white to display what is his little worry." Perhaps the husband worries his wife will get ugly sun spots on her white skin. Or perhaps he has other worries. Her "blinking little nipples" are subject to his "keyhole drift." The man is always referred to as "he" but the woman, whether Anna or the poet herself, is alternately "she" and "you." "You show your present," remarks the narrator, "then he takes it away under that smile and a change of clothes." Is the present the woman's body? Or is she carrying his baby, a more tangible present? The images are concrete but indeterminate: a turquoise bikini replaces the red one; newspapers are scanned, skirts lifted, "she" (another woman?) emerges from the bath "in Hollywood white satin." "The glaze pulled back its gauzy robe," an exhibition that produces envy to the point of "craving" from the other.

Fraser transforms her ordinary scene, a day at the beach, into something "if not," as the title puts it. Throughout her fragmented sentences, there is talk of buying and selling, giving and getting. But of what? Bodies are displayed, touched, longed for. But desire does not lead to communication: the colorful silhouettes remain separate; they have a hard edge.

Tadeus Nyczek has recently edited an anthology called *Humps & Wings: Polish Poetry Since '68* (Invisible City) (San Francisco & Los Angeles: Red Hill Press). on the face of it, nothing could be more different from the "cool" and "hip" impersonality of Laurie Anderson or the aesthetic distancing of Kathleen Fraser than the samizdat political poetry of Krzysztof Karasek, Stanislaw Baranczak, Adam Zagajewski, and other young poets of "the generation of '68." All the more interesting, then, that Stanislaw Baranczak, a former member of KOR, the Social Self-Defense Committee, whose works are banned in Poland and who was dismissed from his lectureship in the philology department at Adam Mickiewicz University (he is now a Professor of Slavic Languages at Harvard) is quoted in *Humps & Wings* as saying that "language is a part of morality . . . for us the most interesting thing was not pure language but 'dirty' language, language spoiled and misused . . . that of mass media, of posters, things like that."

Mass media, political speeches, posters—perhaps it is impossible today for the poet to avoid such "dirty" or contaminated language. One of Laurie Anderson's recent songs play upon the metaphor of the closed circuit; it is called "Let X = X" and it ends on this note:

> I got this postcard. And it read, it said:
> Dear Amigo—Dear Partner
> Listen, uh—I just want to say thanks. So . . . thanks.
> Thanks for all the presents. Thanks for introducing
>   me to the Chief.
> Thanks for putting on the feedbag. Thanks for going all out.
> Thanks for showing me your Swiss Army knife.
>   Oh and uh—
> Thanks for letting me autograph your cast.
>   Hug and kisses. XXXXOOOO

But then the rhetoric of the macho thank-you note gives way to something quite different:

> Oh yeah, P.S.
> I feel—feel like—I am—in a burning building—and I gotta go.

The balloon of mindless clichés ("the Chief," "putting on the feedbag," "going all out") and contaminated idioms ("Hug and kisses") finally pops, leaving us with the reality of the speaker's anxiety ("I feel—feel like—I am—in a burning building"), a "reality" that is, paradoxically, just as inauthentic as the clichés that precede it. It is the space between such versions of the "real" that poets are currently navigating.

CHAPTER 25

Hölderlin Our Contemporary

1

"The poet of the poet"—so Heidegger in a famous lecture of 1937 called Hölderlin. The poet of the poet in the sense that it was Hölderlin's "poetic vocation to write expressly of the essence of poetry," indeed to demonstrate to us "Poetry is the establishing of being by means of the word" (*"Dichtung ist worthafte Stiftung des Seins"*).[1]

But how and when is *Being* so established? "To 'dwell poetically' means," says Heidegger, "to stand in the presence of the gods and to be involved in the proximity of the essence of things." One cannot, such statements imply, *choose* to be a poet; one either is or one isn't. Accordingly, to talk about poetry is to talk about its essence, its mode of being. Thus our *poet of the poet* inevitably and ironically turns into the *poet of the philosopher*.

As such, it has been Hölderlin's fate, especially in American academic circles, to be more often cited than read, more often used to exemplify this or that theoretical point than to influence the work of living poets. One of the great merits of Richard Sieburth's translation is that it refuses to be daunted by the august figure of Hölderlin the Seer, the "inaugural namer of the gods," thus allowing the great German poet to emerge as the actual man who suffered, who was there.

For Sieburth, the author of an excellent study of Pound and Gourmont (*Instigations*, Princeton, 1978), Hölderlin is "the first great modern of European poetry," in that his discourse prefigures such twentieth-century "inventions" as "direct treatment of the thing," metrical and syntactic ambivalence,

Review of *Hymns and Fragments*, by Friedrich Hölderlin, trans. Richard Sieburth. *Parnassus: Poetry in Review* (1985): 144–68.

fragmentation, and parataxis. It is a prefiguration that would be less apparent if Sieburth had included the early Odes and Epigrams, the Hexameters and Elegies, the novel *Hyperion* (1797–1799), and the unfinished tragedy *The Death of Empedocles* (1799). But Hölderlin's modern reputation rests primarily on the great free-verse "hymns" (Hölderlin himself called them "vaterländische Gesänge") and drafts of hymns, written between 1801 and 1806, when, at the age of thirty-six, the poet was committed to a Tübingen clinic for the insane. It is these, together with a generous sampling of sketches or drafts of hymns (*Hymnische Entwürfe*), that Sieburth has chosen to translate. If the emphasis is on what the introduction defines as "Hölderlin's poetics of absence," there is ample precedent for Sieburth's reading in the criticism of Adorno, de Man, and especially in Foucault's discussion in "The Father's 'No'" (1962) of Hölderlin's "madness" as the self-destruction of poetic speech, the creation of "a zone [where] language loses itself in its extreme limits, in a region where language is most unlike itself and where signs no longer communicate." Foucault cites the opening line of "Mnemosyne," "Ein Zeichen sind wir, deutungslos" (A sign we are, without meaning), as an emblem of "the fundamental gap in the signifier."[2]

Attuned as we now are to such "fundamental gaps," Hölderlin's late lyric emerges as peculiarly Modern or, more accurately, postmodern. Consider the opening poem in Sieburth's volume, "Hälfte des Lebens" (Half of Life):

> *Mit gelben Birnen hänget*
> *Und voll mit wilden Rosen*
> *Das Land in den See,*
> *Ihr holden Schwäne,*
> *Und trunken von Küssen*
> *Tunkt ihr das Haupt*
> *Ins heilignüchterne Wasser.*

> *Weh mir, wo nehm' ich, wenn*
> *Es Winter ist, die Blumen, und wo*
> *Den Sonnenschein,*
> *Und Schatten der Erde?*
> *Die Mauern stehn*
> *Sprachlos und kalt, im Winde*
> *Klirren die Fahnen.*

> With its yellow pears
> And wild roses everywhere

The shore hangs in the lake,
O gracious swans,
And drunk with kisses
You dip your heads
In the sobering holy water.

Ah, where will I find
Flowers, come winter,
And where the sunshine
And shade of the earth?
Walls stand cold
And speechless, in the wind
The weathervanes creak.

Hölderlin's "Hälfte des Lebens" is itself divided in half—into two seven-line stanzas, whose lines have predominantly two and three stresses. It begins with the familiar Romantic topos of late fruition—yellow pears and wild roses everywhere, and lovely swans "drunk with kisses" dipping their heads into lake water. The swan image interestingly prefigures Yeats's "The Wild Swans at Coole," in which the poet, similarly stationed on the lakeshore in an autumnal setting (leaves "in their autumn beauty," water "mirror[ing] a still sky"), contemplates the difference between swan life and his own isolated state:

Unwearied still, lover by lover,
They paddle in the cold
Companionable streams or climb the air;
Their hearts have not grown cold;
Passion or conquest, wander where they will
Attend upon them still.

But Hölderlin's "heilignüchterne Wasser" (the oxymoronic force of the adjective comes through sharply in Sieburth's "sobering holy water") is a far cry from Yeats's "cold / Companionable streams." For Hölderlin, the ecstasy of love is threatened, not by loss or old age, as in Yeats, but, unhappily, by the "holy" water itself. And indeed, the opening line immediately introduces a note of dissociation: "Mit gelben Birnen hänget." The verb "hänget," itself left hanging, suspended at the end of the line, is an odd choice: normally, one thinks of the shore as the lake's boundary, providing a kind of stable frame, not as an entity "hanging" on it. Again, Hölderlin's lake water does not, like Yeats's, "mirror" the "still sky" above it; the Romantic notion of correspondences—as above, so below—has no place here. Michael Hamburger, the veteran of English Hölderlin translators, renders the passage as follows:

> With yellow pears the land,
> And full of wild roses
> Hangs down in the lake[3]

And the poet Christopher Middleton gives us:

> With yellow pears the country,
> Brimming with wild roses,
> Hangs into the lake[4]

To render Hölderlin's syntax in English makes for awkward contortion—"With yellow pears hangs / And full of wild roses / The shore in the lake"—and all three translators transpose it accordingly. But Sieburth compensates for this inevitable loss by retaining the original's sense of precariousness: his "shore" (a more literal rendering than Hamburger's "land" or Middleton's "country") "hangs in" but not "into" or "down into" the lake.

The note of unease, only hinted at in the first stanza, with its lovely image of pears and roses, of swans drunk with kisses, now explodes after the stanza break: "Weh mir, wo nehm'ich, wenn / Es Winter ist, die Blumen, und wo / Den Sonnenschein, / Und Schatten der Erde?" Sieburth's rendering of these lines may strike us almost too cool, too abrupt:

> Ah, where will I find
> Flowers, come winter,
> And where the sunshine
> And shade of the earth?

Compare Hamburger:

> But oh, where shall I find
> When winter comes, the flowers . . .

And Middleton:

> Where, ah where shall I find,
> When winter comes, the flower, . . .

Certainly "*Weh mir*" (literally, "woe is me") has more force than a mere "ah." But Sieburth's interpretation is quite consistent. In condensing the original, he gives it a tone of near aphasia; he emphasizes the void that results as the poet contemplates the loss of the very flowers he has just named, the loss not only of sunshine but even of the shade. And indeed, the loss of speech now comes to the fore: "Die Mauern stehn / Sprachlos und kalt" (Walls stand cold / And speechless). It is as if the vision of the flowery and fecund coast can "hang in," so to speak, only "im Winde" where "Klirren die Fahnen" (in the wind / The weathervanes creak).

Both Hamburger and Middleton translate the last line as "The weathervanes clatter." Sieburth's "creak" is more subtle phonetically—a short syllable, its diphthong pointing back to "weather" and its final voiceless stop bringing the reader up short. "The weathervanes creak"—direct treatment of the thing, without a trace of self-pity. If there is no sunshine or shade in winter, if, in the second "half of life," the kissing swans are replaced by creaking weathervanes, who is to blame? The pathos of this and related poems is that there is no one.

2

Why is this the case? Why is Hölderlin's poetry so wholly devoid of visible struggle, of the Romantic longing to assume godlike powers? In his introduction, Sieburth remarks on the "humility or pietas that is perhaps unique to Hölderlin among Romantic poets," on Hölderlin's sense that no mortal could quite "deserve the spendthrift generosity of the gods." To understand this peculiar humility, some biographical facts are necessary.

Johann Friedrich Hölderlin was born in the small Swabian town of Lauffen am Neckar on March 20, 1770. His father, a manager of estates belonging to the Lutheran Church, died in 1772. His mother soon remarried, but his stepfather, the local burgomaster, of whom the boy was evidently very fond, died in 1779. Hölderlin was thus, as Jean Laplanche points out in *Hölderlin et la question du père* (1961), twice deprived of a father. His later adulation of Schiller and of Goethe, who evidently treated the younger poet rather coldly, testifies to a continuing need—and failure—to find a father figure.

From 1788 to 1793, Hölderlin studied for his ordination at the Theological Seminary at Tübingen. Here he wrote his first poems, largely inspired by the French Revolution, developed a passionate interest in all things Greek, and made friends with two of the great philosophers of his time—Hegel and Schelling. Having decided not to enter the ministry, he obtained various tutorial posts, the decisive one as tutor to the four children of a wealthy Frankfurt banker, whose wife, Susette Gontard, whom he called (alluding to Plato's *Symposium*)

"Diotima," became the love of Hölderlin's life. When the French invaded the Rhine Valley in July 1796, Hölderlin accompanied Diotima and her four children to safety in Westphalia, and they were thus together for a brief and passionate idyll. At the same time, he was convinced that the youth of Germany would soon bring about a revolution on the French model.

Four strains thus come together in Hölderlin's work of the late 1790s: theology, Greek culture (as transmitted through modern German philosophy), radical politics, and erotic love. It is important, I think, to stress that the last was by no means an unrequited Wertherian passion; after Hölderlin was asked to quit his post in the Gontard household in 1798, he continued to have secret meetings with Susette Gontard for more than a year. The very moving "Letters to Diotima," included in the standard Hölderlin editions, tell this particular story.

By 1801, the year Sieburth takes as his starting point, the diverse strands I have been discussing no longer meshed:

> Wer war es, der zuerst
> Die Liebesbände verderbt
> Und Stricke von ihnen gemacht hat?

> Who was it who first
> Wrecked the bonds of love
> And transformed them into chains?
> ("Der Rhein")

Napoleon, whom Hölderlin dismissed as "a species of dictator," had come to power. Schiller, Schelling, and Goethe had refused to help him publish a collection of his poetry and in founding a literary journal; his last meeting with Diotima took place in late 1800. By the time he set off on foot for Bordeaux for yet another tutorial post (a journey he was to describe in letters home in harrowing terms, referring to the "baptism of ice" he underwent in a sequence of bitterly cold nights spent sleeping outdoors in the Auvergne mountains), Hölderlin was suffering from serious mental illness. Whatever happened in the South of France (and the late poems contain moving images of its climate and topography), within three months he suddenly reappeared in Stuttgart at the home of a friend, who described him as "pale as a corpse, emaciated with hollow wild eyes, long hair and beard, and dressed like a beggar." In early July, he received word that Diotima had died. This shock seems to have been the final blow: he suffered a complete breakdown and had to be cared for by the local physician in Nürtingen.

By fall 1802, he had recovered sufficiently to visit friends and to begin work on "Patmos," commissioned by the Landgrave of Homburg, after the latter's first choice, the famous poet Klopstock, turned it down. Over the course of the next four years, Hölderlin wrote the bulk of the great hymns and sketches for hymns that were to make him famous. In late 1806, a further breakdown necessitated admission to a psychiatric clinic in Tübingen, where he was placed under "strict observation." After some ten months of unsuccessful treatment at this clinic, Hölderlin was released into the care of a local carpenter and admirer of *Hyperion*, Ernst Zimmer. The physicians gave him "at most three days to live"; in fact, he lived with the carpenter for another thirty-six years. Secluded from the world, he played a little piano, took walks, wrote a few little lyrics, received an occasional guest. Hölderlin died on June 7, 1843.

Numerologists could make much of the fact that Hölderlin was thirty-six when he was certified "insane," thirty-six plus thirty-six when he died, and that his "great" poems were written within a six-year period. Be that as it may, what is especially remarkable about the "precarious dialogue with the Other" (Sieburth's term) of the late poetry is that it remains, to the very end, so peculiarly *lucid*. Hölderlin seems to have been incapable of rambling, witness a late fragment like "Gestalt and Geist" (Shape and Spirit):

> *Alles ist innig*
>> *Das scheidet*
> *So bringt der Dichter*
>
> *Verwegner! möchtest von Angesicht zu Angesicht*
> *Die Seele sehn*
>> *Du gehest in Flammen unter.*

> Everything is inward
>> This is the distinction
> The poet thus conceals
>
> Reckless! wanting to see the soul
> Face to face
>> You go down in flames.

Gnomic as is this abbreviated utterance, it makes perfect sense. To long for total inwardness, for that alien space within that is cut off from concrete reality, is to "go down in flames." Again, the fault is not that of the gods or of society or of the lost father and his substitutes (Hegel, Schiller, etc.). Rather, it is the fate of one who has been "struck by Apollo," overcome by an intensity that cannot be maintained. The poetic act is not willed, perhaps not even desired. For who wants to go down in flames?

3

Richard Sieburth's introduction, which lays out the terrain I have been sketching, is itself a major critical essay on Hölderlin. Sieburth is unusual among translators in also being a sophisticated historical and theoretical critic, as alert to the links between Hölderlin and the English Romantics as to the post-Structural readings of Hölderlin's work by Foucault, de Man, and others. His succinct commentary on the complex thematic strands in the long hymns like "The Rhine" and "Patmos" is especially valuable: for example, the paradox that the "nearest, inmost things are the most arduous to seize" (so that Hölderlin's Greece is to be recovered only through the mediation of Germany), the clash between man's instinctive "drive of unbounded desire" and the order imposed by the gods, the poet's inability to reconcile the order of history with that of divinity with the consequent "terrifying withdrawal of divine presence from the world." In its attempt to mediate between "gods" and "mortals," the poetry thus establishes what Sieburth, here following Heidegger, calls a state of being "always *in between.*" Adorno, tackling this *in between* from an ideological perspective, argues that Hölderlin's poetry explores the modern separation of subject and object, that his parataxis implied the impossibility, given a set of social and cultural conditions, of predicative assertion.

Sieburth's translations of the more formal hymns do, however, pose certain problems. The issue, and it is a knotty one, is syntax. Hölderlin himself remarked in his essay "Reflexion":

It is common practice to have inversions of word order within the period. But clearly much greater effects can be obtained by the inversion of the periods themselves. The logical order of period, in which the basis (the basic period) is followed by its development, the development by its culmination, the culmination by its purpose, and subsidiary clauses are merely appended to the main clauses to which they primarily apply—all this can only rarely serve the poet's ends.

Michael Hamburger, who cites this passage in the introduction to his *Poems and Fragments*, argues that the word "primarily" should caution the translator to refrain from clarifying all but those passages "so obscure as to have baffled and divided the scholarly commentators," that, on the whole, it is the translator's role "to refrain from interpreting . . . passages, so as to preserve their essential ambiguity." Sieburth takes a somewhat different approach:

> Though Hölderlin's radical hyperbata and inversions are feasible in a language such as German (or Greek), where inflection, rather than world order, acts as the ultimate guarantor of grammatical intelligibility, it is virtually impossible to reproduce such syntax in English without falling into an idiom that recalls Milton at his most stilted. In my translations I have therefore tried to convey the particular syntactical torque of Hölderlin's late hymns through means more native to American cadence. My primary ambition has been to retain the overall profile of the phrase while rendering what Hölderlin sometimes termed the "rhythm of representation," that is, the pace at which verbal relations come to be perceived.

Let us see how this transposition works in practice. Here is the opening of "The Rhine," a hymn that structurally resembles such "greater Romantic odes" (Meyer Abrams's term) as "Tintern Abbey" and "Ode to a Nightingale":

> *Im dunkeln Epheu saß ich, an der Pforte*
> *Des Waldes, eben, da der goldene Mittag,*
> *Den Quell besuchend, herunterkam*
> *Von Treppen des Alpengebirgs,*
> *Das mir die göttlichgebaute,*
> *Die Burg der Himmlischen heißt*
> *Nach alter Meinung, wo aber*
> *Geheim noch manches entschieden*
> *Zu Menschen gelanget; von da*
> *Vernahm ich ohne Vermuten*
> *Ein Schicksaal.*

Here a single sentence is draped over the first nine lines, its main clause, "saß ich" (I was sitting), followed by a complex string of temporal, spatial, and casual clauses, as well as the appositive in lines 5–7. The relationship of clausal elements is not, in this case, ambiguous, but the subordination is so complex that by the time we come to "von da" in line 9, we have to retrace our steps and recall the antecedent in line 1.

Hamburger renders the first sentence as follows:

Amid dark ivy I was sitting, at
The forest's gate, just as a golden noon,
To visit the wellspring there, came down
From steps of the Alpine range
Which, following the ancient lore,
I call the divinely built,
The fortress of the Heavenly,
But where, determined in secret
Much even now reaches men.

Here the syntax of the original is generally retained: first the dark ivy, then the person sitting in it, then the larger setting ("at / The forest's gate"), then the epiphanic event ("just as a golden noon"), followed by the naming of the Alpine range as "fortress of the Heavenly" and the allusion to its secret ministry. The fidelity of Hamburger's translation helps the reader to move from the darkness of the ivy to the opening in the forest, to the glimpse of unmediated sunlight perceived from the vantage point of the shade.

Compare this to Sieburth's translation:

I was sitting in the dark ivy, at the gate
Of the forest, just as the spring was visited
With the gold of noon pouring
Down the steps of the Alps
Which I call the fortress of the gods
In the ancient sense, architected
By the heavens, and from which
Many decrees are still mysteriously
Handed down to men.

Poundian translator that he is, Sieburth has a predilection for the natural words in the natural order, and for the maxim that "Dichten = condensare." He wants, as he says in the introduction, to avoid "falling into an idiom that recalls Milton at his most stilted." But here his syntactic transformation produces a casual note that is not quite consonant with Hölderlin's "rhythm of representation": the "dark ivy" and "gold of noon" are subordinated, as they are not in the original, to the activity of the observer ("I was sitting") and to the effect on the spring ("was visited"). Again, Hamburger's "I call the divinely built, / The fortress of the Heavenly" is perhaps more graceful than "Which I call the fortress of the gods /

In the ancient sense, architected / By the heavens." "Architected" strikes me as too glossy for this poem about order and chaos.

The dialectic of "The Rhine" is that between the "One Life"—the Romantic "Unity of Being"—and the fearful sense of isolation experienced by the poet. The course of the river is symbolic of finite consciousness, engendered by the divine principle into the earthy, resistant actuality of the "inert," into the blockage and obstruction of the land through which it must pass. In the course of the hymn, the poet comes to the recognition that the gods purposely frustrate man's potentially fatal desire for immediacy, that suffering is necessary if the One Life is ever to be attained. And even the "Gastmahl," or Bridal Feast, uniting God and man, is transient:

> *Denn schwer ist zu tragen*
> *Das Unglük, aber schwerer das Glük.*

> For misfortune is heavy
> To bear, and fortune weighs yet more.

This wonderful aphorism is all but impossible to translate, there being no way to render the ironic opposition of "Unglük / "Glük" and the concise comparative "schwer, schwerer" in English. Sieburth's version certainly is less awkward than Hamburger's "For hard to bear / is misfortune, but good fortune harder," or Christopher Middleton's "For misfortune is hard to endure, but fortune even harder." The hymn, in any case, now modulates into a coda quite similar to that of "Tintern Abbey," in which the poet turns to his friend Sinclair, even as Wordsworth turns to Dorothy, as one whose innocent piety ensures a state of being in which, no matter how "fierhaft und angekettet" (fevered and chained) life seems, "nimmer ist dir / Verborgen das Lächeln des Herrschers" (the Lord's / Smile never escapes you).

The syntax of the first few lines of this strophe presents Sieburth with a recurrent problem:

> *Dir mag auf heissem Pfade unter Tannen oder*
> *Im Dunkel des Eichwalds gehüllt*
> *In Stahl, mein Sinklair! Gott erscheinen oder*
> *In Wolken, du kennst ihn*

Hamburger writes:

> To you in the heat of a path under fir-trees or
> Within the oak forest's half-light, wrapped
> In steel, my Sinclair, God may appear, or
> In clouds, you'll know him

Which keeps the reader in anticipation of the identity of the addresses even as, in "Tintern Abbey," seven lines elapse between "For thou art with me here upon the banks" and the identification of this "thou," this Other in whose "voice I catch / The language of my former heart," as the poet's "dear, dear Sister."

Sieburth, anxious as he is to avoid the Miltonic period, sacrifices the suspension of the original to a more colloquial and normative English:

> Sinclair, my friend, should God appear
> To you on a burning path under pines
> Or in the dark of oaks, sheathed
> In steel, or among clouds, you would
> Recognize him

Whether this transposition retains what Sieburth calls "the overall profile of the phrase," "the pace at which verbal relations come to be perceived" is open to question. Sieburth is, in any case, much more successful with Hölderlin's more enigmatic and fragmented hymns, the lyrics in which "the configuration of gaps and breaches" becomes increasingly important to the "rhythm of representation."

"Patmos" is a case in point. Here is the opening:

> *Nah ist*
> *Und schwer zu fassen der Gott.*
> *Wo aber Gefahr ist, wächst*
> *Das Rettende auch.*

> Near and
> Hard to grasp, the god.
> Yet where danger lies,
> Grows that which saves.

These lines contain, as Sieburth points out in the notes, a celebrated crux: "Does the danger consist in the very nearness of the divine, or does the peril rather lie in the difficulty of grasping it?" The ambiguity was surely intended: the

Landgrave Friedrich of Hessen-Homburg, to whom "Patmos" was represented as a birthday offering in 1803, had requested a poem that would defend traditional biblical values against Enlightenment impiety and the libertarianism of the French Revolution. Hence the orthodox Christian overlay that pervades the poem as it moves to its affirmative conclusion in stanza 15: "der Vater aber liebt, / Der über allen waltet, / Am meisten, das gepflegelt werde / Der feste Buchstab" (What our Father / Who reigns supreme / Most loves is that we keep the letter / Fast in our care).

"Nah ist / Und schwer zu fassen der Gott." Metrically, these lines have the following shape:

```
/ x
x /  x / x  x /
```

The first line (literally "Near is") is suspended: the reader doesn't know what it is that is near. The answer comes only at the end of line 2, whose rhythm reverses the stress pattern of the preceding line, as if to say that what is near is indeed "Hard to grasp." The rhythm of line 3—"Wo aber Gefahr ist, wächst"—is again metrically "difficult":

```
/ / x  x / x || /
```

and the verb ("wächst") has no subject until line 4 ("Das Rettende").

How to convey the suspensions and difficulties that make Hölderlin's rhythm and lineation so peculiarly expressive? Michael Hamburger renders the lines thus:

> Near is
> And difficult to grasp, the God.
> But where danger threatens
> That which saves from it also grows.

And Christopher Middleton:

> Near and
> Hard to grasp is
> The God.
> But where danger is,
> Deliverance also grows.

Like Sieburth's, these two translations retain the syntax of the first two lines, although Sieburth condenses by omitting the "is," thus re-creating the rhythmic disequilibrium of the original:

> / x
> / x   x / || x /

But it is in lines 3–4 that Sieburth's decision to "retain the overall profile of the phrase," rather than the exact wording and syntax, makes a real difference. Hamburger's translation is wordy, Hölderlin's terse aphorism being stretched out in the stilted, nonidiomatic "But where danger threatens / That which saves from it also grows"—twelve words for Hölderlin's eight. Middleton is more concise, and his positioning of the opening lines nicely conveys the hesitation of the original. But the formality of "Deliverance also grows" is at odds with the curious simplicity, the pietas of Hölderlin's "wächst / Das Rettende auch." Sieburth's "Yet where danger lies, / Grows that which saves" eliminates the "auch" (also), awkward in English, and concentrates on the essence of Hölderlin's statement: the paradox of the salvation that is potential in "danger."

That paradox, it should be observed, is stated in abstract language. It has been argued, both by Sieburth and Hamburger, that in poems like "Half of Life," "Hölderlin anticipates the poetics of Imagism by a century" (Hamburger), that his concern with the modalities of fragmentation and stark juxtaposition, with catalogs of proper names and historical documentation (in, say, "Columbus"), look ahead to Pound's canto structure. But the fact is that, unlike Pound's concretist language, Hölderlin's tends toward abstraction, and that his images, when they do occur, are closer to Beckett's than to Pound's in their indeterminacy, the nonspecificity of their context.

Consider the imagery of lines 5–8 of "Patmos":

> *Im Finstern wohnen*
> *Die Adler und furchtlos gehn*
> *Die Söhne der Alpen über den Abgrund weg*
> *Auf leichtgebaueten Brüken.*

> Eagles dwell
> In darkness, and without fear
> The sons of the Alps span the abyss
> On lightly built bridges.

The opening of "Patmos" has stressed the paradox that the more intensely felt the divine presence, the more threatening it is in actuality. It is the unmediated intensity of divinity, the poem implies, that is so dangerous. In line 5–8, this paradox is now rendered Imagistically: the eagles, traditionally symbolic of strength and hope, the chosen messengers of Zeus, here "dwell / In darkness," and the "sons of the Alps" (natives? mountain climbers? those at home in the world?), who fearlessly cross the abyss, do so by means of "lightly built bridges." "Gefahr" danger) thus goes hand and hand with "Das Rettende" (that which saves).

The implications of this mountain image are now drawn out:

> Drum, da gehäuft sind rings,
> Die Gipfel der Zeit, und die Liebsten
> Nah wohnen, ermattend auf
> Getrenntesten Bergen,
> So gib unschuldig Wasser,
> O Fittige gib uns, treuesten Sinns
> Hinüberzugehn und wiederzukehren.

> Since the peaks of Time lie
> Heaped around us and those we love
> Live near, languishing
> On separate mountains,
> Give us innocent waters
> O give us wings so that, faithful-minded,
> We might cross over and back.

The particle "Drum" (Therefore, On that account) is a typically Hölderlinian false connective, there being no causal link between the "sons of the Alps," spanning the abyss "On lightly built bridges," and the lovers languishing on their separate mountains, who are unable to do so. Here, and in similar cases, Sieburth accordingly omits the connective altogether, thus stressing the qualitative progression, rather than any logical development, from A to B. Imperceptibly, the spatial is temporalized—alps turning into "peaks of Time"—but it is not clear why these peaks "lie / Heaped around us," even as new mountains erect themselves in the poet's field of vision, this time the "Getrenntesten Bergen" (literally, "the most separate mountains") that divide "die Liebsten."

Here the paradox of the opening lines reappears with some variation. "Die

Liebsten" means, literally, "the most loved" (as Hamburger translates it), but it is not clear whether they are "most loved" by the poet or by one another. Again, although they "Live near," they must languish ("ermattend" literally means "growing pale," "growing faint") on the most separate of all mountains. What is clearly a biographical reference to Hölderlin's separation from Diotima (who indeed lived nearby but on the most inaccessible "mountain") is made mysterious: one has a vision of countless lovers able to see one another across the abyss but unable to cross it. Not for them the lightly built bridges of the "sons of the Alps"—those who belong in the world and can negotiate it. So near and yet so far: "Nah ist / un schwer zu fassen."

Sieburth's translation of this passage is typically understated. "Those most loved" becomes "those we love"; the "most separate" mountains become merely "separate." The rationale seems to be—and I think it works—that the superlative form of the adjective is not needed here, that it is quite enough to think of "those we love" and who "Live near" as "languishing / On separate mountains." Again, in condensing the verse texture and eliding extra particles like "most," Sieburth does give us, I think, precisely the texture of Hölderlin's meditation. Its abrupt, cut-off quality comes through.

The stanza's final prayer accords with this tone. "So gieb unschuldig Wasser, / O Fittige gieb uns." The "innocent waters" of baptism or of purification and the spirit wings (Fittige) are desired, strangely enough, not so as to cross over to that other world where the loved ones dwell, but so as to "cross over and *back*" (my emphasis). We long, that is to say, for the Other, for the realm of the gods, not as an escape from the pain of this world, but on the contrary, as an Other that can only be meaningful if we can have it here, on our own ground.

The parallel construction in the original—"Hinüberzugehn und wieder-zukehren"—implies that "here" and "there" are really one and the same. And indeed, the structure of "Patmos" enacts this process of discovery, the crossing over to an Asia, with its "golden haze" and "fragrance of a thousand peaks," leading to the recognition that this "mysterious radiance" can be captured only on native ground and that it exists only in language. The epiphany, at any rate, is brief, for, in the words of "The Rhine," whether by day, "when life / Appears fevered and chained, / Or by night, when everything blends / Into confusion . . . primeval / Chaos reigns once more."

In their clear-eyed vision of a world where, as Yeats put it, "the darkness drops again," no matter what intimations of immortality momentarily pierce the veil, Hölderlin's poems are perhaps the most genuinely painful I have ever read. There is, for example, nothing in English Romantic poetry that can quite match the pure sadness of the final strophe of the late hymn "Mnemosyne." The poet has just described an "Alpine meadow / Where, talking of a wayside cross / Commemorating the dead, / A traveler climbs in a rage, / Sharing distant premonitions with / The other." The traveler is, of course, the poet himself, whose journey to otherness involves extreme suffering (the reference to the wayside cross), as well as the rage of divine inspiration. But in the middle of this account, the line suddenly breaks off:

> Ein Wandersmann geht zornig,
> Fernahnend mit
> Dem andern, aber was ist diß?

> A traveler climbs in a rage,
> Sharing distant premonitions with
> The other, but what is this?

But what is this? The vision breaks, and now we read:

> Am Feigenbaum ist mein
> Achilles mir gestorben

Sieburth's translation:

> By the fig tree
> My Achilles died

does not quite convey the pathos created by the double pronoun "mein"—"mir": a literal reading would be "At the fig tree my Achilles died to me."

In a study of the notebook drafts of "Mnemosyne," Friedrich Beissner shows that these two lines were the kernel of the whole poem, which exists in three different versions. The reference to the fig tree, Beissner expains,[5] was probably prompted by Hölderlin's reading of Richard Chandler's *Travels in Asia Minor and Greece*, where Achilles' grave is explicitly located in a grove of fig trees. But Hölderlin refers, not to the proximity of fig tree and *grave*, but to the fig tree as the place where his Achilles has *died*. It is the death, not of the hero in battle, but of the solitary: Achilles becomes, in other words, the alter ego of the poet. Indeed, in an essay written a few years earlier, Hölderlin declared that what he loved most in the *Iliad* was the character of Achilles, "the genial, all-powerful, melancholy-tender son of the gods."[6] In "Mnemosyne" it is thus "mein / Achilles," with the line breaking off after "mein," and he has not just died, but died for the poet. And now follows the catalog of the deaths:

Und Ajax liegt
An den Grotten der See,
An Bächen, benachbart dem Skamandros.
An Schläfen Sausen ist, nach
Der unbewegten Salamis steter
Gewohnheit, in der Fremd ist groß
Ajax gestorben,
Patroklos aber in des Königes Harnisch. Und es starben
Noch andere viel.

And Ajax lies
By the grottoes of the sea,
By streams, with Skamandros as neighbor.
In the persisting tradition of Salamis,
Great Ajax died
Of the roar in his temples
And on foreign soil, unlike
Patroklos, dead in king's armor. And many
Others also died.

Here, according to Beissner, Hölderlin is referring to Sophocles' *Ajax*, which the poet was translating at the time he was writing "Mnemosyne." In the Sophocles play, Ajax's suicide is prompted by a fit of madness; in his suicide speech, he bids farewell to the grottoes, groves, and streams (like the Skamandros) in the vicinity of Troy, far from his native Salamis. But Hölderlin curiously recounts the death as if it took place twice: the first telling refers to the place ("By the grottoes of the sea"), the second to the cause ("Of the roar in his temples").

If Achilles is what the poet longs to be, Ajax, in his propensity to madness, is closer to what he really is. And Patroklos, "dead in king's armor" (which is to say, in Achilles' armor), becomes the catalyst. For, as Sieburth comments, "The juxtaposition of Ajax and Patroklos is all the more pointed here, given the fact that Ajax killed himself in anger, when, in the wake of Patroklos' death, he was not awarded the armor of Achilles."

"Und es starben / Noch andere viel" (And many / Others also died). One thinks of *The Waste Land*: "I had not thought death had undone so many." Even Mnemosyne, the mother of the Muses, is now defeated:

Der auch, als
Ablegte den Mantel Gott, das abendliche nachter löste
Die Loken.

> And when
> God cast off his cloak, the darkness came to cut
> Her lock of hair.

"These lines," says Sieburth, "speak of the darkness that fell at the close of the ancient Day of divine presence: When even Memory has died, how is poetry possible?"

Notice that Hölderlin neither feels sorry for himself nor blames the gods for his fate. Rather, it is as if he has no choice but to report these deaths, as if they had taken place at the moment of writing the poem. In this context, the cutting of the lock of Mnemosyne's hair represents the final death—that of Poetic Memory itself. "Mnemosyne," evidently Hölderlin's last complete hymn, is thus the poet's elegy for himself in the face of his oncoming madness. Yet even here he tries to control his feelings, to end on a rational and sensible note:

> *Himmlische nemlich sind*
> *Unwillig, wenn einer nicht*
> *Die Seele schonend sich*
> *Zusammengenommen, aber er muß doch; dem*
> *Gleich fehlet die Trauer.*

> For the gods grow
> Indignant if a man
> Not gather himself to save
> His soul, yet he has no choice; like-
> Wise, mourning is in error.

Here Sieburth's translation does not quite convey the tone of the original. "Die Seele schonend" means not so much to save one's soul as to treat it gently, to handle it with kid gloves. Man, having pulled himself together (sich / Zusammengenommen), must spare his soul; he must, in other words, be moderate, avoid extremes: "aber er muß doch." As in English, the German modal usually demands another verb, but here "must" is used in its absolute sense. As Sieburth renders it, "he has no choice." Whatever he does, he is fated to do. To lose control may be to anger the gods, but there is no alternative. For "mourning" (die Trauer), which is to say, uncontrolled grief, is just as futile.

Whether, in other words, the poet rebels against his fate or whether he accepts it sadly and humbly, the result is the same—a final emptiness. We see, as the poet says in strophe 2, "sunshine / On the floor and motes of dust / And the shadows of our native woods and smoke / Blooms from rooftops." But it no longer makes any difference. One way or another, the walls close in. And this is not idle talk, for, in Hölderlin's case, it is precisely what happened.

4

"Mnemosyne" acts as a kind of bridge to the notebook drafts and fragments that are the works most congenial to Sieburth as a translator. Clearly, it is "the aesthetic of the fragment," with its "paratactic character" and its "radical dispossession," that brings out Sieburth's own remarkable poetic talent. As he observes:

> It is largely irrelevant whether the texts that his editors have labeled *Hymnische Entwürfe* ("Drafts of Hymns") or *Bruchstücke* ("Fragments") were indeed actually intended by Hölderlin to stand as self-sufficient entities: what matters is that *we* read them that way . . . To the twentieth-century reader whose taste has been shaped by *The Waste Land* and *The Cantos*, Hölderlin's late drafts and fragments may well be the most accessible portion of his oeuvre, precisely because they seem most modern.

Purists will object that the so-called fragments were, in fact, partial statements or first versions that would have been connected or revised had the poet "finished" them. But, as Sieburth says, in the age of the *Cantos*, it is the very unfinish of these "Drafts and Fragments" (Pound's term) that is attractive. "Auf falbem Laube," for example, becomes, in Sieburth's version ("On pale leaf"), a counterpart to Paul Celan's enigmatic Imagist poems. Again, "Kolomb" (Columbus) contains long catalogs of proper names (e.g., "Anson and Gama, Aeneas / And Jason, the pupil / of Chiron in Megara's caves") and passages that juxtapose Columbus's / own words with French phrases so as to create a Poundian texture:

> And one, an orator,
> Took the floor, a priest or captain
> In a blue jacket
>
> Entière personne content de son
> ame difficulties connoissance
> rapport tire [*sic*]
>
> You out there, calling
> Us from
> This place

One of Sieburth's finest renditions is that of "Heimath" (Home). The poem opens with the short line, "Und niemand weiss" (And no one knows). And no one knows what? The sentence is never completed; instead, the line breaks off and is followed by white space (the equivalent of four lines of print). Then we read:

> *Indessen laß mich wandeln*
> *Und wilde Beeren pflüken*
> *Zu löschen die Liebe zu dir*
> *An deinen Pfaden, o Erd'*
>
> *Hier wo*
>   *und Rosendornen*
> *Und süße Linden duften neben*
> *Den Buchen, des Mittags, wenn im falben Kornfeld*
> *Das Wachstum rauscht, an geradem Halm,*
> *Und den Naken die Ähre seitwärts beugt*
> *Dem Herbste gleich, jezt aber unter hohem*
> *Gewölbe der Eichen, da ich sinn*
> *Und aufwärts frage, der Glokenschlag*
> *Mir wohlbekannt*
> *Fernher tönt, goldenklingend, um die Stunde, wenn*
> *Der Vogel wieder wacht. So gehet es wohl.*

> Meanwhile let me roam
> And pick wild berries
> To quiet my love for you
> Upon your paths, O Earth
>
> Here where
>   and the thorns of roses
> And sweet lindens cast their fragrance
> Beside the beeches, at noon, when the pale rye
> Rustles with the growth of slender stalks,
> Their ears bowed to the side
> Like autumn, but beneath the high
> Vault of oaks, as I muse
> And question the sky, the sound of bells
> I know well

From afar rings golden at the hour
Of reawakening birds. So it goes.

Here Sieburth filters Hölderlin through the locutions and rhythms of Stevens: one thinks of "Sunday Morning" (the "reawakening birds") as well as "The Auroras of Autumn." But the Pound of Cathay is also present. Whereas Hamburger translates "wenn im falben Kornfeld" as "when in the yellowish cornfield / There is a whisper of growth, by the straight stalk," Sieburth opts for the Pound-Fenollosa doctrine that "the cherry tree is all that it does," and writes, "when the pale rye / Rustles with the growth of slender stalks." Again, where Hamburger's "I" "question[s] heavenward," Sieburth's simply "question[s] the sky." The "stroke of the bell, / Familiar to me" (Mir wohlbekannt) becomes "the sound of bells / I know well." Indeed, the fusion of the tolling bell and the renewed birdsong with which the poem concludes, only to end on the deflationary note, "So gehet es wohl," could hardly be more precisely rendered than in Sieburth's

as I muse
And question the sky, the sound of bells
I know well
From afar rings golden at the hour
Of reawakening birds. So it goes

Compare Hamburger:

where I ponder
And question heavenward, the stroke of the bell,
Familiar to me,
Rings out from afar, with a golden ring, at the hour when
The birds awake once more. Then all is well.

Literally, "So gehet es wohl" translates as "It goes well" or "All is well." But idiomatically the phrase is used to say, "That's the way it goes" or, as Sieburth puts it, "So it goes." Surely the second is closer to Hölderlin's larger meaning, which is that, despite the expected beauty of nature, despite the poet's love for the earth, despite his knowledge that the birds will return to sing again, nothing can change for him.

There are other subtle differences. Hamburger's "Rings out from afar" has a Tennysonian cast even as "at the hour when / The birds awake once more" sounds just a shade like Gilbert and Sullivan. "Heavenward"—"yellowish cornfield"—"give out their fragrance"—"Rings out from afar"—these fin-de-siècle locutions, locutions which have made Hölderlin in English cut a somewhat donnish figure, give way, in Sieburth's readings, to the rhetoric of a Celan on an Ashbery. The Poet as Heideggerian Name-Giver is also a Sleight-of-Hand Man.

To conclude: here is a gnomic lyric fragment called "What is the life of man?":

> What is the life of man? An image of divinity.
> As they all wander beneath the sky, mortals
> Look to it. As if reading
> A scripture, men imitate infinity
> And riches. Well, is the simple
> Sky rich? Silver clouds are in fact
> Like flowers. Yet rain down
> Dew and damp. But when the simple
> Blue is effaced, the sky,
> Mat as marble, shines like ore,
> Indicating riches.

It is all very well to talk of the life of man as an image of divinity ("ein Bild der Gottheit"). Yet, when you come right down to it, the signs are deceptive. Silver clouds are like flowers but they rain down dew and damp. And the proverbial blue sky yields nothing of interest. Only when we learn to do without that blue, will the sky shine "like ore, / Indicating riches." But aren't these heavenly "riches" one and the same with the "image of divinity" the poet dutifully offered us to begin with? And if so, how do we avoid the trap of conventional piety? "Nah ist / Und schwer zu fassen."

Notes

1.   See Martin Heidegger, "*Hölderlin und das Wesen der Dichtung*," *Erläuterungen zu Hölderlin's Dichtung*, 5th ed. (Frankfurt am Main, 1981), 34, 41. This essay, translated by Douglas Scott as "Hölderlin and the Essence of Poetry," appears in Heidegger, *Existence and Being*, ed. Werner Brock (Chicago: Gateway, 1970), 270–91.

2.   This essay is reprinted in Michel Foucault, *Language, Counter-Memory, Practice: Selected Essays and Interview*, ed. Donald F. Bouchard, trans. Donald F. Bouchard and Sherry Simon (Ithaca and London: Cornell University Press, 1971), 68–86. See also Paul de Man's trenchant critique, "Heidegger's Exegesis of Hölderlin" (1952), in *Blindness and Insight: Essays in the Rhetoric of Contemporary Criticism*, rev. 2nd ed., ed. Wlad Godzich (Minneapolis: University of Minnesota Press, 1983: Theory and History of Literature, Vol. 7), 246–66; Theodore W. Adorno, "Parataxis Zur späten Lyrik Hölderlins," in *Über Hölderlin: Aufsätze*, ed. Jochen Schmidt (Frankfurt: Insel Verlag, 1970), 339–78.

3.   Friedrich Hölderlin, *Poems and Fragments*, trans. Michael Hamburger, bilingual ed. with preface, introduction, and notes (Cambridge: Cambridge University Press, 1980), 370–71. This new edition of translations, which first appeared in 1966, contains almost all of Hölderlin's extant poetry and is considered the standard work.

4.   Friedrich Hölderlin and Eduard Morike, *Selected Poems*, trans. Christopher Middleton (Chicago and London: University of Chicago Press, 1972), 72–73. This edition is highly selective but, given Middleton's own status as a significant contemporary poet, it is interesting to see what he does with Hölderlin's lyric.

5.   "Hölderlin letzte Hymne," in *Über Hölderlin*, 113–52. See esp. 137.

6.   *Hölderlin Werke und Briefe*, ed. Friedrich Beissner and Jochen Schmidt, Vol. 2: *Der Tod des Empedokles. Aufsätze. Übersetzungen. Briefe* (Frankfurt: Insel Verlag, 1969), 595. My translation.

CHAPTER 26

Of Canons and Contemporaries

E zra Pound was born October 30, 1885, and this autumn his centenary was celebrated from Hailey, Idaho (the place of his birth), to New Haven, Tuscaloosa, Paris, and Tokyo. At Orono, Maine, poets as unlike one another as Donald Davie and Allen Ginsberg spoke of Pound's influence; at San Jose, such younger poets as Michael Palmer and Michael Davidson lectured on Pound's use of language, his stylistic habits, his relationship to earlier writers. However serious the controversy about Pound's politics, his anti-Semitism, indeed his ethics, is today, there can be no doubt that in 1985 Pound is considered one of our great poets—for many people, THE great American poet of the twentieth century and certainly a poet's poet. At the two conferences I myself attended (Orono and San Jose), I was struck by the excitement, erudition, and range of Pound scholarship. No other twentieth-century poet has stimulated such searching and subtle criticism, a criticism, incidentally, that comes not only from around the world but from Left as well as Right, from deconstructionists as well as traditional scholars, from Zen Buddhists and Confucians, as well as committed Christians and confirmed atheists. In the graduate seminar today the debate about the place of the *Cantos*, not only in literary history, but also as an emblem of Modernist culture and society seems to be at its height.

Or is it? At the very moment that the Yale and Alabama Pound symposia were being held, the Harvard University Press published *The Harvard Book of Contemporary American Poetry*, edited by Helen Vendler. This anthology, which begins with the poetry of Wallace Stevens "since he flowered late and came into his own only after the 1955 publication of the *Collected Poems*," systemically and

Review of *The Harvard Book of Contemporary Poetry*, ed. Helen Vendler. *Sulfur* 16 (1986): 155–62.

quietly removes Pound and his circle from the canon. ["Stevens,"] writes Vendler, "is our chief link between the earlier high Modernists (Eliot, Pound, Williams, Crane, Moore) and the later poets," an odd statement indeed in view of the fact that the full text of Pound's *Cantos* did not appear until 1970 and therefore is not likely to have exerted an influence *before* that date. Or again, how could Stevens be the "chief link" between Williams and "the later poets," given the fact that *Paterson* was not completed until 1958, three years after Stevens's death, and *Pictures from Breughel* was not published until 1962? Or, to take a third example, how could Stevens's poetry mediate between a Modernist work like H. D.'s *Trilogy* and contemporary poets, given the fact the first edition of the *Trilogy*, written during World War II, was in 1973?

But of course it all depends on what "later poets" one has in mind. Stevens may well point the way to many of the other thirty-four poets included in *The Harvard Book* for the simple reason that this anthology omits all of the following: Charles Olson, Kenneth Rexroth, Robert Creeley, Robert Duncan, Edward Dorn, Denise Levertov, Louis Zukofsky, George Oppen, Paul Blackburn, Jerome Rothenberg, to mention only the most prominent American poets in the Pound-Williams tradition. Although Vendler is careful to point out that "this anthology can be nothing more than a sampling of what seems to my taste satisfying," her own authority and the Harvard imprimatur clearly make this particular anthology take on canonical aura. And so we must ask the question: what are the contours of a poetry landscape that, on the one hand, celebrates Pound in the fashion I described above and, on the other, authorizes or at least sets the stage for the publication of *The Harvard Book of Contemporary American Poetry*?

The first thing to say, I suppose, is that the current situation is very different from that of 1960, the year Grove Press published Donald Allen's *The New American Poetry*. At that time, there was an identifiable Establishment, whose emblematic anthology, used in classrooms across America, was the two-volume *New American Poets of England and America* (1957), edited by Donald Hall, Robert Pack, and Louis Simpson. Distinguishing his own canon of poets from theirs, Donald Allen could say, quite simply, that what he was calling the "new" poetry had "one common characteristic: a total rejection of all those qualities typical of academic verse" (p. xi). Today, such a distinction would be meaningless because Olson and Creeley have become just as "academic" as were Lowell or Berryman, if by "academic" we mean those poets who teach, and whose work is taught, in the universities. Nor do the old distinctions between "conservative" and "radical" publishers (Harvard University Press, say, versus New Directions) make much sense today. Harvard has just published the selected writings of one of the most radical poets of the twentieth century, the Russian Futurist Velimir Khlebnikov, and it is also the press that brought out Robert von Hallberg's important *Charles Olson: The Scholar's Art* (1978). Again, the University of California Press is responsible for bringing both Olson's *Maximus* and Zukofsky's *"A"* back into print, and for publishing the *Collected Poems* of Robert Creeley, now to be followed by a volume of *Collected Prose*. Even Bruce Andrews' and Charles Bernstein's *The L=A=N=G=U=A=G=E Book*, for that matter, was published, not by some struggling small press or even by New Directions but by the Southern Illinois University Press.

We can no longer, then, talk about the "raw" and the "cooked," or about "closed forms" and "naked poetry," as Stephen Berg and Robert Mezey called it in their excellent anthology of "Recent American Poetry in Open Forms" (1969). This might suggest that the eighties are characterized by a healthy eclecticism, a cheerful pluralism that insures that everyone gets invited to the party. But the fact is that an anthology like the *Harvard Book* is much less eclectic than, say, Richard Ellmann's 1976 *New Oxford Book of American Verse*, which included such poets as Olson, Duncan, Creeley, and Dorn along with the bulk of the poets who appear in the Vendler anthology. Indeed, our total lack of consensus about "the state of the art" testifies less to a generous pluralism than to a curious indifference to the dissemination of poetry on the part of the very persons who should be concerned with it—poetry critics, reviewers, editors, and publishers, as well as those theorists who deal with questions of poetics, and of Modernism and postmodernism.

What we might call the new indifference goes hand in hand with a preoccupation with theory as the literary discourse that really matters. For the very same critics who cannot find a way of discussing whether Pound's *Cantos* is the great poem of the century or merely, in Vendler's words, a "great failed effort," the very same critics who talk repeatedly about "opening up the canon" or "breaking down the old canon" are slavish in their deference to the canonical critics of our day. What self-respecting anthology of contemporary theory, for example, would dare to omit the names of Foucault, Lacan, Derrida, or Kristeva, and, closer to home, of Paul de Man, Harold Bloom, Stanley Fish, Edward Said, Fredric Jameson, or Hayden White? If Harvard were to publish something called *The Harvard Book of Contemporary Criticism* and included, say, only deconstructionists or reader-response critics or Marxist-feminist theorists, there would be an immediate outcry. Or, more probably, the outcry would have been circumvented by the publisher, who would have shown the table of contents to a variety of "respectable" critics and would have been cautioned to make the anthology more inclusive. But in the case of the *Harvard Book of Contemporary Poetry*,

Helen Vendler was evidently given carte blanche to do whatever she liked. Or almost carte blanche: one suspects that she felt at least some pressure to include black poets (hence the otherwise unaccountable inclusion of Langston Hughes who wrote most of his major poems during the 1920s, and of a still-fledgling poet like Rita Dove), a sufficient number of women (I doubt Anne Sexton would otherwise have been included), at least one Beat poet (Allen Ginsberg, who, as a Jewish gay man, also satisfies the minority requirement), and, in the interest of geographical distribution, one West Coast—Zen—minimalist poet in the form of Gary Snyder.

Vendler's introduction, in any case, makes no attempt to justify these inclusions (or their corrective exclusions), opting instead for the large and elegant generalization about "contemporary American poetry." Who, for example, can quarrel with her opening distinction between "the charm of poetry" and its "command," between, that is to say, its linguistic strategies, which she rightly calls untranslatable, and its moral and intellectual content, which can be transmitted even in the poetry we read in translation? Vendler sensibly suggests that contemporary poetry is written both for the eye and for the ear, that visual prosody is now a force to reckon with. And she points out, again very sensibly, that poetry is a "self-hating" form of discourse, that "it insists on a spooling, a form of repetition, the reinscribing of a groove . . . Lyric poetry . . . is profoundly unlinear. It does not advance" (p. 2).

This is very well put, as is the following definition of contemporary American poetic language:

> It is a language that has assimilated the syncopation of jazz, the stylishness of advertising, the technicalities of psychoanalysis, the simplicities of rural speech, the discourse of the university disciplines, the technology of the engineer, the banalities of journalism. (p. 2)

I find myself nodding in enthusiastic agreement, until I start to think about Vendler's choices and ponder why Louis Zukofsky, who understood, as perhaps has no other American Modernist, the "stylishness of advertising," the "technology of the engineer," and the "banalities of journalism," isn't included whereas Howard Nemerov, who writes poems like the following, is:

Snowflakes

Not slowly wrought, nor treasured for their form
In heaven, but by the blind self of the storm

> Spun off, each driven individual
> Perfected in the moment of his fall.

Can this be regarded as the new American language where "the vernacular thrives and where the rhythms of American life . . . have found a place"? Or, to move over a few pages to the Amy Clampitt selection, where are "the rhythms of American life" in "The Kingfisher," which begins:

> In a year the nightingales were said to be so loud
> they drowned out slumber, a peafowl strolled screaming
> beside the ruined nunnery, through the long evening
> of a dazzled pub crawl, the halcyon color, portholed
> by those eye-spots' stunning tapestry unsettled
> the pastoral nightfall with amazements opening. (p. 122)

Surely Clampitt's is, to paraphrase Eliot on Henry James, a mind so fine no journalistic banality has ever violated it. "A peafowl strolled screaming / beside the ruined nunnery" has a faintly Yeatsian ring, just as "those eye-spots stunning tapestry unsettled" recalls Hopkins, but for the "American idiom," we had better go to that other poem called "The Kingfishers" written by Charles Olson:

> What does not change / is the will to change
>
> He woke, fully clothed, in his bed. He
> remembered only one thing, the birds, how
> when he came in, he had gone around the rooms
> and got them back in their cage, the green one first.

The "American idiom," in any case, is described at length in Vendler's introduction, evidently with an eye to the *Harvard Book*'s potential foreign audience. As such, it might be useful to compare the Vendler version of contemporary American poetry to a recent foreign counterpart, specifically the Gallimard bilingual anthology *Vingt poètes américains*, chosen by two prominent poet-critics Jacque Roubaud and Michel Deguy (Paris, 1980). Roubaud's introduction begins with the sentence, "What constitutes American literature; in the second half of the twentieth century, is poetry, indeed the explosion of poetry" (my translation). Implicit in this statement is the assumption that poetry inevitably undergoes historical change (in this case, a rupture), an assumption quite at odds with Vendler's evident faith in the timelessness of poetry. "The symbolic strength of poetry," she writes, "consists in giving presence, through linguistic signs, to absent realities, while insisting, by the very brilliance of poetic style, on the linguistic nature of its own being and the illusionistic character of its effects." That, for Vendler, is what poetry always *is*. Roubaud is more pragmatic: his starting point is the year 1960 in which Donald Allen published *The New American Poetry*, and the "explosion" to which he refers comes out of (1) Black Mountain, (2) the San Francisco Renaissance, (3) the New York School, and (4) Objectivism, as these four related movements affected the work of younger poets. The editor further explains that certain poets already well-known in France (Pound, Williams, Stevens, Cummings, O'Hara, Cage) have been omitted, but that he has included one great precursor, Gertrude Stein, because her work is only now having a decisive effect on poets like John Ashbery, Robert Duncan, Jerome Rothenberg, and David Antin (and, writing five years later, Roubaud might have added the "Language" poets, who have been ardent Stein fans, to this group). The resulting list of "twenty American poets," in the order of their presentation is as follows: Gertrude Stein, Louis Zukofsky, George Oppen, Robert Duncan, Denise Levertov, James Schuyler, Cid Corman, Jack Spicer, Paul Blackburn, Charles Olson, John Ashbery, Larry Eigner, W. S. Merwin, Harry Matthews, Kenneth Koch, Jerome Rothenberg, David Antin, Rosemarie Waldrop, Clayton Eshleman, and Nathaniel Tarn.

There is virtually no common ground between this selection of poets and Vendler's. Only two poets so much as turn up in both the Harvard and the Gallimard anthologies—Ashbery and Merwin. And even here there is an interesting difference, Vendler choosing the later, more "thematic" Ashbery and Merwin poems (e.g., Ashbery's "Self-Portrait in a Convex Mirror," Merwin's "The Asian Dying"), Roubaud and Deguy the more experimental ones like Ashbery's "Sunrise in Suburbia" and Merwin's gnomic epigrams like "The Dream Again."

Does the disparity between the Harvard and the Gallimard anthologies then replicate the old battle between the "academic" (Hall-Pack-Simpson) and the "radical" (Donald Allen)? Not really. For whereas the Gallimard editors are careful to insist, "This anthology makes no claims to *represent* all of American poetry, whose great richness is just beginning to be understood by us" (see dust jacket; my translation), and whereas they make quite clear that they want to introduce French readers to such historical movements as Objectivism and the New York School, to ethnopoetics and the new "performance" poetry, the Harvard anthology purports, according to the dust jacket, to present us with "the range and power of the contemporary American imagination," with the "distillations of twentieth-century perception, feeling, and thought, and reflections of changing social realities."

It is, in short, the Harvard anthology's claim to canonicity that is problematic. Toward the end of her introduction, Vendler observes:

> I have preferred to choose fewer poets, and represent them by more poems, rather than have more poets with few poems each. In this way, readers can see the poets whole. I have had to leave out many poets whose aims were admirable but whose poems seemed thin (whatever their past historical effect).

The parenthesis in that last sentence is especially revealing. For Vendler, poems neither seem to make nor reflect history; they simply *are*. Thus none of the poems in the anthology are dated, and the capsule biographies in the back of the book are likely to be longer on impressionistic description (Louise Glück "writes in a veiled and almost disembodied style at once austere and sensuous"; O'Hara is "a poet of invention, irreverence, and colloquial energy") than on factual information. More important: approximately a quarter of the poems are not, by any stretch of the imagination, "contemporary" at all since Vendler begins with "Sunday Morning" (1915), includes a group of Langston Hughes poems written in the 1920s as well as a selection from Roethke's "greenhouse poems" of the 1940s, and quite a few forties poems by Jarrell, Bishop, and Lowell. Indeed, it is worth noting that twelve of Vendler's thirty-five "contemporary" poets are dead.

But none of this seems to matter for the principle of selection used in the *Harvard Book* has less to do with a period of history (the "contemporary") than with the Harvard of Vendler's early mentors, I. A. Richards and Reuben Brower. In his *The Fields of Light: An Experiment in Critical Reading* (1951), Brower organized his chapters around such topics as "The Speaking Voice (*Dramatic Design*)," "The Aura Around a Bright Clear Centre (*Design in Imagery*)," "Saying One Thing and Meaning Another (*Design in Metaphor and Irony*)," and "The Sinewie Thread (*Key Designs*)." Here is the familiar New Critical demand for organic unity, centering, irony, and indirection, and these are the unstated norms that govern the *Harvard Book of Contemporary Poetry*.

Key design, the "aura around a bright clear centre"—these are further qualified for Vendler by certain thematic values. "There is no significant [contemporary] poet," she writes, "whose work does not mirror, both formally and in its preoccupations, the absence of the transcendent" (p. 11). And again, "The poets included here write—as the earlier Modernists did not—from a Freudian culture" (p. 10), and Lowell is "the first American poet of the family romance" (p. 5). So much for Olson, Duncan, H. D., and Rothenberg, all of them poets who do concern themselves, in one form or another, with "the transcendent"; so much for Zukofsky and Dorn, for Cage and Antin, poets for whom the Freudian family romance is only a small part of the larger sociopolitical world in which we live.

Indeed, to use her own distinction, Vendler herself is more interested in the "moral command" of poetry than in its "linguistic charm." Valuing the Freudian matrix of "the inner life," Vendler quite logically gives precedence to Lowell, Bishop, Berryman, Merrill, Plath, and Rich, to the Ginsberg of *Kaddish* (notably his only "family romance" poem), and to such younger Freudian poets as Frank Bidart and Louise Glück. And even such poets as Ashbery and O'Hara are shadowed by the company they keep in the *Harvard Book*. Framed by countless poems about marriage, infidelity, generational conflict, and psychological trauma, O'Hara's "Why I Am Not a Painter" or Ashbery's "Syringa" undergo an odd process of what Alan C. Golding, in a study of American poetry anthologies (see *Canons*, ed. Robert von Hallberg [University of Chicago Press, 1984]) wittily calls *detoxification*. When, that is to say, we read O'Hara's wonderfully playful, "But me? One day I am thinking / of a color: orange. I write a line / About orange," against the theorem that "the symbolic strength of poetry consists in giving presence, through linguistic signs, to absent realities," we are likely to take O'Hara's "How terrible orange is / and life," as no more than a faint parodic echo of the "late / Coffee and oranges in a sunny chair" of Stevens' "Sunday Morning," the headpiece of the Vendler anthology.

The bright clear center of the "family romance" does not, in other words, allow much room for "aura," much less for difference. A critic of Helen Vendler's authority has, of course, every right to exercise her preferences, to put together a book of her own personal favorites. I myself find the *Harvard Book* a fascinating index to the sensibility and consciousness of one of our most important critics. But to call such a book *The Harvard Book of Contemporary American Poetry* is something else again. What this pretentious title tells us is that our leading publishers, who, in the case of other fields of knowledge, take some pains to establish reasonable guidelines and norms, seem to regard the publishing of poetry as a comparatively trivial pursuit, a more or less marginalized activity, the real action of the moment as being elsewhere. We need to find out how this came to be the case and why. Indeed, what is most urgently needed today is a more adequate discourse about poetry, a discourse that would avoid the bland impressionism that is currently the stock-in-trade of the poetry review. In the absence of a more rigorous poetics, the postmodern, post-Marxist, postculture pantheon will soon include another term—POSTPOETRY.

CHAPTER 27

Agon

The December 1982 issue of the *Yale Review* carried a review of Harold Bloom's *Agon* by none other than Harold Bloom. A joke? Well, not quite. A "poetics of power," as Bloom calls his "Nietzschean polemic," cannot be submitted to anything like impartial summation or judgment: "Most of what we call criticism is not criticism and should be called journalism. Most of what is now called theory is a kind of journalism also. Nearly everything we call literary scholarship is journalism—poor journalism, since it is not news." Bloom's own "revisionist" or "antithetical" stance, it seems, can be defined only by Bloom himself. He explains, for instance, that "our author" has chosen to "remain unphilosophical" because he "knows that philosophy, like religion, is a stuffed bird upon the shelf." Again, he tells us that his interest in Freud (the only "live rival" to criticism) has nothing to do with what is called "Freudian literary criticism"; on the contrary, "the Freudian tropes, having been appropriated from literature, are taken back by criticism when they are seen clearly as being tropes only." Again, "negative theology," as Professor Bloom now calls his critical perspective, defies "all the current covens and sects," which include "skeptics" (deconstructors) and "idolators" ("moldy figs") as well as "feminists, Marxists, Heideggerians" and just about everyone else. "Blessed and cursed by total recall," says Harold Bloom of himself, "there is for him no text anyway, but only that one continuous poem that Shelley prophesied and Borges parodies. His obsession with the trope of transumption reflects his vision of all poetry as being one giant metalepsis, an endless substitution of images of earliness for those of belatedness." As such, Bloom has written a book that is, by his own admission, "not . . . very reviewable."

On this last point the reviewer can only agree, especially since, to apply

Review of *Agon*, by Harold Bloom, *Modern Language Review* 81 (April 1986): 431–35.

Professor Bloom's words to his own book, "there is . . . no text anyway, but only that one continuous poem." The Oxford University Press has unaccountably provided no list of acknowledgements, thus implying that *Agon* is a new work. The fact is that the majority of chapters have been published elsewhere: in the *Oxford Literary Review* (chapter 2), the *New Republic* (no. 12), the *Kenyon Review* (no. 13), and so on. If, as Bloom contends, "nearly everything we call literary scholarship is journalism," what about the other way around? Is journalism (reviewing for weeklies like the *New Republic*) to be construed as literary history or theory?

Surely only "moldy figs" ask such pedantic questions. But suppose we take Bloom at his own word and read *Agon*, not as an exposition of the now famous revisionary ratios or the three crossings, or as his particular version of "Gnostic catastrophe creation" grafted upon "Freudian conflicts of heightened emotional ambivalence," but as a belated version of the critic he cites most frequently as loved precursor (although, according to his own theory of the anxiety of influence, the poet cannot, of course, identify his *real* precursors): namely, Oscar Wilde. Here is Bloom on Wilde:

> The great theorist of [the] voice [of the critic] as voice remains Oscar Wilde, when he reminds us, following Walter Pater, how important it is that the critical imagination never falls into careless habits of accuracy. We must see the object, the poem, as in itself it really is not, because we must see not only what is missing in it, but why the poem had to exclude what is missing. Carlyle and Ruskin, Pater and Wilde are strong critics, but Matthew Arnold is not a critic at all, only a passing bell, or the School Inspector upon his rounds.

And again, with what Bloom considers true Wildean (or Nietzschean defiance):

> Strong reading doesn't ever ask: Am I getting this poem right? Strong reading *knows* that what it does to the poem is right, because it knows what Emerson, its American inventor, taught it, which is that the true ship is the shipbuilder. If you don't believe in your reading, then don't bother anyone else with it, but if you do, then don't care whether anyone else agrees with it or not. If it is strong enough, then they will come round to it anyway, and you should just shrug when they tell you finally that it is a right reading. Of course it isn't, because right reading is not reading well, and can be left, as Yeats grandly would have said, to our servants, except that we haven't got any servants.

Of course Yeats, citing Villiers, wanted to leave, not right reading, which he took seriously indeed, but its very opposite, practical living, to our servants, but presumably the accuracy of the attribution does not matter. What is more important is whether Harold Bloom's own criticism is, as he claims, a form of poetry in the Wildean sense. Here is Wilde's Vivian in *The Decay of Living*, explaining to Cyril that life imitates art rather than the other way around:

Schopenhauer has analyzed the pessimism that characterized modern thought, but Hamlet invented it. The world has become sad because a puppet was once melancholy. The nihilist, that strange martyr who has no faith, who goes to the stake without enthusiasm, and dies for what he does not believe in, is a purely literary product. He was invented by Turgenev, and completed by Dostoyevski. Robespierre came out of the pages of Rousseau as surely the People's Palace rose out of the debris of a novel. Literature always anticipates life. It does not copy it, but moulds it to its purpose. The nineteenth century as we know it, is largely an invention of Balzac.

Compare this to the following statement by Bloom:

Poetry from Homer through Alexander Pope (who died in 1744) had a subject matter in the characters and actions of men and women clearly distinct from the poet who observed them, and who described them and sometimes judged them. But from 1744 or so to the present day the best poetry internalized its subject matter, particularly in the mode of Wordsworth after 1798. Wordsworth had no true subject except his own subjective nature, and very nearly all significant poetry since Wordsworth, even by American poets, has repeated Wordsworth's inward turning.

Wilde's charming and witty aphorisms, embedded as they are in dialogue, are neither true nor false; we read them not as evidence of Balzac's or Dostoyevsky's embodiment of Wilde's own centrally Modern sensibility, a sensibility that views life through the spectacles of art. Then too, Wilde has common sense (the pragmatism that Professor Bloom repeatedly praises but rarely exhibits) on his side, for it is incontestable that, having steeped ourselves in, say, the *Comédie Humaine*, we will begin to see patterns of human behavior that seem to follow Balzacian laws. Wilde is, in other words, calling something to our attention that we already know and making it memorable by means of his superbly elegant rhetoric.

Harold Bloom's generalizations are of a very different sort. By providing a specific date, 1744, as the point at which all poetry turned around and began to internalize its subject matter, he forces us to consider the accuracy of his statement. Exceptions immediately come to mind: was Balzac's "true subject" his "subjective nature" only? If it is argued that Balzac does not count because he is not a poet but a novelist, then what about Joyce? Is Joyce closer to Wordsworth or to the pre-1844 Swift? Does "poetry" mean only "verse" or all imaginative writing? Such questions inevitably present themselves, and Professor Bloom's paragraph, far from allowing itself to be judged as "poetry," appears as literary history manqué—manqué because it strikes us as merely inaccurate. Accuracy, Bloom holds, is not the issue, but the tone of the passage (the hectoring tone of the schoolmaster) suggests otherwise. An expository sentence that tells us that X happened before 1744 and Y afterward demands to be taken seriously.

Similar problems are raised by Bloom's specific readings of texts. Consider the following gloss on the opening of John Ashbery's "Tapestry." The lines are: "It is difficult to separate the tapestry / From the room or loom which takes precedence over it, / For it must always be frontal and yet to one side." Bloom comments:

> Reductively I translate this (with reservations and reverence) as: "It is impossible to separate the poem, Ashbery's *Tapestry*, from either the anterior tradition or the process of writing, each of which has priority, and illusion of presence over it, because the poem is compelled always to 'be frontal,' confronting the force of the literary past, 'and yet to one side,' evading that force." The tapestry, and Ashbery's poem, share an absence that exists in an uneasy dialectical alternation with the presence of the room of tradition, and the loom of composition.

This seemingly neutral translation implies (1) that poems have a paraphraseable content, and (2) that "Tapestry" is valuable because it sets forth a theory of poetic composition that, not surprisingly, echoes Bloom's own: the poem is *compelled* always to be "frontal," *confronting* the force of its precursors. Such analysis is not Wildean or Nietzschean or Emersonian: these "poetic" critics did not bother to "misread" the poems of others so as to make them yield up meanings that were really their own; rather, they left such "translation" aside in the interest of putting forward their own personal vision of the poetic imagination as it relates to life. But Bloom wants it both ways: academic that he is, he wants, on the one hand, to make statements about literary history or about Ashbery's poetic content, while on the other, he wants to be original, daring, and "post-apocalyptic." In "Tapestry," should he not also be able to come to terms with, say, the long two-column poem "Litany"? The latter cannot be forced in the mold of Romantic crisis poem, and so it is more or less dismissed as a failure. But if Bloom were approaching Ashbery's poetry from a Wildean or Emersonian perspective, such incorporation of A and dismissal of B would make no sense. It is as if Wilde has asserted that the nineteenth century is the invention of Balzac and then paused to add that, say, *La Femme de trente ans* is not true Balzac. Again, Wilde does not pick quarrels with fellow critics (surely these drones are not worth the trouble!), whereas Professor Bloom is constantly sparring with such colleagues as Paul de Man ("the critical theorist who [after Nietzsche] troubles and wounds me most"), or Frank Lentricchia, or with "intellectual Paris" *tout court*. The epithet for de Man is telling: surely only in the cloistered world of New Haven would a comparison between him and Nietzsche be taken seriously.

Harold Bloom is, in any case, less the poet he claims to be than the proponent of a particular position that emerges most clearly in his chapter on Emerson. The text he mines most frequently is the famous passage near the opening of *Nature* that begins, "Crossing a bare common, in snow puddles . . . I have enjoyed a perfect exhilaration," and ends with the pithy words, "I become a transparent eyeball; I am nothing; I see all; the currents of the Universal Being circulate through me; I am part or parcel of God." Professor Bloom calls this "a Sublime crossing of the gulf of solipsism" and is quick to add that such a crossing "is *not* into a communion with others." For Emerson's next sentence is: "The name of the nearest friends sounds then foreign and accidental: to be brothers, to be acquaintances, master or servant, is then a trifle and a disturbance." It is this sentence that Professor Bloom repeatedly cites and takes out of context so as to show that "human communion" (impossible after 1744 anyway) is what must be avoided since, as Emerson was to say in his 1866 journal, "for every seeing soul there are two absorbing facts,—*I and the Abyss*." The Abyss is defined by Bloom as "the place of original fullness *before* the Creation," and he remarks that "a second-century Gnostic would have understood Emerson's 'I am nothing; I see all.'" Of "*I and the Abyss*" Bloom further says: "This grand outflaring of negative theology is a major text, however gnomic, of *the* American religion, Emersonianism, which this book aspires to identify, to describe, to celebrate, to join." But "*It cannot become the American religion until it first is canonized as American literature.*"

Why must it be so canonized? This bit of dogma is, as Professor Bloom says, his own, not Emerson's. We can only surmise that the American religion must first appear as literature because Harold Bloom is a professor of literature and he must somehow justify his profession, scornful of academe though he pretends to be. If the reader happens to belong to a church and to believe in a particular religion, so much the worse for the reader. The only true religion is Bloomian Gnostic Emersonianism, which transforms Emerson's "I am part or parcel of God" into "the God that is within me," which is to say, the *pneuma* or "spark" that is the "true oracular and ontological self." Great poetry, by this account, turns out to be "*the knowledge . . . of oneself.*" Ergo, great criticism turns out to be the knowledge of Harold Bloom's self.

In this context it is no surprise that Whitman's *Song of Myself* is described as celebrating "the poetic power of masturbation, not of sexual intercourse." To make his case, Bloom gives a reading of sections 26–30 of Whitman's poem, discovering in the passage that begins with the lines "The orchestra whirls me wider than Uranus flies, / It wrenches such ardors from me I did not know I posses'd them, / It sails me, I dab with bare feet" a "poetic release through a Sublime yet quite literal masturbation." Indeed, "this sublime antithetical flight (or repression) not only takes Whitman out of nature but makes him a new kind of god."

This takes masturbation, whether literal or "Sublime," further than some of us would care to take it. Harold Bloom's *Agon*, it seems, is finally within himself.

CHAPTER 28

Theories of the Avant-Garde

There is a wonderful moment in the revue *Beyond the Fringe* (1964) when Alan Bennett, playing the crusty old public schoolboy who thinks all Americans are boors, says of Lyndon Johnson: "I understand he's now taking steps to federalize the avant-garde." By 1984, the joke has very nearly become a fait accompli. Here are two beautifully produced, expensive, and heavy volumes on the avant-garde, authorized by the *Association Internationale de littérature comparée* (AILC) in conjunction with the Centre d'Étude des Avant-Gardes Littéraires at the University of Brussels. At the same time, the University of Minnesota Press has commissioned a translation of Peter Bürger's controversial *Theorie der Avantgarde* (Frankfurt, 1974), with a scholarly introduction by Jochen Schulte-Sasse that is almost as long as Bürger's essay. Both Schulte-Sasse and Bürger regularly refer to *the* avant-garde as if it were a stable object like a table or a historical event like the French Revolution. Surely such avant-gardists as Tristan Tzara and Marcel Duchamp would have found the solemn assessment of their *praxis* a source for delicious Dada parodies.

The caveat of solemnity aside, the AILC volumes are superb reference books that anyone interested in the literature of the early twentieth century would want to own. Volume 1 begins with a chapter tracing the history of the word "avant-garde"; it is interesting that the first metaphoric use of the military term comes as early as 1596 in Estienne Pasquier's *Les Recherches de la France* (1596): "Ce fut vne belle guerre qu'l'on enterprit lors contre l'ignorānce, j'attribue l'auantgarde à Seue, Beze, & Pelletier, ou si le voulez autrement, ce furent les auantcoureurs des autres Poëtes" (. . . these were the advance-runners of the other poets). But

Review of *Theory of the Avant-Garde*, by Peter Bürger; and *Les Avant-gardes littéraires*, ed. J. Weisgerber. *Modern Language Review* 81 (April 1986): 426–28.

this "avant-garde" instance of the word "avant-garde" is something of an accident: its real use dates from Chateaubriand, Mme de Staël, and especially Sainte-Beuve, and chapter 2 surveys the nineteenth-century background, both literary and cultural, that created the climate for the antithetical "radical" literary movements that we now define as "avant-garde." The heart of volume 1 is the seminal third chapter, which provides the reader with a thorough history of these movements: Futurism, Expressionism, Dada, Surrealism, and, in a minor key, Imagism, Cubism, constructivism, and the "neo-avant-garde" of the sixties. Volume 2 takes up the same material thematically. Chapter 4, "Tendances esthétiques" by Adrian Marino, discusses such categories as "Nihilisme," "Antilittérature," and "Rupture et renversement." Chapter 5, by various hands, is an especially useful survey of genres and forms: "Le Vers libre," "La Dispersion syntaxique," "Les Tableaux-poèmes," and so on. Chapter 6, which relates avant-garde literature to the other arts and to science, is inevitably somewhat superficial. By contrast, chapters 7 and 8 contain a series of incisive and original essays on the political and social dimensions of avant-garde writing and its critical reception today. Here survey gives way to speculation, and the vexed question of the relation of aesthetic to political avant-gardism is discussed from varying perspectives.

According to classic Marxist theory, as Charles Russell observes in his summarizing essay, the avant-garde of 1910–1930 was never more than a symptom of the alienation of art in a dominant bourgeois culture. Having no adequate ties to the real revolutionary forces of society, futurist and Dada poets and painters gave primacy to linguistic innovation, thus producing an even greater split between idea and praxis and depriving the proletariat of an instrument for real revolution. Contemporary Marxists like Russell himself thus reject as "naive" the enthusiasm for the avant-garde of such earlier "liberal" critics as Renato Poggioli, whose *Teoria dell'arte d'avanguardia* (Bologna, 1962) argued that only in an open and democratic society can the agonistic and radical spirit of an avant-garde flourish.

Poggioli's view of an avant-garde "breakthrough" has largely prevailed; indeed, it is doubtful that a team of scholars would undertake a project like *Les Avant-gardes littéraires* without its impetus. Peter Bürger, whom Charles Russell cites respectfully in his essay, takes yet a third position. Himself a Marxist, he wants to recuperate the avant-garde from the harsh critiques of Adorno and Althusser, even as he rejects the notion that the avant-garde ever was or can be politically radical.

The function of the avant-garde, according to Bürger, was to make recognizable for the first time "certain general categories of the work of art"; that is to say, it is only "from the standpoint of the avant-garde that the preceding phases in the development of art as a phenomenon in bourgeois society can be understood." It follows that "the European avant-garde movements can be defined as an attack on the status of art in bourgeois society. What is negated is not an earlier form of art (a style) but art as an institution that is unassociated with the life praxis of men." When Duchamp, for example, signs mass-produced objects (a urinal, a bottle rack) and sends them to art exhibitions, "he negates the category of individual production." As such, the avant-garde could exist only once: today one could send any number of signed urinals or other such objects to art exhibitions and no one would be shocked. For Bürger, the neo-avant-garde "becomes a manifestation that is void of sense and that permits the positing of any meaning whatever."

Bürger's theses are buttressed by precious few concrete examples, and no wonder. If the avant-garde exists only to call into question art as an institution, there is no point characterizing the actual work of Picasso or Picabia, Breton or Broch. Bürger, for that matter, seems to have much less interest in what the avant-garde produced than in family quarrels with Gadamer and Horkheimer, Benjamin and Adorno. It is a pleasure to turn from this programmatic discussion of *the* avant-garde to Weisgerber's extensively annotated and suggestive chapters about cubist aesthetic, Surrealist dream imagery, and so on. And even here one wonders whether *movements* do not have a fatal tendency to swallow up *poets* and whether an "avant-garde" that, by definition, excludes Joyce and Eliot, Stein and Proust, Brecht and Kafka (all designated as "Modernists" rather than as bona fide avant-garde movement members) is a useful category.

CHAPTER 29

The Rise and Fall of English Modernism

> The poetry of England is so much what it is, it is the poetry of the things with
> which any of them are shut in in their daily completely daily island life.
> —GERTRUDE STEIN, "What is English Literature?"

Contemporary criticism, even in its more "advanced" post-Structuralist manifestation, rarely violates the decorum of the academic-literary marketplace. True, there is much talk of revising the canon, of *Neglected Black Woman Poet X* being as important as *Established White Male Poet Y*, and so on. But such revaluation usually works in the interest of what is at least a nominal inclusivity: H. D. must now be read alongside Pound and Eliot, Zora Neale Hurston alongside Faulkner and Richard Wright. Not even the most ardent feminist critic among us, however, is likely to suggest that Pound was no more than a trivial versifier or that Faulkner's narrative strategies were inferior to Hurston's. In such matters, the three *P*'s—prudence, politeness, and professionalism—tend to prevail.

In this climate, Hugh Kenner's new book, *A Sinking Island* is sure to be considered outrageous, especially by English readers. Of Virginia Woolf, who is, at the present moment, perhaps the most widely read and taught twentieth-century English writer, Kenner, remarks, "No, *The Waves* we know from the start, is a Bloomsbury self-congratulation, unreal from end to end, voice after voice, finely straining for fineness of perception" (179). Of Rupert Brooke: "[He was] a promising light versifier who'd toyed with thoughts of fish-heaven and a scaly god." And of W. H. Auden: "He lived without embarrassment in the space where undergraduate callowness merges with unschooled self-esteem, and

Review of *A Sinking Island*, by Hugh Kenner. *Scripsi* 52 (1989): 73–81.

whoever else lived there he could dazzle with syntactic agility while violating no trust in shared attitudes."

Such dismissals of the canonical Modernists almost take one's breath away. But then Hugh Kenner has never worried much about the official canon, being himself perhaps the critic most responsible for creating and disseminating the Modernist canon as we know it. *A Sinking Island* is, however, something of a departure even for Kenner, being his only sustained piece of negative criticism. In his earlier books on Modernism (e.g., *The Pound Era, A Homemade World, A Colder Eye, The Mechanical Muse*), Kenner foregrounded the writers and literary forms that he felt mattered and articulated what he took to be their particular conceptual, verbal, and rhythmic traits. By contrast, *A Sinking Island* is largely diagnostic, a lively, sometimes infuriating, but always challenging study of the demise of English literature in our time, a demise brought on by English insularity and class-conscious tunnel vision, abetted by two World Wars.

Kenner's narrative begins in 1895, when "Red, British red, asserted one island's suzerainty over more than a full quarter of Earth's land, and the blue seas were British too *de facto*." The newly large literate public of the fin-de-siècle Empire could be divided, so Kenner argues, into three groups. The first was the *Tit-Bits* public, the best-known member of which is surely Leopold Bloom, who read the paper in the john ("jakes") and wiped himself with the page that bore Mr. Philip Beaufoy's titillating story "Matcham's Masterstroke." *Tit-Bits* had an "Inquiry Column" in which delicious questions like "Has a duel on bicycles ever taken place?" received succinct answers. In this case, yes, between two Spaniards, Moreno and Perez, "and it ended fatally for the latter." As for *Tit-Bits* fiction, stories like Philip Beaufoy's were read not only by shop girls and advertising canvassers like Leopold Bloom but also by the likes of Joseph Conrad (who once sent in a submission) and the young Virginia and Vanessa Stephen. Kenner reproduces an entire *Tit*-Bits story, "For Vera's Sake," the ancestor of our own B movies and TV scripts, and then shows, with great finesse, how this soap opera account of love and anarchism relates to Conrad's treatment of similar objects.

The second reading public was that of *Everyman's Library*, the brainchild of J. M. Dent and Ernest Rhys, the domain of middle-class respect for "'the classics." How Dent and Rhys developed their list, how the 1911 Copyright Act made it impossible to issue cheap reprints of anything published after 1870, and what impact this emphasis on the tried and true had on British reading habits constitute one of Kenner's most brilliant chapters.

The ideal order of *Everyman* classics, at any rate, left no room for the foreign, the exotic, the avant-garde. These were the domain of a third reading public, which turned to Paris for its aesthetic and its inspiration. Oscar Wilde and

Aubrey Beardsley, Max Beerbohm and Henry James were its emblematic writers; Art with a capital A was its domain. For a brief moment, Wilde managed to combine aestheticism with celebrity status, but such moments could not last, Wilde's obscenity trial marking the turn. "What was new in 1895," says Kenner, "was the popular press, which had learned, like Wilde, to seize moments for those moments' sake. The wages of somebody's sin was now circulation." With Wilde's downfall, the taste for avant-garde poetry went underground and it took two decades to set the stage for so "aesthetic" a poem as Eliot's "Prufrock."

"Three publics, then, at least, the third unfocused and after 1895 demoralized. Such is a serviceable diagram of the England into which a new literature would attempt to insert itself." Kenner's narrative now traces the rise and fall of this "new literature," a literature characterized, first and foremost, by being produced almost exclusively by foreigners: namely, a Pole (Joseph Conrad), a German (Ford Madox Ford), a number of Americans (Henry James, T. S. Eliot, Ezra Pound, Wyndham Lewis, who spent his first six years in America), and a few Irish (George Bernard Shaw, W. B. Yeats, James Joyce). After 1895, so Kenner posits, "innovative books commence to be written by people who've had to learn the written idiom." If an exception like D. H. Lawrence is admitted into this outsider canon, it's because Lawrence was a miner's son who wrote in opposition to the dominant literature, which depended upon class, snobbery, and the use of "correct" names for things ("'Dinner' is an evening meal for a lord, a midday meal for a labourer"). Lawrence, as Kenner views him, was a brilliant writer, driven, partly by the war, partly by harassment from the censor and the press, into more and more strident posturing, his later work often being "close to rubber-shop porn":

> There was available to [Lawrence] no such public as Dickens had. For public norms had been enfeebled; symbiosis with a literate body could be enjoyed and exploited only by hollow best-seller or by hearty bookmen. Deprived of even the illusion of speaking to a public, to any but a *Daily Mail* public such as you'd cow by shouting, after 1920 he ran wild into pseudo-science, pseudo-anthropology: polarities, dark centres, dark gods.

The chapters that deal with the "foreign" contribution to English literature in the early decades of the century are consistently lively and amusing—Kenner writes wonderfully, for example, about the gradual foundering of the literary friendship between Henry James and H. G. Wells, divided as they were on the issue of language in the novel—but the bravura passages of *A Sinking Island* are those beginning with chapter 7, that deal with writers, whom Kenner has not dealt with at any length before: specifically, Bloomsbury, the Leavis–I. A. Richards Cambridge cenacle, the Auden group, and the post–World War II poets.

Bloomsbury, Kenner posits, would never have been what it was, had the Great War not intervened to destroy a fledgling Modernism "just commencing to insert itself" into English consciousness. Kenner's reference is to the cubist revolution as made manifest in the poetry of Pound and Eliot, the artwork of Wyndham Lewis, the publication of *Blast*. This was by no means the Modernism that Virginia Woolf referred to when she announced, "On or about December 1910, human character changed." Her reference was to the famous Post-Impressionist Exhibition at the Grafton Gallery, organized by her close friend and her sister Vanessa's lover, Roger Fry, an exhibition that may have shocked the middlebrow Establishment, accustomed to the painting of a G. F. Watts, but, as Kenner puts it, "What Roger Fry had displayed in 1910 was tame painting by the lights of 1913 . . . it was even old in 1910." If Bloomsbury considered itself terribly "advanced" for daring to admire Cézanne, Van Gogh, Gauguin, and the "blue" and "pink" period Picasso, this is because, so Kenner argues, Bloomsbury's fabled modernity had less to do with the great currents of international Modernism than with style and gesture:

> They were not Victorians, oh no, not they! They were something new, more outrageous then even Lawrence: a self-appreciating superior class that deferred not even tacitly to any communal usage. One Victorian relic they did cherish, acute class-consciousness. Yes, that had to stay. But the Seven Deadly Sins were dead, beginning with pride, which was simply natural, like envy, not to mention lust. The new list of the Virtues was short, and began with snobbery.

The war, which had caused the death of artists like Gaudier-Brzeska and writers like T. E. Hulme, the war in which "of every ten Englishmen under 45, one had died and two more had suffered wounds," and which thus effectively stopped an incipient Modernism all but dead in its tracks, ushered in an era when anti-Victorians could carry on the Victorian tradition in the "village with a fine library" that was Bloomsbury. In that "village," which "someone characterized—as a congeries of men and women all of whom were in love with Duncan Grant," the greatest Bloomsbury writer, Virginia Woolf (Kenner barely mentions E. M. Forster!) wrote primarily "unread" and unreadable novels, the two exceptions being *Mrs Dalloway* and *To the Lighthouse*. Kenner finds Woolf's criticism "seldom meaty" and dislikes her style of qualification, "This *and* that; this *but* that; this *and* (although that) *yet* that too: filled out as they are by her gracefully balanced cadences—these gestures with the left hand and the right serve not to mobilize attention but to lull it." In her now celebrated letters and diaries, published in multiple volumes, "Virginia [reveals herself as] a wonder—as serenely dislikable a lady as English annals afford." She referred to Harriet Weaver as having the table manners of "a wellbred hen." As for Joyce and Eliot, Woolf was struck "by the indecency of the one, and the obscurity of the other." "I cry out," she confessed, "for the old decorums." Rereading the famous "Mr Bennett and Mrs Brown," Kenner wonders whether Bennett's *Hilda Lessways* isn't, after all, a better novel than many of Woolf's own and concludes: "To an Arnold Bennett she could condescend from her safe perch in the upper middle class, but innovation tormented her with jealousy." Reading *Ulysses* in August 1922, she dismissed its author as "a queasy undergraduate scratching his pimples"—a comment Kenner finds especially annoying, given the obvious influences of *Ulysses* on the time scheme (twenty-four hours) and narrative structure of *Mrs Dalloway*.

Kenner's dismantling of the Woolf legend and, by extension, of the Bloomsbury myth is not, of course, without its own pet prejudices. He has a marked distaste for the Bloomsbury lifestyle, with its "intimate hospitality," its Cambridge-insider manner, its strident atheism, and its androgynous bed-hopping. There are those who will no doubt accuse him of being sexist and (here as well as in the Auden chapter) homophobic. True, women and homosexual writers come off poorly in *A Sinking Island*, but then so do most heterosexual male writers like Dylan Thomas and Philip Larkin. Although gender and sexual orientation may play a role, the main question for Kenner is one of writing practice; his Modernist model has always been the Flaubertian one, with its emphasis on *le mot juste*, on concrete particulars and "direct treatment of the thing." He likes writers who get their facts straight, who don't shrink from the "real." So even Woolf's best novel *To the Lighthouse* suffers, Kenner argues, because of its implausible presentation of Mr Ramsay as someone who reputedly talks at dinner "about the square root of one thousand two hundred and fifty-three." Mrs Ramsay, hearing these words, wonders what a square root is and concludes that it is part of "this admirable fabric of the masculine intelligence—upholding the world." Such bogus presentation of what men talk about and how women react to it is an index, so Kenner argues, to a "radical defect of the imagination," an "unwillingness to conjure real plausibility." As a result, *To the Lighthouse* is "a genuine highbrow novel" but not a genuinely great one and its recent sales reflect primarily "classroom procurements"—for Kenner always the sign of mediocrity and conformity.

Outrageous as Kenner's treatment of Woolf may be, his discussion usefully forces us to reconsider some well-worn pieties. For surely (and I say this as someone who wrote her own MA thesis on Virginia Woolf many years ago), the current Woolf cult is excessive, her novels being required reading in courses where, say, Joyce is barely read and Conrad not at all, not to mention Gertrude Stein and Djuna Barnes. In her recent *Sexual/Textual Politics* (Methuen, 1985), Toril Moi criticizes Elaine Showalter for so much as daring to suggest that Woolf's feminism was problematic; if Woolf is found in any way wanting, this argument goes, the fault must be ours for not knowing how to read her correctly. Again, recent Marxist criticism has tried to make a case for texts like *Three Guineas* as constituting a profound critique of capitalism and even fascism, thus shutting its eyes to the anti-Semitic slurs and class-oriented put-downs found on page after page of the letters and diaries, often in the critical essays as well.

Kenner, in any case, regards Woolf, and by extension Bloomsbury, not as the natural culmination of earlier Modernist experimentation by writers like James and Conrad but as a skillfully masked regression to pre-Modernist norms. If we grant this argument, the rest of Kenner's narrative follows quite logically. He writes interestingly of F. R. Leavis, I. A. Richards, and William Empson at Cambridge, suggesting that "critical activity began to seem so urgent in England around 1930 because social fragmentation was being perceived." The self-conscious study of literature began to replace its production. At the same time, the "low, dishonest decade," as Auden called the thirties, was to produce "by a kind of public conspiracy . . . the coalescence of *Everyman's* and *Tid-Bits*: a formula by the way for *The New Yorker*, where Auden was speedily made welcome." This coalescence brought together the worst of both: of *Everyman's*, the hint that Tradition is a closed system to which gentility pays its homage in shillings; of *Tid-Bits*, the premise that attention need not be collected so long as there is some cohering assurance. As for the third reading public, the "aesthetic" one, a Second World War, coming a mere twenty years after the first, marked its final demise, leaving in its wake a nostalgic taste for the "musical" nullities and the pseudo-Georgian images of Dylan Thomas' nature poetry.

Indeed, from Kenner's point of view the English poetry map since the 1950s is a blank. The great exception is Basil Bunting, about whom Kenner has written movingly before, and whose neglect by British publishers and readers he rightly deplores. A second exception is Charles Tomlinson, for whom Kenner makes a brave, if not quite convincing, case as a poet of direct perception in the Pound-Williams-Objectivist tradition. It may be that in the case of Tomlinson, Kenner has let personal friendship color his view; Tomlinson's poems, at least as cited here, will not strike most readers as intrinsically superior to those of such contemporaries as Geoffrey Hill or R. S. Thomas. Kenner's section on Philip Larkin, on the other hand, is devastatingly convincing. *The North Ship* (1955) is dismissed as "a false start, centred as it was on diction forged by Yeats," like "The beast most innocent / That is so fabulous it never sleeps." The later books write bleakly about the "unabashed bleakness" of 1950s England, their "drear view of things" never transcending the dreariness that is their subject. Larkin is characterized as the Laureate of diminished expectations, the proponent of the notion that "foreign languages [are] irrelevant," and that the difficulties of Modernism marked an aberration from the homelier pleasures of reading "easy books." Such narrowness of scope, such intentionally limited horizons lead inevitably, so Kenner concludes, to "the post-war news, that save by factitious cooption—by the sheer illusory power of lists like Faber's and Chatto's—there's no longer an English Literature. Talent has not been lacking, not at all; but, a center absent, talent collects for itself the materials of some unique cosmos . . . Larkin was perhaps the last poet whom "everyone" had heard of, and the "Movement" he was connected with soon didn't contain him." As for the present, "London is no longer the centre of poetry. It's still the centre of opinion. The Hack's Progress, or How to Make It in London with Poetry, is a ready scenario for pointed gossip."

Strong words, these, and sure to arouse ire among English poets and their admirers, both in England and abroad. Can a whole poetry, indeed a whole literature (for Kenner is equally critical of British fiction) be dismissed so summarily? Objectively speaking, certainly not: where, for example, does Harold Pinter fit into Kenner's scheme of things? And why has drama flourished in postwar England whereas the other literary genres have not? Or again, are contemporary English novelists really less interesting than their American counterparts? These are questions Kenner does not address, thus leaving plenty of room for those who want to argue with him.

I myself would want to argue with Kenner about Auden's poetry. "Early Auden," writes Kenner, "was the Cleveland of up-to-date poetry, when he wasn't being the Graham Greene of literature." Further, "Beneath those amusing difficulties of Auden lies a welcome commonality of attitudes. We know how to take everything; the very point of a poem is to assure us we know how to take whatever it may mention." This may be a valid characterization of irony as used by the minor Oxford poets but certainly not of Auden, who soon overcame what Kenner calls his "undergraduate callowness" and went on to write such brilliantly parodic works as *The Sea and the Mirror*, works whose multiple ironies, far from assuring us we know their point, force us to rethink basic problems of syntax, diction, and representation. It can be argued, of course, that the mature Auden was almost an American poet, that he chose to make the United States his home and hence his base of influence. Certainly the poets most influenced by Auden have been Americans like John Ashbery and James Merrill rather than

English ones; indeed, in keeping with Kenner's account of the merger of the *Everyman's* with the *Tit-Bits* public, it may be the case that Auden was too original, too innovative to be appreciated by such New Oxford poets as Craig Raine and Andrew Motion, and that, accordingly, his impact on the "sinking island" has been negligible.

Kenner is not, of course, writing an "objective" history of the Modernist period and he has no obligation to cover all his bases. If he purposely overstates his case, it's because his is a case that deserves to be, indeed must be, made, especially with reference to the current reception of poetry. Week in, week out, after all, the *TLS*, the Poetry Book Society, the Arts Council, the *PN Review*, and any other number of English literary venues introduce us to supposedly new and important poets like Fiona Sampson or Fleur Adcock or Oliver Reynolds. I submit—and here I wholly concur with Kenner—that these are hardly poets at all, merely versifiers. To put it simply, they are poets who never learned the simple lesson, put forward by Pound in 1913, "Do not retell in mediocre verse what has already been done in good prose"—a lesson, incidentally, Philip Larkin never learned either.

For most Americans, as I imagine for most Australians, the current English poetry scene (if not the larger English literary scene) is thus dispiriting. But perhaps no more dispiriting than it was in 1910 or so when Eliot and Pound first appeared on the scene. The *Tit-Bits/Everyman's* public notwithstanding, there are currently signs of an "opening of the field." Andrew Crozier and Tim Longville have published an anthology of alternative poetry for Carcanet Press (*A Various Art*, 1987); and Pierre Joris and Paul Buck have edited an *Anthologie bilingue de la Nouvelle Poésie Anglaise* for Troix Cailloux press, under the title *Matières d'Angleterre*. This second anthology, produced very much under the sign of Ezra Pound, features poets like Ian Hamilton Finlay, Allen Fisher, Veronica Forrest-Thomson, Glenda George, Lee Harwood, Ralph Hawkins, Barry MacSweeney, J. H. Prynne, and Tom Raworth. A fairly active exchange is now in progress between these poets, the Language poets in the United States, Canadian poets like Steve McCaffery and bpNichol, and Australian poets published in these pages—for example, John Tranter. Meanwhile, the dominance of MTV, videocassettes, and C-span is likely to turn reading from its early Modernist status as daily drug to its postmodern status as (once again) occasional luxury. As such, writing shows signs of taking on a new aura. Indeed, if Everyman's Library doesn't publish *Briggflatts*, it is sure to be read, or rather performed, any day now, on the BBC. Island culture, as Gertrude Stein knew well, is enormously resilient.

CHAPTER 30

Sylvia Plath as Cultural Icon

The Haunting of Sylvia Plath represents a challenging new turn in Plath studies and, for that matter, in modern poetry studies. Jacqueline Rose makes clear from the start that hers will be neither a biographical nor an interpretive study of Plath's oeuvre. Indeed, she is much less interested in Plath herself than in her role as cultural icon. Representations of Plath, she argues, fall into "two antagonistic camps": those who "pathologise Plath, freely diagnose her as schizophrenic or psychotic, read her writing as symptom or warning, something we should both admire and avoid," and those, primarily feminist critics, who stress the "representative nature of Plath's inner drama, the extent to which it focuses the inequities . . . of a patriarchal world." The former camp is represented especially by such early Plath critics as A. Alvarez, David Holbrook, and Richard Howard, the latter by Sandra Gilbert and Susan Gubar, Carole Ferrier, and Linda Wagner-Martin, among others. Both camps, Rose believes, are partial; indeed, there can be no "correct" interpretation of Plath's work (much less of her life), since there is, after all, no direct access to the poet. On the contrary, "this book starts from the assumption that Plath is a fantasy."

Rose never cites Michel Foucault but hers is an almost classic Foucaultian analysis. What matters is not what the author "says" but for whom she speaks and under what constraints. What matters is not what Plath's poems mean, much less whether they are "successful," but how "Sylvia Plath is constituted as a literary object on the battleground of cultural survival." This paradigm, complicated by Julia Kristeva's theory of abjection, and various other psychoanalytic models, serves Rose extremely well, at least in the first few chapters.

Review of *The Haunting of Sylvia Plath*, by Jacqueline Rose; and *Rough Magic: A Biography of Sylvia Plath*, by Paul Alexander. *New England Quarterly* (December 1992): 648–52.

The centerpiece of the book is chapter 3, "The Archive," in which Rose carefully weighs the rival claims made about Ted Hughes's role in destroying parts of Plath's journals and changing the order and placement of Plath's poems in the posthumous *Ariel*. Has Hughes acted in the best interests of Plath's reputation and of their children, as Anne Stevenson argues in her biography *Bitter Fame* (1989)? Or has his interference been, as others have viewed it, nothing short of criminal? And what about Aurelia Plath's censorship of the correspondence in *Letters Home*? Rose shows convincingly that there are always at least two sides to the question and that we can never get "at" the "real" Sylvia or know precisely what the "correct" way to handle the Plath archive would in fact be. Her emphasis here and throughout is on the "impossibility of objectivity, the limits of knowledge as such." "To try to construct a single, consistent image of Plath becomes meaningless," she suggests, "because the multiplicity of representations that Plath offers of herself makes such an effort so futile." How, in other words, do we reconcile the contradictory images of "Sylvia Plath" we find in *Ariel, Letters Home, The Bell Jar*, the journals, and so on? And why *should* these images be consistent?

In an interesting discussion of fantasy (chapter 4), Rose shows that the poems have a way of deconstructing their own overt themes. However much violence is condemned, for example, it is also courted. As for the purported move toward transcendence in the later *Ariel* poems, a move critics like myself have praised, Rose argues that even these poems are always in dialogue with one another and that Plath's "transcendence" is problematic, regularly involving as it does the fantasy of the devouring goddess, a vengeful deity whose triumph depends upon the destruction of others.

Convincing as these analyses are, one begins to have the uneasy feeling, midway through the book, that, despite her insistence that there is no "correct" interpretation of Plath's work, Rose thinks *she* is reading Plath the "right" way, correcting previous errors. This becomes apparent in the last two chapters. "Sadie Peregrine" (chapter 5) tries to read Plath's work according to the now fashionable conviction that the "great divide" (Andreas Huyssens's term) between "high" and "low" art does not exist. Since Plath spent so much of her time trying to break into women's magazines (*Ladies' Home Journal, Colliers, Good Housekeeping*, etc.), perhaps we should take the short stories (almost all of them rejected by the magazines in question) seriously, especially since, as recent cultural theory teaches us, the denigration of popular culture goes hand in hand with the denigration of women. Rose thus tries to make a case for the common bond between *Ariel* and the magazine stories, the link being *The Bell Jar*, which has elements of both "high" and "low."

Perhaps this is carrying the antibiographical too far. After all, Plath wanted to break into the "slicks" for a specific reason: to make the money that would support her "serious" writing. In Plath's letters and journals, the lack of money is always a major concern. Then, too, Plath always liked to rise to a challenge: to figure out the winning formula of the *Ladies' Home Journal* stories, for example. One can argue that Plath's preoccupation with magazine fiction tells us something important about the culture of the 1950s, *its* preoccupation with "success," "popularity," and so on. But to say that there is no essential difference between this hackwork and the poetry is, I think, to trivialize the poetry. No one, after all, would so much as know Plath's name today if she had written only or even primarily for the "slicks." And further, Plath's rather unattractive obsession with winning prizes and breaking into the ladies' magazine world was by no means typical of women poets in the fifties; witness Elizabeth Bishop, Denise Levertov, or Adrienne Rich.

Along similar lines, Rose tries to justify Plath's fascist allusions and metaphors (notably in "Daddy"), which many critics (myself included) have attacked as fairly superficial, sophomoric gestures. Again, Rose makes the cultural case: namely, that Plath's fusion of the personal and the political represents a particular stage of feminine consciousness in the fifties and early sixties (e.g., "the equation 'as father to daughter' so 'Nazi to Jew'"). But source is one thing and textuality another, and I persist in thinking that Plath's comparison of her personal plight to that of the Jews being deported to Auschwitz or Dachau represents no more than the cliché version of the Holocaust. This is not the place to argue the point, but, whether or not Rose is right, clearly her analysis of "Daddy" suggests that there is a "right" way to read this poem and that those critics who argue otherwise are "wrong." Imperceptibly, then, the detachment of the early chapters ("Interpretation of a literary work is endless") gradually gives way to the attempt to make Plath conform to the premise of the new Cultural Studies. Although Rose begins by asserting "the right of every reader of Sylvia Plath to form her or his own view of the meanings and significance of her work," some views are clearly judged to be more valid than others.

Despite this caveat, Rose has written an important, highly sophisticated study that casts serious doubts on the biographical studies of Plath to which we are so regularly treated. Paul Alexander's *Rough Magic* unfortunately adds grist to Rose's mill. Billed as "the most objective portrayal yet of the controversial American poet," *Rough Magic* goes over what is by now all too familiar ground: the courtship of Aurelia and Otto, Plath's high school and college successes and problems, the first breakdown, the meeting with Ted, the troubled marriage, the discovery of infidelity and its "tragic" aftermath. True, Alexander's biography is more conscientious and thorough than Edward Butscher's *Sylvia Plath: Method and Madness* (1977) or Linda Wagner-Martin's rather skimpy biography of 1987; and it is certainly less mean spirited and one sided than Anne Stevenson's authorized life of 1989. True, Alexander has some interesting new information about Plath's premarital love affairs, about the actual events leading up to her discovery of the "other woman," and her last days in London. But *Rough Magic* scants the poetry and presents us with highly impressionistic (and often dubious) interpretations of what Aurelia or Sylvia must have thought at this or that juncture, of who was to blame, and so on. In short, Alexander falls into precisely the trap Jacqueline Rose sets for the unwary biographical critic: he writes as if one (namely, he) can "own" the facts of Plath's life.

What we badly need at the moment is a moratorium on Plath biographies. We have now had three (Wagner-Martin's, Stevenson's, Alexander's) in the space of five years. No doubt it is the biographical overkill that prompts Rose to begin her introduction with the sentence "Sylvia Plath haunts our culture." I think this is a great exaggeration, at least as far as the United States is concerned. Indeed, one of the cultural facts that most puzzles me—and Rose has nothing to say on this score—is that interest in Plath is so much greater in her adopted country, Great Britain, than in America. What Rose should ponder is that, at this writing, Plath is taught in very few poetry courses at universities like my own and that the more prominent younger poetry critics in the United States rarely mention Plath's name. Indeed, if she is an icon today, it is less in the literary world than in such popular films as Woody Allen's *Annie Hall*, where Diane Keaton predictably has a copy of *Ariel* on her bookshelf. But even *Annie Hall* is now an old story, and there are no references to Sylvia Plath in *Blade Runner* or, say, in Laurie Anderson's *United States*.

CHAPTER 31

What to Make of a Diminished Thing

S ome months after Philip Larkin, aged twenty-four, began an affair (his first) with a young woman named Ruth Bowman, he wrote to his Oxford friend Kingsley Amis:

> I took Miss Ruth to see . . . Night Club Boom and I should say about 45 seconds of the Club Condon. This was worth the 1/8d. I paid for our admission but not the 5/2d. I paid for our railway fares or the 4/8d. for our scrambled eggs afterwards, or the 4/1d. for subsequent drink. Don't you think it's ABSOLUTELY SHAMEFUL that men have to pay for women without BEING ALLOWED TO SHAG the women afterwards AS A MATTER OF COURSE? I do: simply DISGUSTING. It makes me ANGRY. Everything about the ree-layshun-ship between men and women makes me angry. It's all a fucking balls up. It might have been planned by the army, or the Ministry of Food.[1]

Is the crude nastiness of this remark merely a pose designed to impress the worldlier, more sophisticated Kingsley Amis? Evidently not, for similar sentiments crop up again and again in the letters reproduced in Anthony Thwaite's edition of the *Selected Letters* and in Larkin's private diaries. "Re sexual intercourse:" he wrote in his diary in 1950 (Motion, 119), "always disappointing and often repulsive, like asking someone else to blow your own nose for you."

One of the surprising discoveries made by Andrew Motion in the course of researching his biography was that Larkin evidently had his nose blown for him

Review of *Philip Larkin: A Writer's Life*, by Andrew Motion; and *Selected Letters of Philip Larkin, 1940–1985*, ed. Anthony Thwaite, *Parnassus: Poetry in Review*, 19, no. 2 (1994): 9–29.

a lot more frequently than his poems would have us think. Surprising, because Larkin has generally been viewed as the quintessential poet of "lowered sights and patiently diminished expectations," as Donald Davie put it in his *Thomas Hardy and British Poetry*.[2] In a commemorative volume produced shortly after Larkin's death, Steve Clark declared solemnly, "The sexual politics of Larkin's verse can be seen as one of principled and unillusioned abstention."[3] "Deprivation," the poet himself told an interviewer in 1979, "is for me what daffodils were for Wordsworth."[4]

This image of Larkin as the poet of "principled" deprivation has become legendary. Modest, self-effacing, and levelheaded, so the story goes, Larkin devoted long and demanding days to his position as university librarian, holding posts in a series of dreary provincial cities: first Wellington, then Leicester, Belfast, and finally Hull. A lifelong, retiring bachelor, the poet kept house for himself in a series of digs that ranged from semi-squalid furnished bed-sitting rooms to the cheerless and drably functional house in Newland Park where he ended his days. As for romance, Larkin, so the later poems would have it, "missed out" on the sexual revolution:

> Sexual intercourse began
> In nineteen sixty-three
> (Which was rather late for me)—
> Between the end of the *Chatterley* ban
> And the Beatles' first LP.
>
> Up till then there'd only been
> A sort of bargaining,
> A wrangle for a ring,
> A shame that started at sixteen
> And spread to everything. ("Annus Mirabilis")

It makes for a rueful, wry, and gently humorous tale, but we now know, thanks to Motion's biography, that the Larkin who wrote this poem had recently embarked on an affair with Maeve Brennan, one of his library assistants at Hull, "a sort of superior dogsbody," as Larkin referred to her a few years earlier, "who did a bit of everything" and eventually took charge of the periodical division. This affair was very upsetting to his longtime steady girlfriend Monica Jones (a lecturer in English at Leicester), but Larkin couldn't bring himself to break it off. On the contrary, he eventually resolved the deadlock by taking up with a third woman, his secretary Betty Mackereth. Neither Maeve nor Monica knew about this relationship until after Philip's death and both evidently felt deeply betrayed by it. But then, much earlier, while at Belfast (and already involved in what we would now call a "committed" relationship with Monica) he had had the most passionate of his affairs, a three-year liaison with Patsy Avis, then married to Colin Strang, Larkin's Belfast colleague. While vacationing with Monica in the Scottish Highlands and elsewhere, he wrote sexually charged love letters to Patsy (whom he addressed as his "honeybear" and "fabulous giraffe") as well as arch, flirtatious letters to a young woman named Winifred Arnott, who was working at the Belfast library, and whom Larkin coveted and, one might say, courted for years although she, for one, refused to sleep with him. The affair with Patsy ended when the Strangs moved to Newcastle; later, when an increasingly alcoholic Patsy (her second marriage, to the poet Richard Murphy, did not last long) tried to reestablish intimacy with Larkin, he gently but firmly distanced himself from her pain.

Andrew Motion's own reaction to what seems to be a troubling discrepancy between the Larkin myth and the reality is that the very complexities and contradictions embodied in the poet's life make his lyric all the more interesting. In the introduction to his long, painstakingly researched, beautifully written, and largely fair-minded biography, he declares: "After [Larkin's] death, it's clear that his writing transcends his time rather than merely encapsulating it: he is one of the great poets of the century." And further: "It is part of his poems' strength to speak directly to most people who come across them. He makes each of us feel he is 'our' poet, in a way that Eliot, for instance, does not—and each of us creates a highly personal version of his character to accompany his work."

Again and again one comes across this sentiment: Larkin, for better or worse, is our poet; "we recognize," in Donald Davie's words, "in Larkin's poems the seasons of present-day England, but we recognize also the seasons of an English soul—the moods he expresses are our moods too" (DD, 64). But with the publication of the letters and the Motion biography, a strong countercurrent has set in. Larkin's misogyny, wrote Lisa Jardine in *The Guardian* (December 8, 1992), makes him a dubious contender for the rank of "representative" postwar poet. As for Larkin's politics (of which more in a moment), Tom Paulin was prompted to declare, "For the present, this selection [the *Selected Letters*] stands as a distressing and in many ways revolting compilation which imperfectly reveals and conceals the sewer under the national monument Larkin became," a view more or less echoed by such well-known critics as Terry Eagleton, Peter Ackroyd, and A. N. Wilson. These critics on the Left have, in their turn, been castigated by many on the Right like Martin Amis, who in a *Guardian* piece called "A Poetic Injustice," declared, "The reaction against Larkin has been unprecedentedly violent, as well as unprecedentedly hypocritical, tendentious and smug. Its energy does not—could not—derive from literature: it derives from ideology, or from the vaguer promptings of a new ethos." "In a sense," Amis adds, "none of this matters, because only the poems matter."[5]

Ironically enough, the poet's biographer has concurred with this sentiment. In an *Observer* column written some months after his book's publication, Andrew Motion chastised his critics for their "conflation" of art and life. "Art," he reminded his readers, is not so much the "convulsive expression of personality" as it is the "suppression of personality. . . . [It] exists at a crucial distance from its creator." T. S. Eliot, whose "Tradition and the Individual Talent" (an essay Larkin once dismissed as "piss") Motion's statement about poetry neatly echoes, would have said, "yes, and so why write a biography to begin with?" And why publish a man's personal letters? If, after all, it's the poems, and only the poems, that count, what are we doing with the two very fat volumes under review here?

But of course all of us know, as the terrible controversy over the award of the Bollingen Prize to Ezra Pound in 1949 (and no one ever said of Pound that his moods are our moods too) made clear, "art" and "life" cannot be neatly separated. Amis knows this as well as anyone: it's just that he doesn't think the "life" is all that bad. "The word [racism]," he maintains, "suggests a system of thought, rather than an absence of thought, which would be closer to the reality—closer to the jolts and twitches of stock response. Like mood-cliches, Larkin's racial snarls were inherited propositions, shamefully unexamined, humiliatingly average. These were his 'spots of commonness,' in George Eliot's sense." And there you have it again: Larkin is, after all, "humiliatingly average," a "common" man speaking to men and thus, it turns out, quite endearing.

Indeed, what makes the Larkin controversy so odd is that just when every English major had supposedly learned the lesson that language, especially literary language, is always ideologically charged, that there is no such thing as "neutral" discourse and no hard-and-fast boundary between the writing of a poem and the writing of a letter, the New Critical doctrine of poetic autonomy has once again come into play. A poem, by this notion, is not the reflection of the ideas and beliefs of its author; on the contrary, it creates its own "exemplary" image of what that author is like. Hence all the fuss about "our" poet, the poet who "speaks for us," and so on.

But now that we do, for better or worse, have the poet's biography and letters, how do we relate the seemingly ill-fitting parts of the Larkin puzzle? There are two issues I want to consider here. First, I think it's time to take another look at those "classic" Larkin poems—"Dockery and Son," "The Whitsun Weddings," and so on—to see if indeed they express "our" moods, and if not, whose moods they do express. Second, we must try to understand what the Larkin cult, still going strong in Britain, where his poems are memorized in the schools and assigned on examination papers, tells us about postwar, postmodern British consciousness.

"Fuck and Bugger the War"

The Motion biography provides us with some fascinating clues. Sydney Larkin, Philip's father, was the city treasurer for Coventry, a well-paid post that made it possible for the Larkins to live in a large, if unattractive, suburban house, keep a servant or two, and send their son to the elite King Henry VIII School. Larkin Sr., Motion reports, happened to be an enthusiastic Nazi sympathizer: "He even had a statue of Hitler on the mantelpiece (at home) which at the touch of a button leapt into a Nazi salute. . . . As late as 1939, Sydney had Nazi regalia decorating his office in City Hall." There is no indication that his son, largely apolitical as he tried to be when he went up to Oxford in the first year of the war, disapproved of his father's views. Indeed, the wartime letters make sobering reading. "Germany will win this war like a dose of salts," he writes to his schoolfriend Jim Sutton in December 1940, "and if that gets me into gaol, a bloody good job too. Balls to the war. Balls to a good many things, events, people, and institutions." On April 7, 1942, to Norman Iles, "I am more than ever certain that England cannot win this war: there's absolutely no spirit in the country. I feel everything is a mess." And on July 6 of the same year, again to Jim Sutton: "If there is any new life in the world today, it is in Germany. True, it's a vicious and blood-brutal kind of affair—the new shoots are rather like bayonets. It won't suit me. By 'new' life I don't mean better life, but a change, a new direction. Germany has revolted back too far, into the other extremes. But I think they have many valuable new habits. Otherwise how could D. H. L. [Lawrence] be called Fascist?"

This last remark tells us a lot about Larkin's state of mind during the war. Lawrence was the idol of his youth: not the Utopian Lawrence who wanted to create the ideal community Rananim in some distant exotic place, but the Lawrence of gritty and provincial Nottingham who believed that personal fulfillment is much more important than politics, who recognized that "the ultimate joy is to be alive in the flesh." Larkin's Lawrence, furthermore, is the voice in the wilderness who despised the English bourgeoisie, mistrusted democracy as the rule of the weak, and loathed the idea of war between a petty, snobbish England and the more vital, bold Germany that had given him Frieda. "There's nothing in Wordsworth," Larkin wrote Iles in 1942, "that D. H. L. hasn't done 20 times better."

The fact is that the young Larkin, far from being the man speaking to ordinary men critics later took him to be, was a confirmed aesthete. He hated the war (any war or, for that matter, any political happening) primarily because it was a distraction from the art he wished to practice. Around the time of D-Day, he wrote to Norman Iles:

> I feel that myself & my character are nothing except insofar as they contribute to the creation of literature—that is almost the only thing that interests me now. To increase one's value as a pure instrument is what I am trying to do. I conceive the creative process as depending on an intricate arrangement of little mirrors inside one, & by continual care & assiduity & practice these mirrors can be cleaned & polished, so that in the end artistic perception is a whole-time & not a part-time thing. . . .
>
> You see, my trouble is that I simply can't understand anybody doing anything but write, paint, compose music.

Not Hardy, whom Larkin was later to claim as his model, but Pater stands behind this passage. And there's the rub. For Larkin was born, in the parlance of another idol of his youth—William Butler Yeats—out of phase. It was one thing for Lawrence to detest war when the war in question was an imperialist struggle between rival powers, neither of which could be defined as the clear-cut "good" or "bad" side. But it was quite another to try to avoid the issues posed by the Second World War. Larkin seems never to have understood the differences between the two wars or cared what the Nazis did to whole populations they subjugated, much less what they did to the Jews of Europe. And he seems never to have understood that the "creation of literature" to which he longed to devote himself would have come to a quick halt if Hitler had actually invaded, as he fully planned to do, the British Isles.

It was not a blind spot that could be merely expunged when the war was over. "What [Larkin] most valued in Hardy," Motion remarks, "was the importance attached to suffering." But there is no indication that for Larkin "suffering" applied to anyone but himself. Again and again, as Motion details, he turned a cold shoulder to the suffering of others. When Monica Jones's mother died in 1959, for example, Larkin's first concern was not for her sorrow and pain, but that, as Motion explains, "Without her mother, there was a danger that Monica might rely on him more than she had done in the past. . . . She might even re-open the question of marriage." Under these circumstances, his expressions of sympathy were, in Motion's words, "diluted by cold drops of self-interest."

One might counter that such selfishness is by no means unique to Larkin, that the artist must guard his or her privacy more ruthlessly than do "normal" people. The difficulty arises, however, when the poet's chosen persona is, like Larkin's, a voice of such "decency" and "deprivation." "To write a poem" he insisted in one of his few statements of poetics, "[is] to construct a verbal device that would preserve an experience indefinitely by reproducing it in whoever read the poem" (RW, 83). A curious echo of Eliot's doctrine of the "objective correlative" (which Larkin regularly declared bogus), but what is even more curious is that Larkin, who paid little attention to anyone else's experience, was so eager to have the hypothetical reader sympathize with his own.

On V-Day (May 8, 1945), in any case, Larkin "hardly bothered to raise his eyes from his manuscript book" (M, 133). His contempt for the war effort that brought victory was soon transferred to other political and economic phenomena: Increasingly, Larkin's letters, especially to his great friend and fellow poet Robert Conquest, who furnished him with the porn magazines and pornshop information that so intrigued him, express xenophobic, racist, and class prejudices. A few examples must suffice here.

On the critic G. D. Klingopoulos's dismissal, in his Pelican Guide volume *From Dickens to Hardy*, of William Barnes's metric (in a letter to Monica Jones, 1958):

> I could kick that filthy Greek all the way from the British Museum back to Soho Square if he says Barnes is "clumsy"—the oaf! . . . Fat greasy garlic-slicer! Let him get back to his farced goat cooked in vine leaves and expense-account bills cooked in the stinking "office," and take his filthy maulers off the class writers. (L, 293–94)

On the victory of the Conservative Party and its possible effect on race relations in Britain (in a letter to Robert Conquest, 1970):

> Cracking good news about the election, what? I can hardly believe we've got that little shit [Harold Wilson] and his team of arselicking crooks out of the way. Now Enoch [Powell] for Home Secretary, eh? [. . .] Remember my song, How To Win The Next Election? "Prison for Strikers, Bring back the cat, Kick out the niggers, How about that?" (L, 432)

On worker demands (in a letter to Robert Conquest, 1976):

> The latest campaign is for "the right to work," i.e. the right to get £7 a week for doing bugger all. It's led me to begin a hymn:

> I want to see them starving,
>   The so-called working class,
> Their wages weekly halving,
>   Their women stewing grass,
>
> When I drive out each morning
>   In one of my new suits
> I want to find them fawning
>   To clean my car and boots. (L, 541–42)

On unemployment (in a letter to Colin Gunner, 1981):

> My simple cure for "unemployment" (no such thing really) is to abolish unemployment benefits. If you don't want chaps to do a thing then don't pay them to do it. In the nineteenth century men used to run behind your station growler, following you home to earn a few pence for unloading your luggage. I'd like to see Arthur Scargill [President of Yorkshire National Miners' Union] doing that. (L, 646–47]

On recent strikes by black immigrant workers (in a letter to Colin Gunner, 1984):

> And as for those black scum kicking up a din on the boundary—a squad of South African police would have sorted them out to my satisfaction. (L, 719)

But it is not only "they" ("niggers," "greasy Greeks," immigrants, unemployed miners) who incur Larkin's wrath; one of the surprises of the *Selected Letters* is the nastiness directed to fellow poets. "Yanks," from Eliot and Pound on down, are especially reviled: Robert Lowell, who had praised *The Less Deceived* ("No post-war poetry has so caught the moment"), is dismissed as "Lord-Hairy's Arsehole" (a play on *Lord Weary's Castle*). Emily Dickinson is "Emily Prick-in-son," a "tidy wordlocker"; W. D. Snodgrass, a "dopy kid-mad sod," W. S. Merwin "tripe," Vikram Seth, the producer of a "load of crap . . . [It] comes of being an oriental."

Larkin's fellow-Movement poets don't fare much better. Thom Gunn is "old Feel-of-Stands" (a reference to the poem "A Feel of Hands"); "old [Donald] Davie droning out his tosh" becomes, in response to his critical review of Larkin's *Oxford Book of Twentieth-Century English Verse*, the subject of a song to the tune of "Daisy, Daisy," which trashes "Davie, Davie" as one who panders to fashion and concludes with the lines, "But let's be fair, / It's got you a chair, / And a billet in Frogland too" (L, 499–500). And if Davie is a dishonest critic, Frank Kermode is a pedantic bore, a "jumped up book drunk ponce," who, as one of those "salaried explainers of poetry," finds allusions where there are none (L, 307). As for foreign poets ("Who's Jorge Luis Borges?" Larkin asks Robert Phillips in the 1982 *Paris Review* interview), they simply don't exist, because there is no way "one can ever know a foreign language well enough to make reading poems in it worthwhile. . . . If that glass thing over there is a window, then it isn't a Fenster or a fenêtre or whatever" (RW, 69). "Fiancée," the same complaint Larkin made to Kingsley Amis thirty-five years earlier (L, 180), "why isn't there an English word?"

Larkin lovers defend these remarks, as well as the more scurrilous references I cite above, as largely "macho" bravado, the pose assumed by a painfully shy and stammering schoolboy, who never quite grew up. True, Larkin doesn't write the same way to most of his women correspondents, at least not to Patsy Avis, to whom he writes warmly and wittily, or to Judy Egerton, to whom he is unfailingly polite and thoughtful. But, with rare exceptions like his friendship with Egerton, the common thread that runs through the slurs, digs, racist and misogynist remarks, and proto-Fascist sentiments expressed in the letters and conservations is the absence of any and all generosity of spirit. No doubt this has to do with the strong dose of self-hatred regularly expressed by Larkin; in pop-psychological terms, he couldn't love others because he certainly didn't love himself. But from the reader's point of view, such explanations hardly make the Larkin persona of the letters and recorded conversations more likable.

Andrew Motion makes no bones about Larkin's views. "The Oxford undergraduate who had shown a really remarkable lack of interest in what was happening around him," says Motion, "had grown into a man with no developed political opinions but strong reactionary prejudices." But these prejudices, Motion believes, are transcended in the poetry: "the integrity of his poems depended on his ability to draw on the whole range of his selves, and speak in all their voices." A Larkin poem, in other words, is a formal construct that enables poet and reader to hold contradictory views in suspension. As such, it is not to be confused with mere "life," even though it turns out to "express" what we all think and feel. "The moods he expresses are our moods too." It is this hypothesis I now want to look at.

"Self's the Man"

Suppose we take one of Larkin's best-loved and most frequently "taught" poems, "Dockery and Son," from *The Whitsun Weddings*. Motion provides the background:

Begun on 14 February and completed after fifteen pages of drafts on
28 March [1963], it describes a visit Larkin had made to his old college at
Oxford, St. John's, on the way back from the funeral of Agnes Cuming, his
predecessor as librarian at Hull, almost exactly a year earlier. . . . By permitting itself a great deal of novelistic detail ("Was [Dockery] that withdrawn /
High-collared public-school-boy, sharing rooms / With Cartwright who was
killed?"), and a structure loose enough to give the impression of thinking
aloud ("If he was younger, did he get this son / At nineteen, twenty?"), the
poem makes room for nearly all Larkin's tones and techniques. It is anec-
dotal but lyrical, analytic but expansive, realistic ("awful pie") but metaphorical ("sand clouds"), reminiscent but locked in the present. (M, 333).

What Motion especially admires about "Dockery and Son" is its complex irony.
Visiting his old college, Larkin's speaker is forced to confront his youth and his
decision not to marry and have children. To Dockery, having children evidently
meant "increase"; whereas "To me it was dilution." This is the obvious difference
between himself and Dockery. But, as Motion points out, "Larkin's sense that
his choices are made 'by something hidden from us' smothers the differences
between his own and Dockery's life." It compels him to admit that the fears they
have in common are more striking than the hopes that separate them. "Where,"
asks the speaker, "do these / innate assumptions come from?"

> Not from what
> We think truest, or most want to do:
> Those warp-tight shut, like doors. They're more a style
> Our lives bring with them: habit for a while,
> Suddenly they harden into all we've got.
>
> And how we got it; looked back on, they rear
> Like sand-clouds, thick and close, embodying
> For Dockery a son, for me nothing,
> Nothing with all a son's harsh patronage.
> Life is first boredom, then fear.
> Whether or not we use it, it goes,
> And leaves what something hidden from us chose,
> And age, and then the only end of age.

"Bitterly funny and grievously melancholic," Motion concludes, "'Dockery and
Son' is a compressed autobiography. . . . It grimly sketches the attitudes which

dominated [Larkin's] adult life. Furthermore, its cunning deployment of epigrammatic wisdoms . . . ensure[s] that the poem rises from its authenticating details to spell out general truths."

The reader will have noticed by now that Motion's critical assumptions are almost textbook examples of the New Criticism, as it was practiced, both in the United States and Britain, during the 1950s. A poem, his comments imply, is a "little drama"; it is based on "life," but life heightened, distanced, and thus viewed ironically from more than one angle. Thus "differences" (between the poet and Dockery) turn out to be "similarities," the great irony—evidently a "general truth"—being that either way, we lose: "Life is first boredom, then fear, / Whether or not we use it, it goes, / And leaves what something hidden from us chose, / And age, and then the only end of age."

Repeatedly in discussions of "Dockery," one finds this kind of reading. Barbara Everett, for example, alerts us to such nice ironies as the way the epithet "death-suited" in line three modulates into the memory of having been a "black-gowned" undergraduate in line 4 with the further irony that the poet is symbolically "death-suited" in coming to recognize his own mortality, "the only end of age."[6] As for the ironic enjambment at the end of the first stanza:

I try the door of where I used to live:

Locked. The lawn spreads dazzlingly wide.

P. N. King comments solemnly, "The locked door and lack of recognition emphasize [Larkin's] outsider status in a place where he once felt very much at ease." And in case we miss this meaning, the next line brings it home to us: "A known bell chimes. I catch my train, ignored."

The account of the train journey in stanzas 3 and 4 elicits further admiration. The poet, we recall, dozes off, "waking at the fumes / And furnace-glares of Sheffield, where I changed, / And ate an awful pie, and walked along / The platform to its end to see the ranged / Joining and parting lines reflect a strong / Unhindered moon." "Even the station pie," Everett explains, "has more identity than the speaker: it is 'awful,' it is itself," whereas the poet who eats it is "passive, powerless, subordinate, merely open to experience" (GH, 149). And King notes that the "ranged / Joining and parting lines" of the train tracks metaphorically point to the poem's final epiphany: "Dockery's paternity and the poet's bachelorhood are equal destinies: they are both results of neither choice nor desire but simply the fact of life happening, as it were, behind their backs before they had time to realize the situation they were in. It appears that choice is one of life's major illusions."[7] Or in Everett's words: "The last lines of the poem crystallise this experience [the abrupt sense of failure in life] with an extraordinary blank austerity which at once realises and more largely and humanly generalises: 'this is how it is.' In the knowledge of what each has not got (a son, or an alternative to 'harsh patronage') Dockery and the speaker meet, as they did not appear to have met in college" (GH, 147).

"Dockery and Son," as the critics present it, is, then, eminently teachable: a perfect classroom poem (and, incidentally, not one of Larkin's nastier poems— those that use four-letter words like "This Be the Verse" or "High Windows"), providing food for discussion of the journey motif, the relation of past to present, the difference between reality and appearance, and so on. But the limitation of such New Critical explication is that the assumptions behind the nice ironies (the "black-gowned" become the "death-suited"; the "dazzlingly wide" lawns of memory give way to the "fumes / And furnace-glares of Sheffield") are never called into question. Thus the hard-earned insight to which a given poem supposedly moves—in this case, the recognition that "choice is one of life's major illusions" and that whatever the choice ("For Dockery a son, for me nothing"), the net result is that "Life is first boredom, then, fear, / Whether or not we use it, it goes,"—must be appreciated by the poem's reader as a plausible conclusion to what has preceded it.

But what happens if we aren't disposed to accept the premise that having children is mere "increase?" Or that the poet's "nothing" and Dockery's "harsh patronage" finally add up to the same thing? To ask such questions is to notice that of course poor Dockery is never given a chance in this poem. That someone named Dockery (as in "Hickory, dickory, dock") might just be a proud and loving father, that "Dockery and Son" (with its sarcastic echo of "Dombey and Son") might have an interesting relationship—these possibilities are never entertained any more than it is conceivable to Larkin that Sheffield could signify anything other than "fumes" and "furnace-glares."

The poem's carefully orchestrated details and clever ironies, in other words, will not stand up to real scrutiny. Dockery is just a prop, used to convey the poet's own view of things, his sense that "Life is first boredom, then fear." Far from expressing complex emotions, I would argue, "Dockery and Son" reduces emotion to stock response: The relation of father to son is "harsh patronage," the Oxford of distorting memory ("the lawn spreads dazzlingly wide") cheapens into the hideous industrialization of modern-day Sheffield (compare Lawrence's more complex treatment of the topography), and anyway, whatever choices we make, the end result is death.

But the real death here—and perhaps this is why Larkin is so obsessed with "age, and then the only end of age"—is the curious failure of the imagination, which haunts Larkin's writing. Specificity, the image or phrase or syntactic construction that reveals, this is what we miss in a poem like "Dockery." Oxford, with its "withdrawn / High-collared public-schoolboy[s]," its "Canal and clouds and colleges" is—well—just a postcard Oxford; college life is having to report "unbreakfasted, and still half-tight" to "the Dean," and give "'Our version' of 'these incidents last night,'" and so on. But what Dean, what incidents? Does memory really operate on so generalized a level? Does one, for that matter, remember that, before falling asleep, one yawned, as in:

> Well, it just shows
> How much . . . How little . . . Yawning, I suppose
> I fell asleep . . .

and why "suppose" anything about it except that one needs a rhyme? The "intended laconic flatness" of such passages is merely willed.

This same mood infects "The Whitsun Weddings," where the poet looks with contempt at the bridal couples boarding the train at each station:

> We passed them, grinning and pomaded girls
> In parodies of fashion, heels and veils,
> All posed irresolutely, watching us go,
> As if out on the end of an event
>   Waving goodbye
> To something that survived it. Struck, I leant
> More promptly out next time, more curiously,
> And saw it all again in different terms;
> The fathers with broad belts under their suits
> And seamy foreheads; mothers loud and fat;
> And uncle shouting smut; and then the perms,
> The nylon gloves and jewelry-substitutes,
> The lemons, mauves, and olive-ochres that
>
> Marked off the girls unreally from the rest.

Again, notice the one-dimensionality, the flattening out of human emotion. "They" (the members of the wedding) disgust the speaker: "The fathers with broad belts under their suits / And seamy foreheads," the "loud and fat" mothers, the "cheap" young girls with their perms, nylon gloves and "jewelry-substitutes."

The fathers, we read in the next stanza, "had never known / Success so huge and wholly farcical"; "The women shared / The secret like a happy funeral." As in the case of "Dockery and Son," the poet not only attributes his own emptiness to these others; he simplistically judges what their feelings must be. What could a daughter's marriage represent to a father but farce"? What can such a wedding represent to a mother but a "happy funeral"? Ordinary people, it seems, girls who can't afford real jewelry or leather gloves, who perm their hair and wear "parodies of fashion"—such people are not entitled to happiness, not capable of sorrow or deep feeling. What's worse, they are all alike. Indeed, "The Whitsun Weddings" is no more than a truncated version of the great wedding scenes produced by Larkin's masters, Hardy and Lawrence: the wedding, for example, of Anna Lenski and Will Bragwen in Lawrence's *The Rainbow*, or the great opening scene of Hardy's *Mayor of Casterbridge*, in which Michael Henshard sells his wife Susan for a few quid.

The comparison brings me back to the issue of Larkin's politics, and its relation to the poetry. On the face of it, "Dockery and Son" would seem to be far removed from the nasty extra-literary statements found in Larkin's letters and conversations. In the prose, we may well find such embarrassing statements as "I can hear fat Caribbean germs pattering after me in the Underground" or the complaint made, when Ruth Bowman's cousin came to town, that "it means I have to PAY for TWO women at the PUB and the FLICKS instead of ONE and I DON'T get my COCK into EITHER of them, EVER" (L, 119). But surely, so the common wisdom has it, such sentiments are "transcended" in the poetry.

But are they? To invent characters named Dockery and Son and then to allow those characters no role but to represent the bourgeois choice of "increase," is itself, I would argue, a form of prejudice very like the racism, sexism, or xenophobia Larkin practiced in his life. Not only is Dockery denied any conceivable humanity, the poet himself cannot concede the possibility of a life that might begin in something other than boredom and fear and might lead elsewhere than to oblivion and death.

This cartoon version of "life" is at the heart of Larkin's poetry. In "Self's the Man," for example, he similarly begins by wondering whether "Arnold," who has married and has "kiddies," is less selfish than is the poet himself. The turn comes in stanza 5:

> But wait, not so fast:
> Is there such a contrast?
> He was out for his own ends
> Not just pleasing his friends;

And if it was such a mistake
He still did it for his own sake,
Playing his own game.
So he and I are the same.

Only I'm a better hand
At knowing what I can stand
Without them sending a van—
Or suppose I can.

Here again the intended irony is that the poet's self-justification—his sneering at Arnold's marriage—is only a pose, that his real mood is one of fear, a fear that his own sanity is, after all, no securer than Arnold's. But in order to convey this irony, Larkin again depends on a series of clichés about the other man's choice: Arnold is presented as one who "when he finishes supper / Planning to have a read at the evening paper / It's put a screw in this wall—/ He has no time at all, / With the nippers to wheel round the houses / And the hall to paint in his old trousers / And that letter to her mother / Saying Won't you come for the summer." Thus Arnold is assigned Archie Bunker status, a stereotype for whom struggle, aspiration, and value are reduced to mere tic. Only the poet himself, so it seems, knows what it is to have conflicted feelings.

Now and in England

Given these real limitations, why have so many English readers continued to view Larkin as "one of the great poets of the twentieth century"? Why are young students, as David Gervais reminds us in a new book called *Literary Englands*, more familiar with the end of "Church Going" than with *Paradise Lost*? John Bayley, for one, takes issue with Gervais' suggestion that Larkin's appeal has to do with his particular Englishness. "His greatness," declares Bayley, "consists in the way it avoids not only that label but any other."[8]

For the American reader—at least this American reader—such hyperbole is puzzling. Ninety-five years into the twentieth century, is Larkin really the beacon his admirers claim him to be? And if not, why the insistence that, as Davie put it some decades ago, "Like it or not, Larkin is the centrally representative figure" of postwar England? My own guess is that the Larkin cult has a great deal to do with the strange triangular relationship between both Larkin and Davie, and the figure of T. S. Eliot. Let me explain.

Larkin, as I noted above, was at heart an aesthete who believed that "every poem must be its own sole freshly created universe" (RW, 79), an organic whole made by "construct[ing] a verbal device that would preserve an experience indefinitely by reproducing it in whoever read the poem" (RW, 83). For him, as for Eliot, poetry is not the expression of emotion but the escape from emotion: Feeling must be there in the poem, detached from its creator who really can't talk about its qualities. That this is a latter-day version of Symbolist doctrine, as domesticated by Eliot early in the century, should be obvious to anyone, despite Larkin's own protests to the contrary. Larkin may have declared that he preferred Hardy to the "transcendental" Eliot because "[Hardy's] subjects are men, the life of men, time and the passing of time, love and the fading of love" (M, 141), but, as we have noted, Larkin's own subjects were decidedly not "men, the life of men" or even "love and the fading of love," but rather his own tormented consciousness, his particular sense of isolation, boredom, and loss of opportunity. It was for these emotions that he tried to find the appropriate objective correlative.

In postwar England, much more than in postwar America, where Pound, Stevens, and Williams soon began to take center stage, Eliot was and continues to be the representative Modernist poet. And further, he appears, in accounts of English poetry from F. R. Leavis's *New Bearings in English Poetry* (1932) right up to Motion's 1992 biography, where Eliot is considered as the logical point of comparison, as, of all things, an English Modernist poet, an attribution that seems increasingly eccentric to those of us on this side of the Atlantic, where Eliot's profoundly American ethos is recognized as a matter of course. At the same time, Larkin's own stated animosity toward the "culture-mongering activities of the Americans Eliot and Pound," toward the "myth-kitty" and allusiveness of that "old tin can," as he once called Eliot, reflects the larger animosities to Modernist-Symbolist poetry that first became prominent in the 1950s, thanks to Movement poetics; these animosities have persisted to this day. In postwar, post-Imperialist Britain, the internationalism of the 1910s and 1920s has become deeply suspect, and the "take-over" of English poetry by the Americans (Eliot and Pound) early in the century has come to be seen as something to be resisted.

In this setting, Larkin became the inevitable candidate for the position of "our poet." "Those slow canals," says Davie of "The Whitsun Weddings" ("Canals with floatings of industrial froth"), "have wound through many a poem about England since T. S. Eliot's *Waste Land*, but never under such a level light as this" (DD, 64–65). Thus Larkin represents to certain English critics, a chance to still have the Eliot of "The Fire Sermon," whose typist and clerk surely anticipate the Dockerys and the members of the wedding in Larkin's poetry, and yet an Eliot without the master's notorious difficulty, his foreign phrases and learned allusions. Larkin, in other words, was lauded as an Eliot who had repudiated both America and Symbolist France (with Greece and Rome thrown in for the bargain) and had "come home." "On the literal level," says Davie, "no one denies that what Larkin says is true; that the England in his poems is the England we have inhabited" (DD, 64). Indeed, Larkin may well be the only postwar British poet who carried on the Symbolist tradition that marked the greatness of poetry written in England in the early decades of the century and yet seemed to apply it, half a century later, to the shrunken life lived in the redbrick university towns of the dismantled empire.

This unique position may well have prevented the poet's admirers from noticing that the voice we hear in Larkin's poems is closer to Prufrock's than to that of Prufrock's creator. "My relations with women," Larkin wrote to his friend Jim Sutton in a moment of rare self-insight, "are governed by a shrinking sensitivity, a morbid sense of sin, a furtive lechery" (M, 190). Touché, and this "furtive lechery" finds its outlet in passages like the opening stanza of "High Windows":

> When I see a couple of kids
> And guess he's fucking her and she's
> Taking pills or wearing a diaphragm,
> I know this is paradise
>
> Everyone old has dreamed of all their lives . . .

This "outrageous" opening quickly gives way to the recognition that "everyone young [is] going down the long slide / to happiness," but of course that slide also leads downward to darkness. The "love song" of J. Alfred Prufrock is also a death song, but whereas Prufrock at least has moments of vision, as when he contemplates the "smoke that rises from the pipes / Of lonely men in shirtsleeves leaning out of windows" or when he dreams of the mermaids "singing, each to each," Larkin's "high windows" open only on the "deep blue air, that shows / Nothing, and is nowhere, and is endless." In Eliot's vision, the "awful daring of a moment's surrender / Which an age of prudence can never retract" is carefully grounded (not by Prufrock but by Eliot himself) in the desiccated New England Puritan tradition where "eyes . . . fix you in a formulated phrase" and "Arms that are braceleted and white and bare / (But in the lamplight, downed with light brown hair!)" become threatening presences. But in "High Windows," deprivation and despair are merely posited: there is no palpable context in which to place these gestures.

The very absence of context, of course, has made it possible for critics to point to countless ambiguities and ironies in Larkin's poems, as when Steve Clark, in a discussion of "An Arundel Tomb," explains, "All that distinguishes [the stone sculptures of the unnamed medieval earl and his countess] is their gesture of clasped hands. In a complex and paradoxical development, it is this unconcerned anonymity, their reduction to a single 'attitude,' that allows them to be 'transfigured' into a 'final blazon'" (GH, 271). But what, beyond deprivation, is the poet's relation to this "perfect icon of desire"? An explication like Clark's cannot tell us because the poem's "ironic" premises are never called into question.

And questioned they must be. Reading Larkin in the mid-1990s, one wants to know what has happened that has made life so unremittingly bleak. Why, after all, are fear and boredom the only emotions of childhood? How is it that "Mum and Dad" "fuck you up," that "women are shits," that one's colleagues are "turds," and that one's typical "Dull non-day" is always followed by a "pissy evening"? Why, one wants to ask, doesn't someone just take out the trash?

If Larkin's poetry of "deprivation" does in fact express the quintessential postwar English experience, so much the worse for England. But fortunately (and paradoxically!), Andrew Motion's biography undercuts the very claim for representativeness it overtly makes for its subject. For in placing Larkin in a palpable world, Motion shows that the poet's ethos, far from being "representative" of something larger, may more accurately be seen as a rather special form of paranoia. Thom Gunn and Charles Tomlinson, Jeremy Prynne and Tom Raworth—these poets were not given to the constant name-calling, suspicion, and failure to envision change that we find in Larkin's work. Or again, the expression of bleakness becomes part of a larger complex as it does, for example, in the work of a writer with whom Larkin was acquainted and who once gave a reading from Larkin's work—namely Harold Pinter. From *The Birthday Party* to *No Man's Land* and *Old Times*, and in a series of poems and radio pieces, Pinter takes those same dreary bed-sitting rooms, those nauseating bowls of cornflakes and custard, those scenes where old men are seen "Hoovering" the carpet (even as Larkin once reports to Monica that he got his tie caught in the vacuum cleaner), and invests these details with powerful resonance, providing us with chilling representations of the vagaries of love and friendship, deception, and remorse. Perhaps it has taken an outsider like Pinter (Jewish, London East End, non-university) to take the measure of Britain's postwar accidia. "Home," as Larkin put it in a poem of 1958, "is so sad. It stays as it was left. . . . bereft / Of anyone to please, it withers so" (CP, 119). And perhaps that was Larkin's problem.

Notes

1.   Motion, p. 143. Subsequently cited in the text as M; the *Selected Letters* are subsequently cited as L. *Larkin's Collected Poems*, ed. Anthony Thwaite (New York: Farrar, Straus Giroux, 1989) is cited as CP.

2.   *Thomas Hardy and British Poetry* (New York: Oxford, 1972), p. 71. Subsequently cited in the text as DD.

3.   Steve Clark, "'Get Out As Early As You Can': Larkin's Sexual Politics," *Philip Larkin 1922–1985, A Tribute*, ed. George Hartley (London: Marvell Press, 1988), p. 239. This volume is subsequently cited in the text as GH.

4.   "An Interview with the Observer" (1979), rpt. in *Required Writing: Miscellaneous Pieces 1955–1982* (London: Faber and Faber, 1983), p. 47. This volume is subsequently cited as RW.

5.   Martin Amis, "A Poetic Injustice," *The Guardian Weekly*, August 21, 1993, p. 6. The Paulin statement and the responses by Eagleton, Ackroyd, and Wilson were made in the "Letters" column of the *Times Literary Supplement* a few months earlier and are cited by Amis as is Motion's response.

6.   Barbara Everett, "Larkin and Dockery," GH 149.

7.   P. N. King, *Nine Contemporary Poets: A Critical Introduction* (London and New York: Methuen, 1979), 12–13.

8.   *Times Literary Supplement*, January 21, 1994, p. 3.

CHAPTER 32

The Poetry of Kurt Schwitters

In a 1924 manifesto called "Consistent Poetry," which appears in Jerome Rothenberg and Pierre Joris's beautifully produced and edited selection of Kurt Schwitters's literary works, we read:

> Classical poetry counted on the similarities between people. It considered the association of ideas as unambiguous. It was mistaken. At any rate it built its foci on associations of ideas: "Über allen Gipfeln ist Ruh" ("O'er every mountain peace does reign"). Here Goethe does not only want to indicate that there is quiet on mountain tops; the reader is supposed to enjoy this peacefulness in the same way the poet, tired from his official duties and usually functioning in an urban environment, does himself. That such associations of ideas are not all that commonly shared can be shown if one were to read such a line to someone from Heidjer (a region of two inhabitants per square kilometer). That person would certainly be much more impressed by a line like "lightning hairy zigzags the subway crushes the skyscraper." At any rate, the realization that all is quiet does not bring forth poetic feelings in him because, for him, quietness is the normal state of affairs. I cite this passage because its combination of common-sense. . . .
>
> Abstract poetry separated—and therein lies its great merit—the word from its associations, and played off word against word; more particularly concept against concept, while taking sound into account. That is more consistent than the evaluation of poetic feelings.

Absurd as it is to contemplate the impact of Goethe's nature lyric on the

Review of *pppppp: Poems Performance Pieces Proses Plays Poetics*, by Kurt Schwitters, trans. and ed. Jerome Rothenberg and Pierre Joris. *Sulfur* 34 (1994): 201–8.

hypothetical inhabitant of Heidjer, Schwitters is not being merely playful here. What he sees is that, with the breakdown of the traditional class structures—structures that Goethe could take for granted—the transparency of language as carrier of "poetic feeling," directed toward an audience conditioned to "understand," sharing as it does the poet's own basic feelings, is called into question. No wonder Schwitters longed, as did so many poets of the post–World War I era, to create an "abstract poetry"—a poetry that might remove itself from "concept" altogether. But how to achieve such a poetry? "Not the word but the letter is the original material of poetry," Schwitters declares in the same manifesto. "Consistent poetry is constructed from letters. Letters have no concepts. Letters in themselves have no sound, they only offer the possibility to be given sound values by the performer. The consistent poem plays off letters and groups of letters against each other."

Shades of Khlebnikov's *zaum* poetry and, in our own day, the chance generated work of Jackson Mac Low (who recently wrote his own "*Merzgedichte* in memoriam Kurt Schwitters") and John Cage, who neatly echoes, in his preface to *Mureau*, Schwitters's assertion, "The elements of poetry are letters, syllables, words, sentences." Indeed as Rothenberg and Joris point out, the sound text and concrete poetry of the past few decades can be traced directly back to such works as Schwitters's famous *Ur Sonate*, whose entire text (some twenty-eight pages) is reproduced in this book, waiting for a set of readers to actualize its score. (A recording of Schwitters reading this amazing tour de force is available from *Gelbe Music* in Hamburg.) And certainly Schwitters's alogical and nongrammatical poetry looks ahead to the "Language poetry" of the current generation.

But from the translator's perspective, Schwitters's practice is nothing if not a minefield. For if "not the word but the letter is the original material of poetry," how can translation, usually unable to duplicate the phonemes and morphemes of the original, be adequate? How, for example, to translate a line like "Duumdu" ("Er Sie Es"), whose middle syllable "um" (around) gives us not only the idea of "You on you" but also the paragram "Duum," which is a homonym for "dumm" or "stupid," hence "you stupid you." Pierre Joris translates the word as "Thouroundthou," which nicely duplicates the diphthong but loses Schwitters's double entendre.

Like Khlebnikov's often untranslatable (despite the recent valiant efforts of Paul Schmidt) poetry, Schwitters's poems depend so fully on their linguistic base—on pun and paragram, anaphora and rhyme, onomatopoeia and echolalia, that they seem to defy translation, with the result that this great artist, who is also considered a major poet in the German-speaking world (the scholarly Friedhelm Lach edition, published between 1973–1976, runs to five large volumes), is almost unknown outside Germany. Indeed, such essays as have been written on his poetic composition are primarily the work of art historians, Werner Schmalenbach and John Elderfield, for example, who understand that Schwitters's writings—his early expressionist poems in the vein of August Schramm, the subsequent Dada poems like "An Anna Blume" (the much-anthologized poem which originally made Schwitters famous), the short prose pieces or "proses" as the editors ingeniously call them, the playlets, the visual and sound poems—are not only an integral part of Schwitters's *Merz* (for *Kommerz*) collage art but important in their own right.

The difficulty of translating Schwitters is compounded by the fact that in the last decade of his life when he was living in England, Schwitters translated some of his own early poetry and tried writing new poems in English (see pp. 100–118 of *pppppp*). Poets are not always their own best translators and as Werner Schmalenbach reports, Schwitters's English was always shaky. In 1942, with the help of Stefan Themerson, he translated his 1919 "An Anna Blume," the one poem of his that has made its way into every Dada textbook and anthology. It is the translation unfortunately included by Rothenberg and Joris in *pppppp* as well. I say unfortunately, because I think Schwitters's English version is a travesty of his subtle, witty, playful, and charming 1919 original.

Take the opening line, "O du, Geliebte, meiner 27 Sinne, ich liebe Dir!," which Schwitters translates as "O Thou, beloved of my twenty seven senses, I love thine!" The second-person singular pronoun "Du" is the familiar form of address (vis-à-vis the formal "Sie"), and in German, the pronouns have different endings for every case, singular and plural, whereas our own "you" has no variation, singular or plural, except for the genitive "your." Accordingly, no literal English translation can ever capture the sort of pronoun play in which the German Schwitters regularly indulges. Still, I find the use of "thou" ("thou, thee thee *thine*") questionable, for Schwitters's German is above all distinguished, as are his collages, by its respect for the ordinary, the everyday, the common, the banal. In this instance, the joke is that Anna, addressed quite naturally and colloquially as "O Du, Geliebte" is immediately deflated by the absurd hyperbole of "my twenty seven senses." And this, in turn, is followed by the absurd "Ich liebe dir"—absurd because "dir" is in the dative case whereas "liebe" takes the accusative "dich." "Ich liebe dir" thus turns Anna, who is after all addressed as "Du, ungezähltes Frauenzimmer" (a much less respectful address than "Thou, uncounted woman"!), into no more than the indirect object of the poet's "love." Grammar, let's remember, produces meanings.

By comparison, "I love thine" strikes me as no more than arch, a sort of pseudo–e. e. cummings locution. If one were to retranslate "An Anna Blume," perhaps the solution would be to take the literal option: since English designates the indirect object by means of a preposition, we might render the German as "I love to you" or "for you" and let the ambiguities develop. But Schwitters does other things to weaken his original: Anna's "green bird" becomes "wheels" (which eliminates the double entendre of "bird"), her red dress, literally sawed up (zersägt) into white pleats becomes "thy red dress, clashed in white folds," and so on. Worst of all, the ambiguity of the name Anna Blume—is she an opening bud or a deflowered "schlichtes Mädchen"?—is lost in the coy "Anna Blossom." Schwitters mock-Petrarchan homage to the palindromic Anna of the streets with whom he is sleeping is thus largely deflected.

I mention this particular self-translation because Jerome Rothenberg and Pierre Joris have evidently taken it and related Schwitters's translations at face value. "It's Schwitters," they say in their introduction, "who gives the green light for our extensive use of second-person thou's, sometimes correctly grammatical, sometimes linked to first-person verbs." And indeed, "thee" and "thou" are the pronouns of choice in these translations as are certain other archaisms not quite warranted in the supple and racy language of the original. "Ein Säuferstiel augt dumm das klage Tier," for example, has a comic, sardonic edge that is missing from the line "Drunkard's stem dumbly does eye the doleful beast" (p. 24). "Augt dumm" means "gapes" or "gapes stupidly"; "dumbly does eye" seems unnecessarily contrived. Again, "klage" is a coinage from "klagen" (complain): it can read as the "whining" or "pathetic" animal, but "doleful beast"?

But these are minor flaws in what is often a brilliantly inventive rendering of Schwitters's all-but-untranslatable idiom. Take, for example, Rothenberg's "Subway Poem" (Untergrundgedicht):

> Houses eyeball millions cudgel lamps
> Windows crunch on eyes
> Bellow light the subway-shuttle teeth
> German Daily News sleds past and music (super shoeshines)
> Adding machines spew numbers, Garden City
> Songs tender cannons' gold (physician tested)
> Windows live sans light grow numb
> Sans coal glass woodens
> Flames glass up
> Bellow crunch on light the window
> Flames glass flames

Houses eyeball millions sparkle lamps
And fire woodens coal light bellows forth
(In case of crowds step to the centre aisle)

Häuser augen Millionen peitschen Lampen
Fensten beissen Augen
Brüllen Licht die Untergrundbahn Zähne
Deutsche Tageszeitung rodelt und Musik (bester Schuhputz)
Additionmaschinen wirren Zahlen, Gartenstadt
Lieder zarten die Kanonen Gold (ärtzlich empfohlen)
Fenster leben ohne Licht erstarren
Ohne Kohle holzt das Glas
Flamme glast
Brüllen beissen Licht die Fenster
Flamme glast die Flamme
Häuser augen Millionen funken Lampen
find die Flamme holzen Kohle brüllt das Licht.
(Bei Andrang in den Mittelgang treten.)[1]

This 1920 poem is the counterpart of Schwitters's *Merzbilder*: a catalog of graphic images aligned with a minimum of punctuation in the tradition of the Futurist *parole in libertà*, which Schwitters surely knew, is "cut" by signboards, advertising slogans, and newspaper bits: "super shoeshines," "physician tested," and so on. The cacophony of the original is caught by onomatopoeic words like "cudgel" and "crunch" and compounds like "subway-shuttle teeth." Throughout, Rothenberg's poem replicates the heavy alliteration and assonance and the strong-stress rhythm of Schwitters's poem, his use of idiom (e.g., "Flames glass up") captures the sardonic urbanism of this *Merzbau*, the city where everything has turned into commodity ("German Daily News sleds past"). "Subway poem" is followed by "High Fashion Furs" (Feine Pelzmoden), which takes the cataloging technique of the former lyric even further, juxtaposing a set of images of street scenes (again *parole in libertà* like "Telephones broadcast baskets") with surreal references to the "Boil Intestines Pharmacy," "A-1 intestines" now populating what seems to be the entire city.

"Spice is the variety of life. / Every apron has a wife" has precisely the nursery-rhyme effect of "Würze ist des Witzes Kürze. / Jede Frau hat eine Schürze." And Rothenberg's rendition of the title poem provides a masterful verbal-visual equivalent of the erotic play of the original (p. 81):

P P P P P P P P P

pornographic i- poem

> The   go
> Its bleating   is
> Sweet & peaceful
> And it will   not
> With its   horns

the black line shows where I cut lengthwise into a harmless poem in a children's picture book. From the goat I got the go.

> And it will   not | be provoked
> With its   horns | to shove & poke.

Here "The go" is even more surprising than the original "Die Zie" (cut-up for "Ziege") because "go" is not a syllable in "goat." The "go" that "bleats" is very suggestive, especially when we learn that "Its bleating is / Sweet & peaceful." What is it that the "goa[at]" "will not" presumably "do" [. . .] "with its horns"? Fill in your own story, a story which is then "explained" by reference to the complete page in the children's book:

Here the translation almost betters the original—

> Und sie wird sich   nicht erbossen
> Mit den Hörnern   Eß zo stossen   [FL 95]—

for both the ove of "shove" and the entire word "poke" are found paragrammatically inside "provoked," whereas Schwitters's nursery rhyme has the simpler pattern of the rhyme "erbossen" / "stossen."

But perhaps the most important items in the Rothenberg-Joris book, aside from the great "Ur Sonate," which is reproduced in its entirety, are the "proses" like "The Onion" and "Augusta Bolte," both important precursors for works like Lyn Hejinian's *My Life* or Gilbert Sorrentino's procedural fictions. These works, almost unknown to the English-speaking reader, have Gertrude Stein–like phrasal permutations, intercut by commercial clichés as is the "Subway poem" but on a larger scale. The twenty-eight--page "Auguste Bolte," written in 1923 and published in *Der Sturm*, is the fictional equivalent of Schwitters's *Merzbilder*. The title alludes to the crank Widow Bolte, whom every German schoolchild of the period would have recognized from Wilhelm Busch's famous *Max und Moritz*. In Schwitters's version, Auguste Bolte becomes a young girl, in search of a PhD in "Lif"; indeed the text is subtitled "a doctoral dissertation." Rather than actually collaging clichés and advertising jingles into the text as he did in "Subway poem," Schwitters here interweaves the language of ordinary people in all its absurdity, comedy, and pathos. Beginning with a "wise saying" pronounced by his five-year-old son Ernst ("What one chews turns to mush"), Schwitters declares that his "allegory for good old Aart-ccritcism" is "a natural and faithful reproduction of the critiques in daily papers. The daily press on art, the so-called daily-artpress, wears a little girl's dress. Chaste and modest, it has tied a tiny apron over it, with embroidery trimmings" (p. 139). Like Joyce's Dublin, where Gerty MacDowell is similarly "chaste and modest," the petit-bourgeois "polite society" of Schwitters's Hannover masks a vicious savagery just underneath its placid surface.

As the story opens, "Augusta Bolte saw about 10 people on the street, who all advanced in one and the same direction. This seemed suspicious to Augusta Bolte, very suspicious indeed. 10 people were walking in one and the same direction. 1, 2, 3, 4, 5, 6, 7, 8, 9, 10. Something was going on there." It becomes Augusta's mission to find out where these ten people are going, a mission complicated when the ten break into 2 fives, the fives into 2 + 3 and finally into 5 ones. Along the way, Augusta, "who had been such a brilliant girl, so gifted even back in school" (the phrase is repeated again and again), gets "stuck into a metric pattern," and draws conclusions that "went against her grain. For a moment she wondered what that grain was, against which, in a way, it went." When the ten split into 2 fives, she considers it "a scandalous impertinence of the mass to split up or, better, to divide." "Why indeed," Augusta Bolte wonders, "did 10 people have to split up into groups of 5. That kind of thing was a shrewd tactic of the, in a way, hostile mass." And so on.

The nasty logic and paranoia exhibited in such passages eerily anticipate the Nazi mentality already nascent in Schwitters's Germany. Cliché piles on cliché: Augusta's path now crosses that of one Richard Eckermester, a young ne-er do well who never made it through school: "Neither the carrot nor the stick had had any effect"; Eckermester is seen by Augusta descending from a hackney cab and "abscond[ing] into a house":

The die was cast, and the man absconded into a house. Miss Professor Augusta had her car stop. It was clear that something was going on here. Why else should a man abscond into a house? You can't fit that into a hollow tooth! Why else should a man jump into a hackney cab to abscond into a house? Why? Someone was certain: if nothing was happening here, then nothing was happening anywhere. Although the reverse could be true too. And while Augusta realized the equivalence of all values, as she now realized that, depending on one's taste, everything could prove everything or nothing, a new unheard of realization came to her, namely that it did not matter if one attended it or not.

Nobody could attend to everything. Man had to make a choice. And he had to make a choice. And he had to make a choice, not because he had to make a choice, but because in itself it didn't matter if he made a choice or if he didn't make a choice. (p. 162)

The permutations here are less Steinian than reminiscent of Beckett's *Watt*. And indeed, Schwitters's prose, subtly rendered by Rothenberg and Joris here (although the recurrent rhyme "Auguste wusste . . . das sie . . . musste" is not quite conveyed by "Augusta musta"), anticipates the nervousness, anxiety, illogicality, and comic-horrific irresolution of Beckett's fiction as well as his clown plays.

It is a scandal that this edition of Schwitters's work, produced as it is by two of the finest poet-translators writing today, has not (at least so far) gotten the recognition it deserves. The *New York Times Book Review*, the *New York Review of Books*, the *New Republic*, and comparable periodicals have not reviewed it. But this silence would hardly have surprised Schwitters. For the bourgeois mindset that he so mercilessly parodizes in works like "Auguste Bolte" is the mindset that continues to treat him with "suspicion." He would have shrugged that suspicion off good humoredly with something like the "cadenza" from *Ur Sonata*:

> Priimiititti too
> Priimiititti taa
> Priimiititti too
> Priimiititti taa
> Priimiititti tootaa

Note

1.   Kurt Schwitters, *Das Literarische Werk: Band I. Lyrik*, ed. Friedhelm Lach (Köln: DuMont Shauberg, 1973), 81.

9 780826 362759